DATE DUE

OCT 1 0 1996	

INSTITUTIONAL CHANGE

Studies in Socio-Economics

MORALITY, RATIONALITY, AND EFFICIENCY
NEW PERSPECTIVES ON SOCIO-ECONOMICS
Richard M. Coughlin, editor

SOCIO-ECONOMICS
TOWARD A NEW SYNTHESIS
Amitai Etzioni and Paul R. Lawrence, editors

INSTITUTIONAL CHANGE
THEORY AND EMPIRICAL FINDINGS
Sven-Erik Sjöstrand, editor

INSTITUTIONAL CHANGE

Theory and Empirical Findings

EDITOR
Sven-Erik Sjöstrand

M.E. Sharpe
ARMONK, NEW YORK
LONDON, ENGLAND

Copyright © 1993 by M.E. Sharpe, Inc.

All rights reserved. No part of this book may be reproduced in any form
without written permission from the publisher, M.E. Sharpe, Inc.,
80 Business Park Drive, Armonk, New York 10504.

Library of Congress Cataloging-in-Publication Data

Institutional change: theory and empirical findings /
edited by Sven-Erik Sjöstrand.
p. cm.
Includes index.
ISBN 1–56324–080–7
1. Organizational change. 2. Organizational change—Case studies.
3. Economic conversion—Europe—Case studies.
I. Sjöstrand, Sven-Erik, 1945–
HD58.8I577 1992
302.3′5—dc20
92–40744
CIP

Printed in the United States of America

The paper used in this publication meets the minimum requirements of American National Standard for Information Sciences—Permanence of Paper for
Printed Library Materials, ANSI Z39.48–1984

♾

BM   10 9 8 7 6 5 4 3 2 1

Contents

Part III: Changing Institutions: Focusing on Experiences in Northern and Eastern Europe

Retrospection

Preface

In this volume, *Institutional Change: Theory and Empirical Findings,* there is both an emphasis on basic theory in the area of institutionally oriented research in the social and economic sciences (cf. the initial five chapters included in the introduction and in part I of the book, "Institutional Change: Basic Theory") and a strong accentuation of the empirical efforts addressing the institutional field (cf. not fewer than fourteen chapters consisting of both the second part of this book—"Comparative Analyses of Institutional Structures and Changes"—and the third part—"Changing Institutions: Focusing on Experiences in Northern and Eastern Europe"). In all nineteen chapters attention is given to both social and economic factors when discussing and developing institutionally flavored theories. Thus most approaches in this collection are of a truly socio-economic character.

The theme of this volume—institutional *change*—was selected for both theoretical and empirical reasons. Its empirical relevance is rather obvious. During the beginning of this decade tremendous transformations have been taking place especially in Eastern Europe and in the former Soviet Union but also in the other parts of Europe (e.g., the formation of a larger European Community).

Theoretically, institutional research has been revitalized during the past years, and it has certainly claimed attention from a growing population of researchers in the social and economic sciences. Recently (1991) one of the "founding fathers" of institutional research in the economic sciences, Professor Emeritus at Chicago University Ronald Coase, received the Nobel Prize for his unique contributions in this field. Today there is an almost overwhelming number of scientific writings addressing institutionalization. Contributions focusing on institutional change have, however, been more infrequent, and this volume tries to compensate (somewhat) for that weakness of past institutional research.

The first two major sections of this book—"Introduction" and "Institutional Change: Basic Theory"—include five chapters. Three of them are of a purely theoretical kind, whereas the other two chapters include varying amounts of empirical research and illustrations. Most of the authors discuss institutions both in relation to varying periods of time—with an emphasis on longer or historical perspectives—and in relation to differing territories or *scopes* (e.g., cultures, [across and inside] nations, and [across and inside] single organizations).

In the following part—''Comparative Analyses of Institutional Structures and Changes''—the authors discuss some of the most important institutional developments and transformations that are now taking place *across* nations in many parts of the world, with an unmistakable focus on the European situation. In this part of the book there is an emphasis on empirical material, although in most of the chapters the authors also end up with explicit theoretical conclusions.

''Changing Institutions: Focusing on Experiences in Northern and Eastern Europe'' is the fourth and largest part of this volume. The authors in these chapters provide us with ''inside'' case histories and analyses of what is happening to important (socio-economic) institutions in both the capitalistic economies of the Scandinavian countries (including Finland) and the post-Communist societies of Eastern Europe.

In a short concluding part—''Retrospection''—and chapter—''The Many Faces of Capitalism''—the proposal is put forward that it is time for economic and social scientists to further discuss the varieties and differences among the many and changing capitalistic economic systems in the world, and it is suggested that such comparisons could benefit greatly from both institutional theory and socio-economic thinking.

Most, but not all, chapters in this volume are research efforts originally presented at the Third International Conference on Socio-Economics of the Society for the Advancement of Socio-Economics (SASE) held at the Stockholm School of Economics, Sweden, in mid-1991. At this unique conference, whose theme was ''Interdisciplinary Approaches to Economic Problems,'' more than four hundred papers were presented. From these papers about fifteen were selected for this particular volume. Therefore it does not represent a traditional conference collection but rather a modern type of editorial volume with a distinct theoretical theme and specially invited authors.

The 1991 Stockholm SASE conference certainly made the editor's task more manageable, especially when considering the fact that the twenty-five authors contributing to this volume together represent more than ten different countries. Therefore, it is an honor and a pleasure to thank both the founder and past president of SASE, Professor Amitai Etzioni, and the president of SASE in the year of the 1991 conference, Professor Daniel Yankelovich, for their generous support when in 1989 the SASE decided to select the Stockholm School of Economics for this unique scientific event. Furthermore, for making this Stockholm conference possible, I would also like to thank my colleague and co-organizer of this conference, Professor Karl-Erik Wärneryd.

A lot of assistance to the authors and the editor in improving the included chapters was of course provided by many of the almost five hundred participants at this Stockholm conference. My thanks also go to the researchers at my own institution (Management and Organization Theory) at the Stockholm School of Economics for their assistance in the production of this volume.

This manuscript has been typed and made compatible with computer-based printing techniques by my secretary, Pia Bergman. Her devoted and excellent work has helped to make the relatively swift publication of this large volume possible. Furthermore, all chapters have been scrutinized by Bill Harris of the Department of Professional Communication Skills at the Stockholm School of Economics, a translator, whose careful and devoted language checking has been indispensable.

Finally, I would like to dedicate this volume to Anita and Dan.

Sven-Erik Sjöstrand

Acknowledgment

The editor and the publisher wish to thank *Administrative Science Quarterly* (Cornell University, Johnson Graduate School of Management) for permission to reprint as chapter 5 in this volume the copyrighted article written by Professor Oliver E. Williamson ("Comparative Economic Organization: The Analysis of Discrete Organizational Structures." *Administrative Science Quarterly* 36, no. 2 [June 1991]: 269–96).

Introduction

1. On Institutional Thought in the Social and Economic Sciences

Sven-Erik Sjöstrand

An Overview

There are three main ingredients in this first chapter. First, there is an analysis of some important areas of institutional research with an emphasis on some of the more significant of the existing different institutionally oriented approaches in the social and economic sciences. Organization theory, a rather newly created intersection of several academic disciplines, is at the same time—indirectly—addressed in the survey. This review starts with a survey of sociological writers well known for their institutional orientation and continues with an overview of institutional economics, incorporating what often is labeled the new institutional economics or neoinstitutionalism.

Second, the core concepts of institutionalism—*institution, institutionalization, institutional change*—are carefully described, examined, framed, and defined. Third, these definitions of the core concepts are used as points of reference when describing and discussing the contributions provided in the following nineteen chapters. These three core concepts and their cognates run through all parts of this volume, but their meanings differ slightly both for each individual author and among the disciplines they represent.

Sociological Perspectives

A Core Phenomenon

In sociology institutions have always been on the top of the research agenda. This study of institutions has referred to something very basic in most of the investigations carried out. Institutionalism has been part of mainstream research rather than a kind of alternative to some other, dominating paradigm. Thus, most sociological thinking exhibits at least some institutionalist character. In sociology there is usually assumed some sort of society having an existence (or a function, structure, or history) that transcends individual persons. There is, then, a positive push to perceive local situations as immersed in more general structures.

But much sociological thinking uses institutional ideas only in a limited way. Often macroanalyses in sociology avoid allowing meaning to be organized at the higher (that is, cultural) levels. As much as possible is attributed to the structure of the web of social relations, or if social activity is allowed to be embedded in a meaning system, this system is seldom thought of as organized at levels far beyond the individual (cf. Meyer 1990). In sum, there are researchers who claim that sociology in (too) many cases is insufficiently contextual.

Meyer suggests that a problem that bounds institutional thinking in sociology is the commitment to find some sort of actor in social and economic life. This actor could be an individual but also, for example, a firm or any organization (including the state).[1] Meyer claims that this "actorhood" is a social construct, actually one of the more important institutionalized ways of human thinking and perception of our times.

A Few Classical Writers

In mainstream sociology there are—and have always been—many sorts of institutional theories. Spencer and Weber used the word *institution* but in a way somewhat different from that of most of today's sociologists.[2] Parsons, when formulating his famous functionalistic theory (e.g., 1937, 1940, 1951), emphasized that (all) economic activities take place within an "institutional framework." Then he distinguished institutions from traditional organizational structures and described the former as "normative patterns which define what are felt to be, in a given society, proper, legitimate, or expected modes of action or of social relationship" (1940, p. 190). These normative patterns (institutions) "depend on the support of the moral sentiments of the members of the society" (p. 192). Concrete economic activities then take place in a framework of institutions originated in moral sentiments inculcated in childhood and over time built into the structures of personalities.

Selznick (1957) innovated in this field by emphasizing a historic and contextual perspective, focusing on how values beyond the technical requirements of a task could be infused into organizations and their members (see next section). Berger and Luckmann (1967), inspired especially by Weber and Schütz, very early proposed ideas about institutionalization processes as social constructs. Meyer and Rowan (1977) added to their perspective by explicitly discussing and characterizing institutionalized organizations.

More recent important contributions regarding institutions and institutionalization in sociology include Pfeffer (1982) on organizations and organization theory, DiMaggio and Powell (1983) on institutional isomorphism,

Meyer and Scott (1983) on organizational environments, Perrow (1986) on complex organizations, Thomas et al. (1987a, 1987b) on institutional structures, Zucker (1988) on institutional patterns and organizations, and Etzioni (1988) on the moral dimension and institutions.

Four Kinds of Institutional Approaches

Scott (1987), when analyzing institutionalism in sociological research, identified four different approaches all claiming an institutional focus. One of the earlier and more influential versions of institutional theory presented in sociology was—according to Scott—the one introduced by Selznick (1957). Selznick and his followers regarded institutionalization as a process of instilling value in organizations: "[T]o institutionalize is to infuse with value beyond the technical requirements of the task at hand" (p. 17). Selznick regarded institutionalization as a means of supplying intrinsic worth to a unit (structure or process) that before institutionalization possessed only instrumental utility. By adding value, stability and persistence over time are promoted (cf. Scott 1987, p. 494).

Another important research path in institutionally oriented sociology was established by Meyer and Rowan (1977), who viewed institutionalization as a social process by which individuals come to accept a shared definition of social reality—a conception whose validity is seen as independent of the actor's own view and action but is taken for granted as defining the way things are and/or should be done (Scott 1990, p. 496). This is, indeed, a very general position but one that was elaborated further into the idea that institutional systems correspond to a class of elements, in this case to "belief systems"—that is, to a kind of cultural phenomenon. Later, some researchers proposed the idea of the simultaneous existence of multiple institutional environments for a single organization (DiMaggio and Powell 1983; Meyer and Scott 1983).

Finally, according to Scott (1987), institutions could refer to relatively enduring systems of social beliefs and socially organized practices associated with varying arenas within societies (e.g., religion, the family). This position was elaborated by Friedland and Alfred (1987), who emphasized the importance of introducing a substantive content into any discussion of institutions. They continued by proposing that there are differentiated institutional spheres in a society and no necessary harmony among various institutional complexes. The beliefs (norms) that are appropriate for a certain activity could be dubious. Any activity could have multiple meanings and be the focus of conflicting institutional definitions and demands. Institutionalization then refers to processes that make such sets of rules natural (that is, taken for granted) while eliminating competing or alternative regulations. Institutionalization implies the simultaneous construction of both means and ends and of both actor and activity and the linking of these elements to shared or general beliefs.

Institutional Economics

In the other social sciences, such as political science and law, institutionalism has coexisted with other perspectives in a rather nondramatic and often productive way. For example, in political science many recent writings deal explicitly with institutions. Here Bogason (1987) finds at least three differing approaches: one based on game theory, one founded in theories of collective action (cf. public choice theories), and one inspired by more recent contributions in sociology. Just a few of the recent, more influential writers in political science include—without classification—the following: Kjellberg (1975) on local government, Potter (1979) on the breakdown of certain democratic regimes, Therborn (1980) on the organization of state apparatuses, March and Olsen (1984) on organizational factors in political life, Evans et al. (1985) on "bringing the state back in," and March and Olsen (1989) on the organizational basis of politics.

But in the economic sciences—especially in neoclassical and mathematics-flavored economics—the situation for institutionalists has been both problematic and difficult.

Classical Institutionalism versus the New Institutionalism

In economics we find important writings both in the more classic institutional tradition of thought (e.g., Veblen, Commons, Ayres, Dewey, Myrdal, and Galbraith) and in contributions more connected with the dominant neoclassical (noninstitutionalistic) tradition.

The former tradition refers to new efforts provided by—among others—Sjöstrand (1985) on the organization of Western societies, Hodgson (1987) on economics and institutions, Knudsen et al. (1989) on institutionalism in the social sciences, Bromley (1989) on economic interests and institutions, and Myhrman (forthcoming) on petrified economies. The tradition also refers to new editions of *classical* institutional economists (cf. a recent collection of writings in institutional economics edited by Samuels [1988], or a reissue of some of the writings of Commons [1934/1990]).

The latter tradition refers to neoclassically flavored writers like Williamson (1975, 1985) on the basic institutions of modern United States capitalism, Sen (1981) on "entitlements," Akerlof (1980a, 1980b, 1984) on social customs and "counteracting institutions," Axelrod (1984) on the evolution of cooperation, Leibenstein (1984) on the economics of conventions and institutions, Cyert (1988) on the economic theory of organization and firms, Demsetz (1988) on the organization of economic activity, Rowe (1989) on the economics of rules and conventions, and so forth. Much of this research is sometimes referred to as the new institutionalism, but according to Dugger (1990) and other classical (or orthodox) institutionalists, these efforts are perhaps new but not institutional.

Institutionally oriented socio-economic researchers and research also include (economic) historians like Chandler (1977) and his writings on "the visible hand," Braudel (1982) and his discussion of the "wheels of commerce," Newman (1983) and his descriptions of preindustrial societies, North (North and Thomas 1973; North 1981, 1991) and his grand opuses on structures and changes in modern economic history and on the institutional evolution in Europe, Koot (1987) and his reflections on English historical economics, Fogel (1989) and his analyses of American slavery, and Gustafsson (1991) with his reflections on (transitions to) capitalism.

Institutionalism in Orthodox Theory

The word *institutionalism* has for several decades been used as the standard designation of certain ways of thinking in economics (cf. political economy, institutional economics, evolutionary economics) that differ significantly from those of the ruling majority of the discipline (the neoclassical approach).

One of the original definitions of institutional economics is as follows:

> [T]he study of the structure and functioning of the evolving field of human relations which is concerned with the provision of material goods and services for the satisfaction of human wants . . . the study of the changing patterns of cultural relations which deal with the creation and disposal of scarce material goods and services by individuals and groups in the light of their private and public aims. (Gruchy 1947, pp. 550-52)

This position has been elaborated on by several researchers trying to clarify the differences between this approach and that of mainstream neoclassical economics.

One basic difference between institutionalists and mainstream economists is that the former do not sharply delimit their field of study from the other social sciences but function as more of an open, learning research system. In accordance with its broader perspective, the political and social frameworks for economic activities are not excluded, nor is the past or the future.

Institutional economics also allows for a complex, scientifically based description of humankind. A human being is a social phenomenon that is malleable and developmental. Furthermore, institutional economists also accept the idea that a human being is both a product and a producer of culture and that individual thoughts and actions emerge in a continuous interaction with others and with elements of the embedded culture. Thus, economic activities can only be understood as part of humankind's broader cultural relationships.

In individual situations there is almost always an amount of discretion for the actor, but most of the decisions and actions taken are of a processual kind and significantly culturally determined. This culture is a product of the past, of the present, and of expectations about the future and consists of norms for thoughts and actions embodied in what are often denoted as institutions. Institutions then are constituted by habits and represent prescribed patterns for regulating and stabilizing the performance of different tasks in societies (cf. Tool 1986, ch. 1). Institutional economists then avoid—by approving institutions—an undersocialized explanation of human economic action.

To be more specific, for most institutional economists an institution is identified by *(a)* the individuals who think and act and by *(b)* the rules that provide repetition, stability, and a predictable order. Moreover, there are *(c)* folk views explaining and justifying those activities as well as the rules connected to them.

Thus an institution is a mental construct that cannot be observed as a whole. What one can observe are the activities of people in specific situations. Those situations then include the social rules and the cultural folk views as well as the physical environment and are structured by prior acts. They evolve gradually, connecting the past with both the present and the future. The perception and the demarcation of this total context are defined by the folk views of relevancy (i.e., cause-effect maps). Thus, an institution may be regarded as a grouping of situations in accordance with the organizing ideas of the folk view.[3]

In recent years there has also been an increased interest in institutions for neoclassical writings (cf. the writings listed above). Those researchers have, however, tried to save most of the basic superficial assumptions of neoclassical economics and have therefore only partially modified their theories. Consequently, their efforts have not been accepted by modern orthodox institutionalists as genuine or weighty institutional contributions.

**Toward a Socio-Economic
Perspective on Institutions**

Partially as a consequence of this rapid growth in scientific literature, originating from several disciplines, there have emerged quite different perspectives on the institutional phenomena as such. This situation, however, does not imply that the phenomenon is ambiguous or should be treated as obscure. This variety is not surprising, taking into consideration the fact that several disciplines (economics, institutional economy, economic history, sociology, organization theory, political science, law, and others) are involved in parallel research efforts.

In most of the different applications of the idea of an institution, it is treated carefully and each perspective is usually consistent in its own right. This book to some extent reflects this variety of perspectives on institutions and institutionalization. These somewhat differing perspectives, however, in both this introduction and the concluding chapter are looked upon from an explicit and fairly stable point of reference—a kind of socio-economic definition of institutions and institutionalization.

From the descriptions just presented, which have been chosen from different disciplines, it is clear that both concepts—institution and institutionalization—have been used in different (although not divergent) ways. Perhaps the most striking controversies concern the following basic questions: Is an institution an organization or a system of rules? Does it correspond with ideas of human freedom of action or with more deterministic views? Does it represent a holistic, cultural phenomenon or a rather specific, limited normative system? Is it a formal or informal matter? Does it relate to efficiency considerations in societies or to ideas about how to deal with human uncertainty?

As *institution* is a root concept in this book, it is worth struggling to give it as clear a meaning as possible. Such an explicit and comprehensible definition could be important as a platform for discussing the positions and contributions of all the authors included in this volume.

A Tentative Definition

In this book, both in this introductory chapter and in the concluding chapter, an *institution* is tentatively defined as a human mental construct for a coherent system of shared (enforced) norms that regulate individual interactions in recurrent situations. Then *institutionalization* is the process by which individuals intersubjectively approve, internalize, and externalize such a mental construct.

These two concentrated definitions need some elaboration. First of all, these definitions underline the fact that institutions are not objective phenomena but *mental constructions* of human beings in their (inter)actions. This process of construction is a continuous one, and important inputs in these processes are the social and economic theories produced in scientific work and writings. Such scientific knowledge is to some extent present everywhere in all human interactions and therefore influences human activities. It is part of a field of acquaintances and experiences, of wisdom and folk views. Thus scientific knowledge does not embody everything that constitutes the practice of a field—practice has not been wholly forced into the norms and structures of science—but it is an important force influencing human thought. As institutions are neither objective nor physical phenomena, they cannot be observed as wholes. What can be observed are human activities in various situations (cf. chapter 4 in this book).

Institutions are further defined as coherent systems (of shared norms). The use of the words *coherent systems* refers to the idea that the guiding norms (of a recurrent multipersonal situation) are interrelated in similar ways in the minds of the interacting individuals. These norms could, for example, be secular and derived from an ideology or linked to a moral or religious belief system. In this way the coherent system of norms usually has to be linked either to lengthy historical trends or to long-lasting "cultures" (and their associated lines of thought). In some writings institutions stand for more short-lived and transitory phenomena like professions or procedures. But to qualify here as an institution, a systemic and relatively stable character of the network of (shared) norms is required. Thus, when actors follow more haphazard or arbitrary courses of action, such behavior does not qualify as institutionally regulated behavior.

To apply to an institution this coherent system of norms also has to be *shared (and enforced)*. A shared norm could be taken for granted, implicit, or unconsciously applied, as well as controversial, explicit, and deliberately put into practice among the interacting individuals. If it is shared, it is often a sign of its "efficiency" and of its legitimacy—but there are also norms that dominate recurrent situations in spite of a lack of such qualities. Sometimes norms are known and adjusted to, although they are neither agreed on nor genuinely shared. Every single norm has its own history that has produced its substance and presence. Then that very existence is a result both of the past power conditions and of the former frames of references of various actors of history—individuals as well as collectives.

Those shared (and/or enforced) *norms* consist of many kinds of built-in expectations regarding human actions. Thus, norms tend to stabilize human (inter)action and make individual behavior more predictable. Norms could be reproduced in both formal and articulated forms, as well as in more informal and tacit ones. Many terms have been used by scientists to cover the whole range of possible groupings of norms. Among the terms are the following: *laws, regulations, rules, routines, conventions, traditions, customs, myths,* and *habits.* One could add that these norms—often simultaneously—represent both instrumental qualities (i.e., "efficiency") and values as such (i.e., meaning). Thus, institutions could be looked upon as a kind of "cultural accounts," accumulating ideals and norms as well as capital in a society (cf. Meyer et al. 1987).

In this definition, it is further suggested that an institution *regulates human interactions*, but that does not imply environmental determinism. There is a reciprocity between an individual and an institution in the sense that both of them influence and constitute each other. The institutional setting, therefore, does not define in a unanimous way the actions taken by an individual—there is always some freedom of action. Institutions both restrict and open up for human actions by providing structures for individuals to enforce, trespass, or violate. Moreover, situations are not always similarly known and defined—different individuals could perceive a single situation as belonging to a divergent grouping (and consequently to another institutional setting). Thus, in almost every particular situation there is a choice for the individual among several simultaneously existing—but often unrelated or sometimes even conflicting—norms. An important source for this (partial) individual freedom of action rests on the ability of human beings to discriminate between "what is" and "what should—or could—be." Some scientists claim, however, that this freedom of action is very limited indeed—that most behavior is carried out by routine; whereas others, instead, stress the possibilities inherent in this situation of human discretion.

In the definition stated in this section, it is suggested that institutions regulate individual interactions. By using such an expression, it is emphasized that people believe and assume that they are individual actors. Perhaps one could say that such a perspective ("the social construction of individual actorhood") is an important institutionalized thought in Western culture—but obviously not the only feasible position to take. In this socio-economic definition of institutions, human interaction is focused. In fact, no human action taken could bring about something other than—simultaneously—an interaction. "Pure" individual actions versus Nature are difficult to imagine.

Finally this socio-economically flavored definition relates institutions to *recurrent situations*. The use of the attribute *recurrent* was partly explained in this section. Institutions thus apply foremost to situations that are at least modestly frequent or common in everyday human life. Of course, this reach or scope for institutions varies. Some refer to less habitual but very important situations and others to more frequent, less crucial events.

More problematic is the definition or demarcation of particular, separate situations. Sometimes individuals do not perceive a particular situation in a similar way, and therefore each of them acts on his or her own presumptions (thus, actually as if the individuals were governed by different institutions), something that often creates confusion or tensions. Usually there are rules or norms (folk views) among individuals for how to group or cluster situations. Those rules could be described as *instituting ideas* that impregnate *formal organizations*. These instituting ideas are usually based on notions of necessary and sufficient requisites for identifying and classifying a situation.

It is important to understand that (*formal*) *organizations are not identical with institutions*.[4] On the one hand, organizations are usually manifestations of one dominant institution—or sometimes the arena for several competing ones. On the other hand, organizations simultaneously either reinforce, modify, or alter these institutions. Thus, the members of a particular organization could in their talk and actions express values and rationalities from more than one institutional *sphere* (that is, the scope or extension of a coherent system of shared norms). In sum, it is important to distinguish between institutions as coherent systems of shared norms in a society and organizations as more or less formalized arenas for dominant or competing institutions.

After having elaborated on and explained the ideas behind the definition of an *institution* stated in this section, one must add that there are a few concepts in the economic and social sciences that now and then are used in an analogous way. One of these related concepts is a *convention*. In scientific writings, conventions usually refer to situations where actors share the goals but are indifferent to the means (e.g., driving on the right-hand side of the road; cf. Bromley 1989). Thus, a convention does not, contrary to an institution, reach—that is, provide guidance for action or a meaning—outside the particular situation.

Another of these related concepts is the *game*. It is often substituted for an institution, but such a replacement does not always work out well theoretically.

Games do not allow for what is intrinsic or inherent in institutions—a continuous (but typically very slow and usually gradual) change of the constitutional norms owing to the outcomes of the always ongoing interaction processes among individuals on the microlevel (cf. the game of chess with its *fixed* rules).

Still another related and important concept is *culture*. The use of this term has spread from anthropology to sociology and organization theory, and today it is very much in focus especially in the latter field. Culture is a concept with many meanings. It has been used—particularly in the economic sciences—as a kind of summing up of all the reactions regarding a lack of emphasis on symbolic perspectives in past research. As a consequence, this use has been associated with a lack of interest in the substantial qualities of phenomena (e.g., the content of a norm). Among institutionalists these "hard facts" have always been in focus in their inquiries on social and economic issues. Furthermore, in a general sense, culture is used as the complementary concept—or antipode—to Nature. Often then culture refers to the material and educational levels or characters in a society. Perhaps one could look upon culture as a kind of raw material in the ongoing crystallizations of institutions in a society.

Some Limitations of Institutional
Economic Theory

DiMaggio (1988) stated "The distinguishing contribution of institutional theory rests on the identification of causal mechanisms leading to organizational change and stability on the basis of preconscious understandings that organizational actors share, independently of their interests" (p. 3). Institutional theory has made a unique contribution by "providing explanations of phenomena that do not reflect the behavior of rational [that is, *homo oeconomicus*] actors driven by clearly perceived interests" (p. 7).

There is one basic assumption involved in most institutional approaches in the economic and social sciences. These approaches are founded on the general idea that individuals try to survive, and in doing so, they tend to avoid uncertainty, both by creating as reliable or trustworthy (dependence) relations to others as possible (cf. Sjöstrand 1985, ch. 1) and by trying to find ways of predicting future events (and actions of others). This does not represent a denial of the existence of interests and interest-driven behavior among institutionalists—as suggested by DiMaggio (1988, ch. 1)—but such behavior is less pronounced in their theory building.

Interests are central to almost all theories of human action—in mainstream economics and in some sociological thinking the rather simplistic utilitarian assumption dominates, whereas in institutional economy, many fields of sociology, and most organization theory that assumption is abandoned for others of a slightly more complex—but empirically substantial—sort.[5] One could argue which path to stress the most—interest-driven or uncertainty-reducing behavior. It is important in modern institutional approaches, however, to recognize the presence of both. Maybe it is fair to say that institutionalists, at least of the last decade, to a certain degree have underestimated the merits of interest-flavored perspectives.

Perhaps institutional approaches are especially appropriate for describing intersubjective and exteriorized phenomena and for explaining long-term changes in organizations or societies. Furthermore, institutional analyses could be productive when actors are unlikely to recognize or to act on their interests (and those situations where an individual does not know his or her preferences [preference order] are frequent) or when they are unable to do so effectively (and that, too, is a common situation).

Perhaps one could rephrase the question and try to define when non-institutionalistic approaches could be appropriate and effective. Then one has to find situations where the *homo oeconomicus* type of rationality dominates among the actors—perhaps in the financial sector and in other kinds of strongly price-focusing arenas including auctions. Moreover, such behavior is probably easier to find in arenas where a majority of the actors, or at least the dominating individuals, have been educated in (neoclassical) economics.[6]

The Theme of This Book: Institutional Change

A Theoretical Position

To understand institutional change, one possible starting point is to analyze how institutions are reproduced over time. In the core idea and definition of an institution (provided in the previous section) both stability and pattern maintenance are assumed. Societywide (or Western) constitutive understandings like democracy, rationality, and efficiency are often solidly institutionalized, whereas institutions with a more finite or limited scope, like understandings about procedures, often are relatively unstable. Institutions then have to be reproduced continuously, and their reproduction is often incomplete (cf. Sjöstrand 1985, ch. 5: "On the [Re]production of Institutions in a Society"). Through the idea of reproduction, dynamics is introduced into the theory.

Reproduction does not imply that institutions are replicated over time (that is, simple reproduction) but that the core of the coherent system of shared norms is preserved, allowing for some changes in the positions, roles, and functions of different actors (that is, extended reproduction or [re]production; cf. Therborn 1976). Simple reproduction of institutions occurs when actors have a common perception and definition of a situation and act according to the aroused norms. Such a process is, of course, very much favored if the interests of the single actors correspond to the ones stored in the institutional setting and if (especially additional) individuals are wholly socialized to the prevailing norms. Otherwise, one could expect "distortions," foregoing both extended reproduction and a "swapping" of institutions (and even deinstitutionalization!).

Another possible starting point when discussing institutional change is to try to identify its potential sources. An "innovation generator" is needed, as is a "selection mechanism." Here a gap and a mismatch between microlevels and macrolevels in institutionalization processes are suggested as the initiating force. This gap or mismatch is explained by the distance between, on the one hand, the experiences and thoughts of the many single individuals on the microlevel and, on the other hand, the content and regulations embedded in the more formalized institutions on the macrolevel, reflecting a more holistic perspective on society. These macroinstitutions are continuously (re)produced by the individuals in their daily activities and interactions on the microlevel. As previously indicated by the use of the prefix *(re)*, this reproduction is usually extended (that is, imperfect), and thus over time it now and then undermines the ruling institutions on the macrolevel.

Zucker (1988) claimed that most institutional theory assumes a high degree of simple reproduction on the microlevel. Instead, Zucker—referring to Garfinkel (1967) and others—indicated that "there are significant gaps between the social facts institutionalized at the macrolevel and those institutionalized at the microlevel." According to Zucker (pp. 42–43), this gap or these differences between the two levels first of all emerge from their differing origins of experiences. The microlevel interactive situations rely on first-hand evidences with particular others and environments, whereas those on the macrolevel rely on indicators, on generalized others, or on formal structures. Further, the microlevel tends to be limited in scope, and its coherent system of shared (and enforced) norms often relates to (some/most of) the interacting individuals in the experienced situations (cf. also the existence of groups and other collectives), whereas the macrolevel tends to be grand in scope with a rather abstract and diluted coherent system of shared norms.

As previously mentioned, an individual always has some freedom of action. The norms specified through an institutional setting are always incomplete. Individuals do have a choice between differing (coherent) systems of norms; that is, they sometimes even have the problem of (selecting and) fitting a rule to a situation.[7] Moreover, people have their shortcomings and therefore some variation occurs (sometimes by accident or by chance) in the actions taken in different settings. There is also the possibility that an individual transforms certain disposals for action from one institutional setting to another. Finally—and perhaps most important—individuals discriminate (as previously mentioned) between "what is" and "what ought to be," which stimulates variation.

Other Explanations Regarding
Institutional Change

There are, of course, important complementary (as well as unrelated) explanations suggested for the existence of institutional change and development in addition to the one just described. Excellent recent surveys addressing these research fields have been presented by Bush (1987), Bromley (1989, ch. 2), and Gustafsson (1991, ch. 1).

Quite a few neoclassical economists start from what they describe as "market failures." Institutions then emerge as substitutes for (perfect or efficient) markets. There are several reasons suggested for these market failures. Most of them start from the rather incontestable idea that many exchanges occur in situations of uncertainty and are composed of a finite number of actors. These actors then have a need for information about the rationalities of the others. Such information tends to be incomplete and asymmetrically distributed. All these factors, which are present in most real-life exchanges, make up for the failure of (ideal-type or efficient) markets. A problem here is that these researchers do not consider markets as institutions but rather as a generally superior phenomenon or as a kind of preferable state.

But why not put the basic question the other way around and start with "organizational failures," trying to explain the presence of different kinds of markets? Why not start from the most basic matter of all—the reproduction of human(kind)—and then analyze why close circles (that is, couples, families, friends, and neighbors) and kinship (cf. clans and dynasties) fail? And why not try to disclose how a need for those impersonal, calculative relationships characterizing many markets emerge? Of course, when addressing institutional matters, shortcomings of neoclassical approaches are disclosed, but they will not be discussed here, as there exist many careful descriptions of these delivered by several well-known economic and social scientists.

Apart from market failures, there is much research in the economic sciences that stresses changes in technology as an important exogenous source behind institutional change and development (cf. Bush 1987 for an overview), but most of them simultaneously add other crucial factors in their theory building. Often discussions are introduced about not only "property rights" and "transaction costs" but also factors like resource endowments and product demand (cf., e.g., North and Thomas 1970, 1973; North 1981, 1991; Rowe 1989). In most of these writings, the existence of institutions is explained by a kind of game theory founded on *functionalism*, where the role of an institution is to create order and reduce uncertainty.

A rather general critique against most of these approaches was delivered by both Bromley (1989) and Gustafsson (1991). Their basic criticisms could roughly be summed up in the following way: In these dynamic models, institutional change is essentially produced by the quest for economic efficiency[8], and such thinking is truly circular. This circularity is the result of the fact that it is the institutional arrangements that define what is regarded as efficient. They also refer to and criticize North—the perhaps most distinguished and influential researcher in economic history of the recent decade—for his basic idea that it is the individual's perceptions of possible gains (if combined with certain environmental requirements) that initiate changes.[9] Individuals then merely function as economic entrepreneurs.[10]

North (formerly often together with Thomas) has elaborated on the environmental requirements for such institutional changes. In his more and more sophisticated approach, the emerging institutions are determined by the existing distribution of rights in a society (property rights) and of the way they are enforced (usually through the emergence of a kind of "state"). To specify, establish, and enforce such property rights is associated with (transaction) costs, but these rights could be designed in a way profitable to society. In more recent years, North has added *ideology* to his model, that is, customs, rules, or norms for exchanges produced outside (independent of?) the "state apparatuses." In his later writings, he also discussed changes in relative prices and in individual preferences, as well as consequences of organized actions as crucial sources of institutional change.

Gustafsson (1991) added to this critique also delivered by Bromley (1989). He pointed, in particular, at the fragmented character of most of these neoclassically influenced "neoinstitutional" theories. Explicit descriptions of the relationships among the crucial concepts are too often ambiguous (or even lacking). North was once again the target, although his approach is perhaps the most well elaborated and stimulating one presented. North (according to Gustafsson) neglects or fails—in a straightforward way—to state the relationships among institutions, endowments, and technology (which to him define the opportunity sets for actors altering institutions in a society). Neither does North unambiguously discuss the important relationships among changes in relative prices, preferences, and organizational actions (although all these three factors are suggested by him as those that initiate changes in institutions). Perhaps the most fundamental weakness that emerges, according to Gustafsson, has to do with the lack of information given as to the source of an organizational commitment to change (in) institutions. Neither is there much comment on the tensions and conflicts often involved in these processes of change, nor is there much comment on the explanations for the continuous development and presence of inefficient institutions.

On the Contributions to Institutional Thought Provided in This Book

Part I: Institutional Change: Basic Theory

In Part I of this volume, "Institutional Change: Basic Theory," Douglass C.

North describes his theoretical framework for analyzing the core issue of this volume: institutional change. To him, this kind of theory is essential for further progress in the economic and social sciences because most economic theories of today cannot satisfactorily account for the diverse performances of societies and economies. He challenges the prevailing assumption of frictionless exchange processes in societies and relates friction to institutions, which then are defined as the structures that human beings impose on their interactions—that is, kinds of formal rules or informal constraints that are combined with enforcement characteristics. These institutions (together with other constraints like technology) define the incentives that determine the choices individuals make when shaping the performances of societies over time.

The sources of (deliberate) institutional change are, according to North, the entrepreneurs, who either identify various opportunities in the (changing) environment or acquire new skills over time. Usually institutional change is incremental—revolutionary changes do occur but then merely as a result of gridlock often arising from a lack of mediating institutions.

North illustrates his theoretical framework—that is, the way in which institutions, organizations, and the mental maps of the actors interact to produce institutional change—with an analysis of the history of American land policy. He concludes this empirical discussion by suggesting that the key to institutional change is the ongoing interaction (i.e., competition) between institutions and organizations in the economic setting of scarcity. This competition forces organizations continually to invest in knowledge to survive; what knowledge to invest in is "dictated" by the entire existing institutional framework in a society.

In chapter 3, Amitai Etzioni—like North in the second chapter—addresses institutional change in a very fundamental way when elaborating on the (too) often neglected conception of *friction*. Friction to him is equivalent neither to resistance nor to inertia. Instead, friction refers to the idea that change slows down or even ceases if new (human) energy is not continuously added, and the use of that concept also indicates that adjustments and changes in the institutional structure of a society seldom occur swiftly or unproblematically. Friction refers to the ease and speed with which institutional changes happen.

Etzioni describes the development in Poland during the last decade and in the beginning of the 1990s. Poland was the only country that strictly tried to follow the (neoclassicists') advice to "jump" from one economic system to another. Etzioni relates certain factors that generally tend to affect the speed of transition from one position to another starting with the human factor (including values), adding the problems associated with *capital friction*, the quality of the infrastructure, and labor mobility. He argues that the strategy of trying to jump from a centrally planned economy into a market economy of an Anglo-Sachs(!)ian type must fail. Such a transition—from one institutional setting to another—will (and must be allowed to) take its time, regardless of "external factors" such as foreign aid or forgiveness of debt.

Etzioni ends his chapter by drawing the attention to the problem of "the unevenly paced clocks.'' Thus, he identifies three processes of change differing in their inherent amount of friction: deconstructive processes (that is, relatively rapid ones; for example, closing down state plants), reconstructive processes (slow ones; for example, the development of the infrastructure), and expectancy processes (very rapid ones; for example, ''Western prosperity soon''). Then it is not only the sheer level of friction that is the problem in change or transformational processes in a society but also that there are important differences in pace among the various kinds of socio-economic operations involved.

In chapter 4, I elaborate further on one issue brought up by North in chapter 2. There, North defines institutions as the structures that humans impose on their interactions. I start with an empirical and substantial assumption of the human being, describe such interaction-based institutions and suggest six ideal types (market, corporation, social movement, cooperation/federation, clan, and circle). Furthermore, I show that human beings tend to reduce uncertainty basically in three ways: through the forming or emergence of genuine, idealistic, or calculative relationships with others. I add that such relationships are almost always asymmetrical in their character. Thus, in this way the presence of power relations and the existence of hierarchies is indicated.

When combining relationships and asymmetry, the (three) ways that individuals cope with uncertainty, and the simultaneous presence of asymmetries or power relationships, six different ideal-type and underlying institutions emerge, which govern human exchanges and actions in most organizations and arenas in Western societies.

These six basic institutions characterizing Western societies change—but usually very slowly—over time because the associated reproduction processes are incomplete or imperfect. The distinguishing features of these six basic institutions are, however, their persistence over long periods of time and their various manifestations in organizations and in other arenas (e.g., in legislation), which could be found in many countries and cultures over the centuries. Therefore they could be regarded as ''infrastructures for human interaction.''

In chapter 5, Oliver E. Williamson analyzes a narrower institutional level—that of the arena for institutional dominance or competition, the individual organization. He discusses—in economic terms—the discrete structural alternatives that are available to organizations (i.e., ''the economics of institutions''). Williamson then discusses the comparative efficacy with which alternative forms of governance—markets, hybrids, hierarchies—economize on transaction costs. His approach then is related to, but somewhat different from, the one presented in chapter 4, where alternative forms of exchanges or interactions (i.e., markets, corporations, social movements, cooperatives, circles, and clans) are put into focus. Williamson gives emphasis to research in economics, law, and especially contractual theory, whereas I rely more on findings from the social sciences and organization theory.

Williamson makes a sharp distinction between the two ''pure'' or extreme governance forms, market and hierarchy. What is in between the two is unspecified and named hybrid forms. To Williamson a hierarchy is something other than a continuation of the market mechanism or a contractual act; it is associated with basically different means. Actually he shows not only that each form of governance is defined by its own contract law regime but also that it displays distinctive performance competencies and employs distinctive mechanisms. He exemplifies all this with "the firm," which is subject to the contract law of forbearance and is distinguished in bilateral adaptability respects and works through a combination of fiat, low-powered incentives, and bureaucracy.

Furthermore, Williamson in chapter 5 describes a way of relating in a unified way what too often has been treated separately in (neo)institutional economic research: the institutional environment and the institutions of governance. Perhaps such joining of fields does not solve the whole problem of the defects in embeddedness perspectives in (neo)institutional approaches, but his effort relieves at least some of those objections. An approach combining law, organization theory, and economics has a strong potential, Williamson concludes, for creating an institutionally influenced "new science of organization."

Part II: Comparative Analyses of Institutional Structures and Changes

In Part II of this volume, "Comparative Analyses of Institutional Structures and Changes," Charles Perrow in chapter 6 discusses the ongoing dramatic changes in the institutional forms for economic organizations in Western societies. First of all, he describes the traditional institutional forms; that is, the "integrated" and the "multidivisional" firm, the "holding company," and the "joint venture." Then he introduces the new—emerging—forms: "nondependent subcontracting" and "small firm networks" (SFNs).

Perrow explains the change toward the latter two more decentralized forms by such things as the "efficiencies of deconcentration," "capitalist failure," and "organizational failure." Perrow also clarifies the very existence and growth of the SFN phenomenon, applying roughly the same conceptual framework that I used in chapter 4—the presence and significance of trust relations and cooperation in most organizations (and these qualities usually to a larger extent exist in smaller units).

Perrow ends his chapter by arguing for the possible return of the "civil society." Then the potentials of the SFNs reside in the possibilities of massive disengagements from the big organizations, a spewing out of functions over delimited spaces where they are taken up by small independent organizations. If there are economies offered by trust, networks, and the limitation of social externalities, Perrow claims, then there is no need for one (large) organization to take care of all that. Then there could be a stop to the erosion of the civil society—a halt of the gradual elimination of genuine and idealistic relationships as described in chapter 4.

In chapter 7, Antoni Z. Kaminski and Piotr Strzalkowski discuss the ongoing institutional changes in Central and Eastern Europe. They focus on Czechoslovakia, Hungary, and Poland but also include Bulgaria and Romania in their analysis. They show how the preconditions for institutional change vary among these countries and that these things do matter when trying to transform from one type of economic system to another.

Kaminski and Strzalkowski suggest that the prospects for single countries to convert from planned to market economies rely both on the successful democratization of the political systems—a market economy cannot in the long run coexist with authoritarian regimes—and on the ability to understand and take into account the unique preconditions in the economic system of each country. They emphasize that each country therefore has to choose its own strategy for institutional change and for its transition to a market type of economy.

They compare the critical preconditions for change, especially for Poland, Hungary, and Czechoslovakia (but they also mention Romania and Bulgaria in this context) and add that the success of this kind of transformation of the economy of a society also depends on what external support to expect—and all these five countries do differ in this respect, too. According to Kaminski and Strzalkowski, Poland, Hungary, and Czechoslovakia are in a much better position for receiving foreign aid than are Bulgaria and Romania. They conclude, however, that this conversion to a market economy for all five countries is a task of enormous complexity and certainly a most difficult one and that it will take a long time before a new institutional setting will work acceptably.

John L. Campbell—in chapter 8—makes certain institutional comparisons between Eastern Europe and the United States when discussing property rights and governance transformations. In that analysis, he shows that the state does govern markets also in capitalistic economies. He describes in particular how the United States government manipulates and enforces various property rights, and then he extends his reasoning to the ongoing conversions in most European postsocialist societies.

Campbell regards property rights as an institution that not only defines who owns the means of production but also both who uses them and who appropriates the benefits from their use. Such a theoretical position indicates that the concept is somewhat ambiguous. To change property rights then is not a simple task, because in Western societies there is usually a coherent system of norms associated with these rights—and often these norms are known and shared. In this respect the situation is somewhat different for most Eastern European countries.

According to Campbell, property actions could be powerful tools for reshaping planned economies. But to change property rights is then not only a question of introducing private instead of state ownership of means of production (*privatization*). Such institutional changes are always risky because they will influence most stages and aspects of a transformation process, and in ways that are both complex and hard to understand and predict. Therefore, altering rights of ownership per se is not to Campbell the panacea for Eastern Europe that many others claim. Several other ingredients must be added when using such approaches. He ends his chapter by emphasizing that there are more choices available to Eastern Europe than just command or market economies in their "undiluted" or extreme forms.

Marco Orrù (in chapter 9) compares the institutional settings of Germany (i.e., West Germany) and Japan and finds them—perhaps somewhat surprisingly—to be rather similar in many respects. This comparison is especially interesting, as it considers the two most successful economies in recent decades. Orrù describes the structures of their economies, focusing on business and industry. Furthermore, he discloses the complex organized cooperation in Germany and Japan; among firms, among economic actors in general (i.e., among business associations, cartels, banks, and other financial organizations, and so forth), and between the state and the private sector.

Orrù ends his chapter by stating that the basic presumptions associated with modern neoclassical economics fail to capture and explain the critical institutional textures characterizing the economies of Germany and Japan. These institutional textures are altogether important for the functioning of a particular economic system—whether it is some kind of market economy or not. There are several types of capitalism, and he suggests a typology of "capitalist cooperation" for understanding the different forms. Furthermore, he demonstrates that the successes of German and Japanese capitalism cannot be explained by their extensive use of market relationships or competition but rather can be explained by the planned (!) balance between competition and cooperation. The latter then, Orrù concludes, represents one important distinguishing feature of Japanese and German capitalist structures—an identifiable and unique (?) working logic of the two societies.

Maureen McKelvey in chapter 10 provides us with a rather detailed description of the economic system of Japan, focusing on its national innovative capacity and basic institutional structure. She then compares Japan with both (Western) Europe and the United States and tries to explain the differences that have developed in the institutional structures of these economic regions.

She discusses the structure of Japanese capitalism in relation to four dimensions: Japanese culture, labor, industry (its organization), and government. These four dimensions also provide points of comparison for the description of the other capitalist economies. She shows that the institutional structure of the Japanese economy has important implications for the workings of its market system, particularly in relation to technological development and diffusion.

Capitalism, she concludes, is a general name for a changing mode of production and of society, with the market at the center. The market and the processes of technological change are not, according to McKelvey, separate subsystems of an economy working through mechanical universal laws; instead, an economy is pervaded with institutional structures more or less alike for each society. She ends her chapter by discussing how the Japanese system combines two attributes, namely, (long-term) planning, which enables stable relationships between powerful agents (including organizations), and quick adjustment to change. This dual quality of the socio-economic system is probably especially potent in the area of technological change, she suggests, because it combines the production of knowledge, which is a long-term commitment, with the flexibility of rapid change, which often is associated with technical progress.

In chapter 11, Robert Jessop, Klaus Nielsen, and Ove K. Pedersen extensively describe and compare the development of the economies of Britain, Denmark, and Sweden that have occurred in recent decades. They also try to explain the similarities and differences in the basic institutional frameworks of these countries. Competition (cf. chapter 2, written by North) is at the heart of their analysis.

First of all, they describe four critical economic shifts that, according to them, have affected the nature of competition in the whole world economy. These include the rise of new core technologies, the massive internationalization of financial and industrial flows, the transition from Fordism to post-Fordism (as the dominant model of development shaping economic and political strategies), and the redefinition of the macroeconomic global hierarchy (cf. concepts like European Economic Space [EES] and Pacific Rim Economic Community [PREC]).

Jessop et al. also reflect on the multidimensional character of competitiveness as such and elaborate on that issue on both the microlevel and the macrolevel. They strongly advocate the theoretically controversial position that competition can occur also on the macrolevel (i.e., between countries and economic regions), referring to the idea that although countries or regions are not agents or subjects, they are important socially constructed institutions that to a large extent affect human perceptions and actions.

In the concluding part of their chapter, Jessop et al. describe, for each of the three countries, their modes of growth and regulation, the strategic capacities of their states or governments, their economic problems, and their competitiveness. They end the chapter by stating that the pattern disclosed in this comparative analysis is best understood as an interaction of three sets of variables, namely, the changing modes of growth characteristics of the three national economies, the emerging discourses and strategies concerned with competition, and the capacity of the state for guiding efforts to enhance competitiveness.

Jan Otto Andersson (chapter 12) describes the economies of the Nordic countries that in the 1990s face the single European market, and he focuses on Finland in particular. He analyzes the relationships between internationalization and unemployment and tries to find out whether or not there is a coincidence that the rate of unemployment during the 1970s grew much faster in the countries in the European Community (EC) that it did in the countries in the European Free Trade Association (EFTA) and stayed higher for many years.

For several countries he describes both the degree of "inward internationalization" of the economy and its respective size, and he relates both these figures to the rate of unemployment for each country. Large countries and those that are "inwardly internationalized" surprisingly express a higher rate of un-employment. According to Andersson these findings challenge the view that large country size and inward internationalization are generally economically advantageous.

Both the internal coherence of the national productive system and the simultaneous existence of a corresponding national mode of regulation are suggested by Andersson as institutional explanations for the relative strengths of the smaller, less inwardly internationalized countries when it comes to employment figures. He then analyzes the EC, the United States, and Japan, as well as "the Lilliputians" (e.g,. Iceland, Switzerland, Luxembourg) and EFTA, and concludes that, for each country, there is a balance to find between integration (i.e., as a nation-state) and internationalization (i.e., part of a transnational market sphere). The Nordic countries have for many decades been successful in balancing these divergent forces through a kind of "peninsular democratic corporativism" but—according to Andersson—this may not work in the 1990s.

Part III: Changing Institutions: Focusing on Experiences in Northern and Eastern Europe

In Part III of this volume, "Changing Institutions: Focusing on Experiences in Northern and Eastern Europe," Ove K. Pedersen (in chapter 13) describes the very complex institutional setting of Denmark and its implications for how this country has coped with problems of adaptation and development in the changing world economy. This complex institutional setting is—according to Pedersen—composed of three different institutional spheres: one pertaining to a market economy, one to a "mixed" economy, and one to a "negotiated" economy. He illustrates this theoretical perspective by describing the historical backgrounds of the "wage formation procedures" (i.e., the emergence of a market economy) and the "Welfare State" (i.e., the emergence of a mixed economy), and the changes in the cooperating institutions (i.e., the emergence of a negotiated economy).

The change of the national strategy that occurred in Denmark in the mid-1980s is described by Pedersen using an institutional approach. He explains how a system for general political cooperation has been constructed, a system that has been necessary for achieving this change of national strategy. Pedersen identifies four basic mechanisms for establishing interactions between otherwise unlinked institutions: (1) They were made part of a general field of communication, (2) they were equipped with a generally shared socio-economic ideology, (3) their actions were synchronized regarding both time and level, and (4) their relationships were strengthened by interlocking memberships.

Pedersen then concludes that this system for general political cooperation in Denmark is much more than an arena for decision making and for coordinating a multilayered and policy-centered set of institutions. This overall system of generalized political cooperation can actually be seen as a basic institutional prerequisite for a negotiated economy.

In chapter 14, David Vail discusses one very important example of the institutional changes taking place in Sweden at the beginning of the 1990s: the Food Policy Reform. He carefully describes this fundamental market-oriented reform enacted through the Swedish Parliament in June 1990. Actually, according to Vail, this reform will put Sweden in a vanguard role among the advanced capitalist nations as a nation that really brings market-oriented policy into play in this conservative sector of the economy.

Like Pedersen (chapter 13), Vail describes institutional change in terms of the theory of the negotiated economy (cf. also chapter 11, by Jessop et al.). But—as Vail shows—negotiation during the 1990s is generally losing its importance for the Swedish economy, and more market relations are shifting to previously self-contained areas outside the traditionally market-oriented business sector. Vail explains that this (agricultural) corporativism is being undermined by the increasing influence of traditional democratic institutions (manifested in legislation, interparty collaboration, and election campaigning) at the cost of the negotiations between the government and capacious interest organizations.

When summarizing his chapter, Vail is not sure whether this new development in several sectors of the Swedish economy represents an evolution or a devolution of the negotiated economy. Although a partial de-corporativization could be regarded as a progressive, efficiency-increasing measure, it is also possible that this path will prove socially regressive.

In chapter 15, Ole Berrefjord and Per Heum discuss nonmarket governance of business in another Scandinavian market economy (Norway). In this chapter, they examine the mold in which the compromises between market competition and planning—that is, the actual organization of economic activities in industrialized countries—have been cast in Norwegian firms. In Norway, as in most Western countries, there is a concentration of production into fewer and larger corporations (but for a different perspective cf. chapter 6, by Perrow).

This concentration on large-scale operations also, according to Berrefjord and Heum, could be explained by the increased international competition facing Norwegian firms in the 1980s. These processes of concentration imply that the governance of production increasingly is conducted through "administrative" (i.e., planning) measures (cf. chapter 5, by Williamson). Thus, market governance is in many cases replaced by hierarchical methods.

Berrefjord and Heum also show how corporations organize their external relations and their increasing internal cooperation. Furthermore, they study the interactions between business and government, that is, to what extent firms are not only economic but also political agents in Norway. In the final part of the chapter, Berrefjord and Heum discuss the linkages among corporate growth, intercorporate relations, and business interactions and find positive correlations among all three phenomena. They conclude with a warning: We do not know very much about these nonmarket governance mechanisms, and therefore we have to be careful when applying our theoretical models on small open economies (like Norway). Thus, it is necessary to acquire a deeper understanding of the institutional structures and changes in Western societies when trying to develop economic theory.

In chapter 16, Jerzy Hausner and Andrzej Wojtyna describe how interests are represented in traditional Communist systems like Poland. They claim that a planned economy does not create conditions for the free expression of particular group interests. Formally various political and social bodies take part in the socio-economic planning together with the state administration, but in practice the roles of the former organs are mostly nominal. In the Polish post-Communist economy, new forms of interest representation have evolved, but still the state administration is not an arbiter but an actor in the areas of competition or conflict (e.g., the privatization of state property, the government's policy in various sectors, foreign economic cooperation). The ongoing transformation to a market economy at least temporarily increases the amount of the conflict of interests in Polish society, but the structure of the political system is not yet, according to Hausner and Wojtyna, adjusted to the new situation. Some social groups find no political representation of their interests, they report. An efficient communication between various social groups and political decision makers is lacking, and that brings about a very vague recognition of the authorities from the whole spectrum of economic interests.

Still, the dominance of the state sector is a characteristic of the Polish economy, and therefore the state becomes a party in almost any conflict interests instead of being an arbiter helping in their settlements. What is needed, they conclude, is the creation of new institutions that will serve as efficient mechanisms for negotiations. To achieve this, there is a need for more stable relationships among various representative and decision-making bodies. Current practice is far from such a state. They conclude by discussing whether some kind of "social contract" might be useful for taking the Polish economy through the current transitional period and express a rather favorable attitude to such a (temporary) solution.

In chapter 17, Otakar Chaloupka, Miroslav Klausák, Eva Mašková, and Pavel Mertlík describe the Czechoslovak economic reform and focus on the privatization process and its institutional setting. The designers of the privatization project intend, according to the authors, to transfer about 75 percent of the state enterprises into private hands and at a fast pace. The privatization of state cooperatives is also discussed.

Chaloupka et al. discuss three different methods for privatization: the sale of firms to foreign partners (including "joint ventures"), the free distribution of the shares of the state enterprises to the Czechoslovak population ("voucher privatization"), and—finally—"natural restitution" (i.e., the restitution of nationalized property to its original owners).

Chaloupka et al. also analyze the attitudes of the Czechoslovak people toward these different forms of privatization. By 1989 "the man on the street" considered the economic situation of the society a very problematic one, without seeing the solution to the problem in a speedy (re)introduction of capitalist economic conditions. But during 1990, however, there was a slow but safe change in attitudes, from perceiving private enterprise as something close to black market practices to a kind of productive activity beneficial both to the citizen and to society at large. Thus, they claim, there is an ongoing shift away from decidedly "anticapitalist" orientations.

Finally Chaloupka et al. compare the different logics of privatization and end up being skeptical of the "voucher method." Their mistrust is founded in the lack of educational content in that method. The individual citizen tends to become a kind of "rentier" rather than a convert into an active entrepreneur. Citizens then will be no more than mere consumers lucky enough to be given the chance to increase their consumption by selling the capital shares given to them. A far better approach—according to Chaloupka et al.—is to transfer functions (not assets) less well performed by the state bureaucracy to autonomous economic subjects. The addressed individual in such a case would be the potential bearer of entrepreneurial capabilities: the abilities to develop production, to accept risks and responsibility, and to capitalize his or her income.

Tibor Palankai, in chapter 18, focuses on the current transition and conversion in Hungary. He starts off by stating the main strategic lines of this current transition: marketization, privatization, democratization, and the integration of the country into the world economy. Marketization, he claims, had already started in Hungary in 1968 but has been limited to common goods and carried out in a monopolistic setting (i.e., in a closed economy). But marketization expanded in Hungary during the 1980s to include some parts of both the labor and capital markets. Privatization was encouraged in the late 1980s and gained priority in 1990, and the private sector contributed to something like one-third of the Hungarian gross national product (GNP) in 1991.

Palankai further describes the democratization and liberalization processes in Hungary, and from 1988 this development has accelerated with an institutional setting for a multiparty system, a parliamentary democracy, and human rights, and with the country becoming accepted as a Western democracy (manifested by free parliamentary and local elections in 1990). Palankai also describes the steps that have been taken by Hungary to become a part of the world economy, including entering world economic institutions such as the General Agreement on Tariffs and Trade (GATT).

But the problem for the new Hungary in the 1990s is that it has inherited an obsolete economy in deep crisis. For Hungary, according to Palankai, the main cause of this crisis is the indebtedness of the country. Moreover, Hungary missed the technological revolutions of both the 1970s and the 1980s. Therefore, compared to Western industries, the Hungarian technological level is poor. In addition, the enforced specialization agreements in the Council of Mutual Economic Assistance (CMEA) from 1956 had particularly negative impacts on the

Hungarian economy (some of the successfully operating industries were transferred to other Eastern European countries), and so had the dependence on the Soviet Union.

Palankai ends his chapter by describing the complex transformation problems Hungary is facing in the 1990s, in spite of its achievements in several fields during the 1980s. As in several other Eastern European countries, the military sector has had a strong position and has been closely integrated into the civilian sector. The military budget, however, has to be cut in a dramatic way in the coming decade, and at the same time there is a spectacular collapse of the economies of all the traditional buyers of Hungarian products (i.e., the CMEA markets). The crucial renewal of technologies is hindered— or at least considerably slowed down—by the prevailing pattern of legal, political, and economic institutions. Transforming individuals from one sector (the military sector) of the economy to another (the civilian) will not be easy— especially not against a background of an accelerating rate of unemployment.

Akhmed I. Kitov, in chapter 19, the last chapter of part III of the book, addresses the idea of *friction*, as previously described by Etzioni in chapter 3. Kitov has studied the attitudes among Russian managers toward market economies. Obviously, attitudes of significant agents play an important role in such dramatic transformation processes as the one going on in Russia. Kitov lists more than a dozen doubts, which a selection of Russian managers expressed, ranging from an uncertainty about what a market economy is all about to an anxiety regarding the future for their close circles and families.

This altering of the institutional framework in Russia is also, Kitov shows, among these managers associated with some positive connotations, such as expectations regarding better quality of life and more freedom of action (for the next generation?). At the end of his chapter, Kitov discusses the problems connected to the transfer of ownership from the state to various kinds of new agents. In particular, he identifies and describes some of the problems intrinsic in the present distribution of ownership in Russia.

It is hoped that the twenty chapters in this volume will contribute to the ongoing development of institutionally founded theory in the social and economic sciences, especially regarding institutional change and transformation processes in societies. A particular ingredient present—but not always made explicit— in most of the chapters is stressed in Chapter 20, the book's concluding chapter: "The Many Faces of Capitalism." In this final chapter I in a kind of hypothetical and tentative way briefly discuss some of the many different forms of capitalism and market economies that currently exist all over the world. I end this short concluding chapter by suggesting that more comparative analyses of institutional structures and changes of different countries or regions of the world could be a fruitful way, both for improving socio-economic theory and for a better understanding of the complex economic systems of nations as well as of the structures of the emerging economic regions.

Notes

1. According to Meyer (1990), this "construction of actorhood" in sociological research is—paradoxally—the fundamental process that makes for a world in which institutionalization proceeds rapidly.

2. Max Weber referred both to different collectives like types of families and marriages and to "institutions" of a religious, legislative, economic, or political kind.

3. Neale, combining anthropology and economics (1987, p. 1182), provides us with an operational definition of the concept. He identifies an institution by three characteristics. First, there are people doing; second, there are rules providing repetition, stability, and a predictable order; and third, there are folk views explaining and justifying the activities and the rules. The rules give answers to the question, What? The folk views provide answers to the question, Why? The problem Neale is facing is to identify and describe the sources of the folk views.

4. *Formal* often refers to a delimitation of a unit based on some kind of legislation (cf. employment contracts and related legislation).

5. One example is provided for in chapter 4 of this volume ("complex, interactional man").

6. The latter statement has been supported in several research experiments.

7. Compare the writings on "garbage can" models in decision making (e.g., James March and Johan Olsen, *Ambiguity and Choice in Organizations*, [Bergen: Universitetsförlaget, 1976]).

8. Some writers—like North in his latest books and articles—seem to have abandoned this idea of an evolutionary type of competition eliminating inefficient institutions (Herlitz 1989).

9. In recent writings also collectives.

10. Furthermore: "A view of institutional change that fails to offer any legitimate rationale for change other than that of narrowly constructed economic gains trivializes most collective action; it is further trivialized by the belief that all collective action either contributes to efficiency, or simply redistributes income" (Bromley 1989, p. 32).

Bibliography

Akerlof, George A. 1980a. "A Theory of Social Custom, Of Which Unemployment May Be One Consequence." *Quarterly Journal of Economics* 94: 749–75. Reprinted in Akerlöf 1984.

———. 1980b. "The Economics of Social Customs, Of Which Unemployment May Be One Consequence." *Quarterly Journal of Economics* 95: 749–75.

———. 1984. *An Economic Theorist's Book of Tales*. Cambridge: Cambridge University Press.

Axelrod, Robert. 1984. *The Evolution of Cooperation*. New York: Basic Books.

Berger, Peter, and Thomas Luckmann. 1967. *The Social Construction of Reality*. New York: Doubleday.

Bogason, Peter. 1980. "Institutioner og politologer." *Statsvetenskaplig Tidskrift* 90, 4: 287–97.

Braudel, Fernand. 1982. *The Wheels of Commerce*. Part 2. London.

Bromley, Daniel. 1989. *Economic Interests and Institutions*. New York: Basil Blackwell.

Burns, Tom R., and Helena Flam. 1986. *The Shaping of Social Organization: Social Rule System Theory and Its Applications.* London: Sage.

Bush, Paul. "Theory of Institutional Change." *Journal of Economic Issues.* 20, 3: 1075–116.

Chandler, Alfred. 1977. *The Visible Hand.* Cambridge: Harper and Row, Belknap Press.

Commons, John R. 1934/1990. *Institutional Economics.* Vol. 1. New Brunswick, N.J.: Transaction Publisher.

Cyert, Richard. 1988. *The Economic Theory of Organization and the Firm.* New York: Harvester Wheatsheaf.

Demsetz, Harold. 1988. *Ownership, Control and the Firm. The Organization of Economic Activity.* Vol. 1. Oxford: Basil Blackwell.

DiMaggio, Paul J. 1988. "Interest and Agency in Institutional Theory." In *Institutional Patterns and Organizations*, ed. Lynne G. Zucker. Cambridge: Ballinger Publishing Co., 3–22.

DiMaggio, Paul J., and Walter W. Powell. 1983. "The Iron Cage Revisited: Institutional Isomorphism and Collective Rationality in Organizational Fields." *American Sociological Review* 48: 147–60.

Dugger, William M. 1990. "The New Institutionalism." *Journal of Economic Issues* 24, (June) 2: 423–32.

Elsner, Wolfram. 1989. "Adam Smith's Model of the Origins and Emergence of Institutions." *Journal of Economic Issues* 23, 1: 189–213.

Etzioni, Amitai. 1988. *The Moral Dimension.* New York: Free Press.

Evans, Peter, Dietrich Rueschemeyer, and Thelda Skocpol, eds. 1985. *Bringing the State Back In.* Cambridge: Cambridge University Press.

Fogel, Robert W. 1989. *Without Consent or Contract. The Rise and Fall of American Slavery.* New York: W. W. Norton.

Friedland, Roger, and Robert R. Alfred. 1987. "Bringing Society Back In: Symbols, Structures and Institutional Contradiction." Paper presented at the Conference on Institutional Change, Center for Advanced Study in the Behavioral Sciences, Stanford, Calif., May 15–16.

Garfinkel, Harold. 1967. *Studies in Ethnomethodology.* Englewood Cliffs, N.J.: Prentice-Hall.

Gruchy, Allan G. 1947. *Modern Economic Thought: The American Contribution.* New York: Prentice-Hall.

Gustafsson, Bo, ed. 1991. *Power and Economic Institutions.* Worcester, England: Edward Elgar.

Herlitz, Lars. 1989. *Institutionalismen i Samfundsvidenskaberna.* Gylling, Denmark: Samfundslitteratur.

Hodgson, Geoff M. 1987. *Economics and Institutions.* Oxford: Polity Press.

Kjellberg, F. 1975. *Political Institutionalization.* London: Wiley.

Knudsen, Christian, et al. 1989. *Institutionalismen i Samfundsvidenskaberna.* Gylling, Denmark: Samfundslitteratur.

Koot, G. M. 1987. *English Historical Economics 1870–1926.* Cambridge: Cambridge University Press.

Leibenstein, Harvey. 1984. "Property Rights and X-Efficiency: Comment." *American Economic Review* 73, 4: 831–42.

March, James G., and Johan P. Olsen. 1976. *Ambiguity and Choice in Organizations.* Bergen: Universitetsförlaget.

————. 1984. "The New Institutionalism: Organizational Factors in Political Life."
American Political Science Review 78: 734–49.

————. 1989. *Rediscovering Institutions*. New York: Free Press.

Meyer, John W. 1990. "On Institutions." SCANOR Meeting Conference paper presented at Utö, Sweden, August 29-31.

Meyer, John W., and Brian Rowan. 1977. "Institutional Organizations: Formal Structure as Myth and Ceremony." *American Journal of Sociology* 83: 340–63.

Meyer, John W., and Richard W. Scott. 1983. *Organizational Environments: Ritual and Rationality*. Newbury Park, Calif.: Sage.

Meyer, John W., et al. 1987. "Ontology and Rationalization in the Western Cultural Account." In *Institutional Structure: Constituting State, Society, and the Individual*. London: Sage Publications.

Myhrman, Johan. Forthcoming. *The Petrified Economy*.

Neale, Walter C. 1987. "Institutions." *Journal of Economic Issues* 21, 3: 1177–206.

Newman, K. S. 1983. *Law and Economic Organization: A Comparative Study of Preindustrial Societies*, Cambridge: Cambridge University Press.

North, Douglass C. 1981. *Structure and Change in Economic History*. New York: W. W. Norton.

————. 1989. "Institutions and Economic Performance." Paper presented to the SCASSS Conference, "Rationality, Institutions and Economic Methodology." Uppsala, Sweden, August.

————. 1991. "Institutions." *The Journal of Economic Perspectives* 5, 1: 97–112.

North, Douglass C., and Robert Paul Thomas. 1970. "An Economic Theory of the Growth of the Western World." *Economic History Review* 23: 1–17.

————. 1973. *The Rise of the Western World*. Cambridge: Cambridge University Press.

Parsons, Talcott. 1937. *The Structure of Social Action*, 2 vols. New York: McGraw-Hill.

————. 1940. "The Motivation of Economic Activities." *Canadian Journal of Economics and Political Science* 6: 187–203. Reprinted in *Readings in Economic Sociology*, ed. N. Smelser. Englewood Cliffs N.J.: Prentice-Hall.

————. 1951. *The Social System*. New York: Free Press.

Perrow, Charles. 1986. *Complex Organizations: A Critical Essay*. 3d ed. New York: Random House.

Pfeffer, Jeffrey. 1982. *Organizations and Organization Theory*. Marshfield, Mass.: Pitman.

Potter, A. L. 1979. "Political Institutions, Political Decay and the Argentine Crises of 1930." Ph.D. diss., Stanford University, Department of Political Science.

Rowe, Nicholas. 1989. *Roles and Institutions*. New York: Philip Allan.

Samuels, Warren, ed. 1988. *Institutional Economics*. Vol. 1. Aldershot, England: Edward Elgar.

Schotter, Andrew. 1981. *The Economic Theory of Social Institutions*. Cambridge: Cambridge University Press.

Scott, W. Richard. 1987. "The Adolescence of Institutional Theory." *Administrative Science Quarterly* 32: 493–511.

————. 1990. "Institutional Analysis: Variance and Powers Theory Approaches." Paper presented at SCANCOR's Conference in Stockholm, Sweden, August 29–31.

Scott, W. Richard, and John W. Meyer. 1983. "The Organization of Societal Sectors." In *Organizational Environments: Ritual and Rationality*, ed. John W. Meyer and W. Richard Scott, 129-53. Beverly Hills, Calif.: Sage.

Selznick, Philip. 1957. *Leadership in Administration*. New York: Harper and Row.

Sen, Amartya. 1981. *Poverty and Famines: An Essay on Entitlement and Deprivation.* Oxford: Oxford University Press.

Sjöstrand, Sven-Erik. 1985. *Samhällsorganisation*. Lund, Sweden: Doxa.

Spencer, Herbert. 1899. *The Principles of Sociology*. New York: Appleton.

Therborn, G. M. 1976. "Vad gör den härskande klassen när den härskar?" *Häften för Kritiska Studier* 4: 14–42.

———, ed. 1980. *What Does the Ruling Class Do When It Rules?* London: Verso.

Thomas, George, et al. 1987a. *Institutional Structure*. London: Sage Publications.

———. 1987b. *Institutional Structure: Constituting State, Society, and the Individual.* London: Sage Publications.

Tool, Marc R. 1986. *Essays in Social Value Theory*. New York: M. E. Sharpe.

Williamson, Oliver, E. 1975. *Markets and Hierarchies: Analysis and Antitrust Implications*. New York: Free Press.

———. 1985. *The Economic Institutions of Capitalism*. New York: Free Press.

Wuthnow, Robert, James Davison Hunter, Albert Bergesen, and Edith Kurzweil. 1984. *Cultural Analysis*. Boston: Routledge and Kegan Paul.

Zucker, Lynne G. 1983. "Organizations as Institutions." In *Advances in Organizational Theory and Research*, ed. Samuel B. Bacharach, 2: 53–111. New York: JAI.

———. 1987. "Institutional Theories of Organizations." *Annual Review of Sociology* 13: 443–64. Palo Alto, Calif.: Annual Review.

———, ed. 1988. *Institutional Patterns and Organizations*. Cambridge, MA: Ballinger Publishing.

Part I.

Institutional Change: Basic Theory

2. Institutional Change: A Framework of Analysis

Douglass C. North

A theory of institutional change is essential for further progress in the social sciences in general and economics in particular. Essential because neoclassical theory (and other theories in the social scientist's tool bag) at present cannot satisfactorily account for the very diverse performance of societies and economies both at a moment of time and over time. The explanations derived from neoclassical theory are not satisfactory because, while the models may account for most of the differences in performance between economies on the basis of differential investment in education, savings rates, and so forth, they do not account for why economies would fail to undertake the appropriate activities *if they had a high payoff.*[1] Institutions determine the payoffs. While the fundamental neoclassical assumption of scarcity and hence competition has been robust (and is basic to this analysis), the assumption of a frictionless exchange process has led economic theory astray. Institutions are the structure that humans impose on human interaction and therefore define the incentives that, together with the other constraints (budget, technology, etc.), determine the choices that individuals make that shape the performance of societies and economies over time.

In the following pages, I sketch out a framework for analyzing institutions. This framework builds on the economic theory of choice subject to constraints. However, it incorporates new assumptions about both the constraints that individuals face and the process by which they make choices within those constraints. Among the traditional neoclassical assumptions that are relaxed are those of costless exchange, perfect information, and unlimited cognitive capabilities. Too many gaps still remain in our understanding of this new approach to call it a theory. What I do provide are a set of definitions and principles and a

This essay draws from and builds upon a recent book by the author entitled *Institutions, Institutional Change and Economic Performance* (Cambridge University Press, 1990). I would like to thank members of the Washington University workshop in economic history and particularly Arthur Denzau, Bradley Hansen, and Andrew Rutten for their comments and suggestions. I would also like to thank Elisabeth Case for editing this essay.

structure that provides much of the scaffolding necessary to develop a theory of institutional change.

Institutions and Organizations: Definitions and Descriptions

Institutions consist of formal rules, informal constraints (norms of behavior, conventions, and self-imposed codes of conduct), and the enforcement characteristics of both. The degree to which there is an identity between the objectives of the institutional constraints and the choices individuals make in that institutional setting depends on the effectiveness of enforcement. Enforcement is carried out by the first party (self-imposed codes of conduct), by the second party (retaliation), and/or by a third party (societal sanctions or coercive enforcement by the state). Institutions affect economic performance by determining (together with the technology employed) transaction and transformation (production) costs.

If institutions are the rules of the game, organizations are the players. They are groups of individuals engaged in purposive activity. The constraints imposed by the institutional framework (together with the other constraints) define the opportunity set and therefore the kind of organizations that will come into existence. Given its objective function—for example, profit maximization, winning elections, regulating businesses, educating students—the organization, which may be a firm, a political party, a regulatory agency, a school or college, will engage in acquiring skills and knowledge that will enhance its survival possibilities in the context of ubiquitous scarcity and hence competition. The kinds of skills and knowledge that will pay off will be a function of the incentive structure inherent in the institutional matrix. If the highest rates of return in a society are to be made from piracy, the organizations will invest in knowledge and skills that will make them better pirates; if organizations realize the highest payoffs by increasing productivity, then they will invest in skills and knowledge to achieve that objective. Organizations may not only directly invest in acquiring skills and knowledge but indirectly (via the political process) induce public investment in those kinds of knowledge that they believe will enhance their survival prospects.

The new (or neo-) institutional economics has produced a substantial literature dealing with institutions and organizations. The property rights literature (Alchian 1965/1977; Demsetz 1967), for example, analyzes the implications of institutions and organizations for performance, but in most of it the formation and evolution of institutions and organizations remain exogenous to the analysis. Williamson (1975, 1985), treating the institutional framework as exogenous, explores the transaction and transformation costs of various organizational forms. My objective (North 1990 as well as here) is to put forth an explanation of institutional (and organizational) change that is endogenous, an essential step in my view to further progress in economic history and economic development.

Institutional Change: Agents, Sources, Process, and Direction

The agent of change is the entrepreneur, the decision maker(s) in organizations. The subjective perceptions (mental models) of entrepreneurs determine the choices they make. The sources of change are the opportunities perceived by entrepreneurs. They stem from either external changes in the environment or the acquisition of learning and skills and their incorporation in the mental constructs of the actors. Changes in relative prices have been the most commonly observed external sources of institutional change in history, but changes in taste have also been important. The acquisition of learning and skills will lead to the construction of new mental models by entrepreneurs to decipher the environment; in turn, the models will alter perceived relative prices of potential choices. In fact, it is usually some mixture of external change and internal learning that triggers the choices that lead to institutional change.

Deliberate institutional change will come about, therefore, as a result of the demands of entrepreneurs in the context of the perceived costs of altering the institutional framework at various margins. The entrepreneur will assess the gains to be derived from recontracting within the existing institutional framework compared to the gains from devoting resources to altering that framework. Bargaining strength and the incidence of transaction costs are not the same in the polity as in the economy; otherwise it would not be worthwhile for groups to shift the issues to the political arena. Thus entrepreneurs who perceive themselves and their organizations as relative (or absolute) losers in economic exchange as a consequence of the existing structure of relative prices can turn to the political process to right their perceived wrongs by altering that relative price structure. In any case, it is the perceptions of the entrepreneur—correct or incorrect—that are the sources of action.

Changes in the formal rules may come about as a result of legislative changes such as the passage of a new statute, of judicial changes stemming from court decisions that alter the common law, of regulatory rule changes enacted by regulatory agencies, and of constitutional rule changes that alter the rules by which other rules are made.

Changes in informal constraints—norms, conventions, or personal standards of honesty, for example—have the same originating sources of change as do changes in formal rules; but they occur gradually and sometimes quite subconsciously as individuals evolve alternative patterns of behavior consistent with their newly perceived evaluation of costs and benefits.

The process of change is overwhelmingly incremental (although I shall deal with revolutionary change later in this chapter). The reason is that the economies of scope, the complementarities, and the network externalities that arise from a given institutional matrix of formal rules, informal constraints, and enforcement characteristics will typically bias costs and benefits in favor of choices consistent with the existing framework. The larger the number of rule changes, ceteris paribus, the greater the number of losers and hence opposition. Therefore, except in the case of gridlock (described in the next paragraph), institutional change will occur at those margins considered most pliable in the context of the bargaining power of interested parties. The incremental change may come from a change in the rules via statute or legal change. For informal constraints there may be a very gradual withering away of an accepted norm or social convention or the gradual adoption of a new one as the nature of the political, social, or economic exchange gradually changes.

The direction of change is determined by path dependence. The political and economic organizations that have come into existence in consequence of the institutional matrix typically have a stake in perpetuating the existing framework. The complementarities, economies of scope, and network externalities just mentioned bias change in favor of the interests of the existing organizations. Both the interests of the existing organizations that produce path dependence and the mental models of the actors—the entrepreneurs—that produce ideologies "rationalize" the existing institutional matrix and therefore bias the perception of the actors in favor of policies conceived to be in the interests of existing organizations.

Both external sources of change and unanticipated consequences of their policies may weaken the power of existing organizations, strengthen or give rise to organizations with different interests, and change the path. The critical actor(s) in such situations will be political entrepreneurs whose degrees of freedom will increase in such situations and, on the basis of their perception of the issues, give them the ability to induce the growth of organizations with different interests (or strengthen existing ones).

Revolutionary change occurs as a result of a gridlock arising from a lack of mediating institutions that enable conflicting parties to reach compromises that capture some of the gains from potential trades. The key to the existence of such mediating political (and economic) institutions is not only formal rules and organizations but also informal constraints that can foster dialogue between conflicting parties. The inability to achieve compromise solutions may also reflect limited degrees of freedom of the entrepreneurs to bargain and still maintain the loyalty of their constituent groups. Thus, the real choice set of the conflicting parties may have no intersection, so that even though there are potentially large gains from resolving disagreements, the combination of the limited bargaining freedom of the entrepreneurs and a lack of facilitating institutions makes it impossible to do so.

Revolutionary change, however, is never as revolutionary as its rhetoric would have us believe. It is not just that the power of ideological rhetoric fades as the mental models of the constituents confront their utopian ideals with the harsh realities of post-revolutionary existence. Formal rules may change overnight, but informal constraints do not. Inconsistency between the formal rules and the informal constraints (which may be the result of deep-seated cultural inheritance because they have traditionally resolved basic exchange problems) results in tensions that typically get resolved by some restructuring of the overall constraints—in both directions—to produce a new equilibrium that is far less revolutionary than the rhetoric.

The Framework Illustrated

An extended sketch from American economic history illustrates the way in which institutions, organizations, and the mental models of the actors interact to produce institutional change.

The basic institutional framework of the American colonies that had been carried over from England provided a hospitable environment for economic growth. The incentive structure not only encouraged decentralized and local political autonomy but also provided low-cost economic transacting through fee simple ownership of land (with some early exceptions in proprietary colonies) and secure property rights. The organizations that arose to take advantage of the resultant opportunities—colonial assemblies, plantations, merchant houses, shipping firms, family farms—produced a thriving colonial economy. But the entire colonial period was one of a long learning process—discovering staple exports (tobacco, fish, rice, indigo); developing markets (West Indies, Southern Europe); improving productivity (substituting slaves for indentured servants on tobacco plantations, reducing turnaround time in shipping). In brief, the learning resulted in reducing transaction or transformation costs or in increasing revenues that resulted in improving the efficiency of the colonial economy.

While planters, merchants, shippers, and farmers could and did make modest changes in the institutional framework as their perceived needs changed, they were basically limited by their colonial status—not perceived as a serious burden as long as the threat of French and Indian intervention was present. With the elimination of that threat with the French and Indian War (1755–63), the colonists increasingly perceived their interests as divergent from Britain and its colonial policies. The American Revolution was sparked not only by changes in the institutions such as the Quebec Act (closing off western lands to settlement by American colonists) and the very moderate taxes imposed on the colonists (which produced a violent reaction) but also by the intellectual tradition from Hobbes to Locke that shaped the mental models of the actors. The British never anticipated that the taxes imposed on the colonists would produce such a violent reaction, and the colonists for their part were wrong in their perception that British policy after 1763 would destroy the colonial economy (after all, the colonies that were to become Canada did very well staying within the Empire). It was the perceptions of the colonists in the context of the intellectual traditions of the times that guided Samuel Adams, Thomas Paine, Thomas Jefferson, George Washington, and others on their policies.

The post-revolutionary Northwest Ordinance of 1787 and Constitution codified, elaborated, and modified colonial institutions in the light of contemporary issues (and the bargaining strength of the players). But despite the Revolution, the basic institutional framework of formal rules (including contracts enacted before the war) and informal cultural norms was maintained and continued the incentives for a thriving economy. Productivity increase came not only from high payoff to the acquisition of productive skills and knowledge by economic organizations and from the encouragement of technological change (such as by patent law), but also from induced investment through the polity in public education, land grant colleges, agricultural experiment stations, and so forth. As organizations evolved to take advantage of opportunities, they became more productive (Chandler 1977), and gradually they also altered the institutional framework. The judicial and political framework (the Marshall Court decisions, the Fourteenth Amendment) and the structure of property rights were altered or modified (Munn v. Illinois), but so too were many norms of behavior and other informal constraints altered (reflected in changing attitudes toward slavery and African Americans and toward the role of women in society and temperance, for example).

The price paid for this rapid economic growth was partly inherent in adaptively efficient institutions. The system wiped out losers—farmers who went bust on the frontier, shipping firms that failed as the United States lost its comparative advantage in shipping, laborers who suffered unemployment and declining wages from immigrant competition in the 1850s. It was also partly a consequence of institutions that exploited individuals and groups—American Indians and slaves and not infrequently immigrants, workers, and farmers—to the benefit of those with superior bargaining power.

The political framework resulted in the losers having, albeit imperfect, access to remedies for their perceived source of misfortune—remedies that also altered the institutional framework. Perceived sources consisted of immediately observed grievances filtered through ongoing intellectual currents and ideologies of the actors. The late nineteenth-century farmers could frequently observe price discrimination by the railroad or grain elevator, but the Populist party platform reflected broad ideological views encompassing the perceived burden of the gold standard and widespread monopoly, as well as the pernicious consequences of bankers. Whatever the underlying sources of the farmer's plight that produced discontent, the farmers' perceptions mattered and changed the political and economic institutional framework.

Nor was it just the farmers' perceptions that mattered. So did the subjective models of the other actors or organizations, and these were able to influence outcomes as a result of the institutional matrix. Whether the Supreme Court understood the implications of its 1877 decision in Munn v. Illinois (commonly regarded as a milestone in the growth of federal government regulation) and the many other court decisions that were gradually altering the legal framework depended on the degree to which the information feedback on the consequences of existing laws was accurate and hence gave true models. True or false, the models the judiciary acted upon were incrementally altering the judicial framework.

As with all institutional frameworks, the rules were a mixed bag of those that promoted increased productivity and those that encouraged monopoly, income redistribution, and inefficient resource allocation; but the former have overwhelmingly dominated the institutional framework and produced a path-dependent pattern of economic growth that has persisted for more than three centuries. To illustrate this path-dependent process, I turn from this overarching story to a more detailed examination of one facet of this story—land policy—that will put more meat on the analytical bones of this framework.

The Northwest Ordinance of 1787 was the third in a series of enactments passed by the Congress in the 1780s to establish an overall pattern for the disposal of the vast public lands. The Northwest Ordinance is brief. It provided for rules of inheritance and fee simple ownership of land, set up the basic structure of territorial governments, and provided the mechanisms by which territories gradually became self-governing. Additionally, it made provision for when a territory would be admitted as a state. Then there was a series of Articles of Compact, in effect a bill of rights for the territories. There were additional provisions about good faith to the American Indians, free navigation on the Mississippi and St. Lawrence rivers, public debt, land disposal, and the number of states that could be divided up within the Northwest Territory; finally there was a provision prohibiting slavery in the territories (although the return of runaway slaves was specified).

These provisions can be directly traced to the English and colonial background; many of them, including much of the bill of rights, were explicit provisions of the colonial charters (Hughes 1987). The impetus for the Ordinance was relative price changes stemming from the financial crisis of the new nation and states as they emerged from the Revolution combined with the necessity of developing policies to administer the vast territories that had been acquired as a result of the 1783 peace treaty following independence. Controversial implications for the current and future distribution of political power and (not unrelated) the slavery issue (North and Rutten 1987) shaped specific provisions.

The agents of change (and their organizations) included the following: (1) the Reverend Manassah Cutler (and the Ohio and Scioto companies), who asked Congress to provide a settled plan of self-government for the proposed settlers of the huge blocks of land Congress had granted to those companies—thereby inducing Congress to establish the committee that wrote the Ordinance; and (2) Nathan Dane and Rufus King (representatives from Massachusetts and members of the committee), who wrote many of the Ordinance's provisions and specifically the one barring slavery in the Northwest Territory (Hughes 1987).

The downstream consequences of the Northwest Ordinance were continually being shaped by the relative price changes that reflected the rising implicit rents resulting from the rising value of land together with the government sale prices and weak enforcement policies. The consequent rapid settlement was, in turn, altering the political balance of power. Territories became states with interests different from those of the older states, and their agendas incrementally shaped later public land policies. Claims clubs emerged to thwart competitive bidding (for land that the squatters had settled upon); squatters finally got a general preemption act (giving them first claim on the land they had settled upon); the minimum size of units for sale was reduced, and eventually Congress passed the Homestead Act of 1862 (giving land away free).

Some of the consequences may have been unanticipated. The prohibition of slavery in the new territories, for example, induced a large proportion of settlers to come from New England; they brought with them attitudes that were distinctly different from those of settlers of other regions and from those of immigrants. They were more literate, a lower proportion were tenants, and they possessed greater real estate wealth (Atack and Bateman 1987). Their attitude played a major role in early investment in public education and in other public policies that were in distinct contrast to those that evolved in territories south of the Ohio River where slavery was permitted.

Overall, the history of land policy is only intelligible as a continuously unfolding story of incremental change but one in which the initial path stamped out by the three great land ordinances of the 1780s was decisive in shaping the long-run path. That is, the fundamental features of the three ordinances, which provided for low-cost political and economic transacting, structured the political and economic framework of the territories and led to rapid economic growth, settlement, and integration into the United States economy. Even downstream public policies that produced inefficient consequences such as the Homestead Act of 1862, which imposed inefficient size restrictions on initial land holdings, were mitigated by the low costs of transacting, which led to subsequent consolidations and efficient size units of use.

The Implications of an Institutional Framework

Information processing by the actors as a result of the costliness of transacting underlies the formation of institutions. At issue are both the meaning of rationality and the characteristics of transacting that prevent the actors from achieving the joint maximization result of the zero-transaction cost model.

The instrumental rationality postulate of neoclassical theory assumes that the actors possess information necessary to evaluate correctly alternatives and in consequence make choices that will achieve the desired ends. In fact, such a postulate implicitly assumes the existence of a particular set of institutions and costless information. If institutions play a purely passive role so that they do not constrain the choice of the players and the players are in possession of the information necessary to make correct choices, the instrumental rationality postulate is the correct building block. If, on the other hand, the players are incompletely informed, devise subjective models as guides to choices, and can only very imperfectly correct their models with information feedback, then a procedural rationality postulate is the essential building block to theorizing. Such a postulate not only can account for the incomplete and imperfect markets that characterize much of the present and the past world but also leads the researcher to the key issues of just what it is that makes markets imperfect—the cost of transacting.

The cost of transacting arises because information is costly and asymmetrically held by the parties to the exchange. In consequence, any way that the players develop institutions to structure human interaction results in some degree of imperfection of the markets. In effect, the incentive consequences of institutions provide mixed signals to the participants, so that even in those cases where the institutional framework is more conducive to capturing the gains from trade than was an earlier institutional framework, there will be incentives to cheat, free ride, and so forth that will contribute to market imperfections. The success stories of economic history describe institutional innovations that have lowered the costs of transacting and permitted capturing more of the gains from trade and hence permitted the expansion of markets. But such innovations, for the most part, have not created the conditions necessary for the efficient markets of the neoclassical model. The polity specifies and enforces the property rights of the economic marketplace, and the characteristics of the political market are the essential key to understanding the imperfections of markets.

Just as the efficiency of an economic market can be measured by the degree to which the competitive structure via arbitrage and efficient information feedback mimics or approximates the conditions of a zero-transaction cost framework, so too is a political market efficient to the degree that constituents accurately evaluate the policies pursued by competing candidates in terms of the net effect on their well-being, to the degree that legislators enact only legislation (or regulation) that maximizes the aggregate income of the affected parties to the exchange, and to the degree that constituents and legislators ensure by compensating those adversely affected that no party is injured by an action.

To achieve such results, constituents and legislators would need to possess true models that allowed them to evaluate accurately the gains and losses of alternative policies, legislators would vote their constituents' interests—that is the vote of each legislator would be weighted by the net gains or losses of the constituents—and losers would be compensated such as to make the exchange worthwhile to them—all at a transaction cost that still resulted in the highest net aggregate gain.

I do not wish to imply that the political process in democracies does not sometimes approach such an outcome of nirvana, just as economic markets sometimes approximate the zero-transaction cost model implicit in much economic theory. But such instances are rare and exceptional. Voter ignorance, incomplete information, and, in consequence, the prevalence of ideological stereotypes as the underpinnings of the subjective models individuals develop to explain their environment and make choices result in political markets that can and do perpetuate unproductive institutions and consequent organizations.[2]

Four of the implications for economic theory of the foregoing analysis of institutions and imperfect (or procedural) rationality are the following:

1. Economic (and political) models are specific to particular constellations of institutional constraints that vary radically both through time and cross-sectionally in different economies. The models are institution specific and in many cases highly sensitive to altered institutional constraints. Even more important, the specific institutional constraints dictate the margins at which organizations operate and hence make intelligible the interplay between the rules of the game and the behavior of the actors. If organizations devote their efforts to unproductive activity, the institutional constraints have provided the incentive structure for such activity. Third-world countries are poor because the institutional constraints define a set of payoffs to political/economic activity that do not encourage productive activity. Socialist economies are beginning to learn the hard lesson that the underlying institutional framework is the source of the current poor performance and are attempting to grapple with ways to restructure the institutional framework to redirect incentives that, in turn, will direct organizations along productively increasing paths. And as for the first world, we not only need to appreciate the importance of the overall institutional framework that has been responsible for the growth of the economy but also need to be self-conscious about the consequences of the marginal changes that are continually occurring. We have long been aware that taxes, regulations, judicial decisions, and statute laws shape the policies of organizations, but such awareness has not led economic theory to modeling the political/economic process that produces these results.

2. A self-conscious incorporation of institutions will force social scientists in general and economists in particular to question the behavioral assumptions that underlie their disciplines and, in consequence, to explore much more systematically than we have done so far the implications of the costly and imperfect processing of information for the consequent behavior of the actors. Social scientists *have* incorporated the costliness of information in their models but have not (for the most part) come to grips with the subjective mental constructs by which individuals process information and arrive at conclusions that shape their choices.

3. Ideas and ideologies matter, and institutions play a major role in determining just how much they matter. Ideas and ideologies shape the mental constructs

that individuals use to interpret the world around them and make choices. Moreover, by structuring the interaction of human beings in certain ways, formal institutions deliberately or accidentally lower the price of acting on one's ideas and therefore increase the role of mental constructs and ideological stereotypes in choices. Voting systems, lifetime tenure for judges, indeed the institutional framework of hierarchies in general all provide a setting that alters the price one pays for expressing and acting on one's ideas, convictions, dogmas, or insights.

4. The polity and the economy are inextricably linked in any understanding of the performance of an economy, and therefore we must develop a true political economy discipline. A set of institutional constraints and consequent organizations defines the exchange relationships between the two and therefore determines the way a political/economic system works. Not only do polities specify and enforce property rights that shape the basic incentive structure of an economy; in the modern world the share of gross national product going through government and the ubiquitous and ever-changing regulations imposed by it are the keys to economic performance.

Toward a Theory of Institutional Change

Let me conclude by summing up the key features of this analytical framework of institutional change:

• The continuous interaction between institutions and organizations in the economic setting of scarcity and hence competition is the key to institutional change.

• Competition forces organizations continually to invest in knowledge to survive.

• The institutional framework dictates the kind of knowledge perceived to have the maximum payoff.

• The mental constructs of the players—given the complexity of the environment, the limited information feedback on the consequences of actions, and the inherited cultural conditioning of the players—determine perceptions.

• The economies of scope, complementarities, and network externalities of an institutional matrix make institutional change overwhelmingly incremental and path dependent.

Notes

1. An excellent survey of the new neoclassical growth literature is to be found in "A Contribution to the Empirics of Economic Growth" by G. Mankiw, D. Romer, and D. Weil (National Bureau of Economic Research [NBER] Working Paper no. 3541).

2. See the author's "A Transaction Cost Theory of Politics," *Journal of Theoretical Politics* 2 (Fall 1990) 4: 355–68, for an elaboration of this argument.

Bibliography

Alchian, Armen. 1965/1977. "Some Economics of Property Rights." *Il Politico* 30 (4): 816–29. Reprinted in A. Alchian. *Economic Forces at Work*. Indianapolis: Liberty Press.

Atack, Jeremy, and Fred Bateman. 1987. "Yankee Farming and Settlement in the Old Northwest: A Comparative Analysis." In *Essays on the Economy of the Old Northwest*, ed. D. Klingaman and R. Vedder, Athens: Ohio University.

Chandler, Alfred D. 1977. *The Visible Hand: The Managerial Revolution in American Business*. Cambridge: Harvard University Press, Belknap Press.

Demsetz, Harold. 1967. "Toward a Theory of Property Rights." *American Economic Review* 57: 347–59.

Hughes, J. R. T. 1987. "The Great Land Ordinances." In *Essays on the Economy of the Old Northwest*, ed. D. Klingaman and R. Vedder, 1–18. Athens: Ohio University.

Mankiw, Gregory; David Romer; and David Weil. 1991. "A Contribution to the Empirics of Economic Growth." National Bureau of Economic Research (NBER) Working Paper no. 3541.

North, Douglass C. 1990. *Institutions, Institutional Change and Economic Performance*. Cambridge: Cambridge University Press.

North, Douglass C., and Andrew Rutten. 1987. "The Northwest Ordinance in Historical Perspective." In *Essays on the Economy of the Old Northwest*, ed. D. Klingaman and R. Vedder, 19–36. Athens: Ohio University.

Williamson, Oliver. 1975. *Markets and Hierarchies: Analysis and Antitrust Implications*. New York: Free Press.

———. 1985. *The Economic Institutions of Capitalism*. New York: Free Press.

3. A Socio-Economic Perspective on Friction

Amitai Etzioni

Two Views of Friction

During the deliberations of a faculty seminar on socio-economics at the George Washington University in 1986–87, before the dramatic developments in Eastern Europe occurred, the question of the pace of socio-economic change kept coming up. For a while it seemed that, regardless of the topic to which a particular session of the seminar was devoted, the main difference in perspective between those seminar members who were neoclassical economists and the other social scientists present was their divergent assumptions about the pace of human adjustments to new situations and signals.

The neoclassical economists tended to assume that the adjustments would be swift and basically unproblematic. That is, while foregoing the assumption that economics formerly embraced, of instantaneous and cost-free adjustments, the neoclassicists continued to hold that the hindering factors—or friction—were so low that they did not require significant modifications to the assumptions and basic model nor significant modifications to the lists of factors that need to be systematically studied or to the predictions of neoclassical economics. The possibility of slow and costly adjustments to changes—or high friction—was acknowledged. It was treated, however, as if it did not occur or was rare. Thus, while no one in the seminar denied that behavior was "sticky," when the discussion turned to specifics—for instance, to the effects of price increases on energy conservation—neoclassical economists tended to suggest that conservation would follow once prices were increased. Similarly, it was recognized that prices are sticky on the downside, but that recognition did not leave any discernible imprints on the neoclassicists' discussion about the use of short-order recessions as a way to curb inflation, and so on.

In contrast, other social scientists in the seminar tended to point to a long list of observations that people "just did not behave that way," that they were much slower to adjust than the neoclassical economists expected. Examples abound: Many Americans were slow to open individual retirement accounts (IRAs) (special savings accounts for which the U.S. government allows people to defer taxes on the interest earned) accounts, although it was clearly to their advantage to do so; they were slow to leave jobs in declining industries and move from those parts of the country to new and rising ones; they continued to buy about the same number of tax shelters even after the 1986 tax law made those shelters much less favorable; they keep inefficient corporations going right next to more efficient ones. While these members of the seminar initially put it in terms of absolutes, that is, behavior does not conform to the neoclassical expectations, gradually they came to express it in more relative terms. Rather than assuming that people do not change, the preferred formula became that changes in personal and social behavior, including economic, tend to be slow and difficult—that friction is high.

Once both groups of seminar members became aware that they were focusing on the same kind of factor, friction, the door opened to questions regarding the typical extent of friction, the factors that account for the particular level found, and the implications of high levels of frictions for various models predictions. The seminar stopped, more or less, at this point. This chapter provides a preliminary discussion of these questions.

Another way to highlight the issue at hand is to return to an often repeated analogue neoclassical economists use when challenged that their theories are "unrealistic." They respond that their models are like those of physicists: They formulate laws for perfect conditions, for example, a frictionless slope. These laws provide either an approximation or a model that can then be adjusted to the empirical situation. Socio-economists may respond, at least this one does, that a model may serve as a suitable approximation, when it actually does approximate, that is, comes reasonably close to the reality it seeks to model. However, just as the assumption of imperfect information implies that information is almost fully available, whereas in actuality decisions are made with only small fractions of the needed information, so with friction, the model of a frictionless slope is productive only to the extent that the relevant segments of the world under study are rather low in friction. If friction, like ignorance (in effect a form of friction), is typically high, the suggested logic of model building favors the use of a model of complete friction and adjustments reflecting whatever movement one does encounter.

In the area of decision making, this suggests, first, that one should assume that poor decisions, made with little information and poor processing of the information that is available, are the norm. Well-informed, "good," not to mention optimal, decisions are the exceptions, and the special factors that account for them need explaining. This is, of course, the opposite of the tack usually taken, in which one tries to account for irrationality, assuming rationality to be normal. (For additional discussion, see Etzioni 1988, ch. 6.) Second, unlike physicists, neoclassical economists do not provide, in most areas, transition coefficients, that is, the formulae that allow one to move from generalizations about the idealized state, the frictionless slope, to movement on actual slopes. This omission is unimportant if friction is very low but critical if it is high. As we shall see immediately, at least in some rather important cases, friction is high indeed. Hence, the need for a new approach.

Friction and Post-Communist Transitions

The extent of friction, the ease and the speed with which socio-economic changes can be introduced, is pivotal to the evaluation of the policies pursued and urged on various post-Communist countries since 1989. At the same time, the lessons of these transitions help evolve theories about the levels of friction and the determining factors, theorems that, we shall see, apply to many other areas of socio-economic change from industrial development to movement toward freer trade.

Poland was the first post-Communist country that has followed neoclassicists' advice to jump from a command-and-control system into a free market, or "shock therapy" as others have put it. The most outspoken American proponent of such shock therapy is Jeffrey Sachs, a Harvard economist retained by Solidarity. Sachs's argument is neatly encapsulated by the remark of an Eastern European economist he quotes approvingly: "You don't try to cross over a chasm in two leaps." Sachs also stated in an interview with *The Christian Science Monitor* (3/1/90): "It is repeatedly shown throughout history that gradualism in such a deep crisis doesn't work . . . so if you don't act decisively, it constantly gets ahead of you." He explained earlier:

> My idea is to create the market system as quickly as possible. Let people start to operate. The other idea is to say "Well, we understand that we're punishing the private sector brutally, that none of this makes any sense, but let's only change things very gradually so that maybe in ten years we'll have a normal business environment." That's a crazy idea, frankly. (*The New Yorker* 11/13/89, p. 89)

"The economic textbooks say such a program is to be preferred to a step-by-step program," Heinrich Machewskin, an economist with the German Institute for the Economy in Berlin, stated (*The New York Times* 11/10/90). Gary Becker of the University of Chicago wrote: "Land, housing, retail establishments, and many services can become private property right away. . . . It would even be technically possible to privatize many large factories quickly." And, "the duration of the pain can be reduced and benefits increased if the essentials of a market system are quickly put into place" (*Business Week* 11/24/90).

I predicted that the transition would either be slowed down or repudiated (*The*

New York Times 6/17/90). The prediction was based on observing specific socio-economic factors (discussed shortly) that suggested that the friction level of transition would be high, and therefore attempts to move rapidly would generate stress that could not be overcome (at least within a democratic framework). The first sign that this seems to be a valid prediction might be seen in the results of the November 1990 elections. A *Washington Post* headline (11/27/90) read "Mazowiecki Steps Down as Premier: Government Policies Seen as Repudiated by Polish Electorate."

Neoclassical economists tend to assume that people are the same in all societies, cultures, and historical situations: They are rationally seeking to maximize their self-interest. According to neoclassicists, in Communist societies people are only held back by overbearing statist institutions and scrapping those will free their entrepreneurial spirit and lead in short order to a free economy. Building on these assumptions, urged upon them by neoclassical economists and backed up by pressure from international institutions (such as the International Monetary Fund and the World Bank) as well as from the U.S. State Department and some American banks and private investors, Poland in 1990 slashed government subsidies, made the zloty convertible, closed or privatized a number of state enterprises, deregulated, allowed freedom of labor mobility, and otherwise made room for the market-based allocation of resources. It was assumed that as resources were freed from state control, "privatized," the market would deliver them where they would be used most effectively.

For a short transition period, measured in a year or two, high inflation and unemployment were expected, but thereafter the economy was expected to adjust without any particular state interventions to guide the new resources to this or that place, and without any social safeguards. In Poland, just prior to implementation of the new program, "[g]overnment officials predict[ed] that after a turbulent six months or so the economy should begin to stabilize" (*The New York Times* 12/31/89). "Sure there will be monetary dislocations; prices will undergo a sharp initial rise. But then they'll stabilize. People will know where they stand" (*The New Yorker* 11/13/89, p. 90). The same held for the eastern parts of Germany, where rapid transition has also been attempted. In mid-1990, "[t]he German Economic Research Institute predict[ed] stabilization [for eastern Germany] late next year and a turnaround in 1992" (*The Wall Street Journal* 6/29/90, p. A10). Eight months later, with the bill for economic recovery still rising: "Estimates on the cost of rebuilding eastern Germany have been steadily raised as the region's economic woes multiplied. Many economists now predict that it will cost Bonn more than $1 trillion over the next decade. This year economists estimate, the Government will have to provide close to $100 billion" (*The New York Times* 2/13/91). "Many economists still predict that an upswing will begin next year [for eastern Germany] that could eventually rival the 'economic miracle' of West Germany's postwar reconstruction" (*The New York Times* 2/13/91, p. A1).

The rise of street vendors in Poland was hailed as a sign that the transition was taking place as expected. It was seen also as evidence that Poland was full of entrepreneurs and managers that could run private businesses given a free market.

> Tens of thousands of Poles have turned streets, open spaces, even whole sports stadiums into vast bazaars, selling everything imaginable at rock-bottom prices: from shoelaces to fur coats, plastic flowers to ghetto blasters, denim jackets to skateboards. (*The Independent* 11/2/90, p. 21)
>
> The new free-market forces were at work . . . on the sidewalk in front of an official state grocery store . . . where on Thursday afternoon hundreds of shoppers were crowding about to buy fresh meat, sausage, butter, sugar and coffee. In the not too distant past, inquiries for these goods in stores notable for their bare shelves would bring the response "nie ma," or "we don't have any." The merchandise was being sold on Thursday from more than twenty trucks, private cars and even upturned cartons on the sidewalk clustered about an old sign in front of the government store proclaiming, "It is forbidden to sell around this building" . . . *what is going on here is precisely the kind of capitalist initiative and competition that Finance Minister Leszek Balcerowicz and other officials hope will bring prices down and renew the economy* [italics added]. (*The New York Times* 3/3/90, p. A1)

What are the socio-economic factors that suggest that Poland will be forced to slow down its economic transition or abort its democratic government, and to what extent can they be generalized to other situations?

Human Factors

Far from having fixed self-interested preferences, individuals are penetrated by the institutions and cultures in which they spend their formative years and various parts of their adulthood. True, underneath their acculturation there are elementary basic human features. However, these are not the quest for profit, but the quest for affection, self-esteem, and self-expression aside from the need for basic creature comforts. In addition, these needs can be significantly perverted by the particular societal structures in which people are formed and function.

Many (albeit not all) Poles, citizens of other post-Communist societies, and citizens of many less developed countries, have acquired specific personality traits and work habits that cannot be modified on short order. These include working slowly, without undue exertion; not taking initiatives or responsibilities; stressing quantity over quality; featherbedding; using work time for other purposes (especially shopping); promoting based largely on irrelevant considerations such as party loyalties and connections; bartering of work time and material for other favors; and using low-technology approaches.

The transition to Western style of work and competition will meet resistance. In Yugoslavia, 40 percent of the workers at McDonald's quit because the work was too strenuous (*The New York Times* 6/17/90, p. F13). Others, especially older workers in manual labor such as shipyards and steel mills, are hard to retrain for work in new, high-tech industries such as computer programming. All this holds, only even more so, for the many who serve a lifetime as bureaucrats, party commissars, teachers of Marxism and Leninism, and those who spend their life verifying that others toe the line.

Management and entrepreneurial skills are particularly in short supply. The skills and personality attributes of street vendors, as already pointed out indirectly by Max Weber's discussion of the difference between mercantilism and capitalism, are not those needed. The typical orientation of these street "capitalists" is toward quick bucks achieved by short-order responses to immediate demands, with next to no investments (and hence, no capital management), no management of a significant labor force, and no longer-run planning, innovation, or research and development. They are after quick profits, not reinvesting back into enterprises in order to build major businesses. This observation is supported by the fact that despite the explosive growth of small traders in Poland, the country is very short of managers for sizable enterprises. In Poland, "it is no small feat to find people who are both experienced managers and untarnished by links to the discredited old system. There is a prejudice against filling posts with people who managed state-run enterprises under communist rule. But often they are the most qualified, or the only qualified, people available" (*The New York Times* 7/24/90, p. A8). Many of those that function successfully are repatriated Polish Americans (far from enough to make a difference for the economy as a whole). The shortage of true managers and entrepreneurs is reflected in that the Polish-American Enterprise Fund is reliably reported to have been unable to find qualified takers for most of its funds (according to private communication). Typically loans are below the $50,000 level. (In third-world countries, in similar stages of development, it is common to refer to the lack of or low absorptive capacity.) All this is not to suggest that the needed capitalistic skills and traits cannot be developed in Poland, that its people are somehow inherently inferior; only that their development requires years, if not decades (as it took in the United States under much more favorable circumstances). Introducing large-scale capital, in the form of foreign aid, at this stage is often largely wasted.

Capital

Neoclassic economists tend to assume that if state enterprises are closed or "privatized" (by which they mean legal title is changed from the state to stockholders), the capital assets that are released will float, on their own, where the highest "price" or return is available for them, in the free market. Capital will thus be much more efficiently used and productivity will rise. (They correctly point to "horror" stories of the result of capital being allocated not where users are most willing to pay for it but by government allocations based on national or social ambitions, lending grossly to excessive production of expensive steel, etc.)

Recent experience, however, raises serious doubts about the assumption of the ready transfer of capital either by private corporations using previously state-owned assets or by selling them and using the yield for new investments. As an American economist who works in Poland put it (private communication), an observation also confirmed in eastern Germany and other post-Communist countries: "when you open them to the free market, communists' capital assets dissolve like an Alka-Seltzer pill in a glass of water." Large amounts of the assets, used in Communist economies, are neither transferable nor sellable. Barbara Piasecka Johnson's much publicized plan to buy a controlling share of the Gdansk Shipyard "ran into many of the obstacles that have tripped up other Westerners seeking to invest in Eastern Europe: difficulties in assessing the value of enterprises, daunting investments needed for modernization" (*The New York Times* 4/9/90, p. D5). "Interflug, the East German state airline, once touted as one of the country's jewels, will be shut down. The Treuhand [the holding company created by the government to privatize 8,000 enterprises controlled by the former East German state] could not find a buyer" (*The Washington Post* 3/10/91, p. H1). *The Wall Street Journal* reported that potential investors were reluctant because of "the lack of infrastructure such as telecommunications and transportation, a weak network of suppliers, and East German companies' debt" (6/29/90, p. A10). Hence, often the short-run effect of privatization is not a rise in output, but a sharp decline in the gross national product (GNP), mass unemployment, and recession. In Poland, "[t]he economy also fell into a deep recession, with industrial output falling thirty percent. Farm production slowed and real pay declined by forty percent, according to estimates" (*The New York Times* 5/25/90, p. A10). A year after the new economic program was implemented in Poland, "unemployment has climbed to one million, and next year could reach two million, or more than eleven percent" (*The New York Times* 2/13/91, p. A1).

Like other developing nations, post-Communist societies will have to raise new capital mainly from gradually saving, a very painful and slow process in the face of a sharply declining standard of living. A major socio-economic point needs to be mentioned here. Two facts combine to make such saving particularly difficult in post-Communist societies: First, the standard of living is in part a subjective matter; second, losses raise much more resistance than foregone gains of similar magnitude. (On the first point, see Duesenberry 1952; on the second, Kahneman, Slovic, and Tversky 1982.) Hence, while a country that always had a very low standard of living might be able to save when its standard of living rises above the subsistence level, this is more difficult for a country like Poland that had a higher standard of living but is losing part of it owing to transition.

Theoretically, other counties could provide a steady flow of capital, as the capacity to absorb is gradually increased, but the amounts involved and the long-run commitment needed are such that this is unlikely to obviate the need for slow self-generation of capital.

It should be noted that even under the much more favorable conditions, in the contemporary United States, closed steel mills are not readily converted into high-tech industries, and so on. Results of the notion that capital is readily convertible and that this can be accomplished without substantial losses—a reflection of what might be called capital friction—have been clearly seen when attempts were made to convert corporations that specialize in military production to other usages. Murray Weidenbaum states: "Every comprehensive study of past attempts by large defense contractors to use their capabilities beyond the aerospace market has failed to find a single important example of success" (quoted in *The Christian Science Monitor* 8/7/90, p. 7; for more on economic conversion, see Lynch 1987).

Infrastructure

Generally, for an economy to take off into the higher reaches of development, certain elements must be in place. I spelled out elsewhere (Etzioni 1983) the reasons for the particular list that includes the following: reliable flows of in-animate energy; means of low-cost, expeditious, and reliable transportation and communication; and supportive financial and legal institutions. Post-Communist countries, like many less developed countries, are short on all these. Poland, for example, is suffering from its dependence on oil from the Soviet Union (USSR) and needs time to adjust to the reduction of oil from this source or its rapid increase in price. Poland's telecommunications are woefully unadapted: Poland has seven phone lines for every hundred people (*Business Week* 11/20/89). Its banking system is primitive: Transactions are done in cash; there is no tradition of check writing or bank credits, not to mention stock markets and investments).

> At the PKO bank in Warsaw [Andrzej] Makacewicz [president of the Polish Foundation, a private organization set up to assist economic change] . . . had been standing in line for an hour, trying to deposit one hundred million zlotys—about $10,500—that he had hand-carried from a PKO branch bank in Gdansk, a four-hour drive away, because interbank transfers can take months. (*The Washington Post* 5/9/90, p. A22)

Transportation facilities are inadequate for a modern economy: in eastern Germany, "the region's roads, railways, airports, and telecommunications are so rundown that a recent report by western Germany's Kiel Institute described them as 'wholly inadequate for the rapid development of the five new federal states' " (*The New York Times* 3/12/90, p. A8).

Two of the reasons Western capital has been so reluctant to rush in are the confusion of laws and the dangers of political instability. It will take time to demonstrate to the West a reasonable measure of political continuity. Foreign investors realize that just as it is easy to slash confiscatory and restrictive laws, they can be quickly reinstated, unless they are supported by considerable tradition, political culture, and public support. (The rapid way China flip-flops on its "democratization" is a case in point.)

Labor Mobility

Closing down industries that the state maintained for noneconomic reasons (shipyards, steel mills) and developing new ones, more responsive to the market, often entail labor mobility. In the United States, if the car industry (sustained in part by state supports in the form of bailouts and limitations on imported cars) is in decline and oil on the rise, labor moves from Michigan to Texas. Such movement assumes, first of all, a tradition of mobility that is strong in the United States but much weaker in other countries. People in Poland are much less accustomed to leaving behind their extended families, communities, and graves. Additionally, political conditions often prevented a tradition of free mobility to grow. (The fact that some people do immigrate does not show that the rest are equally mobile; on the contrary, those less adaptable are those who are predisposed to stay.)

Last but not least, there is an interaction effect between labor mobility and the shortage of capital. Since houses, schools, hospitals, shops, and so forth, obviously cannot move with labor, the greater the capital shortage, all other things being equal, the more difficult for labor to move and the slower the transition from one industry to another.

Values

Neoclassical economists assume that once a people overthrow the tyranny of Communist political institutions they exhibit their basic human proclivity: self-interest and quest for self-satisfaction. Actually, while it is true that some Communist followers made a surprisingly rapid transition to Western values (or at least slogans) and that, for some, privatization has acquired the same standing of a simple cure-all that once nationalization had, most members of these societies have kept a variety of social values not easily compatible with capitalism, especially the raw kind of capitalism urged on Poland. Mieczyslaw Kabal, an economist with the Labor Research Institute in Warsaw, stated: "In the Eastern European value system, the right to work and job security are very important values" (*The New York Times* 2/5/90). "There have been reports [in Hungary] of enterprise managers cutting sweetheart deals with Western investors offering to take their firms private for artificially low prices in return for guaranteed jobs and pay" (*The Washington Post* 1/23/90, p. D1). In Poland, Minister of Privatization Waldemar Kuczynski "is also frustrated that many managers of newly privatized companies have sharply raised prices to increase profits, rather than improve production and service" (*The New York Times* 10/29/90, p. D4).

The evidence shows, especially from China and the USSR, that successful farmers and "cooperatives" (private enterprises) do not invoke in others the American desire to keep up with the Joneses and thus multiply the capitalist spirit at "making it." Instead, these ventures frequently bring forth a strong yearning for egalitarianism, combined with pressure to tax heavily those who are successful. Charles P. Wallace reports, "the relatively large sums being earned by cooperatives [in the USSR] have aroused a considerable amount of jealousy, both from state institutions that work far less efficiently and private workers who grumble about the disparity in their take-home pay" (*Los Angeles Times* 5/2/88). These are hardly the sentiments that foster entrepreneurial capitalism.

In Poland, ownership of houses, apartments, land, and factories is returned to those who had title before the Communist takeover, allowing fairness and justice to take precedence over economic efficiency. In Moscow, the city council decided to privatize the ownership of residences. However, instead of selling them—which would have provided the USSR with the ability to increase production and purchasing by increasing the incentives for the Soviets to work harder (so that they could afford to buy a home)—they decided to award them completely free to the current residents, on the social ground that they suffered enough.

My argument is not that economic considerations in these and other cases should have been given precedent. On the contrary, as I have shown in *The Moral Dimension* (1988), all people find some mix that is appropriate to them between their values and their economic needs. The United States is also far from a free market, a country of raw capitalism, but is one mitigated by many social considerations reflected in Medicare, Social Security, unemployment insurance, and numerous other measures.

To urge post-Communist societies to shift to raw capitalism is to ignore the inherent social instability (which led all Western countries to welfare capitalism) of such a system and to invite social tensions that are explosive and will contribute to removing both democratic institutions and—the drive to capitalism. These societies need time and encouragement to find their own balance between whatever social values are dear to them and economic efficiency. To view their rejection of Communist tyranny as an unmitigated taste for raw capitalism is to misunderstand their social orientation and render their transitions much more difficult if not outright impossible.

External Factors

All that has been suggested so far in this chapter must be "corrected" by taking into account external factors that can increase or decrease the levels of friction and associated stress, in the cases of socio-economic transition at hand. There is, however, a tendency to greatly exaggerate what can be accomplished by foreign aid and forgiveness of debt. When an economy is very large, like that of the USSR, and external help is proportionally puny, the ability to ease the transition is particularly small. Even for a country the size of Poland, external help is likely to be far from sufficient to make rapid transition tolerable. This is the case, in part, because some matters cannot be rushed (e.g., retraining of workers, building roads, modernizing ports) and because aid tends to be used for immediate ameliorative purposes such as buying food (as Poland did in the 1970s), which in the longer run builds up demand but no productive capacity. Thus the political gain (sustaining the regime) is temporary. Even in a smaller economy (eastern Germany, population: 17 million; Poland population: 38 million), with a practically unlimited commitment of resources and skills, as well as the infusion of Western values, as is the case for Germany, the transition, though somewhat more hurried, proves to be much more difficult and exacting than has been widely expected. "Henry Maier, a professor at the University of Flensburg and an expert on eastern Germany economics, said the Government had failed to grasp the immensity of the problems in shifting an industrial economy from socialist central planning to free-market capitalism. The Government had the naive notion that the free market would take care of everything," Mr. Maier said "Instead, it has been a disaster" (*The New York Times* 2/13/91, p. A1).

All said and done, transition to post-Communist societies shows the following: First, friction is generally high; second, there are a number of factors that slow down transition, familiar from other less developed economies. The inability to modify most of these factors on quick order has clear policy implications. The main one is that external pressures to rush transitions will cause them to be aborted (as the pain and costs of transition exceed the public tolerance, at least within democracy). It also suggests that foreign aid is best disbursed at a lower level for the longer run than massively for the short run. (Those who argue that our political system is unable to sustain such commitments should examine the long commitments of aid that the United States has maintained to Israel, Egypt, Turkey, and Korea. True, particular mixes of national security considerations and ethnic pressure played a role in these cases, but aid to Poland has its own ethnic base and there are at least as good security reasons to support transition to postcommunism as there are to support Egypt.)

The Unevenly Paced Clocks
and Political Commitment

Aside from the generally high level of friction, difficulties are caused for socio-economic transitions that point to specific policy conclusions from what might be called the problem of the unevenly paced clocks: Some socio-economic processes are inherently more friction laden than others. To the extent that changes must be multifaceted—which all major societal, economic, and political changes are—pushing the relatively quicker processes to proceed at full haste generates major imbalances because the other processes cannot keep up.

In particular at issue is the respective pace of three kinds of processes. Those that can proceed at a relatively rapid pace are *deconstructive* acts such as closing down state plants and collective farms, deregulation, slashing of subsidies, and removing currency controls. Much slower in pace are the processes of *reconstruction*, such as the opening of new plants, development of the infrastructure, and retraining of the labor force. Fastest and most volatile are *expectations*. Expectations are a social-psychological variable that neoclassical economists often assume they can model but actually is one of the least understood factors, precisely because it is highly volatile and driven largely by social and psychological factors and not by economic ones. It seems that one of the few things we can say with certainty about expectations is that they move with less friction than most processes. Thus, very shortly after the beginning of the transition from communism, expectations shot up, with Poles expecting democratization to quickly result in prosperity and a Western life-style. When this did not follow on short order, the mood swung quite sour, resulting in the rejection of the Mazowiecki government in November 1990.

While the knowledge of how to keep expectations realistic is far from established, certainly policies of oversell fan further inflated expectations rather than help keep them closer to reality and more frustration proof. During a 1990 visit to Poland, a social scientist colleague pointed to my published statement that such expectations were unrealistically high by stating that "we are very pessimistic, indeed maybe too much, we do not expect to catch up with the West before the end of the century." At that time the Polish income per capita was a fourth of that of Greece, at roughly $1,750 per capita. Expecting the GNP to increase fourfold was an extremely optimistic projection. For comparison's sake, the United States only doubled its income once every generation, under much more favorable circumstances.

Neoclassical economists sometimes add privately that a main reason they favor rapid transitions is that they fear a lack of political commitment to a longer-run, more gradual transition. If, however, we are correct that *rapid* transition *cannot* be accomplished, one must ask under what conditions a more gradual transition could be attained. The answers seem to be these conditions: *(a)* keep expectations low, so that results would be fulfilling rather than frustrating; *(b)* keep the rewards of the transition high compared to the pain, which a "pull" strategy (see next paragraph) seems to offer; and *(c)* strongly make the moral case for the new regime, which is easier to do for the more humane and less brutal transition.

One way to ensure the slower pace for the total socio-economic change is to build on a "pull" instead of "push" strategy. In post-Communist Poland, this has been suggested in the form of not closing profitable state enterprises but providing favorable terms (say, of credit) to the new, private ones and allowing those, as they grow, to pull labor and other resources (to the extent that they can be salvaged) away from state ones, which will then die on the vine.

The term *profitable state enterprises* may be surprising on two accounts: First, could state enterprises be profitable? Second, if they are, why close them? Poland's mid-sized car industry is useful to illustrate the point. In 1990, after state enterprises were forced to work under commercial conditions (their subsidies abolished, etc.), Poland's auto industry was quite profitable because while they made fewer cars they could more than increase prices because of their monopoly status and the high demand for cars. The champions of the rush to the free market planned nevertheless to close these factories (before the November 1990 elections) because they were state owned and because they were less efficient than Western ones. According to one economist, Polish workers were each making about three cars per year compared with ten cars per worker at Chrysler. It was suggested that plants be privatized or their monopoly status attacked by increasing car imports, even if that would use up scarce foreign currency. However, privatization was delayed because, among other reasons, no investors could be found to take over. A mere privatization would not have increased efficiency because, among other things, Chrysler has a much higher capital outlay per worker than do the Polish plants. While it is true that competition with Western carmakers could have been achieved "right away" by opening the border, the result would have been mainly a decline in Polish production of cars, without any pickup elsewhere. Hence, in the short order, idling more resources, particularly workers, would not have increased output but would have increased pain, costs, and social stress. If instead, private Polish industries, say animation, were given time to grow and expand, they would have drawn workers from the no longer subsidized state industries. As long as the "pulling" industries determined the pace, rather than those being shut, there would be much less transitional imbalance and resulting economic, human, and political strain.

Conclusion

Friction (psychological, sociological, political) is a major social science variable. The beginning assumption in socio-economics should be that friction is high for most changes. The perils of disregarding this generalization are illustrated by examining the transition from command-and-control economies to more free ones.

Bibliography

Duesenberry, James S. 1952. *Income, Saving and the Theory of Consumer Behavior.* Cambridge: Harvard University Press.

Etzioni, Amitai. 1983. *An Immodest Agenda*. New York: McGraw-Hill.
————. 1988. *The Moral Dimension*. New York: Free Press.
Kahneman, Daniel; Paul Slovic; and Amos Tversky. 1982. *Judgment Under Uncertainty: Heuristics and Biases*. Cambridge: Cambridge University Press.
Lynch, John, ed. 1987. *Economic Adjustment and Conversion of Defense Industries*. Boulder, Colo.: Westview Press.

4. Institutions as Infrastructures of Human Interaction

Sven-Erik Sjöstrand

Contractual Person?

In a science like economics, whose basic logic is mainly atomistic, the aggregation of (individual) phenomena is an important issue and illustrates in a somewhat different way the basic controversy regarding the embeddedness of economic action in a society (Granovetter 1985). For many—but not all—modern neoinstitutionalists, aggregation is not the issue: human interactions or exchange processes are the focus (Tool 1988).

When the problem of aggregation is replaced by the focusing of the relationships between actors and systems levels, neoinstitutionalists offer differing explanations. Some discuss dyadic relationships and stress the conception of a *contract* as a basic way of describing how individuals organize their common efforts. Contractual approaches are common in research aiming at explanations of the relative efficiency or effectiveness of various institutional arrangements (Williamson 1985).

One weakness in applying the idea of human interactions and exchanges as something based on contractual relations is the distinct, well-established meaning of the term *contract* in jurisprudence, which differs from the way the term often is used in economic analysis. In the discipline of law, a contract refers to a formal agreement often manifested in a written document. Such a position could be referred to as legalistic and is distinguished by placing more emphasis on form than on substance.

Another basic problem with these contractual efforts is that they neither define their most fundamental concept, that of a *contractual relationship,* nor do they apply a truly (that is, interactional) dynamic perspective. To a certain extent, the former problem could be associated with a tendency to restrict the meaning of the exchange phenomenon in economic theories. Economic theorists all too seldom have included both "the exchange in itself" and "the exchange of something." The latter, utilitarian perspective has dominated economic theory.

In most neoinstitutional analyses, the concept of a contract is used more as a "framework" (Williamson 1985), the execution of which is carried out informally in most cases, and through cooperation between the parties involved. The entire social context surrounding an exchange matters. Individual actions have a meaning that extends beyond the actual exchange of something. This is closely related to a somewhat more differentiated view of human beings. Many neoinstitutionalists do not reduce the human being to something very similar to the classical notion of *homo oeconomicus*. Humankind is also characterized by other qualities and rationalities (cf. as discussed later in the chapter), and therefore exchange processes are more complex.

A contractual approach is fruitful when exchanges are described in utility terms and when people are assumed to be calculative and universalistic (human beings are regarded as interchangeable role players or "gamespersons") in their orientations. But when other human qualities or rationalities are added—e.g., *particularism* (human beings are regarded as unique persons or personalities) and *idealism* (cf. Tönnies 1887/1979, "Gemeinschaft" vs. "Gesellschaft")—the use of a contractual approach is problematic.

This weakness related to the use of the term *contract* is due to the fact that even among neoinstitutionalists using a contractual perspective interpersonal ties often are stylized, average, or devoid of specific content. Individual actions (or, in this context, behavior) are products mainly derived from their named role positions and environmental sets. But individuals do not act according to distinct manuscripts referring to a particular social category that they belong to (Granovetter 1985). They express true dynamics, simultaneously exchanging and creating conditions for exchanges. These problems have been addressed during the last decade, and new concepts have been introduced to adapt to this problem. *Relational contracting* represents one such attempt. The idea of what is often termed *psychological contracts* is another.

Relational contracting stresses the fact that interactions and relations are sometimes lasting and that the importance of the original agreement ("the formal contract") has been de-emphasized in favor of a kind of specific norm system connected to the exchange relationship. This adjustment in theory gives room both for time (lasting relationships) and particularity (unique persons creating a specific relation). The notion of psychological contracting is connected to the already mentioned idea that a contractual agreement is always part of a social context or situation. This context represents a system of norms that is upheld by individuals, and it might be seen as an expression of "internalized agreements," either self-generated from personal experiences or acquired from others. The idea, then, is that society is permeated by more or less voluntary "invisible contracts."

Although both these attempts, which are quite often used by neoinstitutionalists, take care of some of the shortcomings of straightforward contractual analyses, they do not solve at least two fundamental deficiencies: the problem of dynamics and the neglect of the existence of historical asymmetries (power differences). The latter problem raises the notion that the right of every individual to freely conclude an agreement must be related to the fact that individuals face different opportunities and possess different resources.

But some neoinstitutional efforts are more in a "true" processual spirit (cf. Sjöstrand 1985). In such studies, the individual is described as obliged to participate in processes of change. The theoretical formulations often incorporate the idea of processes or of procedures. Social and economic order is regarded as continuously developmental, an ongoing transformation of ordering arrangements. Economic processes are not just explained as a succession of episodic shifts ("contracts"), as many theorists suggest. Furthermore, social and economic change is described as discretionary. Change, then, consists of (re)constructions of cognitive structures and habits of action embedded (and embodied) in institutions. Most forms of cognitive structures (e.g., orders, laws, codes, rules, habits, norms, agreements, and patterns) are discretionary. They were created by individual or organized actors at particular times. They represent historically inherited asymmetries or power relationships (Tool 1981).

Complex, Interactive Person

As mentioned in the first section of this chapter, a crucial problem in economic analysis is related to the choice of assumption about humankind. A focus on the "nature" of human beings implies that single individuals matter. In most neoinstitutional approaches, *homo oeconomicus* is abandoned for other conceptions or at least is modified in some respects. Here, a position that could be summarized as "complex, interactive person" rather than *homo oeconomicus* is suggested. A view of individuals as both complex and interactive encompasses the idea that they could be regarded as actors and that their actions (not behavior!) are important in forming and organizing situations and environments.

When trying to understand the interaction and organizing processes in a society, the approach advocated here is to start with how an individual reduces uncertainty. Uncertainty, then, is related both to environmental change and to environmental complexity. Both—and perhaps especially the latter—are problematic because the cognitive capacity of human beings is assumed to be limited (bounded rationality). Cognitive limitations make it difficult to handle both lack of information and information overload. This human "imperfection"—and some others (to be discussed)—make interpersonal solutions (interaction and organizing) attractive.

Among other "imperfections" of the individual human being, one may start with a few basic and important physical limitations. Obvious examples are the existence of two sexes, the limited strength or energy of a person and his or her insufficient resistance to diseases, injuries, and death (Beckman 1987). These very basic circumstances call for human interaction and organizing. Furthermore, individuals have desires, or at least needs and preferences. There are certain things in life people prefer or enjoy and therefore try to obtain, but individual solutions are insufficient. In such cases, too, there is a need for cooperation, and this is explained by the existence of indivisibles.

Often there is a need for specialization because of the possibilities of acquiring the fruits of large-scale economies. Furthermore, humans are associated with what could be described as a "spiritual" uncertainty, which refers to a concern about identity and identification with basic ideals and values (Sjöstrand 1985, 1986). An individual is trying to find (or create) a meaning for his or her life, and this reduction of uncertainty is mainly carried out through human interaction and communication.

Finally, uncertainty is also reduced through close relationships with other people. There are biological relations such as kinship and family ties but also friendship relations (Sjöstrand 1986). Together, these status relationships are most important in emergent perceptions of identity among human beings. Close relationships and corresponding interactions strongly contribute to people's self-images.

Thus, there are several reasons for people's relating to each other and interacting more or less continuously or closely. At the same time, it has to be emphasized that these interactions or exchanges are accompanied by dependence, and these two phenomena are strongly related. When a person interacts in some way with others, he or she gives up some autonomy, which means that he or she chooses a situation characterized by dependence relations. This choice is accompanied by a hope for relative certainty or some kind of security.

In other words, every individual has a choice. Either he or she looks for independence, and avoids most of the uncertainties that are built into every interaction between individuals, or he or she tries to create dependence relations that are as symmetrical (or as favorable) as possible. The former choice illustrates that any attempt by an individual to reduce uncertainty through interaction or collective solutions simultaneously produces new kinds of uncertainty. Uncertainty is always present, and it is more a question of choosing acceptable degrees of it or trying to minimize it in some selected crucial area. The latter choice, which often includes aiming for symmetrical or even advantageous relationships, illustrates how an individual tries to reduce uncertainty by controlling a situation, an interaction, or another person's environment. The word *power* is often used to denote these asymmetries in human relationships. But it has to be added that human beings also look for certain "controlled forms" of uncertainty and that individuals actually often are stimulated in that way.

Institutions as Infrastructures
of Human Interaction

A distinguishing feature of this approach is that the fundamental institutions in a society are considered to be interaction based (cf. chapter 1). This position is unusual both in neoclassical and neoinstitutional analyses. Most researchers have referred to the term *institution* when describing phenomena that are supposed to simplify human (inter)actions, but not for characterizing significant interaction patterns as such. Instead, substantive elements like "money" or legal entities like the "firm" or "the state" have been stressed (Dillard 1987). For example, "money" is assumed to simplify human action by substituting simultaneous actions for sequential ones, thus making complex and multilateral actions simpler and bilateral. The "firm" is supposed to simplify human actions by reducing the total amount of bilateral relationships necessary to get an overall agreement.

Some researchers (cf. North 1985) emphasize that institutions function like restrictions. They constrain the set of choices available to actors. The definition suggested here is perhaps closer to that of, among others, Heiner (1983), one of the too few researchers who have tried to recharge economic analysis with the complexity that is intrinsic in the institutional approach. An institution, then, might be described as a kind of infrastructure, which facilitates (or hinders) human (re)allocations of resources. Institutions function like "rationality contexts," which emerge in human interactions. What is emphasized here is that these rationality contexts are derived both from historical and emerging (that is, "simultaneously" produced or created) patterns in a society. These infrastructures of human interaction absorb crucial uncertainties, and hence they reduce the demands on the cognitive capacity of the human mind. While these interaction-based institutions stabilize perceptions and actions through the assimilation of certain cognitive maps or charts, they also represent and make room for experiments, trial-and-error processes, and learning.

It is important to understand that, although institutions are mechanisms for the reduction of uncertainty, in their emergent forms they simultaneously reproduce (new) uncertainty. There are two reasons for this; first, because the modifying force of ideals itself is an aspect of the institutional repertoire, and second, because the reproduction is always imperfect (that is, [re]production; the emergent forms vary and change over time; cf. chapter 1). An individual, when interacting and exchanging, faces the institutions of a society, in both its physical and its artificial manifestations. Institutions are embedded in the emergent organizations in a society and in those ideas and concepts that the individual uses to sort out her or his view of reality. This view of the institution and this perception of a society are founded on the idea of society as a "metabolism" of values, power, work, management, resources, and so forth. Everything is closely linked, and the structure of ideas is expressed both in the emergent forms of organizations and in the physical structure of artifacts.

Thus, in a sense, institutions are constituted by human habits. As noted earlier in this chapter, they become prescribed patterns or structures for correlating behavior in the performance of various functions. One kind of purpose or function performed is to facilitate the application of reliable knowledge to the performance of continuing activities, such as production of food and fiber, determination of income shares, and transport of goods and persons, all of which the community has come to regard as significant. Often such an application is the primary reason for the emergence of an institution. When, and to the extent that, institutions operate to affect such application of knowledge to experience, they may be said to be performing an instrumental function.

But institutions perform a different kind of function as well. As already suggested, prescriptive and proscriptive arrangements are sometimes created or retained in order to achieve or preserve hierarchical placement of persons, to preserve status, image, privilege, or rank, to provide and protect discretion over other people's behavior, to erode trust and confidence in others, to imperil or destroy the right to know and understand, to perpetuate custom and tradition solely for its own sake, to provide for the continuity of the institution as such, to define human worth on discriminatory indices, and the like. The exhibition of this kind of activity may be identified as an invidious (dys)function of institutions.

Three Basic Forms for Human Interaction and Organization

Here the manifoldness of human interactions and organizing efforts will be reduced to three fundamental relationships. They are not arbitrarily or randomly selected, but represent an elaboration of some of the suggestions provided by early, classical writers in the social sciences, and they also take into consideration more recent empirical findings (cf. the writings in the area of economic psychology; the writings of Kahneman, Tversky, Kozielecki, and others) and recent empirical Scandinavian research in the area of institutional thought and organization theory (e.g., Sjöstrand 1985; Lundgren 1986; Larsson 1986).

Among distinguished previous scholars publishing in this area, Tönnies (1887/1979) with his distinction between *Gemeinschaft* and *Gesellschaft* stands out (on Tönnies's writings cf. Asplund 1991). The writings of Etzioni (1961, 1966, 1988), both his analysis of compliance relations between individuals and/or organizations and his thinking about ideals and moral obligations, also represent important contributions regarding basic forms for human interaction. Finally, Polanyi (1964, 1967) and his famous descriptions of various societal formations and—more recently—Butler's descriptions (1983) of three ideal types for modes controlling human exchanges, or "transactions," have influenced the following analyses.

Tönnies used the concept of gemeinschaft when he discussed the essential human being. Individuality, perceiving the human being as a person or personality, was something fundamental for Tönnies. Therefore, he regarded the links with family as well as friendship and neighborly ties as fundamental cornerstones when discussing human interaction and organizing processes. He also emphasized custom or tradition as a basic exchange mechanism. On the other hand,

Tönnies associated the gesellschaft more with a person's way of functioning. Phenomena such as scheming, calculation, and autocratic behavior were the distinguishing features of the gesellschaft. In this form, interaction and exchange were determined largely by the law or by an impersonal contract.

Polanyi, in some of his writings, attempted to clarify the position and function of the economy in a society, and more specifically he dealt with the question of which institutional mechanisms encourage human beings to engage in participation and exchange. Polanyi formulated some of his conclusions in terms of transactional modes and found three such modes: reciprocity, redistribution, and market exchanges.

Etzioni stated a number of qualities associated with the relationships and exchanges of individuals when he analyzed different control structures in organizations. Apart from strongly emphasizing the status of hierarchical relationships in this kind of context, he also attempted to describe three types of interactions. Etzioni considered that three "means of power" could be attributed to various positions: physical, material, and symbolic means (coercive, remunerative, and normative power, respectively). These forms of power correspond to three types of interpersonal interactions.

Butler distinguished between three "institutions" for transactional control: namely, market, hierarchy, and commune. Butler claimed that an organization should be regarded as a kind of transactional arena. He suggested three sets of variables for describing the proposed institutions: namely, predilections, bases, and activation. Predilections govern orientations of people and their relationships. They refer to characteristics that the actors in a transactional arena (that is, organization) bring with themselves and that define the favorable prepossessions of mind necessary to enable a particular control mode to operate. Bases refer to a kind of springboard from which appropriate action may occur. Activation defines the type of activity that the corporate body has to engage in to obtain satisfactory service from a task element.

Here, three fundamental (or meta-) rationalities underlying human interactions are suggested, founded on, respectively, *calculative, idealistic,* and *genuine relationships*. On the one hand, this repertoire certainly adds to the complexity of the description frequently used in economic analyses regarding human interaction. On the other hand, it is obvious that this "complexity" should be regarded as an (over)simplification—as one way of stating the more fundamental dimensions. This is especially true if one considers the state of knowledge in this area as presented in economic and social psychology.

Calculative relationships refer to the classical assumption in microeconomic analysis. The assumption of the human being as a kind of *homo oeconomicus* has dominated in neoclassical analysis both in textbooks and in research efforts for a long time. In its pure, original, and most primitive form, *homo oeconomicus* refers to the rationality of a purely self-interested or egoistic person trying to maximize in a certain way. Basically calculative relationships dominate in situations where individuals do not know each other (anonymous relations) and where interactions are of short duration, fragmental, or occasional.

Idealistic relations, on the other hand, make the individual a sharer and a messenger of the ideals and ideologies of some subdivision of humankind. Often these ideals refer to rationalities associated with religious or ideological beliefs. Thus, the individual to some extent compensates for the relative lack of identity, which is provided by pure calculative relationships.

In relationships based on ideals, the actor as a person or as a personality matters. In this kind of relationship, an individual tries to find out what exists, what is good, what is possible, and so forth. Ideals and ideologies usually integrate values, norms, and descriptions and create a kind of security or stability in the individual's orientations in life.

Genuine relations represent a third ingredient in the identity formation processes of a human being. They furnish a personal or even biological identity (kinship) and add both to the social/cultural identity provided through idealistic relationships and to physical survival mainly provided by calculative interactions. The term *genuine* is selected to articulate the very basic human qualities associated with a relationship founded on status (that is, social position). In many ways, the family is the most fundamental of relationships in a person's existence, and in many ways it functions as a prototype for other relationships (Kelley, et al. 1983). Genuine relationships are close, and they are best exemplified by love or friendship. They are characterized by a high frequency of interactions, mutually strong influences, a broad variety in exchanges, and the duration of the relationship. There are also emotional ties implicit in these relationships, and related individuals are unique and important to each other. Phenomena such as trust, authenticity, mutuality, and even intimacy are prevalent.

This argumentation adds up to a different assumption regarding people than is common in most economic analyses. Here, people are assumed to be both interactional and complex. Furthermore, their complexity is specified. Interactions of people are based on three kinds of rationality, which reflect this complexity, namely *calculative, idealistic,* and *status rationalities* (Sjöstrand 1989). See Figure 4.1.

The Presence of Asymmetries

The idea of historically inherited asymmetries of power between individuals has previously been addressed. Thus, human interaction and exchange are characterized not solely by the different rationalities involved (calculative, idealistic, and status) but also by *asymmetric* circumstances as such. Two fundamental forms for human interaction and exchange are *networks* and *hierarchies*. Of course, this focusing on a dichotomy between network and hierarchy represents a simplification of what should be understood as a kind of continuum.

Figure 4.1

Basic Kinds of Relationships in Human Interaction and Exchange

Basic kind of relationship	Assumption of man	Information locus	Transaction mode	Basic function
Calculative	homo oeconomicus	price	exchange	physical survival
Ideational	"religious" man	text (rule)	redistribution	cultural identity
Genuine	social man	status (position)	reciprocity	individual identity

A *network* summarizes the linkages existing among individuals through their predictive and normative expectations and references (Sjöstrand 1975, 1986). A network is a representation of established and mutual expectations among individuals, where "strong" nets correspond to normative qualities and "weak" nets to predictive ones. A pure or ideal type of network suggests a truly symmetrical relationship between individuals.

A *hierarchy*—at least in its pure form—represents something that differs from a network. A hierarchy expresses an asymmetric relationship between parties and could be described as a network with both a center and a periphery. Hierarchies and asymmetric relationships are characterized by relations of super- and subordination and therefore by different levels of restrictions and discretions for individual actors.

Some researchers take the existence of hierarchies as given—something that does not need to be explained. Sometimes they refer to the disciplines of neuropsychology and psychology (e.g., Law Whyte et al. 1969), and sometimes to the cognitive sciences (e.g., Simon 1957). Others try to find and discuss different explanations for these asymmetries and power relationships (e.g., Sjöstrand 1985).

Thus, the existence of hierarchic relationships might be explained in several ways. One way is to start with biological facts and the existence of lineages. Another explanation is related to communicative efficiency ("wheel vs. all channel" solutions, cf. Arrow 1974). Still other explanations are related to differences in human talent (Williamson 1975, 1985) or to the assumption that at least some people tend to behave in an opportunistic way ("free riding") and that therefore some control (that is, hierarchy) of activities is necessary (Williamson 1975). Finally, it has also been suggested that people have and express different ideals in this respect (Sjöstrand 1986). An obvious example is the eternal debate regarding various models for democracy.

Figure 4.2

Six Different Basic Institutions for Human Exchanges in Society

Forms of interaction	Interaction rationalities		
	Calculative	Ideational	Genuine
Hierarchic	corporation	federation (cooperative)	clan
Network type	market	social movement	circle

Six Basic Institutions (or "Rationality Contexts")

What is examined here are the general organizing patterns emerging among individuals in a society. These infrastructures of human interactions have been denoted institutions to emphasize their crucial role for the understanding of human activities and the evolutionary processes of societies. Three basic human interaction and organizing rationalities have been described in the previous section, as well as both symmetric (networks) and asymmetric (hierarchic) relationships between individual actors. If these two basic qualities of human exchange and interaction are combined—the interaction rationalities and the forms for interaction—six ideal-type institutions or infrastructures for human (inter)action emerge (cf. Figure 4.2).

In their most pure or ideal forms, *markets* correspond to a first category, namely, an interaction pattern that combines a calculative rationality with a network format. *Corporations* and *public agencies* combine this calculative rationality with an asymmetric or hierarchic relationship.

Idealistic rationalities, in their pure forms, add up to both *social movements* and *cooperatives* or *federations*. The former refers to networklike institutions, and the latter to hierarchical ones. The distinction between a cooperative and a federation is of minor importance in this context but refers to whether the units or actors involved are physical or legal entities. When individuals organize themselves, the concept of a cooperative is used, but when legal units cooperate the phenomenon is named a federation.

Human rationalities based on genuine relationships combined with symmetrical or networklike forms for interaction correspond to *circles*, whereas the same kind of rationality in combination with hierarchic forms adds up to *clans*. These six ideal-type institutions (or infrastructures of human interactions) then simultaneously function as rationality contexts for individual (inter)actions and—as historically inherited cognitive or habitual structures—partly govern these individual (inter)actions.

The (Re)production of Institutions

A perspective emphasizing reproduction (cf. chapter 1) implies that the organization is perceived as a process, although existing structures to some degree affect the (reproduction) process. Thus, the duality of structure is stressed—structural properties of social systems are both medium and outcome of the actions they recursively organize (Giddens 1984).

In their basic rationalities, organizations reproduce the actual basis for their existence. The basic rationality as such is closely associated with the kind of return the principal values the most. In markets and in corporations, it is *capital;* in the public agency, it is *rules* (or to put it another way: power); in social movements, cooperatives, and federations, it is *membership;* and in circles or clans, it is *trust.*

Reproduction processes enclose everyday routines. When it comes to social movements (and their hierarchical counterparts—cooperatives and federations), membership is reproduced through its physical mediators and their action possibilities. Then the criteria for recruitment and selection (entry/exit) are important, as well as the ways membership is expressed.

Basically there are four ways to behave when relating to an organization (cf. Hirchman 1970, 1982). Either individuals have negative experiences and leave (exit) or protest (verbally) or they relate in a more positive way and stay (loyalty) or even become involved. An ideal movement or cooperative expresses a rationality based on involvement in the forming of the ideals (cf. the importance of recruitment and selection), the membership thereby creating a social or cultural identity.

In sum, it is suggested that the six ideal-type institutions—namely, markets, corporations/public agencies, social movements, federations/cooperatives, circles, and clans—represent fundamental organizing forces and infrastructures in a society. An understanding of these institutions, their embedded rationalities as well as the ways they are reproduced (and changed), will improve our ability to describe and explain actions and strategies of the actual, emergent organizations in society.

Conclusions

In most research efforts in the economic sciences, human exchanges have been reduced to calculative behavior. But this relatively pure utilitarian position is not sufficient when trying to understand and explain what economic institutions have developed through the ages in societies. A more complex view of human beings and human interaction is called for.

Moreover, the importance of human interactions and interaction patterns has for too long been neglected in economic analyses of organization(s) and society. In neoinstitutional approaches, such perspectives have been present, but much more emphasis must be placed on these efforts. There are several reasons. First of all, the view of human beings and human actions as atomized and non-existent outside a social context has to be abandoned. It has been shown that the assumption of *homo oeconomicus* (or "contractual person") has to be replaced by the notion of complex, interactive person, especially when focusing on organizing processes and on the organizational level. The historical and structural embeddedness of relations also has to be brought (back) into the economic analyses of organization(s). The empirical foundations of both these statements are overwhelming. Furthermore, this somewhat more complicated approach, incorporating interaction or dynamics, is claimed to improve significantly both the explanations and predictions of organized actions and the emergence of different kinds of institutions in a society.

In this chapter, it is advocated that perhaps the most important infrastructures in society are interaction regularities or patterns in human exchanges. These interaction-based institutions correspond to the organizing processes of a society, and research focusing on the economics of organization usually only addresses part of this more fundamental issue. Three forces underlying the human interactions or relationships that characterize these infrastructures or institutions in society are deduced, namely, calculative, ideational, and status rationalities. The notion of asymmetries in human interactions and exchanges is also introduced and elaborated on. Two pure forms are described and defined: networks and hierarchies. Of course, these two forms represent an analytical simplification of what is commonly perceived as a continuum.

Six different institutions have been described, combining the two deduced interactional forms (networks and hierarchies) with the three kinds of (inter)action rationalities (calculative, idealistic, and status). The six emergent institutions—namely, markets, social movements, circles, corporations (public agencies), federations (cooperatives), and clans—are described using their basic characteristics, thus adding to the earlier theories presented by several neoinstitutionalists, for example, those theories focusing mainly on the distinction among market and hierarchy (cf. Williamson [1975, 1985] and many others) or between market, intermediate forms, and hierarchy (cf. many industrial economists and network theorists) or between markets and (legal) rules (cf. North [1990] and others working in the area of the economics of law) or, finally, among markets, hierarchies, and clans (cf. Ouchi 1980).

Bibliography

Alchian, Armen, and Harold Demsetz. 1972. "Production, Information Costs and Economic Organization." *American Economic Review* 62, 2: 777–95.

Arrow, K. J. 1974. *The Limits of Organization*. New York: Norton.

Asplund, Johan. 1991. *On Gemeinschaft and Gesellschaft*. (In Swedish only.) Stockholm: Korpen.

Beckman, Svante. 1987. "Classifications of Power." (In Swedish only.) In *Power*, ed. O. Peterson, pp. 118–67. Stockholm: Carlssons Bokförlag.

Brown, B. 1970/1977. *What Economics Is About*. Stockholm: Akademilitteratur.

Butler, R. 1983. "Control through Markets, Hierarchies and Communes." In *Power, Efficiency and Institutions*, ed. A. Francis et al., pp. 286–316. London: Heinemann.

Crozier, Michel, and Erhard Friedberg. 1977/1980. *Actors & Systems*. Chicago: University of Chicago.

Demsetz, Harold. 1967. "Toward a Theory of Property Rights." *American Economic Review* 57, 2: 347–60.

Dillard, Dudley. 1987. "Money as an Institution of Capitalism." *Journal of Economic Issues* 21 (December) 4: 1623–47.

Etzioni, Amitai. 1961. *The Comparative Analysis of Complex Organizations*. New York: Free Press.

———. 1966. "Organizational Control Structures." In *Approaches to Organizational Design*, ed. James March. Pittsburgh: Rand McNally.

———. 1988. *The Moral Dimension: Towards a New Economics*. New York: Free Press.

Foucault, Michel. 1972. *The Archeology of Knowledge*. London: Pantheon.

Furubotn, Eirik, and S. Pejovich. 1972. "Property Rights and Economic Theory." *Journal of Economic Literature* 10, 2: 1137–60.

Giddens, Anthony. 1984. *The Constitution of Society*. Cambridge, Mass.: Polity Press.

Granovetter, M. 1985. "Economic Action and Social Structure: The Problem of Embeddedness." *American Journal of Sociology* 91, 3: 481–510.

Gruchy, Allan. 1947. *Modern Economic Thought: The American Contribution*. New York: Prentice-Hall.

———. 1974. *Contemporary Economic Thought*. London: Macmillan.

Habermas, Jürgen. 1984. *The Theory of Communicative Action*. Vol. 1. Boston: Beacon.

Hedlund, Gunnar. 1986. *The Invisible in Economics and Management*. Stockholm: Stockholm School of Economics.

Heiner, Ronald. 1983. "The Origin of Predictable Behavior." *American Economic Review* 73 (September) 4: 560–95.

Hirchman, Albert. 1970. *Exit, Voice and Loyalty*. Cambridge: Harvard University Press.

———. 1982. *Shifting Involvements*. Oxford: Martin Robertson.

Kelley, H., et al. 1983. *Close Relationships*. San Francisco: W. H. Freeman.

Larsson, Björn. 1986. *Ownership Control and Holding Company Organization*. (In Swedish only.) Stockholm: Stockholm School of Economics.

Law Whyte, L., et al., eds. 1969. *Hierarchical Structures*. New York: Free Press.

Lundgren, Anders. 1986. *Ownership and Competence: A Study of Boards of Directors in Large Swedish Multinationals*. (In Swedish only.) Stockholm: Stockholm School of Economics.

Moss, S. 1981. *An Economic Theory of Business Strategy*. Oxford: Martin Robertson.

Nelson, Richard, and Sidney Winter. 1982. *An Evolutionary Theory of Economic Change*. Cambridge: Harvard University Press.

North, Douglass C. 1985. "Institutions, Transaction Costs and Economic Growth, Political Economy." Working Paper 103. Washington, D.C.: George Washington University.

————. 1990. *Institutions, Institutional Change and Economic Performance.* Cambridge: Cambridge University Press.

North, Douglass C., and Robert Thomas. 1973. *The Rise of the Western World.* Cambridge: Cambridge University Press.

Ouchi, William. 1980. "Markets, Bureaucracies, Clans." *Administrative Science Quarterly* 25, 1 (March): 120–42.

Pfeffer, Jeffrey, and Gerald Salancik. 1978. *The External Control of Organizations.* New York: Harper and Row.

Polanyi, Karl. 1964. *Primitive, Archaic and Modern Economies.* Garden City, N.Y.: Beacon.

————. 1967. *The Economy as Instituted Process.* Lund, Sweden: University (reprint).

Simon, Herbert. 1957. *Models of Man.* New York: Wiley.

Sjöstrand, Sven-Erik. 1975. "A Taxonomic Approach to Some Problems of Company Organization." *Erhvervsøkonomisk Tidskrift* 39, 2: 109–24.

————. 1985. "The Organization of Society." (In Swedish only.) Lund, Sweden: Doxa.

————. 1986. "The Dual Function of Organizations." In *Trends and Megatrends in the Theory of Management,* ed. Erik Johnsen. Copenhagen: Bratt International.

————. 1989. "Institutional Economics—An Overview." In *Perspectives on the Economics of Organization,* ed. Oliver Williamson, Sven-Erik Sjöstrand, and Jan Johanson. Lund, Sweden: Lund University Press.

Therborn, Göran. 1976. "What Does the Ruling Class Do When It Is Ruling?" (In Swedish only.) Häften för kritiska studier 9, 4: 15–46.

Tool, Marc. 1981. "Neoinstitutionalism an Alternative Paradigm?" (Research paper.) London: London School of Economics.

Tönnies, Friedrich. 1887/1979. *Gemeinschaft und Gesellschaft.* Darmstadt: J. Darmstadt Wissenschaft.

Williamson, Oliver. 1975. *Markets and Hierarchies.* New York: Free Press.

————. 1985. *The Economic Institutions of Capitalism.* New York: Free Press.

5. Comparative Economic Organization: The Analysis of Discrete Structural Alternatives

Oliver E. Williamson

Although microeconomic organization is formidably complex and has long resisted systematic analysis, that has been changing as new modes of analysis have become available, as recognition of the importance of institutions to economic performance has grown, and as the limits of earlier modes of analysis have become evident. Information economics, game theory, agency theory, and population ecology have all made significant advances.

This chapter approaches the study of economic organization from a comparative institutional point of view in which transaction-cost economizing is featured. Comparative economic organization never examines organization forms separately but always in relation to alternatives. Transaction-cost economics places the principal burden of analysis on comparisons of transaction costs—which, broadly, are the "costs of running the economic system" (Arrow 1969, p. 48).

My purpose in this chapter is to extend and refine the apparatus out of which transaction-cost economics works, thereby to respond to some of the leading criticisms. Four objections to prior work in this area are especially pertinent.

One objection to prior work is that the two stages of the new institutional economics research agenda—the institutional environment and the institutions of governance—have developed in disjunct ways. The first of these stages paints on a very large historical canvas and emphasizes the institutional rules of the game: customs, laws, politics (North 1986). The second stage is much more microanalytical and focuses on the comparative efficacy with which alternative generic forms of governance—markets, hybrids, hierachies—

Reprinted from "Comparative Economic Organization: The Analysis of Discrete Structural Alternatives" by Oliver E. Williamson, published in *Administrative Science Quarterly* 36, no. 2 (June 1991): 269–96) by permission of *Administrative Science Quarterly*. © 1991 by Cornell University 0001–8392/91/3602–0269. The text has been edited for inclusion in this book.

economize on transaction costs. Can this disjunction problem be overcome?

A second objection to prior work is the criticism that transaction-cost economics deals with polar forms—markets and hierarchies—to the neglect of intermediate or hybrid forms. Although that objection has begun to be addressed by recent treatments of long-term contracting in which bilateral dependency conditions are supported by a variety of specialized governance features (hostages, arbitration, take-or-pay procurement clauses, tied sales, reciprocity, regulation, etc.), the abstract attributes that characterize alternative modes of governance have remained obscure. What are the key attributes and how do they vary among forms?

This is responsive to the third objection, namely, that efforts to operationalize transaction-cost economics have given disproportionate attention to the abstract description of transactions as compared with the abstract description of governance. The dimensionalization of both is needed.

Finally, there is the embeddedness problem: Transaction-cost economics purports to have general application but has been developed almost entirely with reference to Western capitalist economies (Hamilton and Biggart 1988). Is a unified treatment of Western and non-Western capitalist and noncapitalist economies really feasible? This chapter attempts to address these objections by posing the problem of organization as one of discrete structural analysis.

Discrete Structural Analysis

The term *discrete structural analysis* was introduced into the study of comparative economic organization by Simon (1978, pp. 6–7), who observed the following:

> As economics expands beyond its central core of price theory, and its central concern with quantities of commodities and money, we observe in it . . . [a] shift from a highly quantitative analysis, in which equilibration at the margin plays a central role, to a much more qualitative institutional analysis, in which discrete structural alternatives are compared. . . .
>
> [S]uch analyses can often be carried out without elaborate mathematical apparatus or marginal calculation. In general, much cruder and simpler arguments will suffice to demonstrate an inequality between two quantities than are required to show the conditions under which these quantities are equated at the margin.

But what exactly is discrete structural analysis? Is it employed only because "there is at present no [satisfactory] way of characterizing organizations in terms of continuous variation over a spectrum" (Ward 1967, p. 38)? Or is there a deeper rationale?

Of the variety of factors that support discrete structural analysis, I focus here on the following: (1) Firms are not merely extensions of markets but employ different means; (2) discrete contract law differences provide crucial support for and serve to define each generic form of governance; and (3) marginal analysis is typically concerned with second-order refinements to the neglect of first-order economizing.

Different Means

Although the study of economic organization deals principally with markets and market mechanisms, it is haunted by a troublesome fact: A great deal of economic activity takes place within firms (Barnard 1938; Chandler 1962, 1977). Conceivably, however, no novel economizing issues are posed within firms because technology is largely determinative—the firm is mainly defined by economies of scale and scope and is merely an instrument for transforming inputs into outputs according to the laws of technology—and because market mechanisms carry over into firms. I have taken exception with the technology view elsewhere (Williamson, 1975). Consider, therefore, the latter.

In parallel with von Clausewitz's (1832/1980) views on war, I maintain that hierarchy is not merely a contractual act but is also a contractual instrument, a continuation of market relations by other means. The challenge to comparative contractual analysis is to discern and explicate the different means. As developed in later sections of this chapter, each viable form of governance—market, hybrid, and hierarchy—is defined by a syndrome of attributes that bear a supporting relation to one another. Many hypothetical forms of organization never arise, or quickly die out, because they combine inconsistent features.

Contract Law

The mapping of contract law onto economic organization has been examined elsewhere (Williamson 1979, 1985). Although some of that analysis is repeated here, there are two significant differences. First, I advance the hypothesis that each generic form of governance—market, hybrid, and hierarchy—needs to be supported by a different form of contract law. Second, the form of contract law that supports hierarchy is that of forbearance.

Classical Contract Law

Classical contract law applies to the ideal transaction in law and economics—"sharp in by clear agreement; sharp out by clear performance" (Macneil 1974, p. 738)—in which the identity of the parties is irrelevant. "Thick" markets are ones in which individual buyers and sellers bear no dependency relation to each other. Instead, each party can go its own way at negligible cost to another. If contracts are renewed period by period, that is only because current suppliers are continuously meeting bids in the spot market. Such transactions are monetized in extreme degree; contract law is interpreted in a very legalistic way. More formal terms supersede less formal should disputes arise between formal and less formal features (e.g., written agreements versus oral amendments), and hard bargaining, to which the rules of contract law are strictly applied, characterizes these transactions. Classical contract law is congruent with and supports the autonomous market form of organization (Macneil 1974, 1978).

Neoclassical Contract Law and Excuse Doctrine

Neoclassical contract law and excuse doctrine, which relieves parties from strict enforcement, apply to contracts in which the parties to the transaction maintain autonomy but are bilaterally dependent in a nontrivial degree. Identity plainly matters if premature termination or persistent maladaptation would place burdens on one or both parties. Perceptive parties reject classical contract law and move into a neoclassical contracting regime because this better facilitates continuity and promotes efficient adaptation.

As developed later in this chapter, hybrid modes of contracting are supported by neoclassical contract law. The parties to such contracts maintain autonomy, but the contract is mediated by an elastic contracting mechanism. Public utility regulation, in which the relations between public utility firms and their customers are mediated by a regulatory agency, is one example (Goldberg 1976; Williamson 1976). Exchange agreements or reciprocal trading in which the parties experience (and respond similarly to) similar disturbances is another illustration (Williamson 1983). Franchising is another way of preserving semi-autonomy, but added supports are needed (Klein 1980; Hadfield 1990). More generally, long-term, incomplete contracts require special adaptive mechanisms to effect realignment and restore efficiency when beset by unanticipated disturbances.

Disturbances are of three kinds: inconsequential, consequential, and highly consequential. Inconsequential disturbances are ones for which the deviation from efficiency is too small to recover the costs of adjustment. The net gains from realignment are negative for minor disturbances because (as discussed later in this chapter) requests for adjustments need to be justified and are subject to review, the costs of which exceed the prospective gains.

Middle-range or consequential disturbances are ones to which neoclassical contract law applies. These are transactions for which Karl Llewellyn's concept of "contract as framework" is pertinent. Thus, Llewllyn (1931, p. 737) refers to contract as "a framework highly adjustable, a framework which almost never accurately indicates real working relations, but which affords a rough indication around which such relations vary, an occasional guide in cases of doubt, and a norm of ultimate appeal when the relations cease in fact to work." The thirty-two year coal supply agreement between the Nevada Power Company and the Northwest Trading Company illustrates the elastic mechanisms employed by a neoclassical contract. That contract reads in part as follows:

> In the event an inequitable condition occurs which adversely affects one Party, it shall then be the joint and equal responsibility of both Parties to act promptly and in good faith to determine the action required to cure or adjust for the inequity and effectively to implement such action. Upon written claim of inequity served by one Party upon the other, the Parties shall act jointly to reach an agreement concerning the claimed inequity within sixty (60) days of the date of such written claim. An adjusted base coal price that differs from market price by more than ten percent (10%) shall constitute a hardship. The Party claiming inequity shall include in its claim such information and data as may be reasonably necessary to substantiate the claim and shall freely and without delay furnish such other information and data as the other Party reasonably may deem relevant and necessary. If the Parties cannot reach agreement within sixty (60) days the matter shall be submitted to arbitration.

By contrast with a classical contract, this contract (1) contemplates unanticipated disturbances for which adaptation is needed, (2) provides a tolerance zone (of ± 10%) within which misalignments will be absorbed, (3) requires information disclosure and substantiation if adaptation is proposed, and (4) provides for arbitration in the event voluntary agreement fails.

The forum to which this neoclassical contract refers disputes is (initially, at least) that of arbitration rather than that of the courts. Fuller (1963, pp. 11–12) described procedural differences between arbitration and litigation:

> [T]here are open to the arbitrator . . . quick methods of education not open to the courts. An arbitrator will frequently interrupt the examination of witnesses with a request that the parties educate him to the point where he can understand the testimony being received. This education can proceed informally, with frequent interruptions by the arbitrator, and by informed persons on either side, when a point needs clarification. Sometimes there will be arguments across the table, occasionally even within each of the separate camps. The end result will usually be a clarification that will enable everyone to proceed more intelligently with the case.

Such adaptability notwithstanding, neoclassical contracts are not indefinitely elastic. As disturbances become highly consequential, neoclassical contracts experience real strain, because the autonomous ownership status of the parties continuously poses an incentive to defect. The general proposition here is that when the ''lawful'' gains to be had by insistence upon literal enforcement exceed the discounted value of continuing the exchange relationship, defection from the spirit of the contract can be anticipated.

When, in effect, arbitration gives way to litigation, accommodation can no longer be presumed. Instead, the contract reverts to a much more legalistic regime—although, even here, neoclassical contract law averts truly punitive consequences by permitting appeal to exceptions that qualify under some form of excuse doctrine. The legal system's commitment to the keeping of promises under neoclassical contract law is modest, as Macneil (1974, p. 731) explained:

> [C]ontract remedies are generally among the weakest of those the legal system can deliver. But a host of doctrines and techniques lies in the way even of those remedies: impossibility, frustration, mistake, manipulative interpretation, jury discretion, consideration, illegality, duress, undue influence, unconscionability, capacity, forfeiture and penalty rules, doctrines of substantial performance, severability, bankruptcy laws, statues of frauds, to name some; almost any contract doctrine can and does serve to make the commitment of the legal system to promise keeping less than complete.

From an economic point of view, the trade-off that needs to be faced in excusing contract performance is between stronger incentives and reduced opportunism. If the state realization in question was unforeseen and unforeseeable (different in degree and/or especially in kind from the range of normal business experience), if strict enforcement would have truly punitive consequences, and especially if the resulting ''injustice'' is supported by (lawful) opportunism, then excuse can be seen mainly as a way of mitigating opportunism, ideally without adverse impact on incentives. If, however, excuse is granted routinely whenever adversity occurs, then incentives to think through contracts, choose technologies judiciously, share risks efficiently, and avert adversity will be impaired. Excuse doctrine should therefore be used sparingly—which it evidently is (Farnsworth 1968, p. 885; Buxbaum 1985).

The relief afforded by excuse doctrine notwithstanding, neoclassical contracts deal with consequential disturbances only at great cost; arbitration is costly to administer and its adaptive range is limited. As consequential disturbances and, especially, as highly consequential disturbances become more frequent, the hybrid mode supported by arbitration and excuse doctrine incurs added costs and comes under added strain. Even more elastic and adaptive arrangements warrant consideration.

Forbearance

Internal organization, hierarchy, qualifies as a still more elastic and adaptive mode of organization. What type of contract law applies to internal organization? How does this have a bearing on contract performance?

Describing the firm as a ''nexus of contracts'' (Alchian and Demsetz 1972; Jensen and Meckling 1976; Fama 1980) suggests that the firm is no different from the market in contractual respects. Alchian and Demsetz (1972, p. 777) originally took the position that the relation between a shopper and his or her grocer and that between an employer and employee was identical in contractual respects:

The single consumer can assign his grocer to the task of obtaining whatever the customer can induce the grocer to provide at a price acceptable to both parties. That is precisely all that an employer can do to an employee. To speak of managing, directing, or assigning workers to various tasks is a deceptive way of noting that the employer continually is involved in renegotiation of contracts on terms that must be acceptable to both parties. . . . Long-term contracts between employer and employee are not the essence of the organization we call a firm.

That it has been instructive to view the firm as a nexus of contracts is evident from the numerous insights that this literature has generated. But to regard the corporation only as a nexus of contracts misses much of what is truly distinctive about this mode of governance. As developed later in this chapter, bilateral adaptation effected through fiat is a distinguishing feature of internal organization. But wherein do the fiat differences between market and hierarchy arise? If, moreover, hierarchy enjoys an "advantage" with respect to fiat, why can't the market replicate this?

One explanation is that fiat has its origins in the employment contract (Barnard 1938; Simon 1951; Coase 1952; Masten 1988). Although there is a good deal to be said for that explanation, the implicit contract law of internal organization is that of forbearance. Thus, whereas courts routinely grant standing to firms should there be disputes over prices, the damages to be ascribed to delays, failures of quality, and the like, courts will refuse to hear disputes between one internal division and another over identical technical issues. Access to the courts being denied, the parties must resolve their differences internally. Accordingly, hierarchy is its own court of ultimate appeal.

What is known as the "business judgment rule" holds that "[a]bsent bad faith or some other corrupt motive, directors are normally not liable to the corporation for mistakes of judgment, whether those mistakes are classified as mistakes of fact or mistakes of law" (Gilson 1986, p. 741). Not only does that rule serve as "a quasi-jurisdictional barrier to prevent courts from exercising regulatory powers over the activities of corporate managers" (Manne 1967, p. 271), but "[t]he courts' abdication of regulatory authority through the business judgment rule may well be the most significant common law contribution to corporate governance" (Gilson 1986, p. 741). The business judgment rule, which applies to the relation between shareholders and directors, can be interpreted as a particular manifestation of forbearance doctrine, which applies to the management of the firm more generally. To review alleged mistakes of judgment or to adjudicate internal disputes would sorely test the competence of courts and would undermine the efficacy of hierarchy.

Accordingly, the reason why the market is unable to replicate the firm with respect to fiat is that market transactions are defined by contract law of an altogether different kind. There is a logic to classical market contracting and there is a logic for forbearance law, and the choice of one regime precludes the other. Whether a transaction is organized as make or buy—internal procurement or market procurement, respectively—thus matters greatly in dispute-resolution respects. The courts will hear disputes of the one kind and will refuse to be drawn into the resolution of disputes of the other. Internal disputes between one division and another regarding the appropriate transfer prices and the damages to be ascribed to delays, failures of quality, and the like are thus denied a court hearing.

To be sure, not all disputes within firms are technical. Personnel disputes are more complicated. Issues of worker safety, dignity, the limits of "the zone of acceptance," and the like sometimes pose societal spillover costs that are undervalued in the firm's private net benefit calculus. Underprovision for human and worker rights could ensue if the courts refused to consider issues of these kinds. Also, executive compensation agreements can sometimes be written in ways that make it difficult to draw a sharp line between personnel and technical issues. Even with personnel disputes, however, there is a presumption that such differences will be resolved internally. For example, unions may refuse to bring individual grievances to arbitration (Cox 1958, p. 24):

> [G]iving the union control over all claims arising under the collective agreement comports so much better with the functional nature of a collective bargaining agreement. . . . Allowing an individual to carry a claim to arbitration whenever he is dissatisfied with the adjustment worked out by the company and the union . . . discourages the kind of day-to-day cooperation between company and union which is normally the mark of sound industrial relations—a relationship in which grievances are treated as problems to be solved and contracts are only guideposts in a dynamic human relationship. When . . . the individual's claim endangers group interest, the union's function is to resolve the competition by reaching an accommodation or striking a balance.

As compared with markets, internal incentives in hierarchies are flat or low-powered, which is to say that changes in effort expended have little or no immediate effect on compensation. That is mainly because the high-powered incentives of markets are unavoidably compromised by internal organization (Williamson 1985, ch. 6; 1988). Also, however, hierarchy uses flat incentives because these elicit greater cooperation and because unwanted side effects are checked by added internal controls (see Williamson 1988; Holmstrom 1989). Not only, therefore, will workers and managers be more willing to accommodate because their compensation is the same whether they "do this" or "do that," but an unwillingness to accommodate is interpreted not as an excess of zeal but as a predilection to behave in a noncooperative way. Long-term promotion prospects are damaged as a consequence. Defection from the spirit of the agreement in favor of litigiousness is quite perverse if neither immediate nor long-term gains are thereby realized. The combination of fiat with low-powered incentives is a manifestation of the syndrome condition of economic organization to which I referred earlier (and develop more fully later in this chapter).

The underlying rationale for forbearance is twofold: (1) Parties to an internal dispute have deep knowledge—both about the circumstances surrounding a dispute as well as about the efficiency properties of alternative solutions—that can be communicated to the court only at great cost, and (2) permitting internal disputes to be appealed to the court would undermine the efficacy and integrity of hierarchy. If fiat were merely advisory, in that internal disputes over net receipts could be pursued in the courts, the firm would be little more than an "inside contracting" system (Williamson 1985, pp. 218–22). The application of forbearance doctrine to internal organization means that parties to an internal exchange can work out their differences themselves or appeal unresolved disputes to the hierarchy for a decision. But this exhausts their alternatives. When push comes to shove, "legalistic" arguments fail. Greater reliance on instrumental reasoning and mutual accommodation result. This argument contradicts Alchian and Demsetz's (1972, p. 777) claim that the firm "has no power of fiat, no authority, no disciplinary action any different in the slightest degree from ordinary market contracting." That is exactly wrong: Firms can and do exercise fiat that markets cannot. Prior neglect of contract law differences and their ramifications explain the error.

First-Order Economizing

Although the need to get priorities straight is unarguable, first-order economizing—effective adaptation and the elimination of waste—has been neglected. Adaptation is especially crucial. As developed in this section, it is the central economic problem. But as Frank Knight (1941, p. 252) insisted, the elimination of waste is also important:

> [M]en in general, and within limits, wish to behave economically, to make their activities and their organization "efficient" rather than wasteful. This fact does deserve the utmost emphasis; and an adequate definition of the science of economics . . . might well make it explicit that the main relevance of the discussion is found in its relation to social policy, assumed to be directed toward the end indicated, of increasing economic efficiency, of reducing waste.

Relatedly, but independently, Oskar Lange (1938, p. 109) held that "the real danger of socialism is that of the bureaucratization of economic life, and not the impossibility of coping with the problem of allocation of resources." Inasmuch, however, as Lange (1938, p. 109) believed that this argument belonged "in the field of sociology," he concluded that it "must be dispensed with here." Subsequent informed observers of socialism followed this lead, whereupon the problems of bureaucracy were, until recently, given scant attention. Instead, the study of socialism was preoccupied with technical features—marginal cost pricing, activity analysis, and the like—with respect to which a broadly sanguine consensus took shape (Bergson 1948; Montias 1976; Koopmans 1977).

The natural interpretation of the organizational concerns expressed by Knight and Lange—or, at least, the interpretation that I propose here—is that economics was too preoccupied with issues of allocative efficiency, in which marginal analysis was featured, to the neglect of organizational efficiency, in which discrete structural alternatives were brought under scrutiny. Partly that is because the mathematics for dealing with clusters of attributes is only now beginning to be developed (Topkis 1978; Milgrom and Roberts 1990; Holmstrom and Milgrom 1991). Even more basic, however, is the propensity to focus exclusively on market mechanisms to the neglect of discrete structural alternatives. The argument, for example, that all systems of honest trade are variants on the reputation-effect mechanisms of markets (Milgrom, North, and Weingast 1990, p. 16) ignores the possibility that some ways of infusing contractual integrity (e.g., hierarchy) employ altogether different means. Market-favoring predispositions need to be disputed, lest the study of economic organization in all of its forms be needlessly and harmfully truncated.

Dimensionalizing Governance

What are the key attributes with respect to which governance structures differ? The discriminating alignment hypothesis to which transaction-cost economics owes much of its predictive content holds that transactions, which differ in their attributes, are aligned with governance structures, which differ in their costs and competencies, in a discriminating (mainly, transaction-cost-economizing) way. But whereas the dimensionalization of transactions received early and explicit attention, the dimensionalization of governance structure has been relatively slighted. What are the factors that are responsible for the aforementioned differential costs and competencies?

One of those key differences has been already indicated: Market, hybrid, and hierarchy differ in contract law respects. Indeed, were it the case that the very same type of contract law were to be uniformly applied to all forms of governance, important distinctions between these three generic forms would be vitiated. But there is more to governance than contract law. Crucial adaptability differences and differences in the use of incentive and control instruments are also germane.

Adaptation as the Central Economic Problem

Hayek (1945, p. 523) insistently argued that "economic problems arise always and only in consequence of change" and that this truth was obscured by those who held that "technological knowledge" is of foremost importance. He disputed the latter and urged that "the economic problem of society is mainly one of rapid adaptation in the particular circumstances of time and place" (Hayek 1945, p. 524). Of special importance to Hayek was the proposition that the price system, as compared with central planning, is an extraordinarily efficient mechanism for communicating information and inducing change (Hayek 1945, pp. 524–27).

Interestingly, Barnard (1938) also held that the main concern of organization was that of adaptation to changing circumstances, but his concern was with adaptation within internal organization. Confronted with a continuously fluctuating environment, the "survival of an organization depends upon the maintenance of an equilibrium of complex character. . . . [This] calls for readjustment of processes internal to the organization . . . [whence] the center of our interest is the processes by which [adaptation] is accomplished" (Barnard 1938, p. 6).

That is very curious. Both Hayek and Barnard hold that the central problem of economic organization is adaptation. But whereas Hayek (1945) locates this adaptive capacity in the market, it was on the adaptive capacity of internal organization that Barnard (1938) focused attention. If the "marvel of the market" (Hayek) is matched by the "marvel of internal organization" (Barnard), then wherein does one outperform the other?

The marvel to which Hayek (1945, p. 528) referred had spontaneous origins: "The price system is . . . one of those formations which man has learned to use . . . after he stumbled on it without understanding it." The importance of such spontaneous cooperation notwithstanding, it was Barnard's experience that intended cooperation was important and undervalued. The latter was defined as "that kind of cooperation among men that is conscious, deliberate, purposeful" (Barnard 1938, p. 4) and was realized through formal organization, especially hierarchy.

I submit that adaptability is the central problem of economic organization and that both Hayek and Barnard are correct. Both are correct because they are referring to adaptations of different kinds both of which are needed in a high-performance system. The adaptations to which Hayek refers are those for which prices serve as sufficient statistics. Changes in the demand or supply of a commodity are reflected in price changes, in response to which "individual participants . . . [are] able to take the right action" (Hayek 1945, p. 527). I refer to adaptations of this kind as adaptation (A), where (A) denotes autonomy. This is the neoclassical ideal in which consumers and producers respond independently to parametric price changes so as to maximize their utility and profits, respectively.

That would entirely suffice if all disturbances were of this kind. Some disturbances, however, require coordinated responses, lest the individual parts operate at cross-purposes or otherwise suboptimize. Failures of coordination may arise because autonomous parties read and react to signals differently, even though their purpose is to achieve a timely and compatible combined response. The "nonconvergent expectations" to which Malmgren (1961) referred is an illustration. Although, in principle, convergent expectations could be realized by asking one party to read and interpret the signals for all, the lead party may behave strategically—by distorting information or disclosing it in an incomplete and selective fashion.

More generally, parties that bear a long-term bilateral dependency relation to one another must recognize that incomplete contracts require gap filling and sometimes get out of alignment. Although it is always in the collective interest of autonomous parties to fill gaps, correct errors, and effect efficient realignments, it is also the case that the distribution of the resulting gains is indeterminate. Self-interested bargaining predictably obtains. Such bargaining is itself costly. The main costs, however, are that transactions are maladapted to the environment during the bargaining interval. Also, the prospect of *ex post* bargaining invites *ex ante* prepositioning of an inefficient kind (Grossman and Hart 1986).

Recourse to a different mechanism is suggested as the needs for coordinated investments and for uncontested (or less contested) coordinated realignments increase in frequency and consequentiality. Adaptations of these coordinated kinds will be referred to as adaptation (*C*), where (*C*) denotes cooperation. The conscious, deliberate, and purposeful efforts to craft adaptive internal coordinating mechanisms were those on which Barnard focused. Independent adaptations here would at best realize imperfect realignments and could operate at cross-purposes. Lest the aforementioned costs and delays associated with strategic bargaining be incurred, the relation is reconfigured by supplanting autonomy by hierarchy. The authority relation (fiat) has adaptive advantages over autonomy for transactions of a bilaterally (or multilaterally) dependent kind.

Instruments

Vertical and lateral integration are usefully thought of as organization forms of last resort, to be employed when all else fails. That is because markets are a "marvel" in adaptation (*A*) respects. Given disturbance to which prices serve as sufficient statistics, individual buyers and suppliers can reposition autonomously. Appropriating, as they do, individual streams of net receipts, each party has a strong incentive to reduce costs and adapt efficiently. What I have referred to as high-powered incentives result when consequences are tightly linked to actions in this way (Williamson 1988). Other autonomous traders have neither legitimate claims against the gains nor can they be held accountable for the losses. Accounting systems cannot be manipulated to share gains or subsidize losses.

Matters get more complicated when bilateral dependency intrudes. As already discussed in this chapter, bilateral dependency introduces an opportunity to realize gains through hierarchy. As compared with the market, the use of formal organization to orchestrate coordinated adaptation to unanticipated disturbances enjoys adaptive advantages as the condition of bilateral dependency progressively builds up. But these adaptation (*C*) gains come at a cost. Not only can related divisions within the firm make plausible claims that they are causally responsible for the gains (in indeterminate degree), but divisions that report losses can make plausible claims that others are culpable. There are many ways, moreover, in which the headquarters can use the accounting system to effect strategic redistributions (through transfer pricing changes, overhead assignments, inventory conventions, etc.), whatever the preferences of the parties. The upshot is that internal organization degrades incentive intensity, and added bureaucratic costs result (Williamson 1985, ch. 6; 1988).

These three features—adaptability of type A, adaptability of type C, and differential incentive intensity—do not exhaust the important differences between market and hierarchy. Also important are the differential reliance on administrative controls and, as already developed in this chapter, the different contract law regimes to which each is subject. Suffice it to observe here that (1) hierarchy is buttressed by the differential efficacy of administrative controls within firms, as compared with between firms, and (2) incentive intensity within firms is sometimes deliberately suppressed. Incentive intensity is not an objective but is merely an instrument. If added incentive intensity gets in the way of bilateral adaptability, then weaker incentive intensity supported by added administrative controls (monitoring, career rewards and penalties) can be optimal.

Markets and hierarchies are polar models. As indicated at the outset, however, a major purpose of this chapter is to locate hybrid modes—various forms of long-term contracting, reciprocal trading, regulation, franchising, and the like—in relation to these polar modes. Plainly, the neoclassical contract law of hybrid governance differs from both the classical contract law of markets and the forbearance contract law of hierarchies, being more elastic than the former but more legalistic than the latter. The added question is, How do hybrids compare in adaptability (types A and C), incentive intensity, and administrative control?

The hybrid mode displays intermediate values in all four features. It preserves ownership autonomy, which elicits strong incentives and encourages adaptation to type A disturbances (those to which one party can respond efficiently without consulting the other). Because there is bilateral dependency, however, long-term contracts are supported by added contractual safeguards and administrative apparatus (information disclosure, dispute settlement machinery). These facilitate adaptations of type C but come at the cost of incentive attenuation. Concerns for "equity" intrude. Thus the Nevada Power Company–Northwest Trading Company coal contract, whose adaptation mechanics were set out earlier in this chapter, begins with the following: "It is the intent of the Parties hereto that this agreement, as a whole and in all of its parts, shall be equitable to both Parties throughout its term." Such efforts unavoidably dampen incentive intensity features.

One advantage of hierarchy over the hybrid in bilateral adaptation respects is that internal contracts can be more incomplete. More important, adaptations to consequential disturbances are less costly within firms because (1) proposals to adapt require less documentation, (2) resolving internal disputes by fiat rather than by arbitration saves resources and facilitates timely adaptation, (3) information that is deeply impacted can more easily be accessed and more accurately assessed, (4) internal dispute resolution enjoys the support of informal organization (Barnard 1938; Scott 1987), and (5) internal organization has access to additional incentive instruments—including especially career reward and joint profit sharing—that promote a team orientation. Furthermore, highly consequential disturbances that would occasion breakdown or costly litigation under the hybrid mode can be accommodated more easily. The advantages of hierarchy over hybrid in adaptability C respects are not, however, realized without cost. Weaker incentive intensity (greater bureaucratic costs) attend the move from hybrid to hierarchy, ceteris paribus.

Summarizing, the hybrid mode is characterized by semistrong incentives and an intermediate degree of administrative apparatus, displays semistrong adaptations of both kinds, and works out of a semilegalistic contract law regime. As compared with market and hierarchy, which are polar opposites, the hybrid mode is located between the two of these in all five attribute respects. Based on the foregoing, the instruments, adaptive attributes, and contract law features that distinguish markets, hybrids, and hierarchies are shown in Table 5.1.

Discriminating Alignment

Transaction-cost economics subscribes to Commons's view (1924, 1934) that the transaction is the basic unit of analysis. That important insight takes on operational significance upon identifying the critical dimensions with respect to which transactions differ. Without purporting to be exhaustive, these include the frequency with which transactions recur, the uncertainty to which transactions are subject, and the type and degree of asset specificity involved in supplying the good or service in question (Williamson 1979). Although all are important, transaction-cost economics attaches special significance to this last (Williamson 1975, 1979; Klein, Crawford, and Alchian 1978; Grossman and Hart 1986).

Asset specificity has reference to the degree to which an asset can be redeployed to alternative uses and by alternative users without sacrifice of productive value. Asset-specificity distinctions of six kinds have been made: (1) site specificity, as where successive stations are located in a cheek-by-jowl relation to each other so as to economize on inventory and transportation expenses; (2) physical asset specificity, such as specialized dies that are required to produce a component; (3) human asset specificity that arises in learning by doing; (4) brand-name capital; (5) dedicated assets, which are discrete investments in general purpose plant that are made at the behest of a particular customer; and (6) temporal specificity, which is akin to technological nonseparability and can be thought of as a type of site specificity in which timely responsiveness by on-site human assets is vital (Masten, Meehan, and Snyder 1991). This last,

Table 5.1

**Distinguishing Attributes of Market, Hybrid,
and Hierarchy Governance Structures**

Attributes	Governance Structure		
	Market	Hybrid	Hierarchy
Instruments			
Incentive intensity	++[a]	+[b]	0
Administrative controls	0[c]	+	++
Performance attributes			
Adaptability (A)	++	+	0
Adaptability (C)	0	+	++
Contract law	++	+	0

[a] ++ = strong
[b] + = semistrong
[c] 0 = weak

appears to be more akin to a condition of technological nonseparability (Alchian and Demsetz 1972). Asset specificity, especially in its first five forms, creates bilateral dependency and poses added contracting hazards. It has played a central role in the conceptual and empirical work in transaction-cost economics.

The analysis here focuses entirely on transaction costs; neither the revenue consequences nor the production-cost savings that result from asset specialization are included. Although that simplifies the analysis, note that asset specificity increases the transaction costs of all forms of governance. Such added specificity is warranted only if these added governance costs are more than offset by production-cost savings and/or increased revenues. A full analysis will necessarily make allowance for effects of all three kinds (Riordan and Williamson 1985). Only a truncated analysis appears here.

Reduced-Form Analysis

The governance-cost expressions set out herein are akin to reduced forms, in that governance costs are expressed as a function of asset specificity and a set of exogenous variables. The structural equations from which these reduced forms are derived are not set out. The key features that are responsible for cost differences among governance structures are nonetheless evident in the matrix version of the model set out in this section.[1]

Although asset specificity can take a variety of forms, the common consequence is this: A condition of bilateral dependency builds up as asset specificity deepens. The ideal transaction in law and economics—whereby the identities of buyers and sellers is irrelevant—obtains when asset specificity is zero. Identity matters as investments in transaction-specific assets increase, since such specialized assets lose productive value when redeployed to best alternative uses and by best alternative users.

Assume, for simplicity, that asset specificity differences are entirely due to physical or site specificity features. I begin with the situation in which classical market contracting works well: Autonomous actors adapt effectively to exogenous disturbances. Internal organization is at a disadvantage for transactions of this kind, since hierarchy incurs added bureaucratic costs to which no added benefits can be ascribed. That, however, changes as bilateral dependency sets in. Disturbances for which coordinated responses are required become more numerous and consequential as investments in asset specificity deepen. The high-powered incentives of markets here impede adaptability, since each party to an autonomous exchange that has gotten out of alignment and for which mutual consent is needed to effect an adjustment will want to appropriate as much as possible (ideally, all but epsilon) of the adaptive gains to be realized. When bilaterally dependent parties are unable to respond quickly and easily because of disagreements and self-interested bargaining, maladaptation costs are incurred. Although the transfer of such transactions from market to hierarchy creates added bureaucratic costs, those costs may be more than offset by the bilateral adaptive gains that result.

Let $M = M(k;\theta)$ and $H = H(k;\theta)$ be reduced-form expressions that denote market and hierarchy governance costs as a function of asset specificity (k) and a vector of shift parameters (θ). Assuming that each mode is constrained to choose the same level of asset specificity, the following comparative-cost relations obtain:[2]

$$M(0) < H(0) \text{ and } M' > H' > 0 \quad [1]$$

The first of these two inequalities reflects the fact that the bureaucratic costs of internal organization exceed those of the market because the latter is superior in adaptation (A) respects—which is the only kind that matters if asset specificity is negligible. The intercept for market governance is thus lower than is the intercept for hierarchy. The second inequality reflects the marginal disability of markets as compared with hierarchies in adaptability (C) respects as asset specificity, hence bilateral depedency, becomes more consequential.

As previously described, the hybrid mode is located between market and hierarchy with respect to incentive, adaptability, and bureaucratic cost. As compared with the hierarchy, the hybrid sacrifices incentives in favor of superior coordination among the parts. As compared with the hierarchy, the hybrid sacrifices cooperativeness in favor of greater incentive intensity. The distribution of branded product from retail outlets by market, hierarchy, and hybrid, where franchising is an example of this last, illustrates the argument.

Forward integration out of manufacturing into distribution would be implied by hierarchy. That would sacrifice incentive intensity but would (better) assure that the parts do not operate at cross-purposes with one another. The market solution would be to sell the good or service outright. Incentive intensity is thereby harnessed, but suboptimization (free riding on promotional efforts, dissipation of the brand name, etc.) may also result. Franchising awards greater autonomy than hierarchy but places franchises under added rules and surveillance as compared with markets. Cost control and local adaptations are stronger under franchising under than hierarchy, and suboptimization is reduced more under franchising than under hierarchy (as compared with hierarchy), and the added restraints (as compared with the market) under which franchisees operate nevertheless come at a cost. If, for example, quality assurance is realized by constraining the franchise to use materials supplied by the franchiser and if exceptions to that practice are not permitted because of the potential for abuse that would result, then local opportunities to make "apparently" cost-effective procurements will be prohibited. Similarly, the added local autonomy enjoyed by franchisees may get in the way of some global adjustments.

Transactions for which the requisite adaptations to disturbances are neither predominantly autonomous nor bilateral but require a mixture of each are candidates to be organized under the hybrid mode. Over some intermediate range of k, therefore, the mixed adaption (A/C) that hybrids afford could well be superior to the A-favoring or C-favoring adaptations supported by markets and hierarchies, respectively.

Letting $X = X(k;\theta)$ denote the governance costs of the hybrid mode as a function of asset specificity, the argument is the following:[3]

$$M(0) < X(0) < H(0) \quad [2]$$

$$M' > X' > H' > 0 \quad [3]$$

The relations shown in Figure 5.1 then obtain. Efficient supply implies operating on the envelope, whence, if k^* is the optimal value of k, the rule for efficient supply is as follows: I, use markets for $k^* < \overline{k}_1$; II, use hybrids for $\overline{k}_1 < k^* < k_2$; and III, use hierarchy for $k^* > \overline{k}_2$.

In a very heuristic way, moreover, one can think of moving along one of these generic curves as moving toward more intrusive controls. Thus, consider two forms of franchising, one of which involves less control that the other. If $X^1(k)$

Figure 5.1. **Governance Costs as a Function of Asset Specificity**

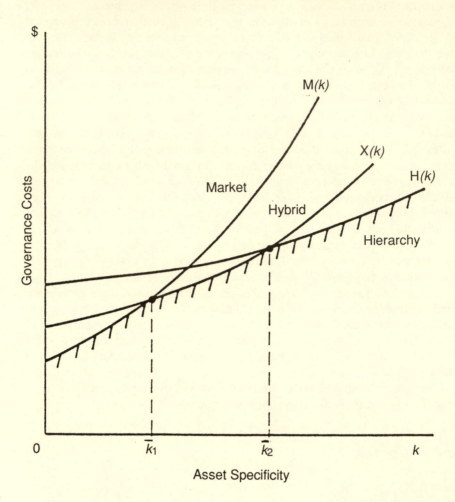

Asset Specificity

and $X^2(k)$ refer to franchising with little and much control, respectively, then $X^2(k)$ will be located to the right of $X^1(k)$ in Figure 5.2. Or consider the M-form (multidivisional) and U-form (unitary or functionally organized) corporation. Because the former provides more marketlike divisionalization than does the latter, the M-form is given by $H1(k)$ and is located closer to $\bar{k}_2$ in Figure 5.2.

A Matrix Representation

Suppose that disturbances are distinguished in terms of the type of response—autonomous or bilateral—that is needed to effect an adaptation. Sup-

Figure 5.2. **Governance Differences within Discrete Structural Forms**

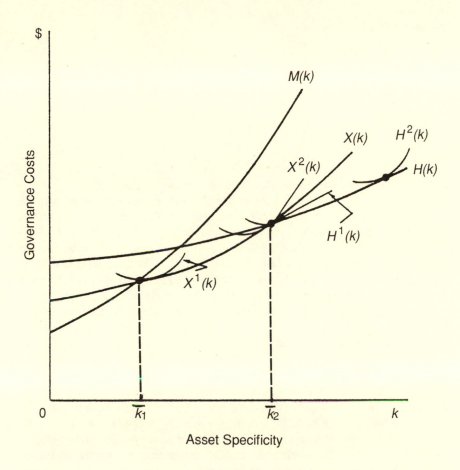

Asset Specificity

pose further that the type of adaptation depends on the degree of asset specificity. Let asset specificity be denoted by k_j and suppose that it can take on any of three values: $k_1 = 0$ (generic investment), $k_2 > 0$ (semispecific investment), or $k_3 > 0$ (highly specific investment).

Assume that adjustments to disturbances can be any of four kinds: I, strictly autonomous; II, mainly autonomous; III, mainly coordinated; or IV, strictly coordinated. Let p_{ij} be the probability that an adaptation of type $i = $ I, II ..., IV will be required if asset specificity condition k_j ($j = 1, 2, 3$) obtains, and let matrix $[p_{ij}]$ be given by Table 5.2.

Note that, the k_1 column excepted, positive probability is associated with every element in the matrix. What added asset specificity does is shift the dis-

Table 5.2

The Matrix [p_{ij}]

[p_{ij}]	k_1	k_2	k_3
I	1.00	.25	.10
II	.00	.25	.10
III	.00	.25	.40
IV	.00	.25	.40

tribution of required responses in favor of greater cooperativeness.

Assume that each adaptation, if costlessly and successfully implemented, would yield identical expected cost savings. For the reasons given above, however, the efficacy with which different modes adapt to disturbances of different kinds varies. Let e_{im} be the efficacy with which mode m ($m = M, X, H$) is able to implement adaptations of type i ($i = $ I, II . . . , IV) and assume that the matrix e_{im} is given by Table 5.3. where 1.0 is the ideal degree of adaptiveness and 0.0 is equivalent (in terms of efficacy) to no adaptation.

The efficacy assumptions embedded in this last matrix warrant discussion: (1) Only the entry e_{IM} has a value of 1.0. This condition—market adaptations to disturbance for which strictly autonomous adaptation is appropriate—corresponds to the ideal transaction in law and economics (classical market contracting). (2) The efficacy of the market falls off as bilateral dependency builds up, becoming negative (worse than no adaptation at all) for the strictly cooperative case (IV). This last reflects the conflictual nature of market exchange for transactions of the bilaterally dependent kind. (3) The hybrid mode is almost as good as the market for strictly autonomous adaptations, is better than the market in all other adaptation categories, and is as good or better than hierarchy in all categories save that for which strict coordination is indicated; (4) Hierarchy is burdened by bureaucracy and never scores high in efficacy for any category of adaptation[4]. What matters, however, is comparative efficacy. The hierarchy comes into its own (comparatively) where adaptations of a strictly cooperative kind are needed. (5) The efficacy of hierarchy is lowest for disturbances requiring a mainly autonomous adaptation. As compared with strictly autonomous disturbances where bureaucratic costs are held in check by an objective market standard, ready recourse to the market is compromised by the need for some coordination. Because, however, the gains from coordination are not great, efforts to coordinate are problematic. If efforts to adapt autonomously are protested (my costs are

Table 5.3

The Matrix [e _im_]

[e_{im}]	M	X	H
I	1.0	0.9	0.7
II	0.7	0.9	0.4
III	0.2	0.5	0.5
IV	−0.2	0.0	0.5

greater because you moved without consulting me), while failures to adapt quickly are costly, the hierarchy is caught between the proverbial rock and a hard place.

Let C_{jm} be the expected maladaptation costs of using mode m to effect adaptations if asset specificity is of type k_j. Since inefficacy is given by $1—e_{im}$, the expected maladaptations costs are as follows:

$$C_{jm} = \Sigma_i p_{ij} (1-e_{im}) \quad [4]$$

That matrix is given by Table 5.4.

The lowest values in each row are realized by matching market, hybrid, and hierarchy with asset specificity conditions k_1, k_2, and k_3, respectively. These costs are consonant with the reduced form relations shown in Figure 5.1. Thus, if ß ≥ 0 is the irreducible setup costs of economic participation, then the bureaucratic costs intercepts associated with zero asset specificity (k_1) for market, hybrid, and hierarchy will be given by ß plus .000, .100, and .300, respectively. Also, the relation between the implied slopes associated with each mode in the matrix (expressed as a function of asset specificity) is that $M' > X' > H'$, which corresponds exactly to the relations shown in Figure 5.1.

Comparative Statics

Transaction-cost economics maintains that (1) transaction-cost economizing is the "main case," which is not to be confused with the only case (Williamson 1985, pp. 22–23; 1989, pp. 137–38), and (2) transaction costs vary with governance structures in the manner already described in this chapter. Assuming that the institutional environment is unchanging, transactions should be clustered under governance structures as indicated. Variance will be observed, but the main case should be as described.

Table 5.4

The Matrix [c_{jm}]

[c_{jm}]	M	X	H
k_1	.000	.100	.300
k_2	.575	.425	.475
k_3	.830	.620	.490

The purpose of this section is to consider how equilibrium distributions of transactions will change in response to disturbances in the institutional environment. That is a comparative static exercise. Both parts of the new institutional economics—the institutional environment and the institutions of governance—are implicated. The crucial distinctions are these (Davis and North 1971, pp. 6–7):

> The *institutional environment* is the set of fundamental political, social and legal ground rules that establishes the basis for production, exchange and distribution. Rules governing elections, property rights, and the right of contract are examples . . . .
> An *institutional arrangement* is an arrangement between economic units that governs the ways in which these units can cooperate and/or compete. It . . . [can] provide a structure within which its members can cooperate . . . or [it can] provide a mechanism that can effect a change in laws or property rights.

The way that I propose to join these two is to treat the institutional environment as a set of parameters, changes in which elicit shifts in the comparative costs of governance. An advantage of a three-way setup—market, hybrid, and hierarchy (as compared with just market and hierarchy)—is that much larger parameter changes are required to induce a shift from market to hierarchy (or the reverse) than are required to induce a shift from market to hybrid or from hybrid to hierarchy. Indeed, as developed in this chapter, much of the comparative static action turns on differential shifts in the intercept and/or slope of the hybrid mode. The critical predictive action is that which is located in the neighborhood of $\bar{k}_1$ (M to X) and $\bar{k}_2$ (X to H) in Figure 5.1. Parameter changes of four kinds are examined: property rights, contract law, reputation effects, and uncertainty.

Among the limitations of the discrete structural approach is that parameter changes need to be introduced in a special way. Rather than investigate the effects of increases (or decreases) in a parameter (a wage rate, a tax, a shift in demand), as is customary with the usual maximizing setup, the comparative governance cost setup needs to characterize parameter changes as improvements (or not). It is furthermore limited by the need for these improvements to be concentrated disproportionately on one generic mode of governance. Those limitations notwithstanding, it is informative to examine comparative static effects.

Property Rights

What has come to be known as the economics of property rights holds that economic performance is largely determined by the way in which property rights are defined. Ownership of assets is especially pertinent to the definition of property rights, where this "consists of three elements: (a) the right to use the asset [and delimitations that apply thereto]. . . , (b) the right to appropriate returns from the asset . . . , and (c) the right to change the asset's form and/or substance" (Furubotn and Pejovich 1974, p. 4).

Most discussions of property rights focus on definitional issues. As is generally conceded, property rights can be costly to define and enforce, hence arise only when their expected benefits exceed the expected costs (Demsetz 1967). That is not my concern here. Rather, I focus on the degree to which property rights, once assigned, have good security features. Security hazards of two types are pertinent: expropriation by the government and expropriation by commerce (rivals, suppliers, customers).

Governmental Expropriation

Issues of "credible commitments" (Williamson 1983) and "security of expectations" (Michelman 1967) are pertinent to expropriation by the government. If property rights could be efficiently assigned once and for all so that assignments, once made, would not subsequently be undone—especially strategically undone—governmental expropriation concerns would not arise. Firms and individuals would confidently invest in productive assets without concern that they would thereafter be deprived of their just desserts.

If, however, property rights are subject to occasional reassignment and if compensation is not paid on each occasion (possibly because it is prohibitively costly), then strategic considerations enter the investment calculus. Wealth will be reallocated (disguised, deflected, consumed) rather than invested in potentially expropriable assets if expropriation is perceived to be a serious hazard. More generally, individuals or groups who either experience or observe expropriation and can reasonably anticipate that they will be similarly disadvantaged in the future have incentives to adapt.

Michelman (1967) focused on cost-effective compensation. He argued that if compensation is costly and if the "demoralization costs" experienced by disadvantaged individuals and interested observers are slight, then compensation is not needed. If, however, demoralization costs can be expected to be great and if losses can be easily ascertained, compensation is warranted. Michelman proposed a series of criteria by which to judge how this calculus works out. Suppose that the government is advised of these concerns and "promises" to respect the proposed criteria. Will such promises be believed? This brings us to the problem of creditable commitments.

Promises are easy to make, but credible promises are another thing. Kornai's (1986, pp. 1705–6) observation that craftspeople and small shopkeepers fear expropriation in Hungary despite "repeated official declarations that their activity is regarded as a permanent feature of Hungarian socialism" is pertinent. That "many of them are myopic profit maximizers, not much interested in building up lasting goodwill . . . or by investing in long-lived fixed assets" (1986, p. 1706) is partly explained by the fact that "[t]hese individuals or their parents lived through the era of confiscations in the forties" (Kornai 1986, p. 1705).

But there is more to it than that. Not only is there a history of expropriation, but, as of 1986, the structure of the government had not changed in such a way as to assuredly forestall subsequent expropriations. Official declarations will be more credible only with long experience or if accompanied by a credible (not easily reversible) reorganization of politics. As one Polish entrepreneur recently remarked, "I don't want expensive machines. If the situation changes, I'll get stuck with them" (Newman 1989, p. A10). Note in this connection that the objectivity of law is placed in jeopardy if the law and its enforcement are under the control of a one-party state (Berman 1983, p. 37). Credibility will be enhanced if a monarch who has made the law "may not make it arbitrarily, and until he has remade it—lawfully—he is bound by it" (Berman 1983, p. 9). Self-denying ordinances and, even more, inertia that has been crafted into the potential process have commitment benefits (North and Weingast 1989).

That this has not fully registered on Eastern Europe and the Soviet Union is suggested by the following remarks of Mikhail Gorbachev (advising U.S. firms to invest quickly in the Soviet Union rather than wait): "Those [companies] who are with us now have good prospects of participating in our great country . . . [whereas those who wait] will remain observers for years to come—we will see to it" (*International Herald Tribune* 1990, p. 5). That the leadership of the Soviet Union "will see to it" that early and late movers will be rewarded and punished, respectively, reflects conventional carrot-and-stick incentive reasoning. What it misses is that ready access to administrative discretion is the source of contractual hazard. The paradox is that fewer degrees of freedom (rules) can have advantages over more (discretion) because added credible commitments can obtain in this way. Effective economic reform thus requires that reneging options be foreclosed if investor confidence is to be realized.

Lack of credible commitment on the part of the government poses hazards for durable, immobile investments of all kinds—specialized and unspecialized alike—in the private sector. If durability and immobility are uncorrelated with asset specificity, then the transaction costs of all forms of private-sector governance increase together as expropriation hazards increase. In that event, the values of k_1 and k_2 might then change little or not at all. What can be said with assurance is that the government sector will have to bear a larger durable investment burden in a regime in which expropriation risks are perceived to be great. Also, private-sector durable investments will favor assets that can be smuggled or are otherwise mobile—such as general-purpose human assets (skilled machinists, physicians) who can be used productively if emigration is permitted to other countries.

Leakage

Not only may property rights be devalued by governments, but the value of specialized knowledge and information may be appropriated and/or dissipated by suppliers, buyers, and rivals. The issues here have recently been addressed by Teece (1986) in conjunction with "weak regimes of appropriability" and are related to earlier discussions by Arrow (1962) regarding property rights in information. If investments in knowledge cannot lawfully be protected or if nominal protection (e.g., a patent) is ineffective, then (1) the *ex ante* incentives to make such investments are impaired and (2) the *ex post* incentives to embed such investments in protective governance structures are increased. As Teece (1986) discussed, vertical or lateral integration into related stages of production where the hazards of leakage are greatest is sometimes undertaken for precisely these protective purposes. Trade-secret protection is an example.

Interpreted in terms of the comparative governance cost apparatus employed here, weaker appropriability (increased risk of leakage) increases the cost of hybrid contracting as compared with hierarchy. The market and hybrid curves in Figure 5.1 are both shifted up by increased leakage, so that $\bar{k}_1$ remains approximately unchanged and the main effects are concentrated at $\bar{k}_2$. The value of $\bar{k}_2$ thus shifts to the left as leakage hazards increase, so that the distribution of transactions favors greater reliance on hierarchy.

Contract Law

Improvements or not in a contract law regime can be judged by how the relevant governance-cost curve shifts. An improvement in excuse doctrine, for example, would shift the cost of hybrid governance down. The idea here is that excuse doctrine can be either too strict or too lax. If it is too strict, then parties will be reluctant to make specialized investments in support of another because of the added risk of truly punitive outcomes should unanticipated events materialize and the opposite party insist that the letter of the contract be observed. If excuse doctrine is too lax, then incentives to think through contracts, choose technologies judiciously, share risks efficiently, and avert adversity will be impaired.

Whether a change in excuse doctrine is an improvement or not depends on the initial conditions and on how these trade-offs play out. Assuming that an improvement is introduced, the effect will be to lower the cost of hybrid contracting—especially at higher values of asset specificity, where a defection from the spirit of the contract is more consequential. The effect of such improvements would be to increase the use of hybrid contracting, especially as compared with hierarchy.

Hadfield (1990, pp. 981–82) has recently examined franchise law and has interpreted the prevailing tendency by the courts to fill in the gaps of an incomplete contract "by according the franchiser unfettered discretion, much as it would enjoy if it [the franchiser] were a vertically integrated corporation" as a mistaken application of forbearance reasoning from hierarchy (where the logic holds) to neoclassical contracting (where the logic fails). Such a failure of franchise law would increase the cost of franchising in relation to forward integration into distribution (Hadfield 1990, p. 954). This would imply a shift in the value of $\bar{k}_2$ in Figure 5.1 to the left.

A change of forbearance doctrine would be reflected in the governance cost of hierarchy. Thus, mistaken forbearance doctrine—for example, a willingness by the courts to litigate intrafirm technical disputes—would have the effect of shifting the costs of hierarchical governance up. This would disadvantage hierarchy in relation to hybrid modes of contracting ($\bar{k}_2$ would shift to the right).

Reputation Effects

One way of interpreting a network is as a nonhierarchical contracting relation in which reputation effects are quickly and accurately communicated. Parties to a transaction to which reputation effects apply can consult not only their own experience but can benefit from the experience of others. To be sure, the efficacy of reputation effects is easily overstated (Williamson 1991b), but comparative efficacy is all that concerns us here and changes in comparative efficacy can often be established.

Thus, assume that it is possible to identify a community of traders in which reputation effects work better (or worse). Improved reputation effects attenuate incentives to behave opportunistically in interfirm trade—since the immediate gains from opportunism in a regime where reputation counts must be traded off against future costs. The hazards of opportunism in interfirm trading are greatest for hybrid transactions—especially those in the neighborhood of $\bar{k}_2$. Since an improvement in interfirm reputation effects will reduce the cost of hybrid contracting, the value of $\bar{k}_2$ will shift to the right. Hybrid contracting will therefore increase in relation to hierarchy in regimes where interfirms' reputation effects are more highly perfected, ceteris paribus. Reputation effects are pertinent within firms as well. If internal reputation effects improve, then managerial opportunism will be reduced and the costs of hierarchical governance will fall.

Ethnic communities that display solidarity often enjoy advantages of a hybrid contracting kind. Reputations spread quickly within such communities, and added sanctions are available to the membership (Light 1972). Such ethnic communities will predictably displace nonethnic communities for activities where interfirm reputation effects are important. Nonethnic communities, to be viable, will resort to market or hierarchy (in a lower or higher k niche, respectively).

Uncertainty

Greater uncertainty could take either of two forms. One is that the probability distribution of disturbances remains unchanged but that more numerous disturbances occur. A second is that disturbances become more consequential (owing, for example, to an increase in the variance).

One way of interpreting changes of either kind is through the efficacy matrix already presented in this chapter. I conjecture that the effects of more frequent disturbances are especially pertinent for those disturbances for which mainly coordinated or strictly coordinated responses are required. Although the efficacy of all forms of governance may deteriorate in the face of more frequent disturbances, the hybrid mode is arguably the most susceptible. That is because hybrid adaptations cannot be made unilaterally (as with market governance) or by fiat (as with hierarchy) but require mutual consent. Consent, however, takes time. If a hybrid mode is negotiating an adjustment to one disturbance only to be hit by another, failures of adaptation predictably obtain (Ashby 1960). An increase in market and hierarchy and a decrease in hybrid will thus be associated with an (above threshold) increase in the frequency of disturbances. As shown in Figure 5.3, the hybrid mode could well become nonviable when the frequency of disturbances reaches high levels.[5]

If an increase in the variance of the disturbances uniformly increases the benefits to be associated with each successful adaptation, then the effect of increasing the consequentiality of disturbances can again be assessed through the effects on efficacy. Since outliers induce greater defection on the spirit of the agreement for hybrid modes, the efficacy of the hybrid is adversely affected by added variance. Unless similar disabilities can be ascribed to market or hierarchy, the hybrid is disfavored by greater variance, ceteris paribus.

Discussion

The foregoing is concerned with the organization of transactions for mature

Figure 5.3. **Organization Form Responses to Changes in Frequency**

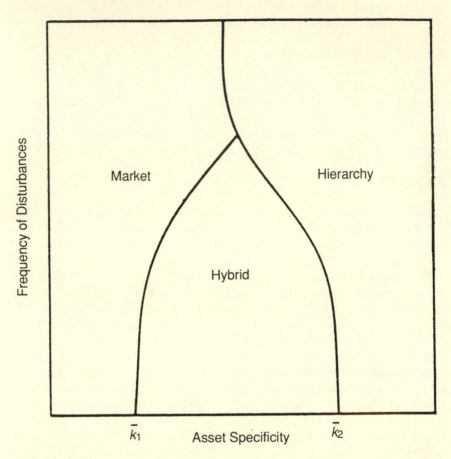

goods and services and introduces parameter shifts one at a time. Added complications arise when innovation is introduced and when a series of parameter shifts occur together.

Innovation

Some of the added problems posed by innovation take the form of weak property rights. These are discussed earlier in the chapter in conjunction with leakage. A second class of problems that confront innovation is that of timeliness. Nonstandard forms of organization, such as parallel research and development (Nelson 1961) and joint ventures, are sometimes employed because these facilitate timely entry.

Timing can be crucial if a party expects to be a "player" when events are fast moving or if learning by doing is essential. Although transaction-cost economics can relate to some of the pertinent issues, such as those posed by tacit knowledge (Polanyi 1962) and the limits of imitation (Williamson 1975, pp. 31–32, 203–7), added apparatus is needed to deal with the full set of issues that arise when responsiveness in real time, rather than equilibrium contracting, is the central concern. Awaiting such developments, the apparatus developed here should not be applied uncritically. For example, joint ventures are sometimes described as hybrids. If, however, joint ventures are temporary forms of organization that support quick responsiveness and if that is their primary purpose, then both successful and unsuccessful joint ventures will commonly be terminated when contracts expire. Successful joint ventures will be terminated because success will often mean that each of the parties, who chose not to merge but, instead, decided to combine their respective strengths in a selective and timely way, will have learned enough to go it alone. Unsuccessful joint ventures will be terminated because the opportunity to participate will have passed them by. Joint ventures that are designed to give a respite should be distinguished from the types of hybrid modes analyzed here, which are of an equilibrium kind.

The need to distinguish continuing from temporary supply does not, however, mean that transaction-cost economizing has application (Williamson 1985). The quasi firms described by Eccles (1981), for example, can be interpreted as the efficient solution to a particular type of recurrent contracting problem. But the details do matter.

Simultaneous Parameter Shifts

The comparative static analysis set out in previous sections of this chapter treats each generic form of organization as a syndrome of attributes and introduces parameter shifts one at a time. Suppose, instead, that a series of shifts were to occur together. Could these be processed as a sequence of independent changes? If such changes were in fact independent, that is precisely what I would propose. If, however, a related set of changes is made simultaneously, it will not do to treat these independently. If strong interaction effects exist, these must be treated as a cluster.

Relying extensively on the recent work of Aoki (1988, 1990), I have elsewhere interpreted the Japanese corporation as follows: (1) Three key factors—employment, subcontracting, and banking—are fundamentally responsible for the success of the Japanese firm; (2) the efficacy of each of these rests on distinctive institutional supports; and (3) the three factors bear a complementary relation to each other (Williamson 1991a).

The search for key factors and their institutional supports is wholly consistent with the spirit of this chapter. Because employment, subcontracting, and banking changes are linked, however, the American corporation cannot expect to replicate the Japanese corporation by making changes in only one of these practices and not in the others. That is not to say that American firms cannot learn by observing subcontracting practices in Japanese firms. Exact replication of individual practices will be suboptimal, however, if linkages are important.

Similar considerations apply to economic reforms in China and Eastern Europe. If, for example, the efficacy of privatization turns crucially on the manner in which banking is organized and on the security of property rights, then piecemeal proposals that ignore the support institutions are fraught with hazard. The study of viable clusters of organization is a combined law, economics, and organizations undertaking. Although the apparatus in this chapter is pertinent, applications to economic reform need to make express provision for contextual differences among alternative forms of capitalism (Hamilton and Biggart 1988).

Conclusion

This chapter advances the transaction-cost economics research agenda in the following five respects: (1) The economic problem of society is described as that of adaptation, of which autonomous and coordinated kinds are distinguished; (2) each generic form of governance is shown to rest on a distinctive form of contract law, of which the contract law of forbearance, which applies to internal organization and supports fiat, is especially noteworthy; (3) the hybrid form of organization is not a loose amalgam of market and hierarchy but possesses its own disciplined rationale; (4) more generally, the logic of each generic form of governance—market, hybrid, and hierarchy—is revealed by the dimensionalization and explication of governance herein developed; and (5) the obviously related but hitherto disjunct stages of institutional economics—the institutional environment and the institutions of governance—are joined by interpreting the institutional environment as a locus of shift parameters, changes in which parameters induce shifts in the comparative costs of governance. A large number of refutable implications are derived from the equilibrium and comparative static analyses of governance that result. The growing empirical literature, moreover, is broadly corroborative (for summaries, see Williamson 1985, ch. 5; Joskow 1988; Shelanski 1990).

Further developments of conceptual, theoretical, and empirical kinds are needed. Taken together with related developments in information economics, agency theory, and population ecology, there is reason to be optimistic that a "new science of organization" will take shape during the decade of the 1990s (Williamson 1990). Whether that materializes or not, organization theory is being renewed in law, economics, and organizational respects. These are exciting times for interdisciplinary social theory.

Notes

1. Developing the deeper structure that supports the reduced forms—by explicating contractual incompleteness and its consequences in a more microanalytic way and by developing the bureaucratic cost consequences of internal organization more explicitly—is an ambitious but important undertaking.

2. A more general optimizing treatment in which the level of asset specificity varies with organization form is set out in Riordan and Williamson (1985). Also see Masten (1982).

3. This assumes that $X(0)$ is less than $H(0)$ to a nontrivial degree, since otherwise the hybrid mode could be dominated throughout by the least-cost choice of either market or hierarchy, which may occur for certain classes of transactions, as discussed later.

4. Hierarchy is able to deal with type I (strictly autonomous) disturbances reasonably well by instructing the operating parts to respond to local disturbances on their own motion and by using the market as an alternate source of supply and of standard.

5. The range of asset specificity is from zero (purely generic) to complete (purely firm-specific). The range of frequency is from "low" (a positive lower bound in a nearly unchanging environment) to "very high."

Bibliography

Alchian, Armen, and Harold Demsetz. 1972. "Production, Information Costs, and Economic Organization." *American Economic Review* 62: 777–95.

Aoki, Masahiko. 1990. "Toward an Economic Model of the Japanese Firm." *Journal of Economic Literature* 28: 1–27.

———. 1988. *Information, Incentives, and Bargaining in the Japanese Economy.* New York: Cambridge University Press.

Arrow, Kenneth J. 1962. "Economic Welfare and the Allocation of Resources of Invention." In *The Rate and Direction of Inventive Activity: Economic and Social Factors*, ed. National Bureau of Economic Research. Princeton, N.J.: Princeton University Press, 609–25.

———. 1969. "The Organization of Economic Activity: Issues Pertinent to the Choice of Market Versus Nonmarket Allocation." In *The Analysis and Evaluation of Public Expenditure*. Vol. 1, *The PPB System*, 59–73. U.S. Joint Economic Committee, 91st Congress, 1st Session, Washington, D.C.: U.S. Government Printing Office.

Ashby, W. Ross. 1960. *Design for a Brain.* New York: John Wiley and Sons.

Barnard, Chester. 1938. *The Functions of the Executive.* Cambridge: Harvard University Press.

Bergson, Abram. 1948. "Socialist Economics." In *Survey of Contemporary Economics*, ed. Howard Ellis. Philadelphia: Blakiston, 430–58.

Berman, Harold. 1983. *Law and Revolution.* Cambridge: Harvard University Press.

Buxbaum, Richard M. 1985. "Modification and Adaptation of Contrasts: American Legal Developments." *Studies in Transnational Economic Law* 3: 31–54.

Chandler, A. D., Jr. 1962. *Strategy and Structure.* Cambridge: MIT Press.

———. 1977. *The Visible Hand: The Managerial Revolution in American Business.*

Cambridge: Harvard University Press.

Clausewitz, Karl von. 1832/1980. *Vom Kriege*. 19th ed. Bonn: Dremmler.

Coase, Ronald H. 1952. "The Nature of the Firm." In *Readings in Price Theory*, eds. G. J. Stigler and Kenneth E. Boulding. Homewood, Ill.: Richard D. Irwin, 331–51.

Commons, John R. 1924. "Law and Economics." *Yale Law Journal* 34: 371–82.

————. 1934. *Institutional Economics*. Madison: University of Wisconsin Press.

Cox, Archibald. 1958. "The legal Nature of Collective Bargaining Agreements." *Michigan Law Review* 57: 1–35.

Davis, Lance E., and Douglass C. North. 1971. *Institutional Change and American Economic Growth*. Cambridge: Cambridge University Press.

Demsetz, Harold. 1967. "Toward a Theory of Property Rights." *American Economic Review* 57: 347–59.

Eccles, Robert. 1981. "The Quasifirm in the Construction Industry." *Journal of Economic Behavior and Organization* 2: 335–57.

Fama, Eugene F. 1980. "Agency Problems and the Theory of the Firm." *Journal of Political Economy* 88: 288–307.

Farnsworth, Edward Allan. 1968. "Disputes over Missions in Contracts." *Columbia Law Review* 8: 860–91.

Fuller, Lon L. 1963. "Collective Bargaining and the Arbitrator." *Wisconsin Law Review* 72 (January): 3–46.

Furubotn, Eirik, and Svetozar Pejovich. 1974. *The Economics of Property Rights*. Cambridge, Mass.: Ballinger.

Gilson, Ronald. 1986. *The Law and Finance of Corporate Acquisitions*. Mineola, N.Y.: The Foundation Press.

Goldberg, Victor. 1976. "Regulation and Administered Contracts." *Bell Journal of Economics* 7: 426–52.

Grossman, Sanford J., and D. Oliver Hart. 1986. "The Costs and Benefits of Ownership: A Theory of Vertical and Lateral Integration." *Journal of Political Economy* 94: 691–719.

Hadfield, Gillian. 1990. "Problematic Relations: Franchising and the Law of Incomplete Contracts." *Stanford Law Review* 42: 927–92.

Hamilton, Gary, and Nicole Biggart. 1988. "Market, Culture, and Authority." *American Journal of Sociology* (supplement) 94: S52–S94.

Hayek, Friedrich. 1945. "The Use of Knowledge in Society." *American Economic Review* 35: 519–30.

Holmstrom, Bengt. 1989. "Agency Costs and Innovation." *Journal of Economic Behavior and Organization* 12: 305–27.

Holmstrom, Bengt, and Paul Milgrom. (In press). "Multi-Task Principal-Agent Analysis." *Journal of Law, Economics, and Organization*.

International Herald Tribune. 1990. "Soviet Economic Development." (June) 5: 5.

Jensen, Michael, and William Meckling. 1976. "Theory of the Firm: Managerial Behavior, Agency Costs, and Capital Structure." *Journal of Financial Economics* 3: 305–60.

Joskow, Paul. 1988. "Asset Specificity and the Structure of Vertical Relationships." *Journal of Law, Economics, and Organization* 4: 95–117.

Klein, Benjamin. 1980. "Transaction Cost Determinants of 'Unfair' Contractual Arrangements." *American Economic Review* 70: 356–62.

Klein, Benjamin, R. A. Crawford, and A. A. Alchian. 1978. "Vertical Integration, Appropriable Rents, and the Competitive Contracting Process." *Journal of Law and Economics* 21: 297–326.

Knight, Frank H. 1941. (Review of Melville J. Herskovits.) "Economic Anthropology." *Journal of Political Economy* 49: 247–58.

Koopmans, Tjalling. 1977. "Concepts of Optimality and Their Uses." *American Economic Review* 67: 261–74.

Kornai, Janos. 1986. "The Hungarian Reform Process." *Journal of Economic Literature* 24: 1687–737.

Lange, Oskar. 1938. "On the Theory of Economic Socialism." In *On the Economic Theory of Socialism*, ed. Benjamin Lippincott. Minneapolis: University of Minnesota Press, 55–143.

Light, Ivan. 1972. *Ethnic Enterprise in America: Business and Welfare among Chinese, Japanese, and Blacks*. Berkeley: University of California Press.

Llewellyn, Karl N. 1931. "What Price Contract? An Essay in Perspective." *Yale Law Journal* 40: 704–51.

Macneil, Ian R. 1974. "The Many Futures of Contracts." *Southern California Law Review* 47: 691–816.

———. 1978. "Contracts: Adjustment of Long-term Economic Relations Under Classical, Neoclassical, and Relational Contract Law." *Northwestern University Law Review* 72: 854–906.

Malmgren, H. 1961. "Information, Expectations and the Theory of the Firm." *Quarterly Journal of Economics* 75: 399–421.

Manne, Henry. 1967. "Our Two Corporation Systems: Law and Economics." *University of Virginia Law Review* 53: 259–85.

Masten, Scott. 1982. "Transaction Costs, Institutional Choice, and the Theory of the Firm." Ph.D diss. University of Pennsylvania.

———. 1988. "A Legal Basis for the Firm." *Journal of Law, Economics, and Organization* 4: 181–98.

Masten, Scott, James Meehan, and Edward Snyder. 1991. "The Costs of Organization." *Journal of Law, Economics, and Organization*.

Michelman, Frank. 1967. "Property, Utility and Fairness: The Ethical Foundations of 'Just Compensation' Law." *Harvard Law Review* 80: 1165–257.

Milgrom, Paul, Douglass North, and Barry Weingast. 1990. "The Role of Institutions in the Revival of Trade." *Economics and Politics* 2: 1–23.

Milgrom, Paul, and John Roberts. 1990. "The Economics of Modern Manufacturing: Technology, Strategy, and Organization." *American Economic Review* 80: 511–28.

Montias, Michael. 1976. *The Structure of Economic Systems*. New Haven, Conn.: Yale University Press.

Nelson, Richard R. 1961. "Uncertainty, Learning, and the Economics of Parallel R&D." *Review of Economics and Statistics* 43: 351–64.

Newman, Barry. 1989, "Poland's Farmers Put the Screws to Leaders by Holding Back Crops." *Wall Street Journal* (October) 25: A1 and A10.

North, Douglass. 1986. "The New Institutional Economics." *Journal of Theoretical and Institutional Economics* 142: 230–37.

North, Douglass, and Barry Weingast. 1989. "Constitutions and Commitment: The Evolution of Institutions Governing Public Choice in 17th Century England." *Journal of Economic History* 49: 803–32.

Polanyi, Michael. 1962. *Personal Knowledge: Towards a Post-Critical Philosophy*. New York: Harper and Row.

Riordan, Michael, and Oliver Williamson. 1985. "Asset Specificity and Economic Organization." *International Journal of Industrial Organization* 3: 365–78.

Scott, W. R. 1987. *Organizations*. 2d ed. Englewood Cliffs, N.J.: Prentice-Hall.

Shelanski, Howard. 1990. "A Survey of Empirical Research in Transaction Cost Economics." (Unpublished manuscript). University of California, Berkeley.

Simon, Herbert. 1951. "A Formal Theory of the Employment Relation." *Econometrica* 19: 293–305.

———. 1978. "Rationality as Process and as Product of Thought." *American Economic Review* 68, 1: 1–16.

Teece, David J. 1986. "Profiting from Technological Innovation." *Research Policy* 15 (December): 285–305.

Topkis, Donald. 1978. "Maximizing a Submodular Function on a Lattice." *Operations Research* 26: 305–21.

Ward, B. N. 1967. *The Socialist Economy: A Study of Organizational Alternatives*. New York: Random House.

Williamson, Oliver E. 1975. *Markets and Hierarchies*. New York: Free Press.

———. 1976. "Franchise Bidding for Natural Monopoly—In General and With Respect to CATV." *Bell Journal of Economics* 7: 73–104.

———. 1979. "Transaction-Cost Economics: The Governance of Contractual Relations." *Journal of Law and Economics* 22: 233–61.

———. 1983. "Credible Commitments: Using Hostages to Support Exchange." *American Economic Review* 73: 519–40.

———. 1985. *The Economic Institutions of Capitalism*. New York: Free Press.

———. 1988. "The Logic of Economic Organization." *Journal of Law, Economics, and Organization* 4: 65–93.

———. 1989. "Transaction Cost Economics." In *Handbook of Industrial Organization*, eds. Richard Schmalensee and Robert Willig. New York: North Holland, 1: 136–82.

———. 1990. "Chester Barnard and the Incipient Science of Organization." In *Organization Theory*, ed. Oliver E. Williamson. New York: Oxford University Press, 172–207.

———. 1991a. "Strategizing, Economizing, and Economic Organization." *Strategic Management Journal* 12 (Winter): 75–94.

———. 1991b. "Economic Institutions: Spontaneous and Intentional Governance," *Journal of Law, Economics, and Organization* 7: 159–87 (special issue).

Part II.

Comparative Analyses of Institutional Structures and Changes

6. Small Firm Networks

Charles B. Perrow

It is clear that the last fifteen years have seen dramatic changes in the form of economic organizations in North America, Europe, and Japan, generally a move toward decentralized structures and loose alliances.[1] I briefly characterize this change in the first section. In the second section, I review three explanations for it, and I argue in the third section that none of them has provided a fully satisfactory account for the changes. One of the new forms to emerge, *nondependent subcontracting*, is discussed in the fourth section. The most interesting form, *small firm networks* (SFNs), will be the focus of the rest of the chapter. It is the least significant form in terms of economic output—on a worldwide basis the output of small firm networks is probably trivial—but I argue in the fifth section that, while it is small and fairly new, it is a diverse and possibly durable economic phenomenon that deserves attention and, in the sixth section, that conventional economic theories and even leftist theories particularly fail with this form. SFNs are significant in three respects that I want to deal with: (1) In the seventh section, I discuss the potentials for what I call the "production of trust," a generally neglected and always unspecified factor of production; (2) in the eighth section, I review the welfare implications, such as effects on the distribution of wealth and power in society, which should be the final referent in all we do, I believe. Before discussing the third significance of SFNs, in the ninth section, I review the fundamental question of whether it is size or networks that are important and conclude that one must have both small size and networking to realize the advantages. (3) In the tenth section, I conclude by discussing the third significance of SFNs, that small-firm networks reverse a 150-year-old trend toward the absorption of society by large organizations, an absorption, I believe, that has weakened civil society.

The Integrated Firm, M-Form, and the Devolution

Figure 6.1 pictures the integrated firm (IF) model. The IF buys out as many of its competitors as it can and also integrates backward and forward to control as much of the "throughput," as Chandler (1977) calls it, from raw materials to

Figure 6.1. **Integrated Firm Model**

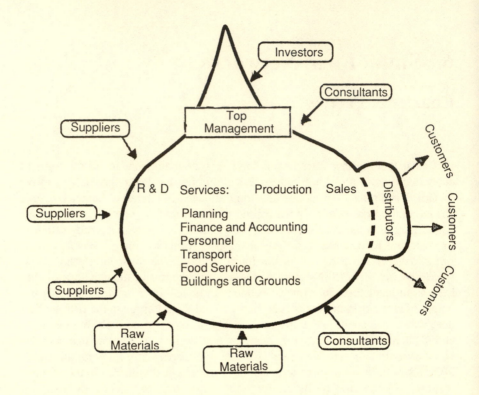

final consumer, as it can. It absorbs the sources of uncertainty in its environment, and in this process, it reduces the number of autonomous organizations in its environment. I have listed a few business and financial service functions to remind us that these also might have been performed by independent organizations before the integration took place. The IF deals with consultants and suppliers, of course, but in order to control transaction costs and throughput coordination, it prefers to make rather than to buy, according to theory. (The onion shape in Figure 6.1 indicates the post-1945 swelling of middle levels and relative decline of the hourly work force.)

Figure 6.2 pictures some of the other forms of economic organizations we should consider. It is shaped like an American football rather than a continuum because in between the two extremes, the IF and the SFN, are a variety of possibilities. Uniting a few integrated firms in different products or in related in-

Figure 6.2. **Forms of Economic Organization**

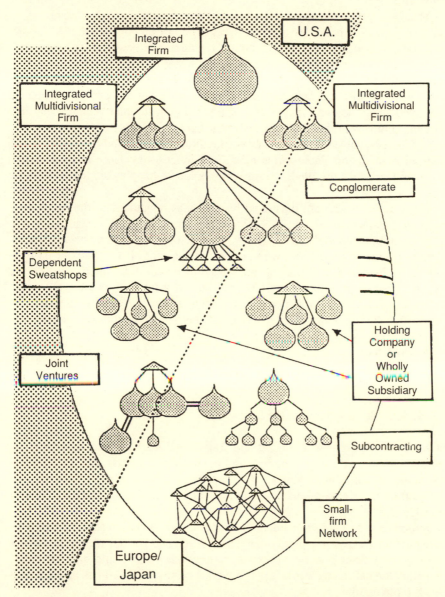

dustries produces the *multidivisional firm (M-form)*, and uniting a multi-divisional firm with some integrated firms, possibly including some with highly dependent subcontractors, or sweatshops, produces the *conglomerate*. If the state owns conglomerates, we have command economies; if they are in private hands, we have command economies; if they are in private hands, we have advanced capitalism.

That is roughly an account of the economic history of the United States from, say, 1850 to 1970 or so. Most of the firms of industrial America are still at the Integrated Production end of the football; the large and powerful ones have become multidivisional (and multinational, of course) or conglomerate firms. But supposedly in response to competition from abroad, U.S. firms have been devolving, downsizing, delaying, breaking up, spinning off, and combining in joint ventures. The two forms in the figure that indicate joint ventures, and the holding company or the wholly owned subsidiary, only feebly represent the variety of forms involved in these changes (See Powell [1990] and Sabel [1991] for indication of these.) These forms have been much in evidence in Europe and Japan at least since the 1960s, but my impression is that they are less evident in the United States.

More radical forms are illustrated by the subcontracting and the small firm network diagrams in Figure 6.2. These are discussed in detail later in this chapter, but for the present it suffices to say that the subcontracting model involves a greater degree of devolution, with perhaps 70 percent of the components produced by independent firms that are generally under 100 employees in size, while the small firm network is the most radical form, with nothing but small firms of under, say, 10 or 25 persons producing a large variety of goods and services, almost everything except extractive goods and basic industrial output.

Why the Change?

Three arguments provide for the change:

1. The *flexible production* school, optimistic about the efficiencies of deconcentration, cite such things as the following:

• A flexible response to changing and fragmented markets because small suppliers have more direct information and have it more quickly than the specialized units of a large bureaucracy.
• Small units have more widely skilled personnel who can be redeployed more quickly.
• Information technology reduces transaction delays and costs when firm A searches for the best supplier among firms B, C, and D, thus offsetting the advantage large firms have from centralized purchasing or in-house suppliers.
• Technological changes make the production of small runs and changes in products more feasible.
• Effort is more directly related to reward in the small firm, and there are more chances of ownership status.
• Nonspecialized tasks in smaller organizations reduce the separation between conception and execution.

(While I have emphasized the role of size theoretically in this list, there is nothing preventing the large bureaucracy from restructuring itself to realize most of the gains of the list.) The grand outlines of this school are best represented by Sabel, Piore, and Zeitlin in the various references to their work in the bibliography.

2. *Capitalist failure*. Less sanguine are the critics of capitalism who cite the externalization of social costs to smaller units. In particular they cite harder work, longer hours, less pay, no union protection, and the absorption of risk by the small firm (see, e.g., Murray 1983 and 1987; Hyman 1988; Smith 1989; Pollert 1988; Sakai 1990; Wood 1988; and for an ambivalent effort to come to terms with flexible specialization by the Left, Thompson 1989). Ironically, for capitalism's critics, as bad as big organizations are, big organizations are better than small ones, if capitalism reigns. They have better labor practices, internal labor markets, and more social services, and there is even evidence from the United States that large, bureaucratic firms promote more cognitive complexity among employees than do small firms.[2] Though I have not seen it discussed, I would anticipate a "self-exploitation" argument here as well; the fetish of consumption drives people to work long hours in order to accumulate and spend.

An additional anticapitalist explanation, independent of the just mentioned claims about exploitation, asserts that the deconcentration in the United States could be explained by the collapse of U.S. industrial hegemony; rather than buying up cheap industrial property to further integrate vertically and horizontally, the giants are getting rid of their own and speculating with the proceeds. Here the response is different from that of other countries; having acquired hegemony though market control and monopsony, the U.S. firms, when faced with superior quality and more efficient production from other countries, can only sell off units and trade with the proceeds. But there is a worldwide decline of profits and intensification of competition, according to this branch of the "capitalism's failure" argument, and it affects the Japanese and European firms that have emphasized flexibility and quality. They are externalizing social costs through contracting out, thus contributing to the changes in organizational forms.

3. A third explanation could be called the *organizational failure* analysis. Along with the first explanation (flexible production), it emphasizes flexibility and speed, but it has fewer of the first's social concerns with broad upskilling, independency, and what we have not discussed as yet, fostering cooperation through networks. Instead, the third explanation has more organizational efficiency concerns that might be associated with management schools, even with "agency theory" (see Perrow [1986a and 1986b] for a critique of agency theory). Here, big firms have gotten too big; internal vested interests create a small-numbers bargaining position that top management cannot cope with; these vested interests create inflexibilities and inefficiencies when markets are fragmenting and technologies changing.[3]

There are two variants of interest, a structural one and an entrepreneurial one. As an example of the first, Swedish organizational theorist Stymne (1989) argues that management is whipped at both ends of the labor market by a "rigid wage structure" which prevents rewarding the specialized people much in demand ("management experts, software experts, engineers, etc."), so they leave to form their own companies. At the other end, the rigid wage structure overpays unskilled workers for such jobs as cleaning, transport, and copying, so outside firms offer cleaning services at lower prices. The second variant cites the stifling of initiative for true entrepreneurs in large firms; they break free and start their own. (They hope to make *their* firms large, and thus stifling never receives comment.)

The cause of the organizational failure in either version of this third view is rather vague—bureaucracy, or "interests." The structuralist, Stymne, implies a surprising inability of those at the top of large, previously successful organizations, to have either the wit to foresee or the power to control the development of internal interests, and implies their inability to find structural alternatives; this view strongly bounds the rationality of management and may verge on a "culture of the firm" explanation of failure. It is not clear why big organizations can reward top management so fully but not reward software experts, even in Sweden with its "wage solidarity" policy. Nor is it clear why big organizations got into the practice of overpaying the unskilled so extensively that they cannot cut their wages but have to fire the lot and rehire them as workers for a separate firm. Presumably, the very high rate of unionization in Sweden may explain why cleaning women are paid well in big firms but paid much less by small contractors, but it is not clear why the wage structure is inflexible for software experts (and not for top management) in Sweden's case, nor why unions could have much impact in the United States with only 17 percent of the work force unionized. In any case, Stymne's thesis about bipolar wage failures deserves testing and fits in with the general organizational failure picture painted by those who favor entrepreneurship.

Most who cite organizational failure as the explanation of deconcentration seem to be entrepreneurial consultants who favor entrepreneurship and seek out the evidence for drive, hard work, creativity, and risk taking and who discuss the entrepreneur's social marginality and family and minority ethnic ties. This is the small-business literature, which I have not found useful, since it rarely conceptualizes networks per se but mostly talks about the importance of "networking" as a personal attribute, and rarely deals with such variables as input and output dependencies, distribution of wealth, hierarchy, and authority structure. There is a related but different cultural argument, though, that may be more important. It stresses the difference between entrepreneurial and proletarian cultures, cites the importance of regions with small farmers and small craftspeople who have business experience and value autonomy above high wages and income security (e.g., Amin 1989; Brusco 1982, 1989); and emphasizes the role of national cultures, for example the Irish culture that allegedly does not favor entrepreneurial styles (O'Farrell 1986).

Inadequacies of the Explanations

All three of these explanations—flexible production, capitalism's crisis, and organizational failure—have their merits. But I am still puzzled by the deconcentration of U.S. firms that is said to be going on, because I should think they would have the wit to capture the profit stream of suppliers and distributors and enlarge that stream because of increased market control that would come from vertical integration. And they certainly could continue their historical role of buying out the best of the entrepreneurs after the niche is discovered and made profitable.

The best explanation, but still unsatisfactory, may lie in one part of the anti-capitalist view. It may be that the business climate in the United States is too unpromising in the long term to avoid decentralization because of low productivity growth, firm debt, an insufficiently skilled work force, and risk-adverse investors and banks who can no longer afford a long-term perspective if too many favor short-term ones. Under these circumstances, where firms cannot control the rate of product change and technological change, markets are more likely to fragment and above-normal returns from oligopoly and the associated mass production of low-quality goods are no longer available. The profits of some units may fall below those of the entire firm, and they will be sold off, even at the expense of losing some market control; lending institutions, resistant to lending for production because of its low returns, may make it harder for the firm to raise money, so the firm has to sell some of its assets; and union or government regulations may be avoided by divesting.

But I am still puzzled by these arguments. True, one sells off low-return units because total return is less important than the rate of return, since poorly performing investments could be redeployed. But the less profitable ones have to be sold at a loss. Since buyers also have alternatives for investing their capital, why buy low-profit businesses? If it is good enough for someone to buy, why sell? And when one's organization is smaller, it will have less political power and less market power.

A second problem with the explanation concerns experience and "fit." Firms sell off incompatible units or ones they have little experience in running. Both are important, of course, but firms are selling off units they have had experience in running; they will lose that experiential investment. If their experience is inadequate we should recall that throughout the history of capitalism firms have found it quite easy to purchase experience; they pay for it and get from those that have it. According to economic arguments, if any good, including experience, is in very short supply, the demand will rise quickly and the supply will rise to meet the demand.

Regarding compatibility with the main line of products, years of successful growth of diversified and divisionalized firms have supposedly taught us the value of synergy, cross subsidization, and hedges against particular market declines and the value of balanced investments. I do not think these arguments rebut those who see a failure of capitalism.

These problems aside, if the pessimistic "capitalism's failure" argument can stand, it can be combined with parts of the optimistic "flexible production" argument. Big firms must downsize in order to even survive because the competition is such that attributes associated with small size—flexibility and product development and quality and speed—are what matter most. It is not vested interests and "bureaucratic red tape" that matter (the organizational failure explanation), but (and this is the central thrust of the present chapter) small size and the advantages of at least some degree of networking among autonomous firms.

Before I explore the evidence for the virtues of small size and networking, I should indicate still another puzzlement: the big firm does not need to spin off or sell off parts of itself and become smaller, to be efficient, as so many say it must; and each time it does so it looses some of the profit stream. Most of the advantages of flexible specialization can be achieved by the judicious restructuring of the big firm: flattening the overall hierarchy by creating many more subunits and giving them considerable autonomy. Furthermore, the firm then keeps the ultimate prize, the contribution to overall profit that the effort of each unit brings. If the firm creates a subsidiary, it must give up part of the profits to the head, who takes the risks; similarly with a joint venture. If the head of the unit is salaried, the firm takes the profits. If downsizing means loss of profit opportunities, why has it happened?

It was only yesterday that we were told by economists that the success of the multidivisional firm and of large firms in general was due to their ability to innovate and provide for a bewildering variety of styles and models; diversification was the appropriate hedge and source of innovative ideas; economies of scale appeared to have no upper bounds, since the bigger the firm, the more power it would have in the capital market, and the more cross subsidization it could do; and the technological changes permitting flexible and decentralized, short product run production should be even more available to rich big firms, permitting "flexible mass production." With all these advantages, and their market power and political power, the need to restructure should be minimal.

One factor that might account for the new competition surely seems to have changed substantially, since such things as better quality, more variety, and rapid styling changes have always been sought: new technologies allow (for) multipurpose machines and equipment and rapid data processing. This undoubtedly facilitates decentralized production. But it also makes it just as possible to have highly flexible *centralized* production with attendant economies of scale in terms of research and development, personnel allocation, and so forth. The technological tide should raise the level of both big and small firms; the big firms should be able to benefit sufficiently so that they do not need to spin off and sell off divisions, contract out projects, and from joint venture. But the technological changes may still favor small firms in the sense that it puts them closer to technological parity with the bit firms; both benefit, but the small firm more.

In any case, integrated production is a way to capture returns while allowing for market and firm growth. It is effective for owners if (1) markets are controlled sufficiently to *control* the rate of product and technological change (it is not necessary to suppress it); (2) if the market is stable for other reasons such as oligopoly, near saturation, technological stability, or government regulation; or, though this is less frequent, (3) if small firms are unable to evade governmental laws and regulations and thus cannot outperform large firms. The first two of these three conditions permit the economies of scale that come from mass production and the possibility of lowering the quality of goods and services in order to increase returns. Mass production is not only the result of market control; mass production itself encourages a firm to seek market control because of the cost of capital tied up in mass production; market control makes it easier to keep investments working. Once a market breaks up into pieces that require different types of activities (such as frequent changes in production lines, producing non-formula motion picture films—see Storper [1989]—or generating new financial services), integrated production firms will be threatened by new firms offering the new goods or services. To these we will finally turn.

Nondependent Subcontracting

The next form in Figure 6.2, subcontracting, is a distinct new form that grew fast in Japan from the 1960s on; it may also be well represented in Europe, but I am unsure about that. I refer to it as the *nondependent subcontracting model*. Here the firm has a first line of subcontractors, perhaps three hundred is the most that can be managed even by a big auto firm, and they in turn have second and third lines of subcontractors, most of them quite small. In some elaborate examples the second and third tiers would have more than one customer; that is, the subcontractor would sell to two or three or more primary firms. Conceivably, the prime contractors could also have other customers. Note that the picture of the subcontracting model is a picture of an integrated firm except for the fact that all of these are independent firms; we lack the all-important line drawn around the firms indicating ownership and retention of profits and responsibility for losses. (Again, some might have other customers, just as units within the IF might sell some of their services outside.) Retaining their own profits, instead of passing them on to headquarters, may be the most important difference between the subcontracting and the IF models. (But that again raises the question of why the parent firm does not just buy up the subcontractors and appropriate their profits. The most pleasant hypothesis is that the owners would not work as hard if they were employees, and the employees themselves would not work as hard for the big corporation as they did for the original owner of the small firm.)

The Japanese favor this form. In general, Japan has a higher proportion of small firms than the United States, though this gross figure can be misleading. More to the point, while General Motors (GM) and most large European auto firms makes 50 percent of the car, the average auto firm in Japan makes only 30 percent of the car. While GM deals directly with 3,500 parts suppliers, the Japanese firm deals directly with between 100 and 300 component suppliers, who in turn deal with about 5,000 subcontractors arranged in tiers (Best 1991, p. 163).

Subcontractors in Japan are no longer dependent upon the big organizations they sell to. In thirty years, subcontractors have gone from the highly dependent positions typical of the United States to quite independent or mutually dependent positions. In Japan, according to Nishigushi (1990), the figure for the following measures went from about 20 percent of subcontractors in all industry in 1950 to about 80 percent in 1980:

• joint determination of prices,
• design input,
• sharing of production information between firm and contractor,
• contracts for large modules rather than single items,
• payment within two months rather than nine or twelve months,
• from about 60 percent of the wage in the big firms to 80 percent or more.

In 1982 subcontractors had an average of 6.5 parent companies, according to figures assembled by Best (1991, pp. 161–63).

There is a quite depressing side to the Japanese miracle in terms of driving labor (Sakai 1990; Dohse, Jurgens, and Malsch 1985) and the exploitation of women, but it is not essential to the *form*, and could be eliminated, and Best and others appear to believe it has been mitigated to some extent.

Small Firm Networks

Finally, there are the small firm networks (SFNs). Imagine breaking up the integrated firm into units whose average number of employees is ten each. For example, instead of 2,000 employees in one firm, there would be 200 firms of 10 employees each. Figure 6.3 captures the essentials of this form. It is new to this half of the twentieth century, but it was evident in the nineteenth century, as Sabel and Zeitlin and Best have argued.[4]

The firms are usually very small—say ten people. They interact with each other, sharing information, equipment, personnel, orders, even as they compete with one another. They are supplied by a smaller number of business service firms (business surveys, technical training, personnel administration, transport, research and development, etc.) and financial service firms. There are, of course, suppliers of equipment, energy, consumables, and so forth, and raw material

Figure 6.3. **Small-Firm Networks**

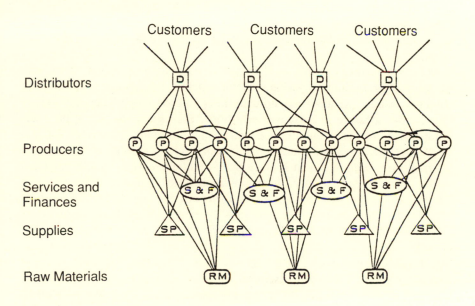

suppliers. Finally, while producers may do their own marketing and distribution, it seems to be more common for there to be a fair number of quite small distributors, which is especially striking since SFNs typically export most of their output.

The small firms are surrounded by an infrastructure that is essential for their survival and for their economies of network scale: local and regional governments provide roads, cheap land, educational services, and even financing; trade associations provide economic information, training, financing, and marketing services; both local and regional governments along with unions monitor unfair business and labor practices.[5] Unfortunately, the issue of economies of scale that attach to a network of firms has received almost no development since it was first discussed in 1919 by Marshall (1919, pp. 283–88). One assumes that while shared investments in equipment may be involved, most of the economies come from shared information and efficient allocation of labor or human resources.

SFNs do not exist in heavy industry or extractive industry In final assembly for large goods such as autos, we have the nondependent subcontracting form rather than a true SFN. SFNs are said to exist in the fields of clothing, food, light machinery, metalworking, electronics, and small- to medium-sized electronic goods, ceramics, furniture, auto components, motorcycles, small engines, machine tools, robots, textile and packaging machinery, mining equipment, industrial filters, and agricultural machinery. But it is not clear from the literature that in all cases *networks* of small firms are involved, though in most cases networks exist.

There is a tendency to dismiss the importance of SFNs by tarring them with the brush of small firms in general, which are held to be exploitative, or limiting them to consumer products from northern Italy, or even simply to textile firms in Prato, Italy, speaking of these as sweatshops. But clearly this is not the case. Small firms are ubiquitous in all countries and generally are havens for low wages, dependency, and exploitation, but I am referring exclusively to networks of small firms with ties to each other and to multiple customers and suppliers. While there is some evidence of exploitation (often self-exploitation through ten- or eleven-hour workdays) in textile firms in Prato and Modena in northern Italy the literature almost always stresses the prosperity of the firms and their locality and the skill of the work force, when these economics issues are discussed.

Amin (1989), for example, finds wages high in "industrial districts," which is another term for SFNs, and discredits the low-wage and exploitation thesis. Capecchi (1989) speaks at one point of "widespread" exploitation, without giving details, but also notes the following about Emilia-Romagna: child labor declined and day-care centers expanded (12 percent of children under three years of age in day care in Bologna, 0.3 percent in Naples); there was a sizable decrease in birthrate and in the proportion of "housewives"; there was an increase in educational level with females surpassing males in high school and university studies; there was a rising demand for instruction in physical exercise, nutrition, and so forth; the region had one of the lowest unemployment rates in Italy; and there was a growing demand for personal and household services. Taplin (1989) notes that employment relations are largely nonadversarial in his study of the textile industry in Prato, Italy, but subcontractors setting up small workshops can impose long hours and poor benefits. Lazerson, in an earlier draft of his 1991 manuscript, offered evidence of long hours and dangerous conditions for some young women in the knitting industry of Modena but also noted the prosperity of the region. One should also note the failure of exploited workers to seek work in nearby textile factories with better wages and benefits.

We have excellent empirical evidence from Italian social scientists and others on the economic reality and success in northern Italy.[6] The next best documented case is a mountain town in Japan, producing machine tools (Friedman

1988). There is less detailed evidence, but at least some, from Germany, Denmark, perhaps Sweden, and France.[7] There is an emerging, struggling case outside Madrid, in electronics (Benton 1986). A debate continues about the character of California's Silicon Valley in the United States, but if we count it, it is about the only SFN I know of in the United States (Florida and Kenney 1990b; Saxenian 1991).[8] There is no evidence of SFNs in Britain (as distinct from small firms; for the growth of these, see Keeble and Wever 1986; for the failure of flexible specialization, Hirst and Zeitlin 1989) or Ireland. So it is not, as many still continue to think, limited to textiles or other soft consumer goods from northern Italy.

Although Figure 6.4 does not faithfully reproduce this, an essential point is that any focal organization has multiple upstream and downstream ties. The next figure makes the basic point. I think Burt (1983) has done the most explicate and empirical demonstration of this, but Pfeffer and Salancik have a cogent discussion in connection with the resource dependency model (1978), and the strategy is as old as capitalism. If you stand at the narrow waist, you can play several customers or suppliers off against each other; they are forced to trade with you—or with your nominal competitor. If you stand in the broad waist of the SFN, however, your customers have choices; so do your suppliers, just as you do. A lot of potential power that is concentrated in the capitalist ideal is dissipated in the SFN.[9]

This is a structural basis for cooperation, I should point out. Firms have no option but to avoid deception and exploitation, because if they do not, another will get the business. The antitrust legislation in the United States was initially intended to create this structural condition but failed to do so for a large number of reasons. But a multiple-tie network may exist not because of the essentially *negative* reason that it forestalls maximizing self-interest with guile, but for the *positive* reason that it provides for the flexibility of the sector or industry, stimulates innovation, and maximizes sector-wide problem solving. The returns come first to the sector, or the local industry, and the health of any single firm is known to be dependent upon the collectivity of competitive firms.

These positive reasons may account for the appearance of the highly successful subcontracting model in Japan. It seems to be able to gain the benefits of multiple ties without actually having multiple ties at all levels. In Figure 6.5 we can see an SFN existing up to the level of the producers, but above that is a structure that would permit the creation of highly dependent relations at the subassembly level and in its ties with final assembly in the parent firm. The fact that the parent does not appear to exploit the subassembly independent firms, nor do the subassembly independent firms exploit their strategic advantage over the producers, suggests that this aspect of trust can be produced without the structural condition of the previous figure—the broad waist. There is other evidence, for example in German firms, of the dominant firm insisting that their subcontractors do no more than one-third of their business with the dominant firm,

Figure 6.4. **Dependency and Independency in Networks**

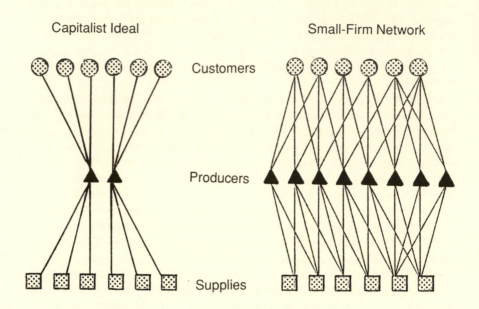

thus voluntarily giving up *strategic* power over suppliers in order to ensure the viability and health of those suppliers. This, of course is just the opposite of the strategy used by the integrated firm (which controls its suppliers to the extent of absorbing them) and contradicts the arguments of transaction-costs analysis.

There are other reasons that networks of small firms do not become "Chandlerized" and end up as one integrated firm. It is not that the members are less greedy or competitive than our industrial ancestors and their present offspring in the United States; it is because competition requires the continual innovation in methods and products. This requires full use and commitment of employees, and this is acheived best by reducing the gap between *conception* and *execution*, the gap introduced by Taylorism. Though the large firm is not incapable of reducing this (see Sabel 1991, on the Möbius trip firm), the small firm does it more as a matter of course. Thus the small firm can react more quickly and fruitfully to change in technology and markets. This has been the consistent explanation for small-firm networks since the initial work of Brusco, Sabel, Piore and Zeitlin.

Explaining Small Firm Networks

Small as the phenomenon of SFNs is, it is theoretically implausible and violates established theories of industrialization of both the Right and the Left.

On the *Right*, we should only have integrated production and the multi-divisional firm according to the magnificent synthesis of Chandler (1977). He emphasizes that *technology* made it possible to greatly increase the size of vertically integrated firms and permit economics of scale; that vertical integration and technology permitted *efficient* throughput coordination from raw material to consumer outlet; and that *bureaucracy* made it possible to exquisitely control the mass of employees and the diversity of processes and products. We can include Williamson here, with his emphasis upon making sure that you will not cheated in your transactions, which is solved by buying out your suppliers and distributors and settling disputes autocratically instead of by bargaining. (See the critique of the markets and hierarchies approach in Lazerson [1988].) But we have the problem of accounting for the apparent decline of the multidivisional-firm (M-form) and the large, integrated production firm, and if that is exaggerated, the problem of the appearance of so many SFNs around the world.

The problem with the account of the *Right* is the quite negligible role it assigns to *trust* and *cooperation*, or what is called "other regarding behavior," in economic affairs, and the dominant role it assigns to the maximization of individual self-interest. We cannot account for SFNs *solely* on the basis of varied and rapidly changing markets and the new technologies that allow decentralized production. If this was so, the big firms would find it profitable simply to decentralize and reward a multitude of small divisions for their flexibility, but retain the "profit stream." They are trying this, of course. In fact, some on the Left feel they will displace SFNs as they spin off wholly owned subsidiaries. The Left argues this way because it has a *power*, rather than an efficiency explanation for the rise of integrated production and the M-form. Market power, and political power, account for the rise. While I share this viewpoint, I feel that the Left also is burdened with an assumption that no longer applies.

The problem with the Left, then, is their view that under capitalism and the capitalist state change can only come from the *organization of the proletariat*, the workers. The only organizational change of much concern for the Left is reorganization of the *labor process* to eliminate exploitation and deskilling. The Left says little about firm size, interfirm networks, marketing techniques, product redesign, trade associations, competition, efficiencies, and the infrastructure that makes networks viable.

But those who created SFNs were not often alienated proletariats, but usually farmers, shopkeepers, and artisans; instead of the organization of the proletarians, we find trade associations that facilitate commercial and industrial interactions. In some cases, especially in northern Italy, unions are im-

Figure 6.5. **The Subcontracting Model**

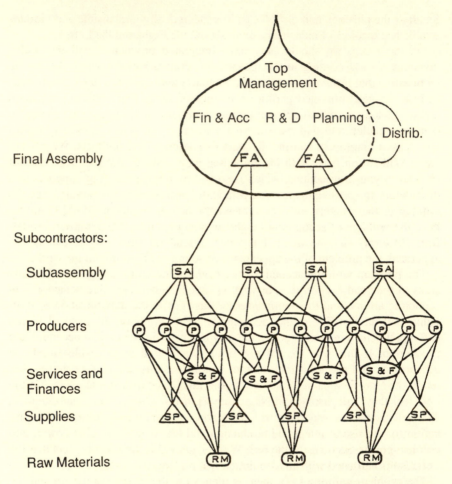

portant—but as regulators of labor conditions in small firms, as providers of business services, and as supporters of such things as autonomous work groups (Herman 1990)—an effort that fell on very rich soil since the small firms had strong inducements already in that direction. No fight by workers against deskilling was needed; the production techniques and the changing market made skills necessary.

Now the Left is correct that exploitation of labor is always a problem, and especially in small organizations. But networks of small organizations supported and regulated by a revitalized local government, by trade associations of the small producers, and in some cases by unions, have managed to limit greatly exploitation in these regions, a job made easier by the low unemployment levels and the remarkable prosperity of these areas.

Thus, powerful theories of both the Right and Left need to be questioned. Both have neglected the economic power of three things that help account for the success of SFNs: economies of scale through networks (still insufficiently theorized), trust and cooperation coexisting with competition, and welfare effects that increase the efficiency of the region and industry. These may be as important as varied markets and new technologies.

The Production of Trust

Let me elaborate on the "production" of trust in SFNs. The production of trust is difficult to demonstrate or even illustrate. As Sabel notes in a remarkable essay (1991), trust seems only to be found retrospectively, never created intentionally. I wish to argue that it is generated by structures, or contexts; these can be deliberately created, encouraging trust, even if trust itself cannot be deliberately created.

Here are some characteristics (see Figure 6.6)—all distinctive of SFNs—that are more likely to generate trusting than self-interest-maximizing behavior in a group of firms:

• Sharing and discussing information on markets, technologies, pay scales, and profits of firms.
• Sufficient similarity in processes and techniques among the firms so that one can understand and judge each other's behavior.
(It's the difference between saying, "I don't know how to make it, so I *have* to trust you," and saying, "I know how to make it, so I *can* trust you.")
• Experience of getting helped by another firm. (In fact, one should design incomplete organizations so they have to ask or borrow.)
• Long-term relationships, but possibly quite intermittent contacts.
• Little difference among firms by size, power, or strategic position.
• Rotation of leadership required to represent a collection of firms.
• Similar financial rewards to the firms and the employees within them.
• Firms having collectively experienced the economic advantages of increased sales and profit margins.
• An awareness of a bounded community of fate generated by trade or professional associations, municipal service groups, unions, or whatever.

Where these conditions exist, the possibility of trust is increased. Now elites have long known this, and ruling classes show many of these characteristics without the trust extending to those they rule.

Employees of large firms generate some trust through unions, but it is small

Figure 6.6. **The Production of Trust**

Characteristics—all distinctive of SFNs—likely to generate trusting rather than self-interest-maximizing behavior in a collection of firms:

- Information, available and discussed, on markets, technologies, pay scales, and profits of firms

- Sufficient similarity in process and techniques among firms so that they can understand and judge each other's behavior

- Experience of getting help from another firm

- Long-term relationships, though possibly intermittent

- Little stratification of firms by size, power, or strategic position

- Rotating leadership where leadership representing a collection of firms is required

- Similar financial rewards to firms and to employees

- Firms collectively experience economic advantages of increased sales and profit margins

- Awareness of a bounded community of fate generated by trade or professional associations, municipal service groups, unions, etc.

---

compared to elite cohesion and trust. One gets trust between owners and employees, and between owners in competing firms, when firms are small and networked. SFNs maximize the possibility for these conditions; the integrated production model does not, and the nondependent subcontracting model does so only partially.

Welfare Functions

Big organizations did not invent *all* the curses of our times, but they certainly had a lot to do with the centralization of power and authority in modern societies. The larger the organization, the more power and authority at the top to hire and fire, develop or enfeeble workers, relocate factories and offices, influence politicians, influence elections, pollute, eliminate competitors, invest money, buy supplies from you or someone else, discriminate ethnically and sexually, and to corrupt. The bigger they are, the more power is generated, and the more concentrated it becomes.

If we take two furniture factories employing 5,000 people each, a total of 10,000 and instead arrange them into 1,000 small firms of 10 each, most producing furniture, but some marketing it, others delivering it, buying materials, doing the accounts, counseling employees and so forth—all things done in the integrated production model *within* the firm—think of the dispersion of power and authority. (The example is not farfetched; the average firm size for the very prosperous furniture industry of the Lombardy province of Italy is under 5; Kozul 1991; Best 1991.)

Another thing that big organizations have not invented but have certainly perfected is *hierarchy*: Rights and privileges and authority and status are clearly defined and differentiated by rank or level in the organization, and movement from one rank to another is guarded by formal criteria. The big furniture firm will have a dozen major grades and many minor ones. It is a fine control device, as well as a rationalizer. But the small firm will have two, perhaps three grades, and movement up and down them will be easy. A study of Japanese blue- to white-collar movement found this to be very high in small firms and low in very big ones (Friedman 1988). In Italy, people move back and forth from owner to worker to owner as demand and styles change.

That takes care of two of the four horsemen of bureaucracy, *centralization*, and *hierarchy*. The other two are *formalization* and *standardization*; these permit repetitive, high-volume production. Fortunately for small firms, formalization and standardization are minimized, simply because high-volume production is not a characteristic of the product markets these firms service. Thus, the four dreadnoughts of bureaucracy dissolve when the large firm does, and neither are they reproduced in SFNs nor do the networks find alternative ways to amass and concentrate power.

Another consequence of moving from integrated production to a network of small firms is that the distribution of wealth in society is affected, and as a result, so are the spending patterns. The heads of 1,000 firms related to furniture production will receive a great deal less in salary and benefits than the two heads of two large firms. I support any development that will make the distribution of wealth more even without significantly changing the total amount, and if it can be done without taking taxes from the rich each year to provide inefficient programs for the poor—a politically expensive effort—all the better. Furthermore, one of the problems of uneven development and uneven economies associated with multidivisional and giant firms is that locally generated wealth is spent or invested non-locally; it is taken from the city, province, region or nation and sent elsewhere, enriching elsewhere and concentrating the wealth of the elsewhere. The wider distribution of wealth reduces this. Very few of the 1,000 owners are likely to make shopping trips from Northern Italy to Paris and New York, and they will use their village banks.

Finally, a network of small firms appears to be associated with strong *local* government institutions. This appears to foster a more responsive educational system, more distributive policies regarding land use and city planning, a wider range of social services including child care, and perhaps more political involvement of the citizens. These are particularly well discussed by Alydalot (1986), and Capecchi (1989). The network of firms and families also generates its own welfare functions in policing labor exploitation, lending money and equipment, and providing informal apprenticeships.

One of the most striking documentations of this comes from a comparison of two fishing towns, New Bedford and Gloucester, in the United States (Doeringer, Mass, and Terkla 1986). In one, the fishing fleet was dominated by boats owned by capitalists who hired captains and crews; in the other, most of the fleet was owned by the individual captains, and family and friends and relatives made up the crew. The latter made longer-term investments in new equipment and methods, shared work instead of using layoffs in slack time, and when forced to lay people off they laid off the oldest who did not have growing families rather than the youngest of first hired, and when business picked up, they responded more quickly, benefiting the community.

Size or Ties

In thinking about the consequences of SFNs—producting of trust; not minimizing the centralization of power and authority, reducing hierarchy, standardization, and formalization; distributing wealth; and reducing uneven development—I am at a loss to specify which of these stems from the "small" and which from the "networks" in the notion of SFNs. Clearly size is very important, and it is the most convenient way of discussing bureaucracy, but small by itself is hardly beautiful. All of these propositions about consequences of *size* become unstable without *ties*—networks. The small firms clustered about one or two mass marketers in the shoe industry in Alicante, Spain, as described by Benton (1986, 1989) are not networked, and they compete fiercely and savagely for the few crumbs that the big corporations hand out. There is so little wealth generated among them that its distribution is insignificant; secrecy and distrust reign, as does the exploitation of workers and family members.

Perhaps it is not size per se that has welfare functions for society, but the network. Yet a network of large firms is familiar to us in cartels, trusts, and interlocking directorates, and in the United States such networks are associated with concentrated power and predatory business practices towards small firms and consumers. Networks as such then, can have few welfare functions for society. An elite that generates trust among its members can be powerful and exploitive. The networks of large firms in Europe and Japan may not be as predatory as those in the United States, but I do not doubt that they generate few if any welfare functions on their own or welcome the state apparatus that requires it of them. Clearly, both characteristics are needed—small units that need to network to produce a good or service to which they all contribute.

Figure 6.7. **Activities That Could Be Performed by Separate Organizations**

Some Production Stages

Retail distribution
Wholesale distribution
Final assembly
Final production
Initial production
Raw materials processing
Raw materials
  extraction

Business Functions

Transportation
Food service
Legal services
Accounting
Advertising
Research & development
Purchasing training
Business travel services

Corporate Services

Medical & dental services
Fitness facilities
Sports programs
Off-site recreational activities
Vacation planning, sites
Child care

Retirement counseling
Career counseling
Legal services
Drug & alcohol
  abuse programs
Psychological counseling

(Note that I avoid discussion of SFNs as a phenomenon of entrepreneurship. That formulation suggests the primacy of motivation and the individual characteristics of leaders. While certainly important, I prefer a more structural approach; what are conditions under which an area is able to shape or give reign to motivations and leadership characteristics favorable to SFNs?)

Phrased this way, in terms of small size and dense networks of firms with complementary skills and functions, and emphasizing the importance of the public and quasi-public infrastructure, the notion of successful small-firm networks confronts directly the received theory and wisdom that the multidivisional firm, with assumed economies of scale and throughput, is economizing and efficient, and that autonomy is required for the pursuit of self-interest.

The Return of Civil Society?

My work on SFNs is part of a larger project (Perrow 1986a, p. 49–52, forthcoming). It traces the development of the Integrated Production firm from the 1820s to the present in the United States. The firm restructured our social landscape and generated externalities that spawned the public and nonprofit organizations which copying the bureaucratic form of the integrated production firm, generated further externalities. I argue that sometimes wittingly but mostly unwittingly the big organizations, public and private, in their role of employers increasingly performed more and more societal functions such as socialization providing occasions for social interactions and handling personal crises, recreation, cultural productions, skill acquisition, and whatever else you wish to ascribe to "society." The units that once performed these functions—families, neighborhoods, schools, independent local governments, small and local guilds, and business and trade associations—were either weakened or made dependent upon the big employing organization. Less and less existed outside the large employing organization or the flock of wholly dependent small firms clustering about them. In effect, society was being absorbed by the big organizations. I am not referring to a welfare-state *government* providing services, but the employer representing society to his or her employees.

The possibility of SFNs is the possibility of massive disengorgement from the big organizations, a spewing out of functions over delimited spaces where they are taken up by small independent organizations. These are linked together with a sense of a community of fate, rather than a link based upon sharing the goals of the owners and top executives of a big organization. Figure 6.7 gives you a bit of an idea of all the opportunities for independent organizations falling out of the big corporation; the same can be done for other big employers, such as big government, big school districts, big unions, and big, centralized church bodies. If there are economies afforded by trust, networks, and the limitation of social externalities, that is, if trust is an alternative way of seeking to reduce transaction costs, if networks are a way of achieving economies of scale, and if we can use community institutions as an alternative to externalizing social costs, then there is no need for one organization to do all the things in the figure; indeed, it is a waste. More important, the fully integrated firm in the figure signifies the erosion of *civil society*, that precious area outside the big organizations, public and private, an area with a minimum either of market-driven behavior or of hierarchy.

Notes

1. The change is celebrated in the more popular management literature, such as the good stories Kanter (1989) tells or the boxes and arrows and injunctions to "strategize" in Morton (1991), analyzed and worried over in compendiums such as the Massachusetts Institute of Technology study edited by Kochan and Useem, *Transforming Organizations* (1992) and imaginatively explored in Powell (1990), and Sabel (1991). Sabel's Möbius strip working paper is perhaps the most intriguing discussion of the variety of variables involved—the evidence is anecdotal and largely European/Japanese. Good Anecdotes and analysis of downsizing in Silicon Valley are found in Saxenian (1991). I have yet to find any definitive statistics of downsizing. Sengenberger et al. (1990) indicate downsizing in all industrial nations, but the figures are too general to allow much interpretation. Badaracco (1988) has weak empirical evidence for deconcentration and joint ventures and gives some case examples.

2. Kohn and Schooler's work (1983, ch. 2) shows that people who work in bureaucratic organizations, blue- and white-collar, are more likely than those in nonbureaucratic organizations to have cognitive complexity and flexibility, open-mindedness, personal re-

sponsibility, and self-direction and to value change. They emphasize the protection that large, permanent bureaucratic organizations provide, rather than the attributes of size per se, but it is still a warning about the dynamics of small organizations in the United States.

3. There is a rueful acknowledgment of these organizational failures in Williamson's work, both the 1975 and the 1985 volumes, but it hardly encumbers his transaction-cost analysis. Similarly, Chandler jolts one out of the somnolence of ever-increasing production figures in the very last pages of his very long 1977 volume, *Visible Hand*, with a plaintive query about the costs of giganticism. Neither acknowledgment deflects its author's relentless efficiency arguments.

4. The classic piece comparing "flexible production" through small firms (what I refer to as small firm networks) in the nineteenth and the twentieth centuries is Sabel and Zeitlin (1985). For a good account of the Springfield Armory as a SFN, or more accurately, a network of small firms serving a final assembler, as in the nondependent subcontractor model, see Best (1991, pp. 29–45). A striking comparison of the putting-out system in the eighteenth and nineteenth centuries with SFNs in the Modena, Italy, knitwear industry today is found in Lazerson (1991).

5. The literature on the infrastructure is now substantial, and it is one of two things that sharply distinguish *networks* of small firms from clusters of small firms about a dominant buyer. (The other is the minimal and very competitive contacts among small firms where they are dependent on a few big customers.) See one of the first articles in the area—Brusco (1982), and Brusco and Righi (1989), Herrigel (1988), Piore and Sabel (1984), Sabel (1989), and Trigilia (1986). Best (1991) provides some of the most detailed discussion of infrastructure in northern Italy, with excellent accounts of business service and financing. Excellent details on computer clones and on box-making and packaging machinery industries can be found in Capecchi (1989). A detailed account of the role of unions in very small firms can be found in Herman (1990).

6. In addition to those already cited, see the just completed dissertation by Kozul (1991), which contrasts the booming SFN furniture industry in northern Italy with the failing integrated production one in Yugoslavia.

7. For several of these countries, see the general discussions in Sabel (1989), Piore and Sabel (1984), and Best (1991). For France, see Lorenz (1988) and forthcoming. For mechanical engineering and machine tools in Germany, see Herrigel (1988 and forthcoming). The Swedish example, the area around Vaxjö, is discussed in Johannisson (1990), but from the point of view of the entrepreneur rather than the relations among firms. It appears that there is no common product in this burst of small-firm industry in a thoroughly agricultural region of Sweden, but there is considerable sharing of entrepreneurial ideas and perhaps resources. This may be true of Jutland (the mainland of Denmark), too, but the information is scanty.

8. See Sabel (1990), "Studied Trust," for one optimistic American study in progress and Saxenian (1991a) for a network description of Silicon Valley. But the account that Florida and Kenney (1990a, ch. 5, 6, and 7) give of the rapacious, shortsighted, individual self-interest-maximizing firms in Silicon Valley is very depressing, even if Saxenian is correct that the trusting network, while limited to the small firms, is still important. Christopherson and Storper (1989) and Storper (1989) find evidence of flexible specialization in the motion picture industry.

9. The matter, of course, is always more complicated. Lyons, Krachenberg, and Henke (1990) and Kamath and Liker (1990) point out that dependent suppliers are more likely to

receive technical assistance from their customer, because of the customer's dependency upon limited suppliers. This is not always the case, however, and depends upon the complexity of the product, its fit with the supplier's product, the length of the relationship, and so on.

Bibliography

Amin, Ash. 1989. "A Model of the Small Firm in Italy." In *Small Firms and Industrial Districts in Italy*, eds. Edward Goodman et al. New York: Routledge.

Amin, Ash, and Kevin Robin. 1989. "Industrial Districts and Regional Development Limits and Possibilities." Unpublished paper. University of Newcastle upon Tyne, February.

Aydalot, Philippe. 1986. "The Location of New Firm Creation: The French Case." In *New Firms and Regional Developments in Europe*, eds. David Keeble and Egbert Wever, 105–23. London: Croom, Helm.

Badaracco, Joseph L., Jr. 1988. "Changing Forms of the Corporation." In *The U.S. Business Corporation*, eds. John R. Meyer and James M. Gustafson, 57–91. Cambridge: Ballinger Publishing Co.

Benton, Lauren. 1986. "The Role of the Informal Sector in Economic Development: Industrial Restructuring in Spain." Ph.D. diss. Johns Hopkins University, Department of Anthropology and History.

———. 1989. "Homework and Industrial Development: Gender Roles and Restructuring in the Spanish Shoe Industry." *World Development* 17, 2: 255–66.

Bessant, John, and Bill Haywood. 1986. "Flexibility in Manufacturing Systems." *International Journal of Management Science* 14, 6: 465–73.

Best, Michael. 1991. *The New Competition*. Cambridge: Harvard University Press.

Brusco, Sebastiano. 1982. "The Emilian Model: Productive Decentralization and Social Integration." *Cambridge Journal of Economics* 3: 167–84.

Brusco, Sebastiano and Ezio Righi. 1989. "Local Government, Industrial Policy and Social Consensus: The Case of Modena (Italy)," *Economy and Society* 18, no. 4 (November).

Burt, Ronald. 1983. *Corporate Profits and Corporation*. New York: Academic Press.

Capecchi, Vittorio. 1989. "The Informal Economy and the Development of Flexible Specialization in Emilia-Romagna." In *The Informal Economy: Studies in Advanced and Less Developed Countries*, eds. Alejandro Portes, Manuel Castells, and Lauren A. Benton, 189–215. Baltimore: Johns Hopkins University Press.

Chandler, Alfred D., Jr. 1977. *The Visible Hand*. Cambridge: Harvard University Press.

Christopherson, Susan, and Michael Storper. 1989. "The Effects of Flexible Specialization on Industrial Politics and the Labor Market: The Motion Picture Industry." *Industrial and Labor Relations Review* 42 (April) 3: 331–47.

Doeringer, Peter B., Philip I. Moss, and David G. Terkla. 1986. "Capitalism and Kinship: Do Institutions Matter in the Labor Market?" *Industrial and Labor Relations Review* 40 (October) 1: 48–60.

Dohse, Knuth; Ulrich Jurgens, and Thomas Malsch. 1985. "From 'Fordism' to 'Toyotism'? The Social Organization of the Labor Process in the Japanese Automobile Industry." *Politics and Society* 14, 2: 115–46.

Dore, Ronald. 1983. "Goodwill and the Spirit of Market Capitalism." *British Journal of Sociology* 34 (December): 459–82.

Fligstein, Neil. 1990. *The Transformation of Corporate Control*. Cambridge: Harvard University Press.

Florida, Richard, and Martin Kenney. 1990a. "High Technology Restructuring in the USA and Japan." *Environment and Planning* A22: 233–52.

———. 1990b. *The Breakthrough Illusion: Corporate America's Failure to Move from Innovation to Mass Production*. New York: Basic Books.

Friedman, David. 1988. *The Misunderstood Miracle*. Ithaca, N.Y.: Cornell University Press.

Goodman, Edward. 1989. "Introduction." In *Small Firms and Industrial Districts in Italy*, ed. Edward Goodman, Julia Bamford, and Peter Saynor, 1–30. London: Routledge.

Harrison, Bennett. 1989. "'The Big Firms are Coming out of the Corner': The Resurgence of Economic Scale and Industrial Power in the Age of 'Flexibility.'" Paper delivered at the 1989 International Conference on Industrial Transformation and Regional Development in an Age of Global Interdependence, Nagoya, Japan, September 18–21.

Herman, Bruce G. 1990. "Economic Development and Industrial Relations in a Small Firm Economy: The Experience of Metal Workers in Emilia-Romagna, Italy." Presented at the Conference on Economic Restructuring, Princeton, N.J., October 5–6.

Herrigel, Gary B. 1978. "Industrial Order in the Machine Tool Industry: A Comparison of the United States and Germany." Conference paper at Social Science Research Council.

———. 1988. "The Political Embeddedness of Small and Medium-Sized Firm Networks in Baden-Württemberg: A Challenge From Above?" Paper delivered at the Workshop on Interfirm Innovation Dynamics, Stuttgart, Germany, October 3–4.

Heydebrand, Wolf V. 1989. "New Organizational Forms." In *Work and Occupations* 16 (August) 3: 323–57.

———. 1989. "Industrial Order and the Politics of Industrial Change: Mechanical Engineering in the Federal Republic of Germany." In *Industry, Politics and Change in West Germany: Toward a Third Republic*, ed. Peter Katzenstein. Ithaca, N.Y.: Cornell University Press, forthcoming.

Hirst, Paul, and Jonathan Zeitlin. 1989. "Flexible Specialisation and the Competitive Failure of UK Manufacturing." *Political Quarterly* 60, 2: 164–78.

Howard, Robert. 1990. "Can Small Business Help Countries Compete?" *Harvard Business Review* (November–December): 88–103.

Hyman, Richard. 1988. "Flexible Specialization and the Competitive Failure of UK Manufacturing." *Political Quarterly* 60, 2: 164–78.

Jaikumar, Ramchandran. 1986. "Massimo Menichetti." Case study for class discussion. Boston: Harvard Business School.

Johannisson, Bengt. 1990. "Organizing for Local Economic Development." Research report presented at Vaxjö University, Vaxjö, Sweden, June.

Johnston, Russell, and Paul R. Lawrence. 1988. "Beyond Vertical Integration— the Rise of the Value-Adding Partnership." *Harvard Business Review* 66 (July–August) 4: 94–101.

Jones, Bryn. 1988. "Work and Flexible Automation in Britain: A Review of Developments and Possibilities.'' *Work, Employment & Society* 2 (December) 4: 451–86.

Kamath, Rajan, and Jeffrey Liker. 1990. ''Supplier Dependence and Innovation: A Contingency Model of Suppliers' Innovative Activities.'' *Journal of Engineering and Technology Management,* 7 (September) 2: 111–27.

Kanter, Rosabeth Moss. 1989. *Teaching Elephants to Dance: The Postentrepreneurial Revolution in Strategy Management and Careers.* New York: Simon and Schuster.

Keeble, David, and Egber Wever. 1986. ''Introduction.'' In *New Firms and Regional Development in Europe,* ed. David Keeble and Egberg Wever, 1–34. London: Croom Helm.

Kern, Horst. No date. ''Trends in Restructuring of the West German Car Industry.'' Sociological Research Institute, University of Goettingen, Federal Republic of Germany.

Kochan, Thomas, and Michael Useem, eds. 1992. *Transforming Organizations.* New York: Oxford University Press.

Kozul, Zeljka. 1991. ''Innovation and Industrial Organization: A Comparative Study of the Dynamics of the Italian and Yugoslav Furniture Industry.'' Faculty of Economics and Politics, Jesus College, Cambridge, England.

Kristensen, Peer Hull, and Charles F. Sabel. 1987. ''Denmark: Chapters Two and Three.'' Draft manuscript, October.

Lane, Christel. 1988. ''Industrial Change in Europe: The Pursuit of Flexible Specialisation in Britain and West Germany.'' *Work, Employment and Society* 2 (June) 2: 141–68.

Lazerson, Mark H. 1988. ''Organizational Growth of Small Firms: An Outcome of Markets and Hierarchies?'' *American Sociological Review* 53: 330–42.

———. 1991. ''A New Phoenix: Putting-Out in the Modena Knitwear Industry.'' Department of Sociology, State University of New York–Stony Brook.

Lorenz, Edvard H. 1988. ''Neither Friends Nor Strangers: Informal Networks of Subcontracting in French Industry.'' In *Trust: Making and Breaking Cooperative Relations,* ed. Diego Gambetta, 194–210. Oxford: Blackwell.

Loveman, Gary, Michael Piore, and Werner Sengenberger. 1988. ''The Evolving Role of Small Business in Industrialized Economies and Some Implications for Employment and Training Policy.'' International Institute for Labour Studies and the Massachusetts Institute of Technology, May.

Lyons, Thomas, et al. 1990. ''Mixed Motive Marriages: What's Next for Buyer–Supplier Relations.'' *Sloan Management Review* 31: 29–36.

Main, Jeremy. 1990. ''Manufacturing the Right Way.'' *Fortune* 121 (May 21) 11: 54–64.

Marshall, Alfred. 1919. *Industry and Trade,* 283–88. London: Macmillan.

Morton, Michael S. Scott, ed. 1991. *The Corporation of the 1990s: Information, Technology, and Organizational Transformation.* New York: Oxford University Press.

Murray, Fergus. 1983. ''The Decentralization of Production: The Decline of the Mass-Collective Worker?'' *Capital and Class* 19: 74–99.

———. 1987. ''Flexible Specialization in the 'Third Italy.''' *Capital and Class* 33: 4–95.

Nasar, Sylvia. 1988. ''America's Competitive Revival,'' *Fortune* 117 (January 4) 1: 44–52.

Nishiguchi, Toshihiro. 1990. ''Strategic Dualism: An Alternative in Industrial Societies.'' Ph.D. diss. Oxford University. Forthcoming as *Strategic Industrial*

Sourcing: The Japanese Advantage (working title). New York: Oxford University Press.

O'Farrell, Patrick. 1986. "The Nature of the New Firms in Ireland: Empirical Evidence and Policy Implications." In *New Firms and Regional Development in Europe*, ed. David Keeble and Egbert Wever, 151–83. London: Croom Helm.

Perrow, Charles. 1986a. *Complex Organizations: A Critical Essay*. Glenview, Ill.: Scott, Foresman, 1972; revised ed., 1979; 3d ed. New York: Random House.

———. 1986b. "Economic Theories of Organizations." *Theory and Society* 15: 11–45.

———. 1991. "A Society of Organizations." *Theory and Society*.

Pfeffer, Jeffrey, and Gerald Salancik. 1978. *The External Control of Organizations*. New York: Harper and Row.

Piore, Michael. No date. "Work Labor and Action: Work Experience in a System of Flexible Production." Draft for Institute of Labour Studies of the International Labour Organization.

Piore, Michael, and Charles Sabel. 1984. *The Second Industrial Divide*. New York: Basic Books.

Pollert, Anna. 1991 "The Orthodoxy of Flexibility." In *Farewell to Flexibility*, ed. by Anna Pollert. London: Blackwell.

———. 1988. "The 'Flexible Firm': Fixation of Fact?" *Work, Employment and Society* 2 (September) 3: 281–316.

Powell, Walter W. 1990. "Neither Market Nor Hierarchy: Network Forms of Organization." *Research in Organizational Behavior* 12: 295–336.

Preece, D. A. 1986. "Organizations, Flexibility and New Technology." In *Managing Advanced Manufacturing Technology*, ed. C. A. Voss, 67–382. Proceedings of the U.K. Operations Management Association Conference, January 2–3, 1986. New York: Springer-Verlag.

Sabel, Charles. 1989. "Flexible Specialisation and the Re-emergence of Regional Economies." In *Reversing Industrial Decline*, ed. Paul Hirst and Jonathan Zeitlin, 17–70. New York: St. Martin's Press.

———. 1990. "Studied Trust: Building New Forms of Cooperation in a Volatile Economy." Paper. Massachusetts Institute of Technology, August 7.

———. 1991. "Möbius-Strip Organizations and Open Labor Markets: Some Consequences of the Reintegration of Conceptions and Execution in a Volatile Economy." In *Social Theory for a Changing Society*, ed. James Coleman and Pierre Bourdieu. Boulder, Colo.: Westview Press.

Sabel, Charles, and Jonathan Zeitlin. 1985. "Historical Alternatives to Mass Prodcution: Politics, Markets and Technology in Nineteenth Century Industrialization." *Past and Present*. 108: 133–75.

Sakai, Kuniyasu. 1990. "The Federal World of Japanese Manufacturing." *Harvard Business Review*, (November–December): 38–49.

Saxenian, AnnaLee. 1991a. "Response to Richard Florida and Martin Kenney 'Silicon Valley and Route 128 Won't Save Us.'" *California Management Review* 33: 136—142.

———. 1991b. "The Origins and Dynamics of Production Networks in Silicon Valley." Prepared for the International Workshop on Networks of Innovators, Center for Research on the Development of Industry and Technology, University of Quebec, Montreal, May 1–3, 1990. Forthcoming in *Research Policy*. Special issue on

"Networks of Innovators."

Sengenberger, Werner, et al., eds. 1990. *The Reemergence of Small Enterprise: Industrials Restructuring in Industrial Economies*. Geneva, Switz.: International Labor Organization.

Smith, Chris. 1989. "Flexible Specialisation, Automation, and Mass Production." *Work, Employment and Society* 3, 2: 203–20.

Storper, Michael. 1989. "The Transition to Flexible Specialisation in the United States Film Industry: External Economies, The Division of Labour, and the Crossing of Industrial Divides." *Cambridge Journal of Economics* 13: 273–305.

Stymne, Bengt. 1989. *Information Technology and Competence Formation in the Swedish Service Sector: An Analysis of Retail Strategy and Development of the Finance Sector*. Stockholm: The Economic Research Institute at the Stockholm School of Economics, 16–17.

Taplin, Ian M. 1989. "Segmentation and the Organization of Work in the Italian Apparel Industry." *Social Science Quarterly* 70 (June) 2: 408–24.

Thompson, Grahme. 1989. "Flexible Specialisation, Industrial Districts, Regional Economies: Strategies for Socialists?" *Economy and Society* 18 (November) 4: 527–45.

Thorelli, Hans B. 1986. "Networks: Between Markets and Hierarchies." *Strategic Management Journal* 7: 37–51.

Trigilia, Carlo. 1986. "Small-Firm Development and Political Subcultures in Italy." *European Sociological Review* 2 (December) 3: 161–75.

Voss, C. A., ed. 1986. *Managing Advanced Manufacturing Technology*. Proceedings of the U.K. Operations Management Association Conference, January 2–3, 1986. New York: Springer-Verlag.

Williamson, Oliver E. 1975. *Markets and Hierarchies*. New York: Free Press.

———. 1985. *The Economic Institution of Capitalism*. New York: Free Press.

Wood, Stephen. 1988. "Between Fordism and Flexibility? The U.S. Car Industry." In *New Technology and Industrial Relations*. Oxford and New York: Basil Blackwell, 101–17.

Zeitlin, Jonathan. 1989. "Local Industrial Strategies: Introduction." *Economy and Society* 18 (November) 4: 367–73.

7. Strategies of Institutional Change in Central and Eastern European Economies

Antoni Z. Kaminski
Piotr Strzalkowski

Introduction

Communist regimes of Central and Eastern Europe (CEE) collapsed within months and were replaced by efforts to (re-)construct a liberal-democratic society. In this chapter, we look into ways societies of the region go about changing their economic organizations, into factors that condition depth, speed, and direction of changes.

The term *strategy* is used here in a loose sense. Strategies of institutional change in the CEE countries are still in the phase of formation. The process of strategy formation does not necessarily consist in consciously constructing a comprehensive blueprint for a transformation in the social order. It may involve a series of independent activities coordinated by a mechanism of mutual adjustments (Lindblom 1964). It may also be a process of muddling through during which preferences and priorities are discovered. Hence, what we consider a strategy adopted by a particular country today can turn out to be a short-term expediency tomorrow.

Undoubtedly, for countries that succumbed to it, communism was a traumatic experience that left hidden, difficult-to-remove wounds in their cultures. Their populations are demoralized; they are short of professions crucial for the market economy to function; and their physical infrastructures have been neglected with traumatic consequences for the economy (e.g., telecommunication) and for social well-being (e.g., ecology). At present, not only are they involved in overcoming economic and social crises difficult to imagine for anyone without direct experience, but they are simultaneously restructuring political and economic institutions that are at the bottom of these crises. Although external circumstances seem to be favorable and foreign assistance forthcoming, the cost of transition must largely be paid by the societies themselves.

We emphasize here the political aspects of economic changes. These aspects prevailed in the design of the Communist system; economic factors acted as loose constraints upon the arbitrary powers of rulers, although they later contributed heavily to the final demise. Moreover, the task of restoring market institutions falls willy-nilly upon the political system.

The discussion is limited to five countries: Romania, Bulgaria, Czechoslovakia, Hungary, and Poland—countries brought together by a geographical proximity and by a feat of destiny sharing in the same historical drama although they are dissimilar in various other respects. Their reactions to the imposition of communism also diverged.

They can be divided into two subgroups. The first consists of Romania and Bulgaria. In 1945, these were the least economically developed. In this subgroup the Communist system was most effectively implemented, and despite moments of relative liberalization, at no time was the system publicly denounced. The second group consists of the westernmost countries of the CEE, which experienced periods of de-Stalinization with open criticism of Communist practice, a thorough examination of shortcomings of the centrally planned economy, and a limited rehabilitation of the market. This group consists of Czechoslovakia, Hungary, and Poland. Looking more closely at particular cases, we notice important variations within each group. It is obvious that communism functioned differently in Bulgaria from the way it did in Romania.

In the second group, Czechoslovakia has traditionally been the most industrially developed, in particular its regions of Bohemia and Moravia. It was there, in 1946, that Communists won parliamentary elections. Later, Czechoslovakia had its period of glory during the Prague Spring of 1968 when it courageously challenged Communist rule. In the decades that followed, the Warsaw Treaty Organization (WTO) invasion suppressed the Czechoslovak society into silence, dissidents notwithstanding. Hence, in the period that followed August 1968, the country saw the political conservatism of its Communist elites and a lasting economic stagnation.

One of the differences between Poland and the remaining countries of the group was that Polish revolts did not provoke a direct WTO invasion. The memory of Polish risings acted as a deterrent both for the Soviets and for the Poles. Soviets were less likely to risk an intervention, and Poles tried not to provoke one. Other differences are well known. Polish society was able to defend the position of the Church, and the private property in agriculture remained. But these successes made its Communist rulers too politically vulnerable to risk a serious economic reform. When pressed too hard by popular expectations, the Polish Communists sought help from friendly Western governments and banks eager to give them credits that would buy their way out of a reform.

Hungary, after more than ten years of a regressive regime that followed the 1956 events, began implementing economic reforms at the end of 1960s. The history of the Hungarian reform abounded in steps forward, backward, and sideways. After twenty years of reforming, Hungary was in a better position than other countries of the region; the share of foreign trade in its gross national product was much higher, and its industry more consumer oriented than in other cases.

The economic liberalization had no parallel in politics. Moscow allowed Poland a measure of political freedom; economically it was conservative. In Hungary, fairly stringent political limitations accompanied some economic freedom.

Before we look at each country's prospects for a successful transition to a market economy, we must emphasize that the transition is not possible without first democratizing the political system. At the level of particular countries, the market economy can coexist with authoritarian regimes. There is, however, an important and often overlooked difference between an authoritarian regime and a Communist regime. A Communist system consists in a close functional correspondence between the organization of the economy and that of the polity. One cannot be changed without changing the other.

Evidently, in CEE, political change is a precondition for a daring economic change. Romania and Bulgaria still struggle to move their economies and polities away from communism, while Czechoslovakia, Hungary, and Poland Communists have been effectively removed from power.

Hungary and Poland implemented a financial reform triggered off by the need to control inflation and to open up internal markets to foreign trade. Polish currency, the zloty, has become for all practical purposes a convertible currency. Other countries have this step still ahead of them. In all countries of the CEE, a huge amount of legislative work must be done and a number of institutions must be established or reformed before construction of the market system is brought to completion.

Structures

The factor that most affected the history of these Communist regimes was the inadequacy of control mechanisms. This led to the gradual disintegration of the state and to economic stagnation or regress.

What were the essential features of the Communist system? In its design, as elaborated by Lenin and applied by Stalin, it was organized from above. Ideally, it was a hierarchy in which freedom of choice belonged to the center, epitomized by the first secretary. In principle, it was a hierarchy of unrestricted control. Guided by this principle the Bolsheviks built their political and, *pari passu,* their economic system. This principle has also been the cause of the dismay over the Communist mode of organization.

The organization design had no other than hierarchical forms of control. It could not rely on bureaucracies because they tend to emancipate themselves and to restrict the powers at the center. The solution found by Stalin was period purges. First, owing to the randomness of terror, purges terrified, and atomized the population. Second, the rapid turnover of personnel prevented officeholders from colluding against the center.

This technique could not survive Stalin because it required the personal power Stalin had won under exceptional circumstances after years of political exertions. Post-Stalinist leaders knew that had they allowed anyone to gain such power, they would be first to fall the victims to it. This eliminated purges as a method of governing and exposed the Communist system to pathologies arising from control deficiencies. Hence, we consider how, and with what results, the five countries dealt with problems posed by the dilemma of control.

The most important distinction between the first and the second group of countries was in the adaptation to the post-Stalin world. In the first group, neo-Stalinist regimes remained in place because of the lack of effective political pressures; on the other hand, Hungary, Poland, and Czechoslovakia experienced, though at different moments, dramatic periods of de-Stalinization. Among countries of the latter group, the legitimacy of the Communist regime was stronger than among those of the former, and the position of rulers more solid.

The main difference between Bulgaria and Romania was in their positions vis-à-vis Moscow and in the personalities of their respective leaders: Zhivkov and Ceauşescu. For Moscow, Bulgaria was politically closer and strategically more important than Romania. In neither country was a market reform seriously considered. Instead, they zealously built their heavy industries according to precepts of Communist dogma.

As mentioned, countries of the second group underwent de-Stalinization at different periods of time and saw it aborted in different ways. In Hungary and Poland, it happened in 1956; in Czechoslovakia twelve years later. In Hungary and Czechoslovakia but not in Poland it ended with a WTO intervention. There were more differences, but these seem the most important. Each traumatic event in the history of these countries provoked learning processes throughout the Communist bloc.

Let us consider countries of the second group where, after de-Stalinization, legitimacy of Communist rule was weakened. We examine these cases with a model of the Communist political system consisting of three elements: the center, the apparatus, and society. Each element can be either strong or weak. The elements are independent; that is, under a strong center, the apparatus has no autonomy, and so society is weak, too. When the apparatus is strong, it effectively restricts the center's freedom of maneuver and oppresses society. Society could be strong only when both the apparatus and the center are weak.

A strong center can select any strategy that does not undermine its strength. The center is strong when the main leader is strong. Then the apparatus becomes its extension. The best strategy for the center was purges. When these became unavailable, the center pursued any strategy that allowed it to maintain some freedom of maneuver in its relationship with the apparatus and the society. Reform, as a way of extending the political bases of support for the center, was within the range of strategies that served this interest.

The apparatus had an interest in defending the status quo, which guaranteed its privileges, and in expanding its influence. Whenever it could, it tended to restrict powers of the center. It opted for oppression of society and rejected reform.

Society, when allowed free expression, supported reforms, condemned arbitrary coercion, and was invariably anti-Communist. This leaves us with three plausible situations: (1) strong center, nonautonomous apparatus, and a weak society; (2) weak center, autonomous apparatus, and a weak society; and (3) weak center, weak apparatus, and a strong society. These three situations correspond to three different strategies in the relationship between the rulers and the ruled: reform, coercion, and corruption (Kaminski 1989).

Reform is a continuous process that does not lead to any definite, qualitatively new system. Communism, as a coherent system of political and economic organization, allows little room for the implementation of a full-fledged market economy. Only few elements of a market can be introduced without fatally weakening its political structures. Thus, a market reform had some positive economic consequences, but it was in fact a political strategy aimed at formally co-opting professional elites in the political system. It was a compromise reached between Communist leadership and professional elites. For this compromise to work, a strong center was required.

The apparatus, whose inner core consisted of the Communist party hierarchy and the security services, had no interest in any liberalization of political or economic life and perceived the professional elements co-opted through reform as a threat to its position. Being an instrument of suppression, the apparatus's interest was to assure the primacy of coercion in the systematization of rule. With coercion dominant, the center had no alternative but to rely upon the apparatus while society was weak. The side effect was the economic inefficiency that the dominance of apparatus entailed.

Corruption dominated when the center and the apparatus were too weak to control the society effectively, their survival depending upon some external circumstances. To attempt an economic reform was too risky to be seriously considered; coercion would not be effective and could bring unacceptable costs. Under such conditions, the ruling elite could only try to maintain itself in power by buying off strategic segments of the society with special privileges. This, eventually, had to result in serious economic imbalances and in shortages even graver than in the former three cases.

The three countries of the second group fit nicely into the three classes. János Kádár in Hungary took over a destroyed party organization and reconstructed it. As party-builder, he acquired a strong personal position and, after some time, embarked upon the path of market reform. Gustav Husak in Czechoslovakia, co-opted by conservatives within the Communist establishment, was at best a *primus inter pares*, presiding over a regime founded on coercion. Finally, the consecutive leaders of the Polish United Workers' Party (PUWP) looked with anxiety at the behavior of the population, trying to insure themselves against the lot of their predecessors by corrupting whomever they could.

Strategies of rule used in each of these cases varied in time and with regard to particular social groups. The Hungarian reform resulted in improvements in the standard of living, and it prepared the country for a real market transition. In itself, it did not institute a market economy.

In Czechoslovakia, the strong apparatus eliminated prospects for an economic reform or a political liberalization. As a leftover from the de-Stalinization episode of the 1968, there were dissidents, but these were not numerous and the security police effectively isolated them from the society. Economically, Czechoslovakia was highly industrialized and played an important role in supplying the USSR with equipment and heavy-industry products. The economic exchange with the USSR still amounts to about 40 percent of all Czechoslovakian foreign trade.

Finally, in Poland, following the events of March 1968 and December 1970, Communist elites were too weak, internally and externally, to risk either an escalation of terror or an economic reform. With the help of Western credits, they tried to satisfy consumer demands, maintain a high level of investments in the wrong industries, and finance rising expenditures of the security services. This further eroded performance of the Polish economy with well-known results. The weak political regime enabled the society to organize itself against it, while the liberal passport policies allowed some exertion of individual initiative.

To say that a strategy of rule was dominant does not mean that it was exclusive. In Poland there was plenty of coercion, and the language of reform abounded in official proclamations. There was much of coercion and corruption in Hungary, and corruption without reform in Czechoslovakia.

How did these strategies affect institutional changes and policies adopted by the governments of these five countries when they abandoned communism? The first impact concerns the ability of political elites to replace the Communist ruling class—their composition and intellectual outlook. The second impact is on the population at large: How did they affect work habits, entrepreneurial talents, respect for the law, the ability to organize for pressure politics, and so forth?

In most Central and Eastern European countries, the exceptions being Bulgaria and Romania, Communist elites were unable to stay in power. All the new elites in the five countries have a disproportionate number of intellectuals among them: writers, journalists, and university professors dominate parliaments and top governmental positions. Opposition to communism was recruited mainly from these groups, and it always looked there for support.

The counterelites were not readily available in Romania and Bulgaria. A loose opposition, when it finally emerged, was unable to win elections. New political forces mature more quickly in Bulgaria than in Romania, but both countries are at the start of a long road.

Poland had a large counterelite rooted in what was called "the underground society" of the 1980s. It consisted of two groups. One involved intellectuals, well educated but lacking necessary administrative and managerial experience and often captives of their ideological presupposition. Some members of this group started small businesses in the late 1980s, but this background is hardly sufficient when the making of global policy decisions or the reforming of state administration is at stake. On the other hand, at least in theory, the Polish counterelites had some idea of the scale of problems that economic and political transformations posed and some idea of the state of the Polish economy.

The other part of the Polish counterelite was a group that included working-class union organizers. Some of them embarked upon the path of political careers. Many remained with the Solidarity trade union and, after a long period of indecision, started to use their union experience in undermining the country's shaky economy.

The new Hungarian elite consists largely of people who had acquired experience with administration and politics during the reform phase of communism. This factor contributed to the relatively fast and smooth change of elites in Hungary. It can be seen in particular in the emergence of a relatively stable political party system, a situation not attained yet in any other country of the region. On the other hand, it seems that Hungarian elites overestimated the usefulness of the reform experience for the post-Communist transformation and consequently underestimated the costs and sacrifices involved in building a market economy.

Finally, in Czechoslovakia, alternative elites were most deficient. For fear of persecutions, only a handful of dissident intellectuals had engaged in open opposition to communism. Some remnants of the Spring of 1968 were allowed to develop abilities in professions for which they were trained, but even they had had problems in communicating with outside academic and professional milieux and could hardly have been expected to create a viable counterelite. The new Czechoslovak political forces have been the least aware of the enormity of tasks facing them.

Thus, we may say only with some exaggeration that the Polish political elite consists disproportionately of college professors, writers, journalists, and other intellectuals possibly with experience in underground work. The Hungarian elite consists of a technocratic detachment of the partisan state mixed with college professors, writers, journalists, and other intellectuals. The Czechoslovak elite includes a mix of similar intellectuals and former party bureaucrats—to do them justice, after more than a year in government, these people have acquired some practical experience.

As to the impact of the strategies of rule on the work habits and entrepreneurial abilities of the population, we postulate the following:

• reform enhances entrepreneurial attitudes and exercises no negative impact upon work culture, but because of the development of the second economy, it may subvert respect for law;
• coercion enhanced passivity both at work and in the ways individuals go about their daily business. It also made people addicted to all sorts of entitlements provided by the Communist state, but it may have been less directly demoralizing than the other two strategies, corruption in particular;
• corruption strengthens individualism and entrepreneurship but at the cost of personal honesty, respect for law, and the habit of serious work and, as already mentioned, teaches the population the art of blackmailing the government.

Thus, we would expect the following: greater initial economic imbalances in Poland than in Czechoslovakia and most of all in Hungary; a lower rate of growth of the private sector in Czechoslovakia than in Poland and in Hungary; higher transaction costs in Poland than in the other two countries, and somewhat less social resistance accompanying reforms in Hungary than in Czechoslovakia and in Poland. In Czechoslovakia, however, this would be a silent subversion by the old structures that can put some effective obstacles on the path of reforms. Last but not least, the more successfully communism had been implemented in a country, the more troubled was its transition away from it. Effects of a particular type of relationship between the rulers and the ruled can only be temporary variations—to be corrected after some efforts—or may become part of a more longitudinal trend.

Policies

Disintegration of the Communist bloc caused by rising economic and political difficulties has left the countries of Central and Eastern Europe without equally viable choices. They can either turn West or face a dramatic debacle. This applies not only to the five countries under consideration but also to the USSR. Turning to the West means that a whole system of institutions must be built anew. This requires material and human assets that none of the countries under consideration possesses to a sufficient degree.

Thus, the degree and the kind of dependence on external actors are of relevance. From this viewpoint, the countries of the first group face the gravest problem. Not only did they fail to remove the Communists from power, but they are less strategically important and are considered less promising than the others. They can count on aid; but for the time being they cannot expect serious financial engagement on the part of international financial institutions of important private foreign investors. The only chance they have is to go on with reforms, against a very strong internal opposition, and hope that the external situation turns to their advantage. And they are trying to do just that.

The three countries of the second group enjoy some priority in terms of economic and political interest. They depend in their efforts on Western know-how and financial support. All three may offer fairly good economic prospects, provided sufficient assistance is forthcoming and their populations are ready to suffer a long period of deferred gratifications. For what is required of them is hard work rewarded with a low standard of living.

Each of the three countries is differently related to the international environment. Hungary, with its long history of reform and stimulation of foreign exchange, has experience of international markets and enjoys a favorable image in the world financial community. Czechoslovakia seeks recourse in its prewar history and the long tradition of industrialization. Poland may be proud of its record of anti-Communist resistance but, with huge, albeit now substantially reduced debt, has a credibility problem.

Financial support, on which access to modern technologies and to the institutional know-how depends, hangs in great measure on the acceptance of the adopted programs by the World Bank and the International Monetary Fund (IMF). The World Bank, in particular, plays an important role in assessing the value of government programs and policies.

A country's freedom in devising its own transition strategy depends on its bargaining power with the World Bank, and this, in turn, is affected by its international image, by the size and structure of the foreign debt, and by its ability to serve it. In this respect, Poland's position is fairly weak, for it could not bear the burden of meeting its financial obligations. The positions of Hungary and Czechoslovakia are relatively stronger. In our view, this factor, as well as the hyperinflation of 1989, has affected the speed and the depth of the Polish reform: Poland had to demonstrate its readiness to meet its problems head-on.

The fact that the World Bank is the main arbiter of the reform gave to it a monetarist streak. Consequently, Poland succeeded in taming inflation and equilibrating the market but at the cost of deepening recession. Critiques of the program say that market equilibrium can be reached at any level of production and unemployment. The priority should be, then, stimulation of economic growth and not the market equilibrium. Another criticism points to an overemphasis on policy measures to the neglect of structural changes.

The Gross National Product (GNP)/debt ratio is lower in Hungary than it was in Poland (62.2 percent and 74.3 percent, respectively, in 1990). In terms of the debt structure, the Hungarian position is worse off, because the main part of its debt comes from private banks. However, it has so far succeeded in meeting its obligations, which has no doubt helped its image.

Hungarians seem to have assumed that the reform policies of the Communist government made their task of building a market economy easier than in other countries of the region. Thus, their program of change is more gradual and less radical. The Czechoslovak government, which initially cherished the illusion that it was easy to overcome the Communist heritage, has now changed its mind and is trying to move quickly ahead with its privatization and reprivatization program.

The trivial truth is that it is easier to destroy the market than to restore it. One of the main problems involved in its restoration is the privatization process. To privatize an economy that is from 80 to 100 percent owned by the state, one needs not only an efficient administration but also a good game plan. For the purpose of the undertaking is not only to change the ownership structure and to help develop a class of owners but most of all to create capital markets.

If privatization means an increase in the share of privately owned enterprises in the national economy, this can be achieved in various ways. First, it can be done through the growth of the private sector, both through endemic process and through joint ventures or sale of firms to foreign owners. This had started in Hungary and Poland well before the end of communism and has continued ever since. (The share of the GNP produced in 1990 by the private sector was less than 2 percent in Czechoslovakia, less than 20 percent in Hungary, and about 30 percent in Poland; an exact figure is lacking.)[1] Second, it can be done through acquisition of state-owned resources by the "privatization of nomenklatura," a process that began in Poland and Hungary, albeit in slightly different ways, in 1988 and finished at the end of 1990. Third, it can be done through the return of assets nationalized during the Communist revolution to their rightful owners: reprivatization. Finally, it can be done by transferring state-owned companies to private owners through sales on the open market.

Characterizing the five countries in terms of these four types of privatization, we may say that the endemic version of the first type characterized until recently only Poland and Hungary, and these countries first embarked upon the path of attracting foreign capital.[2] The "privatization of nomenklatura" took place in all the countries of Central and Eastern Europe with the possible exception of Czechoslovakia. The reprivatization of property poses a lot of technical problems, but it is a logical solution if the principle of private property is accepted. This method will probably be applied in Hungary and Czechoslovakia and to a lesser degree in Poland.

Within the last solution two different policy approaches are discernible. First, there is the approach involving the small privatization of shops and small- or medium-sized establishments, which can be bought through open market bidding. This is easy and does not require specialized administration. Another approach relates to the privatization of big enterprises, which abound in a Communist economy. It is a difficult task demanding administrative and banking resources, which are hard to find in these countries. Moreover, if the direct sale of an important portion of the national wealth is to make sense, there must be enough private capital, and private wealth is lacking. In Czechoslovakia, for instance, individually owned savings are estimated at 3 percent of all national wealth. Hence, other schemes are considered such as the distribution of share vouchers among the adult population. This method will be applied in Poland and Czechoslovakia but probably not in Hungary. In Poland and Czechoslovakia, all enterprises, no matter what their economic prospects, are going to be sold. The last solution places the risk on the buyer.

It is our position that the really effective roads to privatization are the endemic development of the private sector and the inflow of private capital from abroad, which carries with it organizational patterns and a cultural ethos essential to an economic recovery. Only these two methods can lead, in our view, to an effective mobilization of society for economic activity.

Conclusions

It is important to realize what a difficult task societies of CEE face. To make it clear, let us conclude with a metaphor based upon a real-life incident. Once the swamps of Polesye, were the biggest swamps in Europe; they had unique scenery. In the 1960s, Soviet authorities decided to dry the swamps and to turn them over to agriculture. Huge investments were made, and the swamps were eventually dried. Then the authorities discovered that the swamps were turning into wasteland: the soil was unfit for agricultural usage. Moreover, the undertaking had a disastrous impact upon hydrological conditions in the region. Then it was decided to restore the swamps. This proved impossible because swamps are extremely complex biosystems.

The Communist experiment with societies is no different from the story about the Polesye swamps. Although we assume that rebuilding the civil society—and this includes institutions of political democracy and of competitive markets—is a task that may succeed, it is a task of enormous complexity.

Notes

1. The information on Czecholsovakia comes from *Rzeczpospolity* February 1, 1991; on Hungary, "Interview with the Director of the State Property Agency, Mr. Lajsa Csepi," *Rzeczpospolita* April 15, 1991; for Poland, *The Statistical Yearbook* 1991. In Poland, between the end of 1989 and the end of 1990, the share of the private sector in total industrial production grew from 8.5 to 13.4 percent. The proportion of the labor force (outside of agriculture) that was employed in the private sector grew from 12 to 16 percent of the total. During that same time period the production of the state sector fell by about one-quarter.

2. At the end of 1990, in Hungary there were about 1,500 joint ventures with assets valued at about $1 billion; in Poland there were about 2,800 joint ventures with a capital of $400 million.

Bibliography

Kaminski, Antoni Z. 1989. "Coercion, Corruption, and Reform: State and Society in the

Soviet-Type Socialist Regime.'' *Journal of Theoretical Politics* 1, 1: 77–102.
Lindblom, Charles. 1964. *The Intelligence of Democracy*. New York: Free Press.

8. Property Rights and Governance Transformations in Eastern Europe and the United States

John L. Campbell

Eastern European states are beginning to build postsocialist market economies. The state's capacity to redefine property rights is an important tool in this process not only because it enables policymakers to transfer ownership from the state to private actors but also because it enables them to influence the degree to which economic exchange and production is coordinated, or *governed*, by markets, vertically integrated corporations, joint ventures, cartels, and other organizational forms. Students of capitalism have recognized that the state has shaped economic governance in the West through the manipulation of property rights (e.g., North 1981, 1990) and that this has occurred even in comparatively *neoliberal economies,* such as the United States (e.g., Fligstein 1990; Lindberg and Campbell 1991). By neoliberal economies I mean ones that are based largely on private free-market competition where the state's role is generally restricted to regulating competition among private actors (cf. Jessop, Nielsen, and Pedersen; chapter 11 in this volume). However, scholars have not examined the implications of these insights about the West for the development of postsocialist societies and, as a result, have not recognized the full impact that property rights actions will have on the transformation of Eastern European economies.

This chapter explains briefly how the U.S. state shapes economic governance by manipulating and enforcing property rights, and the chapter then extends the analysis to the development of postsocialist societies. In doing so, it makes several additional points. First, because property rights are rules that define not only who *owns* the means of production but also who *uses* them and *appropriates the benefits* from their use (e.g., Bromley 1989, pp. 187–206; Barzel 1989, p. 2; Caporaso 1989), the state's property rights actions, such as establishing and enforcing antitrust, regulatory, tax, labor, and contract law, can in-

Thanks go to Jerzy Hausner, Bob Jessop, Scott Lash, Klaus Nielsen, David Ost, and particularly Robert Jenkins for helpful comments.

fluence economic governance in postsocialist societies even when they do not affect ownership per se. Second, through its property rights actions postsocialist states can create pressures for change that cause actors to begin looking for new forms of governance, and they can constrain and influence how these actors select different forms once they start to look for them. Thus, property rights actions are multidimensional policy tools that affect the governance transformation process in different ways as it unfolds. Third, although property rights actions afford policymakers powerful tools for shaping postsocialist economies, there are risks involved in using these tools. Finally, the application of Western concepts of property rights and theories of governance transformation to postsocialism provides important insights not just about the changes occurring in Eastern Europe but about these concepts and theories themselves.

**The U.S. State and the Transformation
of Governance Regimes**

Property rights actions influenced the transformation of *governance regimes* in various sectors of the U.S. economy. Governance regimes are combinations of specific organizational forms, including markets, corporate hierarchies, associations, and networks (e.g., interlocking directorates, long-term subcontracting agreements, bilateral and multilateral joint ventures, pools, cartels) that coordinate economic activity among organizations in an industry or economic sector. Individually these forms are called *governance mechanisms* (Lindberg, Campbell, and Hollingsworth 1991). Thus, governance transformations involve the reorganization of a particular regime. Corporate hierarchies, for example, may emerge to replace a competitive market as the governance mechanism responsible for allocating certain goods or services in a sector, formal cartels may give way to informal price-leading arrangements for collectively setting prices, and so on.

Governance transformations are typically initiated by actors who respond to changes in markets, technology, and other conditions in their environment, including political ones. These *pressures for change* may cause actors to seek a new governance regime for coordinating their economic activity. However, the development of a new regime is not automatic because it involves a complex *selection process* that involves experimentation, bargaining, and struggle over the structure of a new regime. Furthermore, the selection process does not always result in a new regime because some actors may block whatever alternatives others may seek. In the United States, the state has contributed to governance transformations through its property rights actions by creating pressures for change and by engaging the selection process in several different ways.[1]

The state created pressures for change by altering, or threatening to alter, property rights regarding ownership and use of the means of production. For example, Congress deliberately created pressures for the development of a market-based governance regime in the commercial nuclear energy sector by passing legislation in the 1950s that permitted private firms to own nuclear technology. Although this failed to encourage marketization, policymakers succeeded by restricting the liability a firm could incur in the event of an accident and by threatening to permit the construction of government-owned nuclear plants that would compete directly with private utilities (Campbell 1991). In telecommunications, the federal government transformed American Telephone and Telegraph's (AT&T) monopoly in long-distance telephone service into a competitive market by permitting other companies to connect their long-distance microwave transmission services with AT&T's local telephone grid (Bickers 1991).

The state also manipulates property rights to influence the selection process by *assisting* and *leading* private actors who are engaged in the selection process. To stabilize market-based milk prices during the early twentieth century, dairy farmers tried to establish cooperatives and corporatist price bargaining with distributors, but they succeeded only after the Justice Department stopped invoking antitrust law to block the process (Young 1991). Similarly, the state offered antitrust exemptions during the 1980s to help major steel producers reorganize governance through mergers and joint ventures to prevent the further erosion of market shares to foreign competitors (Scherrer 1991a). In contrast, the state led the selection process after pressures for change developed in the automobile industry by promoting a government-industry joint venture in 1978 designed to improve automobile quality and help the auto industry cope more effectively with foreign competition (White 1982). The state-led selection process was most dramatic in the railroad sector where the federal government created its own rail companies, Amtrak and Conrail, by nationalizing and reorganizing several private railroads to remedy the sector's financial problems and maintain services for customers—a governance transformation that shifted ownership from private to public hands and consolidated previously dispersed firms into two corporate hierarchies (Kennedy 1991).

In addition to being an actor, the state's institutional structure also affects the selection process. Federalism affords subnational governments leeway in devising property rights and defining distinct *locations for economic activity.* In the steel sector during the 1960s and 1970s, lower wages and taxes in the South, resulting from differences in state property rights, facilitated the establishment of small, independent minimills that created market competition for specialty steel products in a sector that had been dominated by an oligopoly (Scherrer 1991a). Movement to the South also helped firms in auto, steel, and meatpacking undermine formally organized, collective governance mechanisms (corporate-union bargaining) and contributed to more market-based mechanisms for establishing wages and benefits (Portz 1991; Scherrer 1991a, 1991b). Long-term subcontracting relations between independent parts suppliers and large automobile manufacturers were also facilitated by these regional differences in property rights (Scherrer 1991b). Thus, in contrast to cases where state actors helped to select a specific governance regime directly, here the state's effect was indirect and *unintentional* because it established the range of governance options from which private actors could choose.

The state also influences the selection process through its capacity to *ratify* new governance regimes. Ratification occurs when the government formally approves a new regime or upholds resultant transactions. Ratification often involves a ruling on property rights, such as when Congress passed legislation in 1922 that formally exempted dairy cooperatives from antitrust prosecution, thereby institutionalizing this form of governance (Young 1991). When ratification is not forthcoming, the emergent regime is destabilized and the selection process continues. For example, railroad operators formed associations, pools, and cartels during the nineteenth century to solve scheduling and pricing problems. Although Congress passed legislation supporting these governance mechanisms, the courts refused to uphold the resulting agreements on antitrust grounds (McCraw 1984, p. 49). As a result of these contradictory property rights policies emanating from different parts of the state, rail companies continued to search for solutions to their problems and finally selected corporate mergers, a governance mechanism that both Congress and the courts accepted (Chandler 1977, ch. 6).

Implications for Postsocialism

To summarize, the U.S. state transforms and permanently shapes economic governance through property rights actions that create pressures for change and influence the selection process. Although the U.S. state is often described as being "weaker" than other Western states because it lacks many capacities for influencing economic activity through the direct allocation of critical resources, such as investment capital (Hamilton and Biggart 1988, pp. 87–88; Samuels 1987, p. 17; Zysman 1983, ch. 2), economic activity is, nevertheless, permanently embedded within the state's property rights structure. Thus, the U.S. state constantly influences and occasionally triggers governance transformations—effects generally attributed only to strong states (Krasner 1978, ch. 3). Ironically, through its property rights actions the relatively neoliberal U.S. state occasionally produces institutional outcomes, such as producer cooperatives, corporatist price bargaining, cooperative research consortia, and long-term subcontracting arrangements, that deviate from the free-market ideal often associated with neoliberalism.

This bears directly on the transformation of state socialist economies. Advocates of neoliberal reform in Eastern Europe (as well as many students of Western political economy) fail to appreciate how extensive the state's role is in affecting governance in *all* Western economies, including those that resemble the neoliberal model (Czekaj and Owsiak 1990). Recognizing the significant effects that property rights actions had on governance in the United States helps to correct this misperception and reveals how even relatively neoliberal states can foster a much wider range of governance options than just markets or corporate hierarchies—the governance mechanisms generally associated with neoliberal economies (e.g., Edmonds 1983). This is especially important at a time when property rights actions are becoming the key policy tools for shaping new governance regimes in postsocialist societies.

Eastern European states have relied heavily on the provision and allocation of credit, subsidies, and other resources to plan economic activity under state socialism. This planning has helped shape economic governance, but often with disastrous results. For example, Kornai (1980, 1989) showed how extravagant allocation policies create soft budget constraints, that is, the ability of firms to secure resources and investment without demonstrating creditworthiness or profitability. In turn, these constraints contributed to the expansion and perpetuation of large, but inefficient, bureaucratic state enterprises and reduced the incentives for actors to develop more efficient governance regimes. However, through the privatization of state enterprises and banks, the development of capital markets, and the increasing provision of capital and technology by the West, the resources available to postsocialist states for influencing governance arrangements through direct allocations are diminishing. By default, then, property rights actions are becoming more important for shaping governance in Eastern Europe. However, little attention has been paid to the different types of property rights actions that are available to postsocialist states and how the mix of property rights actions will have important consequences for governance outcomes.[2]

Three Types of Property Rights

The current debate in Eastern Europe about building postsocialist economies focuses almost entirely on how to transform governance arrangements by altering property rights that cover *ownership* of the means of production. For example, there is much discussion about which state enterprises to privatize and whether to privatize by selling enterprise shares to employees through employee stock ownership plans or to private investors through auctions, vouchers, or the sale of shares in holding companies. In contrast, little, if any, attention is paid to how property rights shape governance by defining how the means of production are *used*, or by whom, once privatization is accomplished (e.g., Blanchard et al. 1990; Hausner and Wojtyna 1990; Ost 1991; Pankow 1990; Rudolf 1991; Stark 1990). Yet both types of property rights have important consequences for governance transformations. In fact, when property rights influenced governance transformations in the United States, it was usually because they redefined how and under what conditions the means of production were used, not who owned them.

Several governments are trying to build postsocialist market economies through privatization schemes without having developed antitrust, labor, environmental, and other property rights laws to regulate the use of private property. Under these conditions, privatization has had undesirable consequences in terms of economic governance. For example, in the Soviet city of Sverdlovsk, an industrial stronghold in the Urals, the Communist old guard was voted out of power in the city council, after which the city tried to stimulate the development of small enterprises and legalized several free-market stores that sold Finnish boots and Western beer, cigarettes, and other goods. However, these would-be entrepreneurs were crushed by a few large industrial trading firms that did not want competition. These firms were organized and run by former high-ranking Communist party officials who managed to transfer their power from political to commercial organizations (Keller 1990). This has also occurred in Eastern European countries (e.g., Blanchard et al. 1990; Ost 1991; Stark 1990; Seleny 1991), much to the dismay of the new regimes and their supporters. Even some of those who support the idea of relatively spontaneous privatization warn against transforming centralized political power into economic power through the formation of these so-called *nomenklatura* companies (e.g., Kornai 1990, p. 90).[3]

Had state officials established property rights, such as antitrust laws, that protected small firms by regulating the *use* of private property, economic competition might have been preserved. This is important insofar as the goal of many reformers is not only to privatize the economy but also to create competitive markets that eliminate soft budget constraints. Indeed, some argue that the existence of large, oligopolistic enterprises, even if they are privately owned, threatens the development of competitive markets in Eastern Europe (e.g., Kornai 1989). This is not to deny the importance of property rights that define ownership per se. After all, property rights actions that prevented the creation of large trading companies in the first place could have prevented the *nomenklatura* from translating their political power into economic power and would have increased the chances for competitive markets to flourish.[4] This is why the Solidarity government passed legislation nullifying attempts to create *nomenklatura* companies in Poland (Hausner and Wojtyna 1990). Nevertheless, property rights actions that redefine ownership, but not how the means of production are used, will not necessarily ensure the kinds of governance regimes that policymakers desire.

It is worth noting that privatization without regulating how the means of production are used may lead to additional problems. For instance, acceptance of entrepreneurial market activity in Poland quickly led to the development of so-called mafia taxis in Warsaw that frequently overcharged their customers—an abuse all the more likely given in absence of property rights regulating how people conduct business in the taxi industry. It is easy to imagine how the lack of property rights covering the use of property could lead to the development of a market economy with many of the same corrupt and deceptive practices that plagued late-nineteenth- and early-twentieth-century capitalism in the West (e.g., Weinstein 1968). However, the broader point is that to accomplish their goals and avoid problems of *nomenklatura* companies, consumer abuses, and the like, policymakers will have to devise appropriate *mixtures* of different *types* of property rights.

In addition to defining who owns and uses the means of production, property rights also define who appropriates the benefits, including profits, that are derived from using the means of production. This third type of property right has already affected governance arrangements in Eastern Europe. For instance, Hungarian policymakers passed special legislation in 1982 that ratified and, thus, successfully encouraged the development of "enterprise business work partnerships" (VGMs) in state firms (Stark 1989). VGMs are an officially sanctioned version of an inside subcontracting arrangement that existed informally prior to 1982, often on a clandestine basis. In VGMs some of the firm's employees contract with management to use the firm's equipment during their spare time to produce various commodities or services that the firm needs, such as parts, design work, and product research and development, but that were previously subcontracted out to other firms. Because these employees are allowed to keep the profits from their work, VGMs generally operate more efficiently than the state enterprises within which they are located. Indeed, as VGMs proliferated, economic leaders saw them as a way to enable large enterprises to compete more successfully in international markets (Stark 1986, p. 497).

VGMs flourished after 1982 because the state changed property rights regarding who could claim benefits derived from using state-owned means of production. The state neither relinquished ownership to the workers in its factories nor changed who was allowed to use its equipment, although managers and employees renegotiated the ends to which this equipment was put. Conversely, rules making the private appropriation of profit illegal in Hungary and elsewhere in Eastern Europe undoubtedly limited the expansion of commercial activity located outside the state and organized through VGMs and other so-called second-economy activities where people privately, and often surreptitiously, supplemented the income they earned in the state sector.[5]

Although VGMs emerged under conditions of state ownership, postsocialist governments can manipulate property rights covering the appropriation of benefits, such as tax laws, to encourage the development of similar governance mechanisms after privatization. Indeed, flexible subcontracting arrangements developed under conditions of private property in Italy after World War II owing, in part, to the provision of ten-year exemptions from income taxes to artisans and small industrial enterprises. By temporarily relinquishing its claim to a fraction of future income, the state, dominated by a Christian Democratic party intent on expanding its middle-class electoral base, deliberately manipulated these property rights to create a large sector of small firms—a sector that gradually evolved elaborate subcontracting arrangements, rather than vertical integration, in order to preserve their special tax status (Lazerson 1988; Weiss

1988, 1984, p. 224). To the extent that Eastern European firms will have to operate in a post-Fordist international economy (Maier 1990), where flexible production, subcontracting among smaller firms, and less hierarchically organized economic activity are desirable, understanding how property rights actions lead to this type of governance arrangement will become very important.

In sum, redefining ownership of the means of production is not the only type of property rights action that can produce more efficient forms of governance in postsocialism. Indeed, if the problem is to improve economic efficiency through the creation of market competition or long-term subcontracting arrangements, then just redefining ownership may not be the solution at all. On the one hand, in Sverdlovsk privatization without additional property rights reforms *reduced* competition by eliminating small entrepreneurs. On the other hand, in the VGM case subcontracting flourished without privatization and competition *increased*. Some enterprise managers encouraged the development of several VGMs within the firm and let them compete, and some engineering and design VGMs became so efficient that they eventually competed with their parent firms for contracts with other enterprises (Stark 1986, p. 501). Furthermore, if privatization becomes difficult in the first place because investors refuse to buy inefficient firms, as occurred in Poland recently when the state was unable to sell some of its outdated enterprises (Engelberg 1991), then property rights actions that improve the firm's efficiency by redefining how the means of production are used, or who controls the benefit stream, may have to *precede* transfer of ownership.[6] After all, Conrail, the U.S. state-owned railroad company, was privatized only after it had been transformed into a profitable enterprise (Kennedy 1991).

One caveat is in order. Regardless of the desired institutional goals, creating the appropriate mix of property rights is a tricky business. Property rights crafted at different times may contradict each other in ways that undermine the goals of policymakers. In the United States this occurred when common law undermined the congressionally supported efforts of railroads to form associations and cartels. Similar problems have already materialized in Eastern Europe. Although legalization encouraged the spread of VGMs, the imposition of relatively steep personal income taxes in Hungary in the late 1980s threatened this governance mechanism. Because VGMs are legal, they are among the most visible parts of the second economy (e.g., Stark 1989, p. 161) and people who participate in them are more vulnerable to tax collection than are those whose activity in the second economy is less conspicuous. As taxes increase and reduce the net income people earn by working in VGMs, the incentives for participating in them deteriorate. Moreover, to the extent that privatization forces the state to rely increasingly on taxation as a revenue source, people may be scared away from private business in general, particularly insofar as the state resorts to highly progressive tax codes that undermine incentives at the margin for extra entrepreneurial effort (Kornai 1990, pp. 126–32; 1989, p. 56).[7] In short, when devising various mixtures of property rights policymakers must carefully examine the effects the *interactions* among property rights will have on governance outcomes.

The Governance Transformation
Process in General

Property rights actions in Eastern Europe will influence all stages of the governance transformation process. First, privatization and other property rights actions will constitute pressures for change to which actors will respond by selecting different governance regimes. The *nomenklatura* have already reacted in some countries to privatization by trying to create their own large companies. Furthermore, some states have already created competitive markets on a limited basis through the sale of state assets, such as restaurants, boutiques, and retail stores (Venys 1991). Second, property rights actions will affect the selection process. In addition to ratifying different governance mechanisms, as occurred in Sverdlovsk and Hungary when the state legalized various forms of entrepreneurial activity, property rights actions will enable the state to lead, assist, and structure the selection process in ways designed to solve some of the most critical problems facing postsocialist economies, such as the need to attract investment capital.

Capital is essential for privatization, but there is not enough domestic capital in Eastern Europe to achieve privatization. The assets of Polish state enterprises, for example, are estimated to be worth between $50 billion and $100 billion (Rudolf 1991). To fill the gap and to attract technology and managerial expertise, several Eastern European states have started to adopt legislation to encourage the formation of joint ventures between state enterprises and Western firms (e.g., Robinson 1991). Poland and Hungary, the two countries in Eastern Europe carrying the largest hard currency debts since 1984, have devised particularly lenient joint venture regulations. For instance, Hungarian policymakers passed the 1989 Act on the Transformation of State Enterprise to encourage the development of East–West joint ventures and partnerships by requiring that in some cases at least 20 percent of the enterprise's capitalization come from external sources (Seleny 1991). As a result of these property rights actions, Hungary and Poland each now have several hundred more joint ventures than the rest of their Eastern European neighbors combined (U.S. General Accounting Office 1990), and in Hungary over half of all foreign investment has come through joint ventures (Seleny 1991).

Property rights actions can also facilitate the development of industrial consortia and cartels among domestically owned enterprises so that these firms can pool capital and other resources. Policymakers in the United States occasionally try to foster such strategies as, for example, when Congress passed special antitrust legislation in 1984 permitting U.S. computer and semiconductor firms to form collective research organizations where the costs of research and development would otherwise have been prohibitive (Gabor and Dworkin 1989). Thus, in addition to creating pressures for change by selling state-owned enterprises and then letting private actors autonomously select governance regimes, property rights actions also afford postsocialist states the capacity and opportunity to influence the selection process as it unfolds.

Property Rights Actions and the Risks of Foreign Capital

Of course, trying to attract foreign capital with which to create markets, joint ventures, and other governance mechanisms involves risks. Foreign lenders and investors will often require a quid pro quo before investing in the new postsocialist economies (Czekaj and Owsiak 1990). The International Monetary Fund has already agreed to provide Hungary and Poland with lines of credit in order to help them ease their balance of payments problems, but only after they consented to reduce demand, increase exports and hard currency balances, cut state budgets, and stabilize their currencies through a variety of conservative monetary and fiscal policies. The Bush administration in the United States has recently proposed to provide financial assistance to Eastern European governments if they agreed to take similar economic actions (U.S. General Accounting Office 1990). Noticeably absent from these discussions, particularly those regarding currency stabilization and inflation management, are policies that would encourage business and labor to organize through industry or peak associations and negotiate solutions to these problems through corporatist arrangements—an approach that was adopted with some success in Western Europe during the 1970s and 1980s (Lindberg and Maier 1985), but that is often at odds with the kinds of austerity policies Eastern European governments are currently pursuing at the behest of foreign lenders. As a result, negotiations to attract foreign capital seem to have limited de facto the range of property rights and governance options that Eastern European governments are considering.

There are other risks associated with attracting foreign capital that will be exacerbated insofar as the institutional structure of postsocialist states facilitates the creation of different sets of property rights. Foreign corporations are likely to demand special property rights before agreeing to invest in Eastern Europe. Much the same thing happens in the United States at the *subnational* level where public officials negotiate with corporations to invest in the local or state economy. Corporations tend to invest in places with the most liberal, that is, nonrestrictive, labor, environmental, tax, and other regulations (Newman 1984) or where local governments agree to provide liberal exemptions to these rules. This has led to bidding wars among subnational governments competing for the same investment capital. Concessions, such as forgoing tax revenue, are often granted to the corporation at great expense to the community and the state (Bluestone and Harrison 1982; Harrison and Bluestone 1988). In addition, state governments have occasionally passed anti-union laws that undermine the ability of labor to organize and bargain collectively with business (Goodman 1979, pp. 73,

99)—property rights covering the conditions under which labor is used that inhibit governance through associations and long-term labor–management contracts and foster market-based transactions for labor.

Similar competition among subnational governments through the manipulation of property rights could develop in Eastern Europe, especially where local governments begin to gain autonomy from the national state, as they have recently in Poland (Hausner and Wojtyna 1990), and where they assume more responsibility for developing their own revenue base and enjoy the capacity to define distinct locations of economic activity through localized property rights. In Yugoslavia, for example, general privatization laws are interpreted in different ways by Slovinian, Croatian, Serbian, and other subnational governments (Djelic 1991). The same thing may occur in former East Germany, to the extent that the old Lander governments are resurrected in the wake of reunification (Hoene 1991), and throughout the rest of Eastern Europe. As in the West, this could lead to governance regimes relying primarily on markets and corporate hierarchies rather than on associations and other collective governance mechanisms, an outcome that would disappoint those who favor governance regimes relying more on corporatist negotiation.[8]

Property rights competition could materialize among *national* governments in Eastern Europe for the same reason and with similar consequences. Indeed, multinational firms and organized business groups have lobbied national governments throughout the European Community in search of more favorable investment climates. This so-called policy shopping rarely includes negotiations with labor or consumer representatives and thus tends to undermine the corporatist arrangements that are in place in many of these countries. It also results in multinational firms investing in countries with less expensive and more flexible social benefits (Pestoff 1991, p. 33).

There are additional problems associated with attempts to attract foreign capital through property rights concessions. Lax environmental and tax codes could exacerbate the environmental degradation and fiscal problems these countries already face, as often occurs when third-world governments try to attract capital from multinational corporations, the World Bank, or the International Monetary Fund (Barnet and Muller 1974, pp. 136–39; Payer 1974). Some Eastern Europeans also worry that massive infusions of foreign capital will precipitate sudden and widespread unemployment as new owners lay off workers to reduce labor costs and improve the efficiency of firms (Stark 1990). Indeed, to attract foreign capital and technology Czechoslovakia has allowed employers to lay off as many workers as they want and has granted a variety of tax concessions in cases where firms are partly foreign owned (Robinson 1991). Moreover, labor–management problems could result particularly in the absence of property rights, such as labor and occupational safety law, that further protect the interests of workers. These are especially severe problems to the extent that their resolution in favor of investors could undermine the political stability of the new

Eastern European governments. In fact, recognition of the costs of attracting foreign capital has led to fierce debate in Eastern Europe over property rights regarding the investments of outsiders (Ost 1991).[9]

Postsocialist Implications for Western Theory

The preceding discussion raises several theoretical issues regarding property rights and economic governance as treated by Western scholars. For example, the conventional literature on property rights argues that it is the specification of different bundles of property rights that determine governance arrangements (e.g., Barzel 1989). However, the contents of these bundles are rarely explored in conceptual detail. Generic definitions of property rights are frequently offered in discussions about the effects of property rights on economic governance, and these definitions often list different types of property rights, such as those regarding ownership, use, and appropriation of benefits. Yet these types are rarely examined individually, in relation to each other, or in terms of their individual or interactive effects on governance arrangements (e.g., Barzel 1989; Caporaso 1989; North 1990, 1981; but see Bromley 1989, ch. 7). In short, different types of property rights are recognized, but not *theorized*. By exploring how three distinct types of property rights influence governance in Eastern Europe, this chapter begins to disentangle the concept of property rights and specifies how different types of property rights affect the governance of economic activity.

Scholars have recently criticized the property rights literature for assuming that property rights are created and enforced only by the state (Barzel 1989, p. 64). For example, in his earlier work North (1981) argued that inefficient property rights develop precisely because the process of defining them is a political one conducted by rulers interested in maximizing their revenues but not necessarily the output of the economy. The development of Hungarian VGMs, however, suggests that policymakers are not always the ones who establish property rights. In this case, property rights were initially renegotiated between enterprise managers and workers behind the backs of party officials. Indeed, development of the second economy in general suggests that private actors are often responsible for creating and enforcing property rights.

The fact that the adoption of official property rights ratifying VGMs occurred only after this form of governance had become relatively common also suggests that there is an important distinction between *formal* and *informal* property rights and that there are significant relationships between them and governance transformations. Recently, North (1990, p. 45) argued that the selection of governance arrangements is constrained by both formal and informal rules. Formal rules include those established, sanctioned, and enforced by the state, such as property rights. Informal rules include cultural norms and unwritten codes regarding economic activity. Although North does not suggest it, these norms and codes constitute informal property rights insofar as they regulate the ownership, use, and appropriation of benefits of the means of production, but do not involve the state in their delineation and enforcement. According to North, informal rules change more slowly than formal ones, particularly during war, revolution, or other social upheavals when formal rules are rapidly transformed. This lag, he argued, creates tensions between formal and informal rules that policymakers must eventually ease by bringing the former into closer alignment with the latter (North 1990, pp. 89–91). It follows that informal property rights act as a *brake* on the development of formal ones.[10]

This may be true. However, the case of VGMs and the second economy suggests that the *opposite* is also possible. Major alterations in informal property rights through the creation of private and unofficial subcontracting arrangements eventually diverged so much from formal property rights that state officials adopted a new set of formal property rights that permitted and encouraged the operation of VGMs. Furthermore, official privatization policies are now being promulgated, in part, because the state could no longer ignore the relative success of private market activity that had been occurring informally for years in the second economy. Thus, shifts in informal property rights may also serve as a *catalyst* for change in formal ones.[11]

North's attempt to theorize the relationship between formal and informal rules and their effects on economic governance represents an important innovation in thinking about how property rights contribute to governance transformations—one that is reminiscent of recent work by sociologists who have demonstrated how economic activity is embedded in and mediated by broader social relations (e.g., Baker 1984; DiMaggio 1990; Dore 1983; Granovetter 1985, 1990). Despite his insights, however, North makes no attempt to explain the *origins* of these informal constraints (North 1990, p. 44)—a surprising omission given his earlier attempts to theorize the political origins of formal property rights (e.g., North 1981). It is ironic, then, that one of the keys to understanding the origins of informal property rights is to recognize how economic behavior is embedded in social relations.

For example, clandestine entrepreneurialism, tax evasion, and other forms of private economic activity have existed for years in Eastern Europe, not only because citizens had an economic interest in pursuing these activities but also because it was a culturally sanctioned form of resistance to an oppressive political regime. In Hungary, tax evasion became rampant, in part, because it was a socially acceptable way of cheating the government—a cultural code that will linger for years regardless of the efforts of politicians to stop it (Kornai 1990, p. 118). In effect, private citizens, responding to an unofficial culture that condoned political resistance, gradually created informal property rights regarding appropriation of benefits from the means of production.

Some scholars have suggested that private actors define and enforce property rights as part of their constant search for more efficient production and exchange and because it is too expensive for the state alone to manage all property rights (e.g., Barzel 1989, p. 64). In contrast, North (1990, p. 42) argues that informal constraints cannot always be reduced to wealth or efficiency maximization. The example of tax evasion suggests that both views may be partially correct. Although it was efficient for citizens to withhold taxes, in the sense that they benefited financially from doing so, this behavior also had cultural origins. Thus, an explanation of the origins of informal property rights requires an analysis of economic *and* social determinants.

However, social embeddedness also influences the creation of formal property rights, although less directly. Entrepreneurs and others active in the second economy have hesitated to form visible interest groups under postsocialism because the conspiratorial conditions in which they worked and the networks of corruption in which they were embedded during state socialism made them distrustful of each other as well as of the authorities. As a result, laws prohibiting the development of *nomenklatura* companies notwithstanding, it has generally been difficult for these groups to push for the creation of property rights that protect their interests under postsocialism (Ost 1991, p. 21).[12] Thus, although some argue that actors can delineate property rights to whatever degree they desire as they pursue their maximization strategies (Barzel 1989, p. 114), the evidence presented here indicates that there are substantial political and social limits on the range of formal and informal property rights from which actors choose and that a theory of property rights and governance transformation must include an analysis of these limits.[13]

Conclusion

Scholars have asked whether concepts from Western social sciences can be fruitfully applied to the study of Eastern Europe (Stark 1989). This chapter demonstrates that they can and that Western concepts and theories can be improved in the process. First, examining how changes in property rights have led to governance transformations in the East helps to clarify the vague concept of property rights that characterizes much of the Western literature on the subject. Specifically, it is important to differentiate among rights that define ownership, use, and appropriation of benefits from the means of production. Second, the application of a more clearly articulated concept of property rights to the development of postsocialism illustrates how altering rights of ownership per se is not necessarily the panacea for Eastern Europe that some predict. Some governance mechanisms, such as VGMs, that seem to have worked quite well were created without privatization of state assets, as have other organizational forms under state socialism (e.g., Dabrowski, Federowicz, and Levitas 1990). Finally, this lends credence to the idea that there are more choices available to Eastern Europe than just command or market economies, depending on how property rights are defined. Those who pose the choices at these two extremes, either for the East (e.g., Kornai 1990) or for the West (e.g., Wolf 1988), ignore many other important and interesting forms of governance that have worked in the past and that can be crafted through the delineation and enforcement of property rights.

Notes

1. For further discussion of the governance transformation process, see Campbell and Lindberg (1991). An extended discussion of the material that follows in this section appears in Campbell and Lindberg (1990).

2. Because property rights and allocative actions represent different types of *policy tools*, the distinction between them is one of *means*, not ends. Indeed, both types of state action may have similar effects on economic outcomes, such as the distribution of resources in the economy (e.g., Barzel 1989) and governance arrangements. For example, the government may grant tax breaks, which is a property rights action, or provide subsidies, which is an allocative action, to automobile manufacturers in order to get them to develop collectively more fuel-efficient cars. Both types of actions may redistribute resources and lead to the creation of research consortia. However, changing the tax code does so by altering *rules*, in this case those governing the appropriation of benefits from the means of production. Subsidies do so through the *direct provision* of resources as transfer payments. For further discussion of the distinction between property rights and allocative actions, see Lindberg and Campbell (1991).

3. The problem of *nomenklatura* companies is a tricky one. Although many oppose the creation of *nomenklatura* companies, the *nomenklatura* are among the few who have accumulated substantial capital under the old regime—capital that is now desperately needed for privatization (Ost 1991).

4. See Szelenyi (1986–87, 1988) for further discussion about the emergence of parallel structures of economic inequality in the state and private sectors of Eastern Europe.

5. Despite these legal obstacles, the second economy constitutes a significant proportion of economic activity in the East. In Hungary, for example, it is estimated to account for 25 percent of gross domestic product (Seleny 1991). For further discussion of the development and significance of the second economy, see Szelenyi (1989; 1988, pp. 40–41; 1986–87, pp. 124–27) and Stark (1986, 1989).

6. For this reason, the final failure of the command economy may be its inability to create a market economy through command marketization.

7. See Schumpeter (1918/1991, pp. 112–14) for a discussion of how taxation can undermine entrepreneurialism in the West and how this is a problem that constrains the ability of Western states to meet their revenue needs. Indeed, this could be a severe problem for postsocialist states that need revenues to modernize infrastructure, but must not deter entrepreneurialism.

8. For a comparison of neoliberal, corporatist, and other possible governance outcomes in Eastern Europe, see Ost (1991) and Rudolf (1991).

9. Kornai's (1990, pp. 167–68) position highlights the tensions surrounding the issue. In contrast to others, he argued that it is precisely because Eastern European countries need to attract foreign capital that they should *not* grant special property rights, such as tax breaks or licensing privileges, to foreign investors. To do so, he argued, would discourage foreign investment by conveying the impression of a politically unstable and unpredictable investment climate. Political compromises will surely result, such as the legislation passed in Czechoslovakia (Venys 1991) and Poland (Rudolf 1991) that limits the amount of state assets that can be acquired by foreign investors.

10. See MacCaulay (1963) for a discussion of formal business contracts and informal codes of business ethics that closely parallel the distinction between formal and informal property rights.

11. The juxtaposition of North's view of the relationship between formal and informal property rights, derived from his reading of Western economic history, and mine, based on a view of Eastern Europe, supports Stark's (1986) methodological claim that comparisons of capitalist and state-socialist systems often result in "mirrored comparisons."

12. See Ost (1991) for a discussion of additional reasons why civil society has not become better organized politically, even in Poland where Solidarity has been in existence for a decade (Ost 1987).

13. This sort of error is made possible by deliberately omitting an analysis of the role of culture and the state in the formation and enforcement of property rights (Hodgson 1988, ch. 7–8)—an omission presumably necessary in order to produce clean and parsimonious models (e.g., Barzel 1989, p. 10). For further discussion of the problems associated with constructing excessively clean models, see Hirsch, Michaels, and Friedman (1990).

Bibliography

Baker, Wayne. 1984. "The Social Structure of a National Securities Market." *American Journal of Sociology* 34, 4: 459–82.

Barnet, Richard J., and Ronald E. Muller. 1974. *Global Reach*. New York: Simon and Schuster.

Barzel, Yoram. 1989. *Economic Analysis of Property Rights*. New York: Cambridge University Press.

Bickers, Kenneth. 1991. "Transformation in the Governance of the American Telecommunications Industry." In *Governance of the American Economy*, ed. John L. Campbell, J. Rogers Hollingsworth, and Leon N. Lindberg, 77–107. New York: Cambridge University Press.

Blanchard, O., R. Dornbusch, P. Krugman, R. Layard, and L. Summers. 1990. "Reform in Eastern Europe and the Soviet Union." Written for UN-wider (unpublished paper).

Bluestone, Barry, and Bennett Harrison. 1982. *The Deindustrialization of America*. New York: Basic Books.

Bromley, Daniel W. 1989. *Economic Interests and Institutions: The Conceptual Foundations of Public Policy*. New York: Blackwell.

Campbell, John L. 1991. "Contradictions of Governance in the Nuclear Energy Sector." In *Governance of the American Economy*, ed. John L. Campbell, J. Rogers Hollingsworth, and Leon N. Lindberg, 108–37. New York: Cambridge University Press.

Campbell, John L., et al. eds. 1991. *Governance of the American Economy*. New York: Cambridge University Press.

Campbell, John L., and Leon N. Lindberg. 1990. "Property Rights and the Organization of Economic Activity by the State." *American Sociological Review* 55, 5: 634–47.

———. 1991. "The Evolution of Governance Regimes." In *Governance of the American Economy*, ed. John L. Campbell, J. Rogers Hollingsworth, and Leon N. Lindberg, 319–55. New York: Cambridge University Press.

Caporaso, James A. 1989. "Microeconomics and International Political Economy: The Neoclassical Approach to Institutions." In *Global Changes and Theoretical Chal-*

lenges, ed. Ernst-Otto Czempiel and James N. Rosenau, 136–59. Lexington, Mass.: Lexington Books.

Chandler, Alfred D. 1977. *The Visible Hand: The Managerial Revolution in American Business*. Cambridge: Harvard University Press.

Czekaj, Jan, and Stanislaw Owsiak. 1990. "Social Limitations for Efficient Allocation of Resources in the Post-Socialist Countries." Paper presented at the Conference on Market, Politics, and the Negotiated Economy—Scandinavian and Post-Socialist Perspectives. Cracow, Poland (December).

Dabrowski, Janusz M., Michal Federowicz, and Anthony Levitas. 1990. "Stabilization and State Enterprise Adjustment: The Political Economy of State Firms after Five Months of Fiscal Discipline, Poland 1990." Program on Central and Eastern Europe Working Paper Series, no. 6. Center for European Studies, Harvard University.

DiMaggio, Paul. 1990. "Cultural Aspects of Economic Action and Organization." In *Beyond the Marketplace*, ed. Roger Friedland and A. F. Robertson, 113–36. New York: Aldine de Gruyter.

Djelic, Bozidar. 1991. "Privatization in Yugoslavia: From Self-Management to Socialism?" Paper presented at the Conference on Dilemmas of Transition from State Socialism in East Central Europe. Center for European Studies, Harvard University.

Dore, Ronald. 1983. "Goodwill and the Spirit of Market Capitalism." *British Journal of Sociology* 34, 4: 459–82.

Edmonds, Martin. 1983. "Crisis Management in the United States." In *Industrial Crisis: A Comparative Study of the State and Industry*, ed. Kenneth Dyson and Stephen Wilks, 67–102. Oxford: Martin Robertson.

Engelberg, Stephen. 1991. "First Sale of State Holdings a Disappointment in Poland." The *New York Times*, January 14, D1, D6.

Fligstein, Neil. 1990. *The Transformation of Corporate Control*. Cambridge: Harvard University Press.

Gabor, Andrea, and Peter Dworkin. 1989. "High Tech's United Front." *U.S. News and World Report* 10 (July), 43.

Goodman, Robert. 1979. *The Last Entrepreneurs: America's Regional Wars for Jobs and Dollars*. Boston: South End Press.

Granovetter, Mark. 1985. "Economic Action and Social Structure: The Problem of Embeddedness." *American Journal of Sociology* 91, 3: 481–510.

———. 1990. "The Old and the New Economic Sociology: A History and an Agenda." In *Beyond the Marketplace*, ed. Roger Friedland and A. F. Robertson, 89–112. New York: Aldine de Gruyter.

Hamilton, Gary, and Nicole Biggart. 1988. "Market, Culture, and Authority: A Comparative Analysis of Management and Organization in the Far East." *American Journal of Sociology* 94: S52–S94.

Harrison, Bennett, and Barry Bluestone. 1988. *The Great U-Turn: Corporate Restructuring and the Polarizing of America*. New York: Basic Books.

Hausner, Jerzy, and Andrzej Wojtyna. 1990. "Evolution of Interest Representation in Poland." Paper presented at the Conference on Market, Politics, and the Negotiated Economy—Scandinavian and Post-Socialist Perspectives. Cracow, Poland.

Hirsch, Paul, Stuart Michaels, and Ray Friedman. 1990. "Clean Models vs. Dirty Hands: Why Economics Is Different from Sociology." In *Structures of Capital*, ed. Sharon Zukin and Paul DiMaggio, 39–56. New York: Cambridge University Press.

Hodgson, Geoffrey. 1988. *Economics and Institutions*. Philadelphia: University of Pennsylvania Press.

Hoene, Bernd. 1991. "Reconstructing Labor Markets in Eastern Germany." Paper presented at the Conference on Dilemmas of Transition from State Socialism in East Central Europe. Center for European Studies, Harvard University.

Jessop, Bob, Klaus Nielsen, and Ove K. Pedersen. 1990. "Structural Competitiveness and Strategic Capacities: Scandinavia, Great Britain and West Germany." Paper presented at the Conference on Market, Politics, and the Negotiated Economy—Scandinavian and Post-Socialist Perspectives. Cracow, Poland.

Keller, Bill. 1990. "In Urals City, the Communist Apparatus Ends But Not The Communist Power." The *New York Times*, December 13: A24.

Kennedy, Robert D. 1991. "The Statist Evolution of Rail Governance in the United States, 1830–1986." In *Governance of the American Economy*, ed. John L. Campbell, J. Rogers Hollingsworth, and Leon N. Lindberg, 139–81. New York: Cambridge University Press.

Kornai, Janos. 1980. *Economics of Shortage*. Amsterdam: North-Holland.

———. 1989. "The Hungarian Reform Process: Visions, Hopes, and Reality." In *Remaking the Economic Institutions of Socialism: China and Eastern Europe*, ed. Victor Nee and David Stark, 32–94. Stanford, Calif.: Stanford University Press.

———. 1990. *The Road to a Free Economy: Shifting From a Socialist System—The Example of Hungary*. New York: W. W. Norton.

Krasner, Stephen D. 1978. *Defending the National Interest: Raw Materials Investments and U.S. Foreign Policy*. Princeton, N.J.: Princeton University Press.

Lazerson, Mark. 1988. "Small Firm Growth: An Outcome of Markets and Hierarchies." *American Sociology Review* 53, 3: 330–42.

Lindberg, Leon N., and John L. Campbell. 1991. "The State and the Organization of Economic Activity." In *Governance of the American Economy*, ed. John L. Campbell, J. Rogers Hollingsworth, and Leon N. Lindberg, 356–95. New York: Cambridge University Press.

Lindberg, Leon N., and Charles Maier. 1985. *The Politics of Inflation and Economic Stagnation*. Washington, D.C.: Brookings Institution.

MacCaulay, Stewart. 1963. "Non-Contractual Relations in Business: A Preliminary Study." *American Sociological Review* 28, 1: 55–67.

McCraw, Thomas K. 1984. *Prophets of Regulation*. Cambridge: Harvard University Press.

Maier, Charles. 1990. "Why Did Communism Collapse in 1989?" Paper presented at the Seminar on the State and Capitalism, Center for European Studies, Harvard University, Cambridge.

Newman, Robert J. 1984. *Growth in the American South: Changing Regional Employment and Wage Patterns in the 1960s and 1970s*. New York: New York University Press.

North, Douglass. 1981. *Structure and Change in Economic History*. New York: W. W. Norton.

———. 1990. *Institutions, Institutional Change and Economic Performance*. New York: Cambridge University Press.

Ost, David. 1987. "The Transformation of Solidarity and the Future of Central Europe." *Telos* 19 (Spring): 69–94.

———. 1991. "Shaping a New Politics in Poland: Interests and Politics in Post-

Communist East Europe.'' Program in Central and Eastern Europe Working Paper Series, no. 8. Center for European Studies, Harvard University.

Pankow, Julian. 1990. ''Prospects for Employee Ownership in the Process of Privatizing the Polish Economy.'' Paper presented at the Conference on Market, Politics, and the Negotiated Economy—Scandinavian and Post-Socialist Perspectives. Cracow, Poland.

Payer, Cheryl. 1974. *The Debt Trap: The International Monetary Fund and the Third World*. New York: Monthly Review Press.

Pestoff, Victor. 1991. ''The Demise of the Swedish Model and the Rise of Organized Business as a Major Political Actor.'' Paper presented at the Annual Conference of the Society for the Advancement of Socio-Economics, Stockholm, Sweden (June).

Portz, John. 1991. ''Economic Governance and the American Meatpacking Industry.'' In *Governance of the American Economy*, ed. John L. Campbell, J. Rogers Hollingsworth, and Leon N. Lindberg, 259–92. New York: Cambridge University Press.

Robinson, Anthony. 1991. ''Czechs Hang 'For Sale' Sign in 50 of Republic's Key Companies.'' *Financial Times*, June 14: 2.

Rudolf, Stanislaw. 1991. ''Economic and Social Aspects of Privatization in Poland.'' Unpublished manuscript, University of Lodz, Poland.

Samuels, Richard J. 1987. *The Business of the Japanese State*. Ithaca, N.Y.: Cornell University Press.

Scherrer, Christoph. 1991a. ''Governance of the Steel Industry: What Caused the Disintegration of the Oligopoly.'' In *Governance of the American Economy*, ed. John L. Campbell, J. Rogers Hollingsworth, and Leon N. Lindberg, 192–208. New York: Cambridge University Press.

———. 1991b. ''Governance of the Automobile Industry: The Transformation of Labor and Supplier Relations.'' In *Governance of the American Economy*, ed. John L. Campbell, J. Rogers Hollingsworth, and Leon N. Lindberg, 209–35. New York: Cambridge University Press.

Schumpeter, Joseph. 1918/1991. ''The Crisis of the Tax State.'' In *Joseph A. Schumpeter: The Economics and Sociology of Capitalism*, ed. Richard Swedberg, 99–140. Princeton, N.J.: Princeton University Press.

Seleny, Anna. 1991. ''Property Rights in Transition: State and Private Sectors in Hungary.'' Paper presented at the Conference on Dilemmas of Transition from State Socialism in East Central Europe. Center for European Studies, Harvard University.

Stark, David. 1986. ''Rethinking Internal Labor Markets: New Insights from a Comparative Perspective.'' *American Sociological Review* 51, 4: 492–504.

———. 1989. ''Coexisting Organizational Forms in Hungary's Emerging Mixed Economy.'' In *Remaking the Economic Institutions of Socialism: China and Eastern Europe*, ed. Victor Nee and David Stark, 32–94. Stanford, Calif.: Stanford University Press.

———. 1990. ''Privatization in Hungary: From Plan to Market or From Plan to Clan?'' Working Papers on Transitions from State Socialism, no. 90.2. Ithaca, N.Y.: Center for International Studies, Cornell University.

Szelenyi, Ivan. 1986–87. ''The Prospects and Limits of the East European New Class Project: An Auto-critical Reflection on 'The Intellectuals on the Road to Class Power.' '' *Politics and Society* 15, 2:103–44.

———. 1988. *Socialist Entrepreneurs: Embourgeoisement in Rural Hungary*. Madison: University of Wisconsin Press.

————. 1989. ''Eastern Europe in an Epoch of Transition: Toward a Socialist Mixed Economy?'' In *Remaking the Economic Institutions of Socialism: China and Eastern Europe*, ed. Victor Nee and David Stark, 208–32. Stanford, Calif.: Stanford University Press.

U.S. General Accounting Office. 1990. *Eastern Europe: Donor Assistance and Reform Efforts*. GAO/NSIAD-91-21. Gaithersburg, Md.: U.S. General Accounting Office.

Venys, Ladislaw. 1991. ''The Political Economy of Privatization in Czechoslovakia.'' Paper presented at the East Central European Study Group, Center for European Studies, Harvard University.

Weinstein, James. 1968. *The Corporate Ideal and the Liberal State*. Boston: Beacon Press.

Weiss, Linda. 1984. ''The Italian State and Small Business.'' *Archives Europeennes de Sociologie* 25, 2: 214–41.

————. 1988. *Creating Capitalism: The State and Small Business Since 1945*. New York: Basil Blackwell.

White, Lawrence. 1982. ''The Motor Vehicle Industry.'' In *Government and Technical Progress: A Cross-Industry Analysis*, ed. Richard Nelson, 411–50. New York: Pergamon Press.

Wolf, Charles. 1988. *Markets or Governments: Choosing Between Imperfect Alternatives*. Cambridge: Massachusetts Institute of Technology Press.

Young, Brigitte. 1991. ''The Dairy Industry: From Yeomanry to the Institutionalization of Multilateral Governance.'' In *Governance of the American Economy*, ed. John L. Campbell, J. Rogers Hollingsworth, and Leon N. Lindberg, 236–58. New York: Cambridge University Press.

Zysman, John. 1983. *Governments, Markets, and Growth*. Ithaca, N.Y.: Cornell University Press.

9. Institutional Cooperation in Japanese and German Capitalism

Marco Orrù

In recent decades, the capitalist economies of Japan and Germany have shown unmatched strength and resilience in the face of international economic downturns that have prompted the decline of other major industrial nations like the United States and the United Kingdom.[1] Economists, business experts, political scientists, students of organizations, and economic sociologists have in various ways sought to identify the distinguishing features that make some economies more successful than others in the international arena, and the German and Japanese economies have received a good share of attention in their own right (for Germany cf. Katzenstein 1987, 1989; Leaman 1988; for Japan cf. Dore 1987; Sato and Hoshino 1984; Caves and Uekusa 1976). But a direct, detailed comparison between these two major economies has been absent (a rare exception: Shigeyoshi and Bergmann 1984). This neglect is particularly puzzling since the capitalist structures of the two countries show a remarkable number of similarities when observed side by side.

Both Germany and Japan are poor in natural resources and have a relatively small agricultural sector. Their industrial activities are concentrated mostly in similar manufacturing areas like electrical products and electronics, automobile manufacturing, mechanical engineering, and steel, and in each area a few large corporations stand out as sector leaders. Both countries have a highly educated, highly skilled, well-paid, and disciplined labor force. Also, in both Germany and Japan a significant share of economic activities is devoted to the export of goods that are valued around the world for their high quality. The role of each country within its own economic region also displays similarities: Japan dominates the East Asian and Southeast Asian region and is making significant inroads into mainland China, and Germany dominates Western Europe and the former Soviet Union. Similar relations of regional interdependence can also be observed, for instance, between Japan and Taiwan on the one hand, and between Germany and Italy on the other hand. And yet no study has sought to explain systematically the remarkable affinity between the economic structures of two countries, which are geographically and culturally so far apart.

The neglect of a Japan–Germany comparison is easy to explain. In the past twenty years, especially in the United States, researchers have been fascinated by the East Asian economic miracle and have sought to identify broad cultural features like the Confucian work ethic to account for East Asia's success story (cf. Nakane 1970 and Silin 1976). In the process, the distinctive variation of economic structures in different East Asian countries like South Korea, Taiwan, and Japan was often lost by the wayside (an exception: Hamilton and Biggart 1988). In a parallel fashion, less attention was devoted to the success stories of Western economies like Germany, France, and Italy, and the variation in Western capitalist economies was likewise downplayed. The emphasis fell, instead, on the sharp contrast between capitalism in East Asia and capitalism in the West, especially in the United States (cf. Berger 1984).

Another major reason for the neglect of Japan–Germany comparison derives from the fragmentation of approaches to the study of economic structures. Political scientists have often claimed a primacy for the role of the state, or of other political institutions, in directing and shaping economic structures (cf. Weiss 1988; Evans, Rueschemeyer, and Skocpol 1985). Economists have looked at domestic and international markets and competitive advantages to infer the direction taken by different economies (cf. Porter 1990). Anthropologists have sought to identify sets of values or cultural practices that can be shown to influence economic development (cf. Redding 1990). Each approach provides worthwhile insights, but when taken by themselves, they prevent one from conceiving the possibility that, in fact, countries with different political structures, with varying competitive advantages, and with widely different cultures, could develop remarkably similar economic structures.

Recent trends in economic sociology (cf. Dore 1986; Hamilton and Biggart 1988), in organizational analysis (cf. March and Olsen 1984; DiMaggio and Powell 1991; Gerlach 1991), and in political sciences (cf. Zysman 1983; Samuels 1987; and Katzenstein 1989) have sought to overcome the problems of a sectorial, unidirectional analysis of economic and political structures in favor of an approach that incorporates several levels of analysis and their interrelations. The focus on an institutional approach and on the study of patterned interrelations among institutions has developed simultaneously (and often independently) as the way for different social science disciplines to advance the understanding of ever more complex economic, political, and social structures. The common argument is that markets, cultures, state policies, or formal organizational features cannot isolatedly provide a satisfactory account for the emergence or persistence of an observed type of capitalist economy. Instead, researchers advocate the need to integrate multiple levels of analysis to show how different institutional spheres are interconnected and have a cumulative interactive effect in shaping economic structures.

In this chapter I seek to identify the overarching logic of German and Japanese capitalist structures by utilizing an institutional approach that incorporates and analyzes the interactions within and among political, economic, and organizational factors, among others. Focusing on the broad features of these interactions, I highlight a pervasive organizational logic of mutual adjustment that characterizes the economic and social structure of both countries. Mutual adjustment pervades German and Japanese economies with regard to a broad range of institutional actors: industrial organizations, educational institutions, labor unions, financial institutions, educational institutions, federal and state bureaucracies, and political bodies. What is striking in both societies is the extent to which different institutional actors are able to develop a shared community of intents that are translated into widely supported national economic policies. In the economic structures of both Germany and Japan, institutional cooperation appears within institutions (e.g., work organization within firms, internal structure of labor unions, business groups' arrangements) and between institutions (e.g., between labor unions and industrial corporations, between educational institutions and industrial firms, among subcontracting firms, and between political bodies and business associations). Institutional cooperation can be identified as a key feature of the overarching organizational logic of both economies.

To show how institutional cooperation is a major feature in the capitalist structures of Japan and Germany I present my argument in four parts. First, I provide national statistics for both countries to assess how the two economies compare side by side in general terms. Second, I analyze each country's industrial structure to highlight their organizational distinctiveness. Third, I compare Japan's and Germany's capitalist structures in terms of contributing institutional sectors, and I highlight the patterns of close interaction and collaboration within and among these sectors. Fourth, I summarize the comparative overview of the Japanese and German economies by further elaborating the concept of capitalist cooperation as a key framework for understanding the institutional foundations of both economies.

The Economies of Japan and Germany

Germany's unification is today a political reality, but the forty-five years of division into East Germany and West Germany since World War II created two very different economies. It would be misleading to treat the German economic structure as a unified whole; instead, West Germany will be our comparative case. As unification becomes an economic reality, the traits of West Germany's economic structure will likely come to characterize Germany in its entirety. My analysis of Germany therefore is based on West Germany's economic structure.

Japan and Germany are, respectively, the second- and third-ranking capitalist economies in the world. Both countries, having suffered total devastation during World War II, proceeded in the postwar decades to a vigorous rebuilding of their shattered economies. Today, their economic and financial strengths challenge

Table 9.1

Summary Statistics on Germany and Japan, 1986

Category	West Germany	Japan
Area (sq. km.)	248,667	371,857
Population (1986)	61,080,000	121,490,000
Population density	246	327
Total civilian employees	25,267,000	58,530,000
Percentage in agriculture	5.3	8.5
Percentage in industry	40.9	34.5
Percentage in services	53.7	57.1
GDP (billion US$)	892	1,956
GDP per capita (US$)	14,611	16,109
Exports as percentage of GDP	27.2	10.8
Imports as percentage of GDP	21.3	6.5
Literacy rate (in percent)	99	99
Population per physician (1982)	431	735
Television sets per 1,000	373	580

Sources: OECD Economic Surveys, Germany (July 1988); *Japan Statistical Yearbook,* 1988; *Statistisches Jahrbuch 1988 für die Bundesrepublic Deutschland; Information Please Almanac 1990* (Boston: Houghton Mifflin).

and sometimes come out ahead of the United States. For example, a 1988 rank ing of the world's fifty largest commercial banks shows that twenty-three of them are from Japan and five are from Germany, while just four are from the United States.[2] Table 9.1 shows major comparative statistics for Germany and Japan.

Japan's population is twice the size of Germany's, and its gross domestic pro duct (GDP) is over twice as large; but overall size aside, the two countries show similar aggregate statistics. Both economies have high civilian employment (41 percent in Germany, 48 percent in Japan) when compared with other industrial ized countries like France (38 percent) or the Netherlands (35 percent). More over, as Table 9.2 shows, Japan and Germany display the highest share of workers employed in industry among industrialized countries (41 percent for Germany, 35 percent for Japan). This compares with 31 percent in the United Kingdom, 28 percent in the United States, and 25 percent in Canada.

The economies of Japan and Germany rest indisputably on a very strong in dustrial manufacturing base, and this fact is all the more significant when one considers that the same two countries pay some of the highest wages for indus trial workers around the world. Both countries boast a highly educated labor force, with Japan having the highest number of scientists and engineers (around 70 per 10,000 workers), ahead of the United States and Germany[3]. Data on 1987 nonmilitary research and development activities also show a larger share of the gross national product (GNP) invested in Japan (2.8 percent) and Germany (2.6

Table 9.2

**Share of Civilian Employment in Industry for
Selected Industrialized Countries, 1986**

Country	Percentage
Germany	40.9
Japan	34.5
Italy	33.1
France	31.3
United Kingdom	30.9
United States	27.7
Canada	25.3

Source: OECD Labor Force Statistics for 1986.

percent) compared with the United States (1.8 percent).

Not only do Germany and Japan lead industrialized nations in their share of manufacturing activities, they also lead industrialized economies in the absolute size of export activities. In 1986, Germany exported goods worth $242 billion, and Japan's exports amounted to $211 billion, compared with France's $119 billion and the United Kingdom's $107 billion. The United States' 1986 exports added up to slightly more than Japan's in absolute terms, but amounted to only 5 percent of the United States total GDP, compared to Germany's whopping 27 percent and Japan's 11 percent.[4] The destination of exports from the two countries differs geographically, according to regional market structures. Most German exports (75 percent) go to other European countries, almost 10 percent go to the United States, and only 2 percent go to Japan. Japanese exports are more widely distributed. Thirty-seven percent of Japanese exports go to the United States, 30 percent to the rest of Asia, and 22 percent to European countries. Despite their geographic diversity, the content of Japanese and German exports is remarkably similar. The largest shares of Germany's exports are in machinery (23 percent), automobiles (19 percent), chemical products (13 percent), and electronics (6 percent). Japan's largest exports are in automobiles (28 percent), machinery (23 percent), and electronics (18 percent).[5] The similarity is not accidental; Japanese industrial policy has sought to emulate Germany's industrial structure for several decades. Magaziner and Hout report: "By 1985, the Japanese Economic Planning Agency hopes that Japan will have a structure similar to the structure of Germany's exports of manufactured goods in the mid-1970s" (cf. Magaziner and Hout 1981, p. 8).

The industrial structure of Japan and Germany is similar in yet another respect. In both countries, large industrial corporations are the leaders of their national economies in both domestic and international markets. Brand names like Toyota, Toshiba, and NEC are household words in Japan and abroad, just in the same way as Volkswagen, Siemens, and Basf are well known in Germany and throughout the world. Table 9.3 lists the top twenty industrial businesses from Japan and from Germany in 1988 to illustrate how the top corporations in the two countries compare. Except for the presence of large German chemical companies (Basf, Hoechst, and Bayer), the makeup of the two lists is remarkably similar. The top twenty corporations in both countries span six major industrial sectors: motor vehicles and parts, electronics, metal industries, computers, industrial and farm equipment, and oil refining.

Automobile manufacturing constitutes a large share of top corporations in both countries (five for Germany, six for Japan), illustrating an additional similarity of industrial strategies in the two economies.

Research and development activities are given high priority (cf. Porter 1990). Research and development investments by private corporations are heavily emphasized, especially within large industrial firms in both Japan and Germany. Table 9.4 shows top-ranking corporate research and development spenders in both countries; all firms listed rank within the top twenty corporations included in Table 9.3.

While large manufacturing corporations dominate the economic activities in both countries, state ownership of manufacturing firms is nearly absent. Of Japan's 159 corporations listed in Fortune's International 500 in 1988, only one (Japan Tobacco) was government owned. Of Germany's 53 top corporations, only 2 (Salzgitter and Saarbergwerke) belonged to the government. This compares with 14 government-owned industrial corporations from France, 7 from India, and 5 from Finland in the same International 500 list. A similar absence of state ownership can be observed with regard to financial institutions. Of the largest 100 banks outside the United States in 1988, 31 are Japanese, but only one of these banks is government owned; Germany lists 11 banks, of which only 2 are owned by the state. This compares with 7 government-owned banks from Italy, and 4 from France in the same top 100 list. Overall, with respect to both industrial and financial activities, the Japanese and the German governments seem, comparatively speaking, to keep their direct involvement in their national economies to a minimum.

Indisputably, both Japanese and German large corporations play a major role in the international economy as well as in their respective domestic economies. But it would be misleading to think that they alone account for these economies' industrial prowess. Porter remarks: ''While there is a mixture of large and small firms, German international success is built to a surprising extent on small- and medium-sized firms, something often not well understood by observers of the German economy'' (Porter 1990, p. 374). Data on the distribution of manufacturing enterprises by number of employees from 1986 show that even when ex-

Table 9.3

Top Twenty German and Japanese Corporations in "Fortune's International 500" 1988

	West Germany			Japan			
Name	Sector	Sales	Employees	Name	Sector	Sales	Employees
Daimler-Benz	40	41,818	338,749	Toyota	40	50,790	86,082
Siemens	36	34,129	355,000	Hitachi	36	41,331	263,996
Volkswagen	40	33,696	252,066	Matsushita	36	33,922	134,186
Basf	28	24,960	134,834	Nissan	40	29,097	108,716
Hoechst	28	23,308	164,527	Toshiba	36	25,441	122,000
Bayer	28	23,026	165,700	Honda	40	22,236	58,320
Thyssen	28	16,796	127,778	NEC	36	19,626	102,452
Bosch	33	15,747	167,778	Nippon Steel	33	17,109	67,766
BMW	40	11,762	58,000	Mitsub Elec	36	16,857	75,795
Ruhrkohle	10	11,750	120,341	Mazda	40	15,151	28,027
Mannesmann	45	11,620	121,782	Fujitsu	44	14,797	94,825
Ford-Werke	40	10,951	49,530	Mitsubishi Mot	40	14,183	25,600
Adam Opel	40	9,936	52,675	Mitsubishi H.I.	45	13,398	56,100
Metall G.	33	8,757	25,132	Nippon Oil	29	12,773	10,178
Man	45	8,639	61,901	Sony	36	10,134	60,500
Krupp	29	8,385	63,391	Sanyo	36	9,376	39,179
Veba Oel	27	6,788	17,156	Bridgestone	30	9,296	88,148
Bertelsmann	44	6,539	41,961	IBM Japan	44	9,270	21,061
IBM Deutsch	28	6,471	30,712	Isuzu	40	9,268	24,443
Henkel	28	5,833	35,943	Nippondenso	40	8,962	47,359
Total sales in millions of $		320,911				383,017	
Total employees			2,382,958				1,514,733
Average sales per firm		16,046				19,151	
Average employees per firm			119,148				75,737
Average sales per employee		134,669				252,861	

Sector codes:: 10 = Mining; 27 = Publishing and printing; 28 = Chemicals; 29 = Petroleum refining; 30 = Rubber products; 33 = Metals; 36 = Electronics; 40 = Motor vehicles and parts; 44 = Computers; 45 = Industrial/Farm equipment; Sales are in millions of US$.

Table 9.4

**Top Corporate Research and Development
Spenders in Japan and Germany, 1989**

	Japan			Germany	
Firm	US$ (million)	Sales (in percent)	Firm	US$ (million)	Sales (in percent)
Hitachi	2,190	9.9	Siemens	3,684	11.2
Matsushita	2,140	7.9	Daimler-Benz	2,927	8.2
Toyota	1,190	3.9	Bayer	1,404	6.1
NEC	1,780	10.2	Hoechst	1,379	5.9
Fujitsu	1,740	12.8	Volkswagen	1,198	3.5

Source: Business Week, June 15, 1990, pp. 75, 122.

cluding manufacturing firms with less than 20 employees, large German firms (with 200 or more workers) account for less than 17 percent of the total number of enterprises. Large Japanese firms, then, make up an even smaller share of the total (a little over 6 percent).

Table 9.5 shows significant differences in the two countries' structure of manufacturing enterprises. Overall, Japan has stronger industrial muscle than Germany, but it has relatively fewer large corporations, and their average size is smaller than that of their German counterparts. Later in this chapter, we focus on the organizational features that account for differences between the two countries. For now it should suffice to point out that industrial collaboration among firms of different sizes is a distinctive feature of both the German and Japanese economies—although a much stronger feature in Japan than in Germany.

Collaborative arrangements among large industrial corporations and top financial institutions have been described by the business press as characteristic features of both German and Japanese capitalism. The casual reader is well acquainted with the notion of ''Japan Inc.''—the dense web among large banks, industrial corporations, national bureaucracies, and business associations that make the Japanese economy behave as one integrated conglomerate. But a similar metaphor is also extended to Germany, as in this journalistic report: ''In West Germany, major industrial groups are interlocked in a web of big banks and government ministries, sharing board members and shareholders. They are often called on to help bolster Germany Inc.''[6] In a recent *Business Week* cover story on Mitsubishi, the giant Japanese conglomerate, the authors compared the interdependence of Mitsubishi member firms with ''Deutsche Bank's large industrial holdings in Germany.''[7] What is most intriguing about the similarity in the industrial structures of the two countries is that colla-

Table 9.5

**Manufacturing Enterprises by Number of Employees
in Germany and Japan, 1986**

			West Germany		
Size	Firms	Percent	Employees	Percent	Average
20–49	16,634	43.5	545,682	7.9	32.8
50–199	15,183	39.7	1,466,708	21.3	96.6
200+	6,436	16.8	4,869,853	70.8	756.7
Total	38,253	100.0	6,882,243	100.0	179.9
			Japan		
20–49	76,415	65.2	2,297,000	24.3	30.1
50–199	33,494	28.6	2,999,000	31.7	89.5
200+	7,226	6.2	4,154,000	44.0	574.9
Total	117,135	100.0	9,450,000	100.0	80.7

Sources: Japan Statistical Yearbook, 1988; Statistiches Jahrbuch 1988 für die Bundesrepublic Deutschland.

boration between giant Japanese and German business groups is soon going to be an economic reality. Talks between Daimler-Benz and Mitsubishi top executives, reports *Business Week*, "could lead Germany and Japan's two largest business groups into joint ventures ranging from building a car plant in the Soviet Union to designing hypersonic planes able to fly in space."

It is clear that Germany and Japan are among the most successful industrialized countries in the world, and it should be equally clear from this section's overview that there are many similarities in the characteristics of these two economies. Yet it would be erroneous to assume that if the two countries have achieved similar results they must have utilized similar strategies throughout. In fact, if one looks closely at the organizational patterns of business in the two countries, one will detect along with numerous similarities clear, remarkable differences. I want to highlight organizational differences and similarities in the next section.

The Structure of Japanese and German Business

Studies of Japanese and other successful Asian and non-Asian economies have often been offered as examples of economic structures that disprove the superior efficiency of vertically integrated business activities based on the reduction of transaction costs (cf. Dore 1987; Hamilton and Biggart 1988; Lorenzoni and Ornati 1988). The attempt to show how subcontractual arrangements can display a reduction of transaction costs equal or even superior to vertically integrated, in-house production arrangements was worthwhile; but such attempts might have gone overboard by assuming that the deep structure of the two production models would have to be as different from each other as their variation in the surface structure. On the one hand, Granovetter (1985) endeavored to show that opportunism and deceit are in no way absent from economic transactions among vertically integrated businesses. On the other hand, Dore (1983) demonstrated that subcontractual relations among manufacturing firms in Japan can be as nearly free of any opportunistic and deceitful economic behavior. However, it would be unwarranted to use these authors' evidence to turn transaction-cost theory on its head and claim that subcontractual relations are necessarily more cost-efficient than vertically integrated relations. Simply put, matters of economic efficiency cannot be settled either way in theoretical, abstract terms.

The organizational structures of industrial sectors in Japan and Germany provide empirical evidence that subcontractual arrangements are not necessarily superior to vertical integration or vice versa. One needs to go beyond the external structure of firms to meaningfully understand the economic logic that drives them. Table 9.6 illustrates external organizational differences by comparing paired sets of German and Japanese industrial and financial corporations.

Across a variety of sectors, from banking to motor vehicles and parts manufacturing to electronics to steel, Japanese corporations with equal or higher sales figures of a paired German corporation employ, on average, one-third to one-half the number of workers. Automation of production is one significant factor in reducing the size of the work force in large Japanese firms; but the main reason for the variation in firm size between Japan and Germany is to be found in the extensive subcontracting arrangements that characterize the entire Japanese production system, compared with the vertically integrated and internalized manufacturing system of most German firms. The automobile industries of the two countries provide a good comparative illustration.

In a study of Japan's automobile industry, Shimokawa (1985) describes the production system as "based primarily on a powerful *keiretsu* relationship between automobile manufacturers and technologically advanced primary parts manufacturers and secondarily on numerous small and medium-sized parts producers" (p. 6). Thus, Shimokawa assesses one large automobile manufacturer in Japan as having 168 primary subcontractors, 4,000 secondary subcontractors, and 31,600 tertiary subcontractors. This contrasts sharply with the German automobile manufacturing patterns described by Streeck:

> West German auto assemblers are highly vertically integrated, and this [is] one major difference from their Japanese competitors. . . . The apparent preference for making rather than buying parts seems in part to be accounted for by pressures from the works councils for high and stable employment. . . . There is also a preference for large, integrated plants; the biggest German plant, VW Wolfsburg, employs no less than sixty-five thousand people. (1989, p. 121)

To be sure, there is variation within the German organizational landscape. Manufacturers in Germany's southern region are more likely to operate on the

Table 9.6

Paired German and Japanese Corporations by Sector, 1988

Sector	Japanese firms	Employees	German Firms	Employees
Autos	Toyota	86,082	Daimler-Benz	338,749
Auto parts	Nippondenso	47,359	Bosch	167,780
Banking	Dai-Ichi Kangyo	18,663	Deutsche Bank	54,769
Computers	IBM Japan	21,061	IBM Deutschland	30,712
Electronics	Matsushita	134,186	Siemens	353,000
Ind. Equip.	Mitsubishi H. I.	56,100	Mannesmann	122,782
Oil	Nippon Oil	10,178	Veba Oël	17,156
Steel	Nippon Steel	67,766	Thyssen	127,778

Source: Fortune, July 31, 1989, pp. 291–94 and 320–21.

basis of interfirm networks than their counterparts in the Ruhr Valley in the north; but when they are compared with the extensive Japanese subcontract patterns, even southern Germany's production networks of Daimler-Benz, BMW, Bosch, and others in the Baden Württemberg region appear as internalized production systems. BMW, with 58,000 employees, is a relatively small automobile manufacturer by German standards, but Japan's Mazda, with only 28,000 workers, posted nearly 30 percent higher sales figures than BMW in 1988. (See Table 9.3.)

The organizational differences between German and Japanese manufacturing were already suggested by the figures in Table 9.5. Germany has almost as many firms with 200 or more workers as Japan, but half as many firms with 50 to 199 workers, and only one-fifth the number of small firms with 20 to 49 workers. In this last category, Japan counts over 76,000 manufacturing firms employing close to 3.3 million workers, while Germany counts fewer than 17,000 firms employing a little over half a million workers. Small entrepreneurship is much more widespread in Japan than in Germany; 1983 data on the percentage of salaried employees in industry show Japan, Italy, and Belgium at the low end with 71 to 74 percent, while Germany, Canada, and the United States rank at the high end with 87 to 90 percent salaried employees (cf. Nanetti 1988, p. 12). The difference between German and Japanese organizational patterns is emphatically underlined by these statistics.[8]

The surface differences between Germany and Japan are obvious, but we would be mistaken in equating the internalization of production by large German manufacturers with the mass-production style of United States manufacturers who also tend to internalize production processes. Herrigel (1989) described the organizational pattern of German industrial corporations, especially in northern areas, as one of "autarkic-firm-based industrial order." Herrigel explains that in Germany, "Firms grew very large very rapidly because the lack of surrounding infrastructure forced them to incorporate most of the stages of manufacture under their control" (p. 193). But with regard to these autarkic firms, Herrigel (1989) argues:

> The logic behind production organization was the opposite of that in large series and mass production processes: instead of building rigidity into process organization in the plant to produce a large series standard product efficiently, these firms sought to create structures—workshops—that enhanced the firm's ability to reorganize production quickly. (p. 194)

Herrigel characterizes these large industrial firms as "a collection of specialized workshops." Thus, despite the difference in the external structure of German and Japanese manufacturing, they are internally much closer to each other organizationally than either of them is to large firms in the United States. Both German and Japanese firms appear to emphasize flexible production and specialization of tasks. Piore and Sabel (1984) detected the similarities between the two economies despite different external patterns of organization, remarking:

> In West Germany the changes [toward craft production] are often centered in the large firms, rather than in the network of their suppliers. West German firms are decentralizing internally, instead of dissolving into their supplier networks (the limiting case in Italy) or functioning as assemblers of customized components (the limiting case in Japan). (pp. 229–30)

If both German and Japanese manufacturers are able to achieve high levels of flexible specialization through the different avenues of extensive subcontracting (in Japan) and of large autarkic firms (in Germany), then the reasons for their similar economic efficiency must be sought below the surface, in the deeper institutional features that characterize the organization of each economy.

Institutional Cooperation in Japan and Germany

It should be apparent, by now, that the economic organizations observed in Germany and in Japan are by no means identical; instead, they differ substantially in how they set the boundaries of individual corporations and to what extent they rely on subcontracting with external firms. Japan's manufacturing structure is often depicted as a giant production pyramid. The Ministry for International Trade and Industry (MITI) estimates that more than 50 percent of manufacturing firms with 300 or fewer workers are subcontractors for larger Japanese manufacturing firms. "One of Japan's top electronics makers has well over 6,000 subcontractors in that pyramid."[9]

The picture in German manufacturing is quite different. The ten largest manufacturing enterprises in Germany literally dominate the industrial landscape, and their dominance has increased substantially in recent decades. In 1965, the top ten industrial firms accounted for 15.6 percent of Germany's total industrial turnover and for 13.4 percent of total employment in industry. In 1980, the same top ten firms accounted for 20.7 percent of turnover and for 22.7 percent of industrial employment (Leaman 1988, p. 66). In comparison, the 1,001 firms belonging to Japan's largest business groups employed, in 1985, only 9.4 percent of the industrial work force.[10]

The striking differences in the industrial structure of Germany and of Japan are too obvious to be overlooked; yet, these differences are not as significant as the similarities that underlie, in both economies, the internal structure of industrial firms and the relationship among the various institutional actors in the economy. I call the similar overarching characteristic of both countries' economic structure *institutional cooperation*—that is, a formulation of economic strategies and a practice of production based on the emergence of collectively shared responsibilities. This phenomenon of institutional cooperation can be shown at three distinct analytical levels: It characterizes (1) industrial relations within firms, (2) relations across institutional realms pertinent to economic action, and (3) relations between the private sector and the state in the two societies. Let us compare the Japanese and German economic structures in each of these areas in turn.

Internal Cooperation of Business Firms

Japan's labor relations have often been considered culturally unique for their emphasis on lifetime employment, seniority-based advancement, consensus-building decision making, and the structuring of manufacturing activities around responsible production teams. These organizational traits have often been contrasted with industrial relations in Western economies (especially in the United States and Britain), which emphasize elasticity in hiring and firing workers, performance-based job classifications that set advancement careers, highly stratified hierarchies for decision making, and narrow interpretation of job-related tasks and responsibilities. Such divergence in labor relations models, however, is neither universal nor unchanging.

Streeck (1984) identified a convergence trend between German and Japanese models of industrial relations, where German firm relations have increasingly come to resemble those of the Japanese. Streeck lists four evolving features of

German industrial relations:

> (1) The emergence of a system of stable and secure (guaranteed) employment for workers in large companies. . . . (2) The adoption of a "human resources" approach to manpower management by large companies [which] aims at increased flexibility of manpower use in spite of employment stability. . . . (3) The works council has been incorporated into the management of the manpower function of large companies. . . . (4) There is a growing identification of the interests of workers in large firms with the interests of their employing organization as a production unit competing in the market. (pp. 112–13)

These four characteristics of their industrial relations lead Streeck to argue that German firms are moving toward a cooperative model of firm management approaching that of the Japanese—although Streeck is quick to qualify: "Clearly, the large enterprise as an interest community between capital and labor is much more apparent in Japan than it is in Germany" (p. 113).

Recent empirical studies have shown that organizational features of German manufacturing firms differ significantly from those of other European economies. Maurice et al. (1980) highlighted German firms' distinctive organization of manufacturing, compared with British and French firms. The authors observed, "In the works the flexibility and cooperation between different production jobs was greater in Germany than in the other countries" (p. 70). Hartmann et al. (1983) compared British and German manufacturing firms' skill utilization in introducing computerized machine tools, and argued:

> In Germany CNC was more visibly used to reduce training differentials between technical staff and the shop-floor personnel, to increase the tradesman's status, to encourage even greater flexibility in production, and to reduce the "decision-making overload" on top management. (p. 229)

With a similar thrust, Schumann (1990) studied the trends emerging in Germany's automobile, machine building, and chemical industries and identified an increasing reliance of German firms on "teams of workers collectively responsible for a whole system of automated machinery" (p. 4) Schumann writes:

> Nowhere in our empirical research did we come across an intensifying division of labor. Actually, the contrary is predominant. . . . Current attempts at gaining efficiency rely on the integration of functions and more complex responsibilities. (p. 24)

As it pertains to their internal organization, it seems evident that both Japanese and German firms similarly emphasize the diffusion of responsibilities throughout the production process, the flexibility and interchangeability of tasks, the substantial reduction of managerial hierarchies, and consensus-based decision making.

Historically, different factors accounted for the development of similar organizational features in Germany and Japan. The German model is greatly indebted to the emergence of distinctive labor–management relations in German industry after World War II, sanctioned by the Co-Determination Act of 1951 and the Works Constitution Act of 1952. Streeck (1984) describes these two pieces of legislation as follows:

> Two different channels of employee representation in German industrial organizations: co-determination at the workplace . . . which is exercised through work councils, and co-determination in the enterprise, which is exercised through work force representatives in the supervisory board and, to an extent, the management board. (p. 95)

Streeck's assessment of co-determination is that, on the one hand, it narrowed the organizational control of management over hiring and firing but, on the other hand, it broadened the potential utilization of a firm's stable work force. "Co-determination has contributed to growing organizational rigidities and at the same time has provided the organizational instruments to cope with such rigidities without major losses in efficiency" (p. 105).

Park (1984) describes Japan's distinctive firm relations as having emerged historically to address the need for democratization of the economy, increased productivity, elimination of management/workers imbalances, and strengthening of the labor movement. The result was a Labor–Management Consultation System, which first emerged in 1920 but did not see extensive adoption of implementation until the 1950s. The Japanese participatory system borrowed from the German Works Council and from the British Whitley Committee. But Park remarks: "Even though this system originated in Western Europe, there is no doubt that it has absorbed some typical Japanese traits" (p. 154). The German system, in comparison, keeps worker participation from entering top- or even middle-level managerial decision making.

The Japanese type of participation is a priori embedded into a management-centered economic system, whereas the Western European concept of participation is directed toward expanding the strength of labor unions representing workers' and employees' interests (Park 1984, p. 165).

Significantly, some German managers look with envy at industrial relations in Japan, wishing German workers would emulate their Japanese counterparts in being loyal to their firm, ready to sacrifice, and prone to consensus; yet, comparatively speaking, industrial relations in Germany are much closer to the harmonious Japanese model than to the belligerent industrial relations found in other European countries.

> West German unions . . . have mastered the crises of the 1970s and 1980s far bet-
> ter than their counterparts in countries like Italy or the United Kingdom. . . .
> Their less flamboyant approach helped West German unions build a foundation
> for union power strong enough to outlast the institutional dislocations and struc-
> tural breaks in Western political economies after the first "oil shock." (Streeck
> 1990, p. 2)

Industrial relations in Japan and Germany display some differences, but overall,
they are comparatively similar to each other in the clear emphasis they give to
consensus seeking and cooperation in their industrial organizations. But the
cooperation within firms is significantly amplified and strengthened by the
larger framework of cooperation among the major institutional actors in the capitalist economies of both Japan and Germany. I turn to this economywide
cooperation in the next section.

Institutional Cooperation of Economic Actors

Researchers, especially in the United States, have been bewildered by the economic miracle that is Japan. But the more closely they look at the structure of
Japan's economy the less are they willing to see it as in any way comparable to
Western economies. The title of a business column by Blinder (1990) captures
the feeling: "There are Capitalists, then there are the Japanese." He explains:

> According to American doctrine, monopolies and cartels are economic
> pathologies. We are also wary of vertical integration, because captive suppliers or
> retailers may serve the interest of the dominant company rather than those of con-
> sumers. We worry that cozy relationships between upstream and downstream
> companies may lead to inefficiencies, so we favor arm's-length deals in which
> buyers seek the lowest prices.[11]

But the Japanese, Blinder argues, do business differently. When they need parts
supplied in their production process, or capital for business expansion, or a
network of retail outlets, the Japanese do not search in the market for the best
deal, but turn to the firms in their own business group. "To their way of thinking, long-term, reliable relationships cut costs as business partners learn from
and help one another." The Japanese government reinforces the cooperative
thrust of the private sector by allowing cross-holding of stocks among grouped
businesses to keep out foreign competition, by favoring domestic companies for
significant national projects, and by cooperating in research and development
activities.

Blinder's and other writers' descriptions of Japanese business practices are accurate, but researchers are mistaken in considering Japan's economic structure as unique and eminently non-Western. Too often, capitalism is equated with U.S. capitalism, disregarding a wide variation in the economic structure of such countries as France, Italy, and Germany. If we compare Germany's economic structure to the United States, it will be apparent that it differs from U.S. capitalism as much as Japanese capitalism does and that, in fact, it more closely resembles the latter than the former. In Germany, as in Japan, close ties and intensive collaboration obtain among industrial firms, financial institutions, local and central government, business associations, and labor unions. Zysman (1983) describes the cooperative quality of the German economic structure:

> The distinctive character of the German system of "organized private enterprise" depends on the combination of four elements: concentration, tolerated cartel-like arrangements, centralized semiofficial trade associations, and a tutelary banking system. (p. 252)

It is significant that the same four features Zysman attributes to the German economic structure also characterize Japan's economy. Let us examine each one in both countries.

Industrial concentration was already apparent when we assessed the extent to which large industrial firms dominate Germany's economic landscape.[12] Over 70 percent of industrial workers in Germany are employed by firms with 200 or more workers. But Japan also displays industrial concentration obtained through dense subcontracting; although small industrial firms are numerous, most of them do subcontracting work for large industrial firms. One insider reports: "Most people don't realize how extensive this system is. Many products are made entirely by smaller companies and simply labeled and packaged to look as if they were manufactured by one of Japan's 'giants.' "[13]

Historically, cartel like arrangements have also been a feature of German capitalism. German business historian Kocka (1897/1941) provided a detailed account of the emergence of cartels:

> Cartels were mostly voluntary agreements between concerns which remained independent and they had the aim of establishing a common policy in the market . . . . They served to limit competition, to stabilize prices and profits, and they tender toward a monopoly control of the market. In 1897 the legality of cartels was confirmed by the highest court of the Reich. (p. 563)

According to Kocka, the number of cartels rose dramatically, from only 4 in 1875, to 385 in 1905, to about 2,100 in 1930. Collusion among business enterprises was seen favorably by the Germans. Hardach (1980), for instance, points out that "labor unions usually expected better job security from cartels than from unrestricted competition . . . [they] regarded [them] as an intermediate stage in the industrial evolution toward socialism'' (p. 148). Hardach (1980) reasons as follows:

> Quite in contrast to the Anglo-American view, which connected competitive markets with equilibrium and monopolistic situations with indeterminacy and disorder, it was held [in Germany] that unrestricted competition was ''destructive'' and that cartels were an ''element of order.'' (p. 148)

Japan followed a different road to cartelization by organizing its financial and industrial structure around a limited number of large business groups to which most large corporations in Japan belong. The six largest groups are Mitsubishi, Mitsui, Sumitomo, Fuyo, DKB, and Sanwa. The historical roots of some of these business groups go back a long way. The House of Sumitomo was founded in 1590; the House of Mitsui goes back to 1615. But the emergence of the modern industrial groups occurred during the Meiji era, in the last third of the nineteenth century (cf. Gerlach 1991). Preferential financial, production, and trade operations obtain among members of each business group (cf. Orrù et al, 1989). Dore (1986) describes the business group philosophy: ''It is a bit like an extended family grouping, where business is kept as much as possible within the family, and a certain degree of give and take is expected to modify the adversarial pursuit of marked advantage'' (p. 178).

Business associations are major partners in shaping industrial policies in both Germany and Japan. Germany lists three powerful institutions: the Federation of German Industry (BDI), the Federation of German Employers' Association (BDA), and the Diet of German Industry and Commerce (DIHT).[14] As Zysman (1983) describes them, ''these organizations link German business to the government in an elaborate and centralized fashion. The federal constitution gives these associations consultative or semiofficial status that draws them into policymaking'' (p. 253). Japan lists four major business associations (the so-called *zaikai*): (1) *Keidanren* (the Federation of Economic Organizations), (2) *Keizai Doyukai* (Japan's Committee for Economic Development), (3) *Nikkeiren* (the Federation of Employers' Association), and (4) *Nihon Shoko Kaigisho* (Japan Chamber of Commerce and Industry). These four business associations interact closely with the Japanese government and the business bureaucracies, especially MITI and the Ministry of Finance, in the development of national industrial policies (cf. Taira and Wada 1986). Traditionally, these business associations have been headed by leaders of Japan's largest industrial and financial corporations (cf. Johnson 1982; Samuels 1987).

The banking system plays a ''tutelary role'' in the economic structures of both Germany and Japan. Schmiegelow and Schmiegelow (1990) point out the similarity between the two economies:

> The prevalence of indirect financing (of debt over equity financing), which char-

acterized Japan's "overborrowed" corporate sector until the mid-1970s, may have seemed vertiginous from the point of view of the Anglo-Saxon countries, but basically similar conditions prevail in West Germany even today. Both in Japan and in West Germany, this system has been the cornerstone of the formation of long-term corporatist relationships in which management performance of participating enterprises is controlled by banks rather than by the capital market. (p. 568)

"The German 'universal' banks, preeminent players in all financial markets, contrast sharply with the more specialized banks of the Anglo-American system. For 'universal' banks equity investments and loans are alternative means of providing corporate finance" (Zysman 1983, p. 64). The automobile sector provides a good illustration of Germany's tutelary banking system. Streeck (1989) explains:

> Bank representatives sit on all supervisory boards, either as shareholders or representing the proxy votes for shares they have in deposit. Each manufacturer has a long-standing relationship with one bank, which serves as *Hausbank*. (p. 120)

Deutsche Bank is the main bank for Volkswagen (VW) and for Daimler-Benz, Dresdner Bank for BMW, Bayerische Vereinsbank for Audi, Landesgirokasse for Porsche. The *Hausbank* often evaluates the financial and managerial soundness of industrial companies and takes decisive action when problems arise. Streeck reports: "In the VW crisis of 1974 the Deutsche Bank was crucial in stimulating reorganization by threatening, in a supervisory board meeting, to withhold further credit and let the company go to the receiver" (p. 120).

Large Japanese industrial firms are also under the tutelage of major financial institutions. The three largest shareholders of Toyota Motors are Mitsui Bank, Sanwa Bank, and Tokai Bank; Nissan Motors' largest shareholder is the Industrial Bank of Japan. Mazda Motors' main bank, Sumitomo Bank, was instrumental in rescuing Mazda from bankruptcy in the mid-1970s, when the bank absorbed Mazda's huge default risks (Sheard 1984). But beyond the one-on-one relations between individual banks and individual industrial firms, both German and Japanese banks have a privileged role in orchestrating their national economies.

As Ziegler, Bender, and Biehler (1985) report, "The efficiency of the German banking system and its close links with industry have often been cited as partial explanations for periods of rapid growth in German economic development" (p. 91). Historically, the authors explain, banks were actively involved in shaping Germany's industrial structure:

> The banks took an active part in founding new firms, issued shares and bonds on behalf of industrial enterprises, held financial participations, provided long- and

> short-term loans and kept close personal connections, especially through repre-
> sentation on supervisory boards of the joint stock companies which were the
> dominant legal form among large industrials. (p. 92)

Three banks dominate the financial landscape in today's Germany: Deutsche
Bank, Dresdner Bank, and Commerzbank. Germany's Ministry of Finance
estimated in 1979 that these three banks "held seventeen percent of all
participants and thirty-eight percent of the total stock value" (cited in Ziegler et
al. 1985, p. 106). In their analysis of interlocks in the boards of financial and industrial companies, Ziegler and colleagues argue:

> There seems to be a hierarchical structure: executives of the three big banks sat
> on the supervisory boards of production companies, while the reverse occurred
> much less frequently. . . . [However,] this structure may well be the result of co-
> optive efforts from the side of production companies rather than the banks' at-
> tempts at control. (pp. 106–7)

Compared to other industrialized countries, both Japanese and German industrial
corporations (especially the largest firms) rely more heavily on banks' long-term
credit rather than on equity to raise capital. The largest three banks in Germany
exert influence over about one-third of non-isolated industrial firms; thus, they
have strong direct links with industrial corporations. However, Ziegler and colleagues interpret the overall picture as follows:

> This does not seem to indicate one-sided bank control but more likely a coales-
> cence of major interests from both the financial and the non-financial sectors.
> Banks act more like integrators cross-connecting industrials from various eco-
> nomic sectors and other fractional interests. They even seem to avoid too close a
> relationship with any particular group of enterprises. (p. 110)

Japanese banks also play a central role in their economy. As in Germany, Japanese firms rely more heavily on bank loans than on equity. Each Japanese business group has its own main bank, which provides the bulk of loans for industrial firms belonging to the group and which dispatches directors to group firms. In
1985, Mitsubishi Petrochemical, a member of the Mitsubishi group, borrowed
32 percent of its capital from Mitsubishi financial institutions which held 20 percent of the firm's stocks. Three directors on Mitsubishi Petrochemicals were dispatched by the banks. Similarly, Sumitomo Cement borrowed 39 percent of its
capital from Sumitomo financial institutions, which held 19 percent of the firm's
stocks and had two directors dispatched to it by Sumitomo Bank.[14] The web
spun by major Japanese banks is not restricted to the influence over members of
their own business groups. For instance, Nippon Steel, the largest steel manufacturer that constitutes an independent industrial group, received financial loans

from Mitsubishi (9.6 percent), Mitsui (5.6 percent), Sumitomo (8.5 percent), Fuyo (8.9 percent), Dai-Ichi Kangyo Bank (DKB) (2.3 percent), Sanwa (8.2 percent), Tokai (3.2 percent), and Industrial Bank of Japan (IBJ) (9.6 percent). Accordingly, most lending financial institutions held somewhere between 1.6 and 3.4 percent of Nippon Steel's stocks.[15] The coordinating core of the Japanese economic structure, in the end, is constituted by Japan's largest financial institutions—which include life insurance companies, city banks, trust and banking institutions, and marine and fire insurance companies (Orrù 1991).

When considered together, the four structural features just outlined (concentration, cartels, business associations, and tutelary banking) all point to cooperative arrangements as characteristic of both Germany's and Japan's economic structures—especially when these are compared with the economic structures in most other industrialized countries. The uniqueness of Japanese and German capitalism resides in the close collaboration among large industrial firms, financial institutions, labor unions, business associations, and the government. Such collaboration rests on a view of national economic goals and priorities that is shared by all parties involved.

Cooperation of State and Private Sector

Political institutions in both Japan and Germany act as facilitators in the formulation and implementation of national industrial policies. On the one hand, they avoid direct involvement in industrial activities (as in France's *dirigiste* state) or in massively financing private industrial conglomerates (as in South Korea's powerful state banks); on the other hand, they avoid taking a minimalist stance of "governs best who governs least" typical of Anglo-Saxon economies (especially the conservative regimes of United Kingdom and the United States in the 1980s). Instead, the role played by both the German and the Japanese government is typically to facilitate the merging of interests among economic actors, rather than imposing unilateral decisions from the top down or keeping out of private businesses' way altogether.

The major political theme guiding the German economy since after World War II has been the principle of *Soziale Martktwirtschaft* (social market economy). Müller-Armack (1965) provided its classic definition:

> The Social Market Economy is a social and economic order. . . . The co-ordinated functions of the Social Market Economy do not conform exclusively to the mechanical rules of competition. Its principles of organization relate to the State and to society, both of which impress their notions of value and responsibilities on the whole system. . . [It is] a co-ordination . . . between . . . the market, the State and the social groups. (pp. 90–91)

The cooperation of institutional economic actors in Germany rests on the *Soziale*

Marktwirtschaft principle that the conflict of unrestrained competition should be mitigated by coordination and mutual adjustment. Müller-Armack argues that economic goals such as currency stability, full employment, growth, and equilibrium in the balance of payments require that "the institutional co-operation within the Government be organized on a permanent basis" (p. 101). With a slightly different vocabulary, but referring to the same principle, Körner (1971) speaks of "co-operative co-ordination . . . embracing the relevant State executive organs and representatives of several industries, sectors and groups" (p. 204). For example, Germany's policy of concerted action—Hardach (1980) explains—"sought to bring labor and management representatives together under the chairmanship of the minister of economies" (p. 202). As Katzenstein (1987) describes it, "Government by coalition, a system of cooperative federalism, and parapublic institutions are the three institutional nodes around which the politics of economic policy has unfolded in the Federal Republic" (p. 84). Katzenstein provides an example of the government's cooperation with the private sector during the 1960s coal-mining crisis:

> The West German approach . . . amounted to concentration through cooperation . . . . The federal government bought out on favorable terms virtually all private owned mines and consolidated the industry under a holding company in which it owned substantial equity. . . . Significantly, both business and unions were centrally involved in the development of energy policy. The government neither imposed its preferred solution on the industry nor permitted market forces simply to dictate outcomes. (p. 102)

The same attempt to strike a balance between competition and coordination found in German economic policy characterizes Japanese industrial policy. Johnson (1985, pp. 59–68) labels the dynamics of Japanese business "collusive rivalry"—a hybrid of competitive and cooperative forces. The organization of Japan's industrial structure around a few very large business groups makes it possible to simultaneously promote competition among large corporations in the same industrial sector while favoring close cooperation among firms that span across industrial sectors. The role of the government and of the national bureaucracy is not to impose its legislative fiat in private business, but rather to provide "administrative guidance." As Johnson describes it, "The Japanese government is extremely intrusive into the privately owned and managed economy, but it does this through market-conforming methods and in cooperation rather than confrontation with the private sector" (p. 61). In a similar vein, Samuels (1987) characterizes the relation between private business and the Japanese state as a "reciprocal consent" where the market and the state come to mutual accommodation. Reciprocal consent implies the mutual co-optation of private business in political economy issues and of the national government in the supervision of the industrial structure in the service of national interests.

The Japanese pattern of interaction between political institutions and the private sector is one of orchestrated consent and reciprocal support. For example, when Texaco took over Getty Oil in 1984, it sought to dispose of Getty's 50 percent shares of Mitsubishi Oil. The Mitsubishi Group decided to negotiate with Texaco for the purchase of Getty's shares. MITI supported Mitsubishi's move by announcing that it would use Section 27 of Japan's Foreign Exchange Law to block the sale of Mitsubishi Oil shares to foreign buyers (Sheard 1984, p. 23). This and many other examples of reciprocal support between the state and private business in Japan reflect "the explicit recognition of the indivisibility of economy and politics" (Johnson 1985, p. 64). The Japanese government considers it its own business to facilitate private businesses' pursuit of economic goals. Similarly, the German state's policy has been chiefly to promote economic growth and stability by providing the appropriate climate for a thriving and internationally competitive private business.

It should by now be apparent that if researchers are willing to abandon the preconceived notion that a unique "Asiatic" group centeredness characterizes Japan's economic structure, it then becomes possible to see how much of what we observe in Japanese business can also be observed in German business. Thus, it becomes possible to speak of typologies of capitalism, rather than resorting to culturally idiosyncratic models that vary endlessly from country to country. In relation to the German and Japanese economies' reliance on a centralized private sector and on an ideology of social partnership, Schmiegelow and Schmiegelow (1990) rightly observed that "analysts could speak of 'German Inc.,' at least as easily as of 'Japan Inc.' " (p. 570).

Conclusion

Neoclassical economic theory assumes that economic actors (whether individuals, firms, or other social groups) compete in the marketplace as isolated entities in their rational pursuit of self-interested, utilitarian goals. Adam Smith (1776/1977) identified the principles underlying modern capitalism's ideal type of economic action. Economic action is motivated by self-interest: "It is not from the benevolence of the butcher, the brewer, or the baker that we expect our dinner, but from their regard to their own interest" (p. 18). Economic order, accordingly, emerges from individualistic competition: "The individual intends only his own gain, and he is in this, as in many other cases, led by an invisible hand to promote an end which was no part of his intention" (p. 477). The neoclassical paradigm dominates economic theory and is embodied (to some extent) in the economic structures of countries like Great Britain and the United States. But it is questionable that the same paradigm could be said to apply to the economic structures we just examined in Germany and in Japan. Wallach (1985) argues the German case:

> Adam Smith's "invisible hand" and the support for the ultimate "laissez-faire" idea that government should not be involved in economic affairs has hardly had

> strong support in Germany, for early artisans felt they were protected by the government, and later corporations found government backing advantageous. (p. 236)

Dore (1983) makes the case for Japan:

> The Japanese, in spite of what their political leaders say at summit conferences about the glories of free enterprise in the Free World . . . have never caught up with Adam Smith. They have never managed actually to bring themselves to *believe* in the invisible hand. (p. 470)

One cannot easily dismiss the Japanese and German economies (the second and third largest, respectively, in the capitalist world) as simple aberrations from the ideal type of fully competitive free markets—much less so, since most other capitalist economies around the world are just as removed (although in different ways) from such an ideal type. The institutional cooperation characterizing Germany and Japan needs to be studied and understood in its own right, as a distinctive pattern of economic action with status equal to that of other typologies of modern capitalism like the laissez-faire economies of Great Britain and the United States, the family entrepreneurship economies of Italy and Taiwan, and the state-orchestrated economies of France and India. In this chapter, I concentrated on the German and Japanese economic structures to evince a typology of capitalist cooperation and to highlight its distinguishing features as illustrated by the two case studies.

Table 9.7 shows synoptically how cooperation is a significant component across a variety of organizational dimensions—within firms and across institutional sectors of the economy—in both Japanese and German capitalism. Cooperation is not a secondary feature, but a structural constant of both economies; it is not a behavioral afterthought of individuals but an institutionalized principle that guides economic action at different structural and organizational levels.

The institutional cooperation characterizing the Japanese and the German economies demonstrates that their economic success does not come from competition alone, but also from a planned and balanced integration of individual and institutional actors, of private and public policies, of different social classes and political groups, in both the economic and the social arenas. Katzenstein (1989) describes the historically resilient consensus of Germany's political economy: "social welfare and economic efficiency are not antithetical but mutually reinforcing" (p. 353). Accordingly, cooperation among labor unions, industrial corporations, financial institutions, governmental agencies, and other institutional actors is taken to be the obvious way of doing business. Dore (1983) comments that in Japan economic action is pervasively accompanied by the "need to be benevolent as well as self-interested." Dore explains: "It is not just that benevolence is the best policy . . . the best way to material success. . . .

Table 9.7

A Typology of Capitalist Cooperation

	Japan	Germany
Intra-firm organization	Team responsibility Quality training	Flexibility of tasks Highly skilled workers
Labor-management relations	Consultation system	Codetermination
Production networks	Extensive subcontracting	Autarkic internal workshop or regional subcontracting
Inter-firm relations	Collusive rivalry	Cartelization
Ownership networks	Corporate crossholdings	Multiple-bank stockholding
Corporate networks	Intermarket business groups	Oligopolies and cartels
Capital sources	Extensive bank loans and corporate profits	Extensive bank loans and corporate profits
State/business relations	Administrative guidance and reciprocal consent	Cooperative coordination and concerted action

But that . . . benevolence is a duty'' (p. 470). Individuals and institutions in economic and noneconomic action alike are required to display mutual consideration, to think of collective goals and benefits rather than individual ones. Thus, the inclination in economic action is to seek success through cooperation and mutual reinforcement, through the merging of interests, rather than seeking success through all-out competition.

The institutional analysis of economic structures relies on the inclusion of significant institutional factors without univocally assigning causal primacy to any single dimension (whether political, or cultural, or economic). The combination of factors is here given priority over their analytical separation. The advantage of the institutional approach is that it makes it possible to identify the organizational logic that characterizes two economies with vastly different cultural and political histories without getting caught in the search for the ultimate causal factor (whether it be the culture, the state, or the market). Cooperation as a distinctive feature of Japanese and German capitalist structures was shown here to be not the outcome of cultural or political or economic factors alone; rather, it was shown to constitute an identifiable working logic of economic action that is empirically observed throughout the economic structure of the two societies. The identification of a pattern of capitalist cooperation and of other distinctive forms of capitalism around the world, I claim, will advance in new directions our understanding of economic structures as socially constructed institutions—beyond the pointless search for one, undifferentiated model of world capitalism.

Notes

1. For basic economic statistics, see the *OECD Economic Surveys on Japan and Germany* (both July 1988).

2. *Fortune*, July 31, 1989, p. 286.

3. *Business Week*, June 15, 1990, p. 35.

4. *OECD Economic Surveys, Germany* (July 1988), International Comparisons.

5. Data are from *Japan Statistical Yearbook*, 1988, and *Statistisches Jahrbuch 1988 für die Bundesrepublik Deutschland.*

6. *Business Week*, February 12, 1990, p. 55.

7. *Business Week*, September 24, 1990, p. 100.

8. Leaman's *The Political Economy of West Germany, 1945–1985*, p. 70, presents the following statistics on numbers of suppliers of large German firms: AEG 30,000, Siemens 30,000, Krupp 23,000, Daimler-Benz 18,000, Bayer 17,500, BASF 10,000, Opel 7,800. The data are from the 1960s, and I find the figures provided unbelievably high; but I have not been able to check Leaman's sources. Still, if one considers that the 1986 figures show a total of 38,254 manufacturing firms with twenty or more employees in the entire Federal Republic, it becomes apparent how unlikely Leaman's supplier figures appear.

9. *Business Tokyo*, April 1990, p. 24.

10. Dodwell Marketing Consultants. 1986. *Industrial Groups in the Japanese Economy*. Tokyo: Dodwell, p. 41.

11. *Business Week*, October 8, 1990, p. 21.

12. For historical overview, see Richard Tilly, "The Growth of Large-Scale Enterprise in Germany since the Middle of the Nineteenth Century," in *The Rise of Managerial Capitalism*. ed. Herman Daems and Herman Van der Wee (Louvain: Leuven University Press, 1974). For a comparative perspective, see Alfred D. Chandler and Herman Daems, eds. *Managerial Hierarchies* (Cambridge: Harvard University Press, 1980).

13. *Business Tokyo*, April 1990, p. 24.

14. See note 10.

15. See note 10, p. 341.

Bibliography

Berger, Peter. 1984. "An East Asian Development Model." *The Economic News* no. 3079 (September,17–23).

Caves, Richard, E., and Masu Uekusa. 1976. *Industrial Organization in Japan*. Washington, D.C.: Brookings Institution.

DiMaggio, Paul, and Walter W. Powell. 1991. *The New Institutionalism in Organizational Analysis*. Chicago: University of Chicago Press.

Dore, Ronald P. 1983. "Goodwill and the Spirit of Market Capitalism." *British Journal of Sociology* 34 (December): 459–82.

———. 1986. *Flexible Rigidities*. Stanford: Stanford University Press.

———. 1987. *Taking Japan Seriously*. London: Athlone Press.

Evans, Peter. B., Dietrich Rueschemeyer, and Theda Skocpol. eds. 1985. *Bringing the State Back In*. Cambridge: Cambridge University Press.

Gerlach, Michael, L. 1991. *Alliance Capitalism*. Berkeley: University of California Press.

Granovetter, Mark. 1985. "Economic Action and Social Structure." *American Journal of Sociology* 91: 481–510.

Hamilton, Gary G., and Nicole Woolsey Biggart. 1988. "Market, Culture, and Authority." *American Journal for Sociology* 94 (Supplement): S52–S94.

Hardach, Karl. 1980. *The Political Economy of Germany in the Twentieth Century*. Berkeley: University of California Press.

Hartmann, Gert, Ian Nicholas, Arndt Sorge, and Malcolm Warner. 1983. "Computerised Machine-Tools, Manpower Consequences and Skill Utilisation." *British Journal of Industrial Relations* 21, 2: 221–31.

Herrigel, Gary B. 1989. "Industrial Order and the Politics of Industrial Change." In *Industry and Politics in West Germany*, ed. Peter J. Katzenstein. Ithaca, N.Y.: Cornell University Press.

Johnson, Chalmer. 1982. *MITI and the Japanese Miracle*. Stanford: Stanford University Press.

———. 1985. "The Institutional Foundations of Japanese Industrial Policy." *California Management Review* 27: 4.

Katzenstein, Peter J. 1987. *Policy and Politics in West Germany*. Philadelphia: Temple University Press.

———, ed. 1989. *Industry and Politics in West Germany*. Ithaca, N.Y.: Cornell University Press.

Kocka, Jürgen. 1897/1941. "Enterprises and Managers in German Industrialization." In *The Cambridge Economic History of Europe*. Vol. 7, part I.

Körner, Keiko. 1971. "The Social Dimensions of Political Economy." *The German Economic Review* 9: 3.

Leaman, Jeremy. 1988. *The Political Economy of West Germany, 1945–1985*. New York: St. Martin's Press.

Lorenzoni, Gianni, and Oscar A. Ornati. 1988. "Constellations of Firms and New Ventures." *Journal of Business Venturing* 3: 41–57.

Magaziner, Ira, and Thomas Hout. 1981. *Japanese Industrial Policy*. Berkeley: University of California Institute for International Studies.

March, James, and Johan P. Olsen. 1984. "The New Institutionalism." *Political Science Review* 78: 734–49.

Maurice, Marc, Arndt Sorge, and Malcolm Warner. 1980. "Societal Differences in Organizing Manufacturing Units." *Organization Studies* 1, 1: 56–89.

Müller-Armack, Alfred. 1965. "The Principles of the Social Market Economy." *The German Economic Review* 3: 2.

Nakane, Chie. 1970. *Japanese Society*. Berkeley: University of California Press.

Nanetti, Raffaella Y. 1988. *Growth and Territorial Policies*. London: Pinter Publishers.

Orrù, Marco. 1991. "Practical and Theoretical Aspects of Japanese Business Networks." In *Business Networks in East and Southeast Asia*, ed. Gary G. Hamilton. Hong Kong: University of Hong Kong Centre of Asian Studies.

———. 1991. "Institutional Logic of Small-Firm Economies in Italy and Taiwan." *Studies in Comparative International Development* 26, 1: 3–28.

Orrù, Marco, Gary G. Hamilton, and Mariko Suzuki. 1989. "Patterns of Inter-Firm Control in Japanese Business." *Organization Studies* 10: 4.

Park, S. J. 1984. "Labour-Management Consultation as a Japanese Type of Participation." In *Industrial Relations in Transition*, ed. Tokunaga Shigeyoshi and Joachim Bergmann, 53–67. Tokyo: University of Tokyo Press.

Piore, Michael J. 1984. *The Second Industrial Divide*. New York: Basic Books.

Porter, Michael E. 1990. *The Competitive Advantage of Nations*. New York: Free Press.

Redding, Gordon. 1990. *The Spirit of Chinese Capitalism*. Berlin: De Gruyter.

Samuels, Richard. 1987. ''The Business of the Japanese State.'' In *The Political Economy of Japan*, ed. Kozo Yamamura and Yasukichi Yasuba. Stanford: Stanford University Press.

Sato, Kazuo, and Yasuo Hoshino, eds. 1984. *The Anatomy of Japanese Business*. Armonk, N.Y.: M. E. Sharpe.

Sheard, Paul. 1984. ''Financial Corporate Grouping, Cross-Subsidization in the Private Sector and the Industrial Adjustment Process in Japan.'' Discussion Paper no. 44. Osaka University: Faculty of Economics.

Schmiegelow, Henrik, and Michele Schmiegelow. 1990. ''How Japan Affects the International System.'' *International Organization* 44: 4.

Schumann, Michael. 1990. ''New Forms of Work Organization in West German Industrial Enterprises.'' Paper presented at the World Congress of Sociology, Madrid (Spain).

Shigeyoshi, Tokunaga, and Joachim Bergmann, eds. 1984. *Industrial Relations in Transition*. Tokyo: University of Tokyo Press.

Shimokawa, Koichi. 1985. ''Japan's *Keiretsu* System.'' *Japanese Economic Studies* 13, (Summer) 4: 3–31.

Silin, Robert H. 1976. *Leadership and Values*. Cambridge: Harvard University Press.

Smith, Adam. 1776/1928. *Wealth of Nations*. Chicago: University of Chicago Press.

Streeck, Wolfgang. 1984. ''Guaranteed Employment, Flexible Manpower Use, and Cooperative Manpower Management.'' In *Industrial Relations in Transition*, ed. Tokunaga Shigeyoshi and Joachim Bergmann, 81–116. Tokyo: University of Tokyo Press.

———. 1989. ''Successful Adjustment to Turbulent Markets.'' In *Industry and Politics in West Germany*, ed. Peter J. Katzenstein. Ithaca, N.Y.: Cornell University Press.

———. 1990. ''More Uncertainties: West German Unions Facing 1992.'' Paper presented at the Seventh Conference of Europeanists, Washington, D.C., March.

Taira, Koji, and Teiichi Wada. 1986. ''The Japanese Business–Government Relations.'' In *The Structural Analysis of Business*, ed. Mark Mizruchi and Michael Schwartz. New York: Cambridge University Press.

Wallach, Peter. 1985. ''Political Economies.'' In *West German Politics in the Mid-Eighties*, ed. H. G. Peter Wallach, and George K. Romoser. New York: Praeger.

Weiss, Linda. 1988. *Creating Capitalism*. Oxford: Basil Blackwell.

Ziegeler, Rolf, Donald Bender, and Hermann Biehler. 1985. ''Industry and Banking in the German Corporate Network.'' In *Networks of Corporate Power*, ed. Frank N. Stockman, Rolf Ziegler, and John Scott, 48–64. Cambridge: Polity Press.

Zysman, John. 1983. *Government, Markets, and Growth*. Ithaca, N.Y.: Cornell University Press.

10. Japanese Institutions Supporting Innovation

Maureen McKelvey

Concepts and Theories

This chapter has a dual aim in discussing Japanese institutions supporting technical change. On the one hand, there is the aim of further developing an understanding of the workings of *capitalist economies*, with an underlying argument about the vitality of technology as the engine of capitalism (Nelson 1990). On the other hand, there is the aim of understanding the development of *technology* in society, in specifically capitalist societies. Technology can be defined as artifacts or material objects that incorporate some systematic knowledge about how objects function in the world. Technology may be thought of as discrete objects or as systems; it is often hard to separate one technological item from its surrounding systems of technologies. Another distinction is between product technology, which is or is part of a product, and process technology, which is used in the production process. The two aims of this chapter are closely related but represent two perspectives.

The analytical starting point of this chapter is that capitalist nations differ. This statement is far from radical in most social science research, with the exception being mainstream economics, where all markets are assumed to be equivalent if not equal. Additionally, neoclassical economics often assumes that a free market is a natural state of affairs, composed by the sum of individual actions (buying and selling), where each individual tries to maximize his/her own interest but the outcome is to the good of the whole group. Within their conceptual framework, government action is therefore considered unnatural intervention that distorts the workings of the market—except in cases of market failure. The two types of policy most directly concerned with innovation—science and technology policy and industrial policy—are therefore defined as needing state intervention in the case of market failure (Arrow 1962; Komiya 1987, pp. 33–34).

In contrast to this characterization of the market, this chapter argues that capitalist economies vitally differ. No single idealized type of economic interaction called a free market exists as an isolated subsystem of a society—although one can identify universal characteristics of the market mechanism. Rather, in practice, many different forms of market-based interaction exist, and each form affects that country's economic performance in regard to different variables. Important differences exist in the organizations of markets and of market-based relations, in relations between companies and noncompany actors important to the economy, and in institutional arrangements, both formal—research and development system, regulation of the labor market—and informal, such as habits or conceptual understanding. The actual functioning of the economy must therefore be understood in relation to the overall functioning of a modern industrialized society, particularly in the sense of structured interaction. The market itself can also be understood as an institution (cf. chapter 11 of this book; Hodgson 1988).

This understanding of the capitalist system in relation to technological change can be called a national system of innovation. Although definition of this concept varies and is dependent on the underlying theory (McKelvey 1991), the common nexus is that technological change is a—or the prime—mover of capitalism and that relations are vital for technology. One key assumption is that change is a fundamental part of the economy and that economic change is usually related to creation and diffusion of innovations. Another argument is that the national context affects and is affected by the process of creation and diffusion of innovations. The national context can include social and cultural factors, but in particular, factors relating to the functioning of a modern market system such as user–producer relations (Lundvall 1988), the research and development system, the key industrial sectors (Edquist and Lundvall 1992), and/or societal adaptation of the new technoeconomic paradigm (Freeman and Perez 1988). Recent empirical research (Nelson 1991) quite strongly indicates that national systems of innovation do differ in terms of which formal institutions produce knowledge, their specialization in knowledge production, the organization and functioning of diffusion mechanisms, and the relations between different institutions.[1]

Freeman (1987, p. 1) defines a *national system of innovation* as ''the network of institutions in the public and private sectors whose activities and interactions initiate, import, modify and diffuse new technology.'' A full analysis of the Japanese national system of innovation would include the actors who aid in creating and diffusing new technologies, their goals and motivations, and the external pressures for technological change. The aim of this chapter is more modest in that instead of describing the entire system, I wish to show how the specific organization of relations can encourage or discourage innovation. Therefore, my definition is that a national system of innovation is the structured interaction between agents in a nation involved in the search for innovation, or new economically successful technology. Their interaction is structured in the sense that relations are often repeated or stable—either between individuals or between members of groups—and in the sense that formal and informal institutions often regulate or influence (but do not determine) behavior.

This chapter argues these points by concentrating on a specific group of economic relations in Japan—those related to technological change. In the case of Japan after World War II, the creation and sustainment of high rates of economically successful technological change has been favored by the particular organization of Japanese capitalism. The organization of Japanese capitalism is here discussed in relation to four points:

1. Japanese culture—in the broad sense of common thought patterns which condition interactions, not least economic transactions.

2. Japanese labor—especially its relation to companies, the state, and education.

3. Japanese industry—its organization partly in the sense of industrial structure and partly in the sense of nonmarket interaction.

4. Japanese government—the type of political framework it provides for the functioning of the economy as well as its relations with industry through policy.

These four elements can provide points of comparison for the functioning of other capitalist economies.

Japanese Culture

> Culture includes the dual interaction between individual and the collective. . . . The . . . culture of any group or social unit is . . . the total of the collective or shared learning of that unit as it develops its capacity to survive in its external environment and to manage its own internal affairs. Culture is . . . taught to new members as the correct way to perceive, think about and feel in relation to [internal and external] problems. . . . The power of culture is derived from the fact that it operates as a set of assumptions that are unconscious and taken for granted. (Schein 1985, pp. 19–20)

As one begins to read generally about Japanese culture, certain aspects usually reappear in any list of how Japanese culture differs from European and American culture.[2] These are the following: perception of their own uniqueness, suspicion of foreigners, drive for self-sufficiency, and group orientation.

For people from Euro-American cultures who have been raised to believe in the rights, dignity, and equality of all individuals regardless of race, creed, or sex, it is very odd and striking that many Japanese perceive themselves as genuinely unique. By some accounts, many Japanese perceive themselves as different from the rest of homo sapiens—as a people and a culture. According to Prestowitz, there has been almost an obsession with reasons why they differ from everyone else; for example by the mid-1980s, there were about a thousand books explaining why the Japanese are unique—books called *nihonhinron* (Prestowitz 1988, p. 81).[3]

The Japanese perception of their own uniqueness is closely related to the other cultural values. A group by definition excludes nongroup members; suspicion of foreigners, therefore, is a more extreme expression of strong group identity. In Japan, this suspicion even extends to Japanese who have lived out of the country for a long period (Prestowitz 1988, p. 85); these returnees may have a very hard time being integrated into the group again and accepted. Seeing themselves as a unique group also means that abstract, impartial economic processes—which affect all parties equally—is not an appealing thought. I by no means intend to suggest that the Japanese are not affected by or are not aware of the importance of the market, the benefits of international trade, and the problems of international competition. Rather, the point is that the emphasis on the unique group could lead the Japanese to take a more active role in trying to readjust economic forces to their favor and not just accept the dictates of economic theory or the distribution of an "impartial and unimpeded" market. This can be related to the Japanese drive for self-sufficiency.

During much of the postwar period, there has been a societal progrowth consensus in Japan, and in contrast with the corresponding American-European ideology about free international markets, the Japanese have highly valued economic self-sufficiency. There are many examples in the postwar period (and today) where the Japanese have protected their domestic market in order to produce objects within the country rather than buy them from a foreign country. Thus, this perception of uniqueness can have directly affected the goals of government and the formation of the Japanese capitalist society. Undoubtedly as a result of the unique postwar circumstances, much of the drive for Japanese self-sufficiency has centered on national economic security rather than military security.

The group orientation of the Japanese has also been noted in many contexts. Prestowitz goes so far as to argue that "in Japan there is virtually no life outside groups, which define a person's existence" (Prestowitz 1988, p. 82). The meaning of the group in Japan is not a group in opposition to the individual, but instead, the group is an intense set of personal relationships, which must be carefully cultivated.[4] This general group orientation of culture means that business relations, business–government relations, economic behavior, and so forth, are quite different from their counterparts in cultures that emphasize the individual and more impartial, arm's-length transactions (see Dore 1987).

The four traits of Japanese culture—group orientation, drive for self-sufficiency, suspicion of foreigners, and perception of own uniqueness—have had some important influences on Japanese economic success and diffusion of innovation.[5] The group orientation, for example, may lead to mobilization of the largest group—the nation—for the common goal of modernization. Modernization has been largely based on creation and above all diffusion of innovation, including both incremental and radical changes. If culture is seen as a complicated interconnection of individual and structure, where culture is reproduced through actions in relationships, then culture is important for structuring relationships—for example, between labor and management—as the next section demonstrates.

Japanese Employees, Education, and Innovation

It is an obvious truth that it is human beings who perform economic activities, with the help of constructed machines and social organization. At the same time, diversity among humans at work is often reduced in theory to a uniform mass called "labor," which is interchangeable and can be replaced by capital.

However, there are two main arguments against accepting interchangeability of labor as a general statement describing humans' work. First, in most work, each person's characteristics, not least their "tacit knowledge" (Polanyi 1967) about how to do things, can make a great deal of difference to the output. Second, work is not a mechanistic linear input–output scheme where the managers give orders, the workers do the physical labor, and out pops the product. Work is, instead, dependent on interactions among persons. Buraway (1985), for example, analyzes the worker–manager interaction in conflicts and cooperation as games or "the politics of production." However, social interaction in the workplace can also be understood by examining how the organization of interaction provides incentives and disincentives for certain kinds of behavior. In the transformation of Eastern Europe, many people have focused on the new economic (market-based) incentives versus the old noneconomic (prestige, political power) ones. However, different ways of organizing within a market-based system of incentives will also reward or discourage different kinds of behavior. This argument is further developed in connection with technological change in Japan.[6]

General Overview of the Japanese Labor Market

The Japanese labor market can hardly be mentioned without addressing "lifetime employment." The positive implications of Japanese lifetime employment in regard to technology and economic development are often mentioned, whereas the possible negative consequences are rarely if ever mentioned. There are postulated positive effects on both highly educated managers and blue-collar workers.

For managers, there may be two positive effects. The first effect is at the psychological level of managers; they may work harder to increase long-term profitability because they know their future lies with that particular firm. In Japan, managers' ability to make these decisions about research and development investment and new technologies are positively affected by the fact that many managers are technologically competent and that many identify with employees and the survival of the company rather than with the shareholders (Odagiri and Goto 1989, pp. 9–12). Second, the "lack of interfirm mobility of managerial staff" leads to "the consequent need to ensure a sufficient growth to keep internal planning resources fully employed" (Ergas 1987, p. 220). Ergas argues that this "creates insistent pressure to diversification" (ibid.), which would lead the firm into adjacent research and development activities. Okimoto, however, argues that old industrial sectors like steel and textiles diversify into related fields, whereas more medium- and high-technology sectors stay within bounded limits, owing to their high debt situation and hence firm vulnerability (Okimoto 1989). At the same time, however, high-tech products themselves cross many traditional industry boundaries. Whatever the extent to which companies diversify, the existence of permanent managers and workers does create pressures within the company to survive, preferably through growth. One means of growth is innovation or technological change.

In the case of manual workers, lifetime employment provides them with the opportunity to acquire skills through in-company training. Even though wages are linked to seniority, training can lead to fringe benefits and diverse promotion possibilities in the internal labor market (Koike 1987, p. 327).[7] Committed, skilled workers, particularly those with a wide knowledge base, have a better possibility of making incremental improvements to products and processes than unskilled workers or workers who feel little loyalty to a company. However, the lifetime employees may also lose all incentive to make improvements because they know wages are tied to age, not effort, or because they are tired of or bored with their jobs but know they cannot change companies; therefore, other methods of reinforcing loyalty are concurrently used by Japanese employees. Companies—usually large ones—benefit as well from training the lifetime employees. Because these workers will stay with the firm, the company that invested in training will also reap the benefits.

Although (relative) lifetime employment does apply to a small number of employees, it is misleading to conceptualize the whole Japanese labor market in terms of it. First, the guarantee of lifetime employment is more implicit than explicit.

> Contrary to much Western belief, there are no formal "lifetime," "permanent" or even "long-term" employment contracts in Japan. Such matters are tacit understandings, sometimes called "implicit contracts," even in large firms. (Brofenbrenner and Yasuba 1987, p. 600)

Although these contracts may not be spelled out, Japanese companies and workers do often act as though they are "binding" contracts in the common sense of the word. There are a minority of Japanese managers and workers who are covered by such rigid (but informal) lifetime agreements. Because of this agreement, both the employee and the employer reduce their respective uncertainty about the future, and each has a responsibility toward the other.

Moreover, although the term *lifetime employment* has become part of our common understanding of Japanese labor, it obviously cannot apply to all workers in Japan. If all workers only worked for one company throughout their lives, the whole economic system would be in a state of rigor mortis. By moving between cities, firms, and industries, workers diffuse their skills, move (ideally) from less to more productive sectors, and enable change in the economy.

How many Japanese workers are, then, covered by this well-known lifetime employment system? Because lifetime employment is an implicit agreement, estimates are difficult and uncertain, but all estimates point to very low percentages as a total of the Japanese labor force. Ergas (1987, p. 238) refers to Tachibanki (1984), who "estimates that lifetime employment applies to no more than ten percent of the Japanese labor force, almost entirely at higher levels of educational attainment." Okimoto (1989, p. 45) writes that "estimates generally place the percentage . . . at somewhere between twenty-five and thirty-five percent." Therefore, between 90 percent and 65 percent of workers in Japan are *not* covered by lifetime employment.

One can argue that the lifetime employed have much power vis-á-vis their company compared with the more temporary workers. This argument is reinforced by the structure of labor unions in Japan. Union policy limits "membership to a size which [makes] absolute security of uninterrupted employment possible at all times." This means that unions are generally limited to these same "permanent regular workers and exclude temporary and casual workers, and part-timers" (Kawashima 1987, p. 600). Therefore, unions mostly represent men employed in large companies.

If only a minority of workers have implicit lifetime employment, how do the other workers fare? According to Kawashima's (1987, p. 609) calculations, about 50 percent of all wage workers in the nonagricultural sectors in 1982 were temporary and casual workers or part-time workers; the great majority of these were women.[8] These periphery workers do not enjoy the same benefits, wages, or stability as core workers. Kawashima argues that because permanent core workers make firms' labor costs and number of workers very rigid, these periphery workers are necessary to allow the system to adjust to the fluctuations of a capitalist economy.

Thus, while persons who have implicit lifetime employment may use their capabilities to the full, the majority of workers who do not fall into this category probably do not use their capacities to the full in their working lives. As in other capitalist systems, the skill and training potential of a substantial portion of the working population is not met. Neither do these workers have much incentive to aid technological development—whether of process or product technology—in their present jobs. In the long run, lack of trained workers can mean shortages of specific skilled employees, which can be an important constraint on economic growth and transformation in a country in the long run. On the other hand, the stability given to the lifetime employed can facilitate the introduction of new process technology because they do not experience this technology as a direct threat to their jobs.

Education

Within the broad term *education/training*, certain types of education are particularly important for innovation in the modern society:

• General overall education. General education levels provide a base for further training and may enable workers to make more incremental improvements through learning by doing.
• Specialized occupation-related skills. Specialized skills enable employees to master and develop process technology in their work.
• Specific engineering/science skills. Engineers and scientists are able to directly influence the creation and improvement of technological change.

The following discussion of education in Japan briefly takes up the structure of education, what groups take responsibility for education, and the implication for innovation.

As to general education levels, the Japanese government provides only nine years of free education. After these nine years, both public and private high schools and universities charge tuition fees, although public fees are somewhat lower than private ones (Bronfenbrenner and Yasuba 1987, p. 113). This system is similar to the American one, although public high schools are free in the United States.[9] Thus, the Japanese government finances a small proportion of total education costs, in contrast to most European countries.

Instead of the Japanese government investing heavily in education, individuals in Japan invest in education because of its high rewards. The importance of schooling at all levels of society is related to the meritocratic nature of Japanese society. Dore argues that "it is the role played by effort . . . which gives legitimacy to the system, creates the presumption that people 'deserve' the material and prestige and power rewards which, by virtue of their qualification label, society accords them" (Dore 1987, p. 204). Most Japanese accept the individual basis of success instead of attributing success to socially conditioned factors. Additionally, Japan's renowned high rate of savings is partly correlated with the high price (and prestige) of schooling. "Many people, even if they have middle-class incomes, consume at near-poverty levels since they are forced to save because of debts contracted to purchase real estate after 1970 or for the education of their children" (Bronfenbrenner and Yasuba 1987, p. 114). Obviously, at least middle-class Japanese families must place a high value on education.

In line with this idea that success is the reward for those who work hard, the Japanese education system divides students according to ability. Up until the age of fifteen, Japanese students are educated in mixed-ability classes. After this point, competitive exams sort them into different ability levels in high school, which pretty much determines which university and type of job each person will get. The bottom level has the highest level of dropouts and dimmest future prospects, the middle gets into vocational and junior colleges, while the top have a very bright future (Dore 1987, p. 205). The cream of secondary school attend Tokyo University, and many of the cream of Tokyo University graduates seek jobs in top Japanese firms or at the Ministry for International Trade and Industry (MITI). Thus, the type of schooling an individual receives is extremely important to his/her future prospects, and it is important to note that both business and the government attract top students with similar educations; this can later facilitate communication about government policy.

The purpose of education is, of course, not only to educate the individual but also to create skilled labor; different educational systems are more or less successful at this. Ergas (1987) interprets the Japanese school system as promoting a high level of general skills—that is not specific to one occupation or one firm. However, Ergas is concentrating on those who "succeed" as he refers to postsecondary education, which contains a large measure of general education, as in the United States (p. 216). Bronfenbrenner and Yasuba (1987, p. 114) argue that much of the Japanese educational system, including cram schools, is directed toward passing competitive exams to come up to the next level of schooling; they mean that education is thereby narrowly concentrated on academic subjects and does not meet the needs of less talented students.

However, Japanese firms—particularly large ones—also play an important role in training workers at all educational levels after formal schooling. Corporation-based training may be where less talented students receive educational—or at least occupational—skills.[10] Japanese firms play an important role in increasing the technological skills of the labor force, and they know they will recover the training investment in stable workers. If companies know that the labor market is highly mobile—as in the United States—then they will rightly fear that their newly trained employees might quit to find a more lucrative job elsewhere; thus, companies in a mobile labor market, which is organized differently, may have fewer incentives to offer training than do Japanese companies.

Specific engineering and science skills are also particularly important to innovation. Although Japan is beginning to emphasize basic science to a greater extent than previously, the Japanese educational system still produces many more engineers then scientists. (See Table 10.1.)

Prestowitz argues that the emphasis in Japan on engineering education is the result of deliberate policies emphasizing those occupations that an industrial society most needs. In general, the Japanese education and training system seems successful at training persons for jobs, including highly skilled ones. This system is partly supported by the meritocratic view of education, where individual effort is highly prized, and partly by the fact that companies see direct benefits from training long-term employees. The government plays only a minor role. A certain level and type of training and education are a necessary condition of high technology, especially in industries facing massive changes in technologies.

Table 10.1

First University Degrees (United States, Japan) in Science and Mathematics and in Engineering as a Percentage of Total, 1982

Degree	United States	Japan
Sciences and Mathematics	60 percent	14 percent
Engineering	40 percent	86 percent

Source: Prestowitz 1988, p. 126.

This discussion is intended to increase our understanding of the diversity in the Japanese labor market; this diversity may help us understand the social interaction around production. In addition, the organization and functioning of the labor market and opportunities for skill acquisition are essential components of industrial production and as such can influence workers' acceptance of new technology, their ability to make incremental improvements, and loyalty to a company—for better or for worse.

Japanese Industry—Organization and Research and Development Intensity

Obviously, the aggregate Japanese economy is made up of diverse firms—small and big ones, successful and bankrupt ones—and of diverse sectors—internationally successful to extremely ineffective. As in the case of lifetime employment, the most visible aspect of the Japanese economy—consumer electronics and basic microelectronic components—are only part of a much greater diversity. Additionally, however, the organization of Japanese industry is complex, as it is in all industrialized countries, but Japan has some specific characteristics that help add nuance to the picture of autonomous firms competing in a free market. Instead, both firms and industries are organized in a very special way, which I can argue is crucial to technological development and diffusion; although some characteristics are uniquely Japanese, others can be found in similar forms in other countries.

To begin with, the managers—particularly those of large firms—have a much longer time perspective for investments in capital and in research and development than do their counterparts in Europe and America. One important reason for this is the organization of stock ownership in Japan. In contrast to the West, Japanese companies hold a large percentage of each other's stock. "Over seventy percent of outstanding Japanese shares are held by corporations and less than thirty percent by individuals'' (Okimoto 1989, p. 43). Much shareholding is reciprocal, which means the two corporate owners keep their stock for long periods of time; short-term returns to stocks as an indicator of success are much less important to firms' ability to raise capital than in Western Europe and the United States. This adds stability to managers' calculations about the environment their firm will face in the future.

In fact, industrial relations among companies are even more formally organized in Japan than these reciprocal shareholdings suggest. A basic organizational feature of Japanese industrial organization is the *keiretsu* groups, which are loose affiliations of firms, including major banks, manufacturers, and trading companies. Membership in a keiretsu means "extensive intra-keiretsu stockholding, reliance on the main keiretsu bank for external indirect financing, and stable but by no means exclusive business transactions" (Okimoto 1989, p. 133). Most of the major Japanese firms are linked to one of these groups, although they often have ties with other groups as well. Within these groups there is a tendency toward group autonomy, in that each tends to build up a strong position in the major industrial sectors (in competition with other keiretsus) and, for example, in their regular meetings to discuss business strategy (Prestowitz 1988, p. 159). These loose—but sometimes strong—groups provide stability for the member firms in terms of selling relations, capital finance, and orientation toward common goals, all of which enable a more long-term evaluation of a firm's position. Long-term planning and reduction of uncertainty can encourage investment in risky enterprises such as technological development.

A related form of organization in Japanese industry connects a firm with firms in its backward-and-forward-linked industries and is called *kigyo keiretsu* (enterprise groups). These enterprise groups "consist of a large manufacturer and its suppliers and distributors" (Prestowitz 1988, p. 164), often within a larger keiretsu. Many of these relationships are captive, meaning that the supplier and distributor are mutually dependent and their relations are long-term rather than based on lowest price competition.[11] In important ways, the links between large companies and subcontractors help diffuse technology and the results of research and development (Odagiri and Goto, 1989, pp. 9–12).

These different sorts of organized economic interaction—instead of money-based transactions—provide some advantages from the standpoint of innovation. For one thing, these keiretsu groups made up for the deficiencies of an underdeveloped capital market by providing capital and funding within the group, as well as by providing stable buyers. If a firm cannot borrow money, then investment in research and development is difficult. The stable ownership pattern with reciprocal shareholding and mutual risk taking in groups has also provided insurance against—or else has enabled—the traditionally high debt financing of Japanese firms. It also enables long-term planning, including investment in costly and risky research and development as well as in process technology.

However, despite these examples of organized markets and collusive practices, Japan has had intense competition. In fact, the Japanese have a term that seems contradictionary to Western readers—*excessive competition*. Excessive competition is defined as:

> a zero-sum situation in which an excess number of producers possess supply capacities that far exceed demand. Such disequilibrium gives rise to dysfunctional competition between firms, leading to severe price slashing, "forward" or "predatory" pricing, a rash of bankruptcies, and industrial disorder. (Okimoto 1989, p. 38)

There is a debate over the causes of excessive competition, including the positions that it is a result of industrial policy that encourages overinvestment, that it is caused by the market strategy of Japanese corporations, and that it is caused by the desire of the firm to maximize profit by maximizing market share (Okimoto 1989, pp. 38–48). Each of these explanations is valid to some extent, but whichever is most "correct," it is important to note that excessive competition and the corresponding collusion to prevent havoc have been essential features of the Japanese economy.

This concept of excessive competition displays a Japanese dislike of such untidy in-fighting and calls for an actor to mitigate disorganization on the market. Excessive competition was probably the result of two things in the pre-1973 period:

1. The declining long-run average cost curve in Japan's specialization in heavy industries in the 1950s and 1960s.[12] The dynamic in this part of the Japanese system "was principally due to the availability of readily borrowable, successively more advanced foreign technology. Thus each firm in a typical industry could outcompete its rivals by investing more and producing more than others in the sector" (Yamamura 1988, p. 175). Those Japanese firms with a protected home market had artificially high prices and stable market shares—a situation caused by government policy—and then they could afford to increase production and exports and sell at a price lower than the world market price.[13]

2. However, the prevention of excessive competition required a coordinator who did not allow firms to go bankrupt; otherwise, competition would have forced a shakeout and a consolidation of firms. Yamamura (1988) argues that the Japanese government "guided" investment by not allowing firms to invest more than their current market share. In the rapid growth period up to about 1973, Japanese industrial policy "consisted first of a widespread protection of domestic markets and of oligopolization of major industries" (1988, p. 174). This protection was exemplified in high tariffs on many products, by restrictive

quotes over imports, and in MITI's control of foreign exchange, among other things.

However, in the post-1973 period, a number of economic and political changes have occurred domestically and internationally to make such governmental control of markets more difficult. Government control over industrial decisions has weakened considerably. In addition, the current high-technology industries differ from heavy industry in some fundamental ways such as costs of research and development, level of uncertainty, high investment costs, and so on. This means that the nature of the new technologies makes governmental guidance of industry more difficult. At the same time, however, a general atmosphere of "buy Japanese high technology" still potentially provides Japanese high-tech firms with relatively certain markets. This consequently reduces the future uncertainty such firms face and helps the economy as a whole to gain technology and skills through learning by doing and learning by using (see Rosenberg 1982).

Another important issue concerning Japanese industry is the current industrial structure, considering both specialization in high technology as well as less efficient and/or protected industries. Most researchers would probably instinctively agree that Japan is specialized in high-tech industries; this intuition is backed up by the five graphs (see Figures 10.1–10.5). In them, high tech is defined, following the OECD, as the five industrial sectors that invest 4 percent or more of sales into research and development. These are the five sectors: International Standard Industry Classification (ISIC) 3522 (drugs and medicine), ISIC 3825 (office machinery and computers), ISIC 383 (electrical machinery and components), ISIC 3845 (aerospace), and ISIC 385 (scientific instruments). Figures 10.1–10.5 show the share of each research-and-development-intensive product in production as a percentage of the OECD average, in Germany, Japan, the Netherlands, Sweden, and the United States. The figures are taken from Edquist and McKelvey (1991).

Japan was in 1986 the most specialized country in production of manufacturing products in three out of five of these research-and-development-intensive product groups—in ISIC 3825, ISIC 383, and ISIC 385. These figures are, of course, interesting in themselves, but considering the relatively backward economic and technological position of Japan after World War II, they also sustain my argument that the Japanese system of innovation has been quite successful in importing, developing, and producing technology.

In addition, another important point about the Japanese economy is that not all industrial sectors are internationally successful, and, in fact, many "fall far behind [the standards of the best worldwide competitors]" (Porter 1990, p. 394). Agriculture, for example, has long been protected—partly for political reasons—and the costs are much higher than if the Japanese bought comparable food products at world prices. As discussed earlier in this chapter, in many industries, protection of the Japanese market combined with heavy investment and

Figure 10.1. **Share of ISIC 3522 (Drugs and Medicine) in Production in Five Countries as a Percentage of the OECD Average, 1971–86**

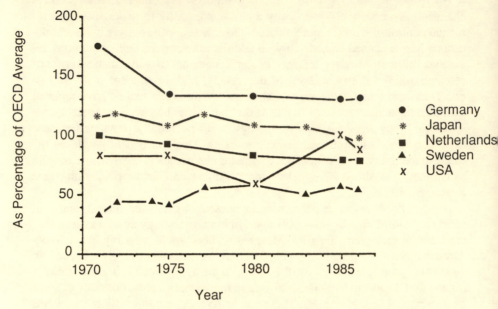

Figure 10.2. **Share of ISIC 3825 (Office Machinery and Computers) in Production in Five Countries as a Percentage of the OECD Average, 1971–86**

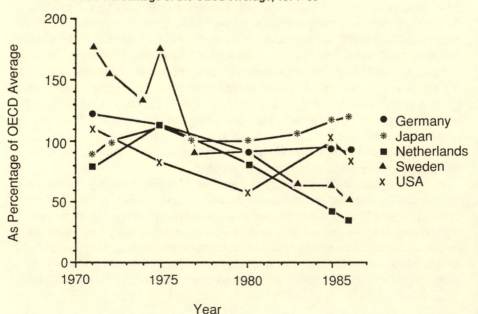

Figure 10.3. **Share of ISIC 383 (Electrical Machinery and Components) in Production in Five Countries as a Percentage of the OECD Average, 1971–86**

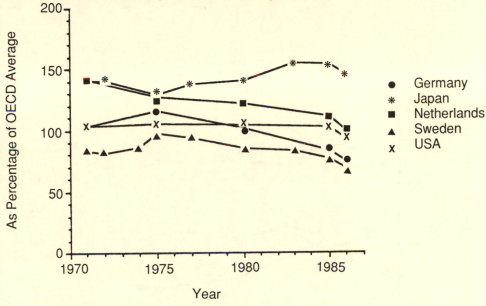

Figure 10.4. **Share of ISIC 3845 (Aerospace) in Production in Five Countries as a Percentage of the OECD Average, 1971–86**

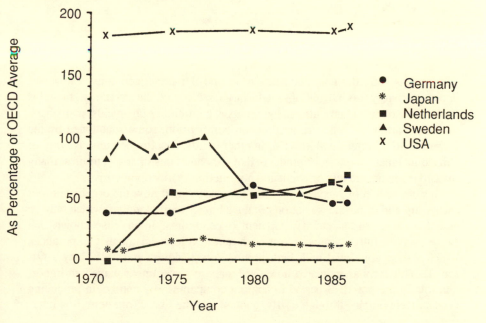

Figure 10.5. **Share of ISIC 385 (Scientific Instruments) in Production in Five Countries as a Percentage of the OECD Average, 1971–86**

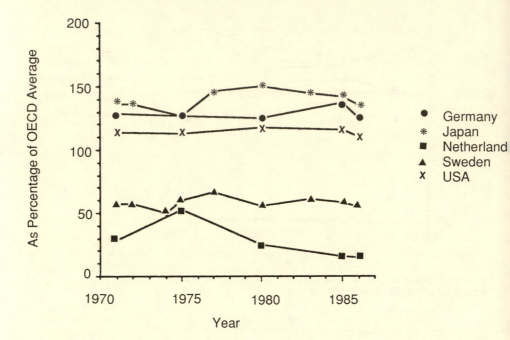

exports has led to great competition in the Japanese economy. However, domestic rivalry "is all but absent in large sectors of the economy. In fields suchas construction, agriculture, food, paper, commodity chemicals, and fibers, there are cartels and other restrictions on competition, some sanctioned by the government" (Porter 1990, p. 413). In other words, despite the high visibility of "made in Japan" consumer products like cars and consumer electronics, many industrial sectors are less efficient and not internationally competitive.

This discussion of Japanese industry has highlighted how the organization of ownership and of business relations enables longer term planning, which may be essential for research and development expenditures. It has also shown that Japan successfully produces research-and-development-intensive products, which can be correlated with high productivity (Edquist and McKelvey 1991, sec. 4). Third, it has indicated how the Japanese government played an important role in the pre-1973 period in helping companies buy and begin producing product technologies through tariffs, quotas, and the like. From here, it is interesting to move the analysis to the organization of government and its activities directly related to the development and diffusion of technology in industries.

Japanese Government

The Political Setting for Japanese Policy

Because the political situation in Japan is not very well known in the West but affects government behavior, including policy, a very brief overview is given here.[14] The three most relevant parts of the Japanese system of innovation are the following:

• A general overview of the political parties and political system.
• The relationship between politics and the bureaucracy.
• The Ministry of International Trade and Industry (MITI).

In Japan, the Liberal Democratic party (LDP) has dominated the *Diet* (parliament) for almost the whole postwar period. Although the LDP barely has a majority in the Diet, they work closely with some of the opposition parties and are in reality a solid majority. The opposition parties are, in fact, deeply divided and are unable to work together. At the same time, none of the opposition parties can seriously threaten the LDP by themselves. This means that many voters feel there are no serious alternatives to the LDP.

In this dominant one-party system, the LDP has a broad base of electoral support—much broader than any of the opposition parties. At the same time, however, this party is overrepresented in the Diet because of the peculiarities of the Japanese system of electoral districts. Agricultural and semiurban areas are greatly overrepresented, which has two consequences. First, it increases the LDP's power because rural areas support the LDP to a greater extent than do urban areas; second, agricultural interests have power in the party and the government well beyond their representation in society. Other staunch supporter groups of the LDP include small businesses, fishermen, the construction industry, and the like, and they also receive political favors in return for votes.[15] Thus, the current political setup does not a priori favor high-technology industries.

In fact, the activities of most Japanese ministries are likewise quite politicized, where politicians and parties give favors or use the legislative branch to further their own interests. MITI is unusual in that it has had greater freedom from politicians and from political bargaining power.[16] Following Okimoto (1989, p. 181), two major reasons for its relatively low politicization are that MITI and industry have been able to reach consensus and that the LDP has been dependent on labor-intensive groups for votes and therefore has partly ignored other sectors. An important point of this discussion is that the Japanese government is not identical with MITI as some books about Japan seem to argue. Many of the other ministries are very politicized, and the economic-minded MITI is unusual in its efficiency and rationality.

Although Japanese government is not identical with MITI, MITI does have enormous power within the bureaucracy and within Japan. MITI is in charge of almost all industrial sectors "from energy security to retail distribution, textiles to aircraft, heavy manufacturing to leisure activities, and regional development to international trade and investment" (Okimoto 1989, p. 113). Because MITI has such a broad range of industries, it is in fact essentially responsible for the Japanese economy. MITI also has the power to resist special sectors that want protection of special subsidies. Instead of MITI having to fight for power with other ministries about "their" industries and instead of interest groups being able to capture power in a fragmented policymaking system, the concentration of power in one ministry enables that ministry to take a broad view of the economy. However, if MITI makes a wrong decision, the organization of the Japanese government does not provide much in the way of checks and balances.

Overview of Government Policy

In the pre-1973 period, the Japanese government undoubtedly had some powerful tools to influence industry's choice of technology and the structure of the Japanese economy. Each *genkyoku* in MITI (or ministerial bureau, division, or section under whose jurisdiction a given industry falls) had almost full power over "its" industry. Up to the end of the 1960s, they drew up policy, made proposals on tax provisions, tariffs, imports, foreign investment, approved patent and technology agreements, and issued licenses (Komiya 1987, p. 14). Thus MITI's vertical divisions (by industry) had both the responsibility and the power to propose technology and industrial policy.

Two very important laws also enabled the Japanese government to influence domestic and international investment decisions: the Foreign Exchange Control Law of 1949 and the Foreign Investment Law of 1950. Using these, MITI also had the power to screen and restrict direct foreign investment in Japan. Spero (1985) argues that this was also intended to "prevent the repatriation of earnings and capital of foreign investors" (p. 153). Keeping profits and capital within Japan thus enabled domestic accumulation of technology embedded in capital. This encouraged diffusion of process technology to Japan. Within Japan, MITI encouraged sharing of knowledge and of patents in order to diffuse technology. In addition, MITI had the power to influence Japanese companies' purchase of foreign technology through its control of foreign exchange; MITI had a relatively clear policy to encourage "Japanese firms [to] purchase advanced technology through licensing agreements instead of acquiring technology through foreign control" (Spero 1985, p. 153). Licensing thus meant that Japanese firms could acquire knowledge and expertise through producing; simply buying technology from abroad would not have given Japan companies the know-how to produce it.

What sort of industry was MITI interested in supporting using these and other policies? Most researchers agree that in the pre-1973 period, the Japanese government's "vision" in manufacturing was based on supporting industries that met the dual criteria of rapid increase in productivity and producing goods with a high income elasticity of demand. However, a divergence then arises between those who interpret these criteria and the resulting government policy as a successful economic strategy to shape the industrial structure and those who felt support went to politically important industries.

Komiya (1987) argues that certain industries such as tourism and fast-food, which fulfilled this dual criteria, were not supported because they did not correspond to what bureaucrats felt Japan should have. In other words, the criteria were actually *ex post facto* rationalizations for subjective decisions, based on political criteria such as industries "symbolic of industrial might, that had already been pursued by countries more advanced than Japan [and industries of a] certain size, so that the theme of their development could garner people's attention" (p. 8). Imitation and symbols thus overweighed economic criteria in selecting targeted industry. Komiya does not deny that government protection and promotion policies may have helped those industries that were selected. Rather, he argues that government aid is only part of the truth because many other industries manufacturing products like color TV, clocks, and robots grew without government help.

Allen also questions how much these dual criteria were applied beforehand and how much they have been inferred from the results, but he implicitly argues that Japan—with a common purpose of bureaucrats and industry—continuously made economically wise decisions.

> At a time when her problem was to catch up with the West, heavy expenditures on basic research would have been a waste of scarce resources badly needed for new equipment. For the same reason she was under no temptation to squander her substance of "prestige" products or those "on the frontiers of knowledge." (Allen 1981, p. 77)

According to this argument, the objectives of Japanese policy were concentrated in economic rationality rather than in political prestige or other factors. However, this analysis of Japanese behavior does not really explain why Japan was able to act so rationally when many other countries—both developed and developing—have succumbed to "prestige" projects, often in the name of charismatic leaders.

Allen (1981) concludes that "the government's most important role has been first to see that finances were available to enable private firms to develop on the lines that they had persuaded the officials to approve, and secondly to provide incentives to investment in the most up-to-date equipment" (p. 73). In other words, industrial policy reflected the goals of industry and followed market dictates, but the government did encourage investment in technology to raise the level of productivity.

Consensus in the sense of overall societal consensus of progrowth policy has also been used to explain the success of pre-1973 policy. Eads and Yamamura (1987) argue that

> the ability of the government to pursue the pro-growth strategy was substantially strengthened by the effective disenfranchisement of the Left. This, together with the policy of "lifetime employment" increasingly practiced by large firms, made labor a supporter rather than an opponent of the rapid growth strategy. (p. 432)

Eads and Yamamura suggest that in order for industrial policy to be successful, some mechanism outside the policy process itself must lead to consensus; when the process and purpose of policy itself becomes politicized, then it is more difficult for industrial policy to lead to the desired results. They argue that consensus has turned into internal fragmentation in the post-1973 period, with more questioning in Japanese society of the social costs of high growth—price setting, pollution, urban overcrowding—and more questioning about the distribution of growth. They claim that this disintegration of a priori agreement of the objectives of (industrial) policy is one of the factors that has reduced the possibilities for effective Japanese policy today.

Additionally, many of the formal tools that the *genkyoku* had while Japan was industrializing have been blunted or lost in more recent years. In 1979 and 1980, Japan passed the Foreign Exchange and Foreign Trade Control Law. This "liberalized foreign exchange controls, removed formal entry restrictions on foreign direct investment, with the exception of restricted sectors . . . and permitted one hundred percent foreign control" (Spero 1985, p. 154). Thus, the strength and very existence of some Japanese policy tools changed over time, and the role of government in industrial policy has diminished greatly in the post-1973 period.

Japanese Science and Technology Policy

A specific area of government action that is relevant for a national system of innovation is science and technology policy. One of the most striking things about Japanese technology policy—which contrasts with all assumptions about the enormous influence of the Japanese government—is the low level of research and development support directly given to the private sector. The most relevant figure here is the proportion of total private sector research and development expenditures that are directly supported by the state. As Table 10.2 shows, the Japanese government supports a lower percentage of private research and development than the other countries listed. Including indirect government support to industry,[17] the total government share of private expenditures in research and development was still only 2.6 percent in 1983 (Odagiri and Goto 1989, p. 4). What this demonstrates, of course, is that direct Japanese technology policy and indirect policy provided a negligible percentage of research and development funds in the 1980s compared with the other countries. The trend holds for earlier periods as well, with a high of 13.7 percent in 1958—when payment for import of technology is included under private expenditures. However, the differences between Japan and the other countries are reduced tremendously if one excludes government support to defense-related industries. By doing so, the percentage for the United States in Table 10.1 is reduced from 32.7 percent to 7.7 percent (Odagiri and Goto 1989, p. 3).[18] Thus, throughout the postwar period, it does not appear that direct Japanese government support to "push" technological development has been particularly important.

However, there are also less direct ways in which the Japanese government can support research and development. Examples include the Bicycle Racing Fund[19] and energy-related taxes, which are funds "hidden" within MITI's internal budget and which therefore give MITI some discretion in allocating money rather than resorting to a legislative decision (Okimoto 1989, pp. 76, 82).

Another way in which the government can support industrial research and development is through organizing national research projects. Japan has apparently organized these very successfully, in terms of technical results and increasing interactive learning. MITI has organized many such national projects, in diverse fields, and most of them are in very risky and costly precommercial technologies, which companies alone might not invest in (Sigurdson and Tågerud 1989). Although there are some positive effects of large-scale, government research and development projects, much of the most intensive and important research is still carried out within the companies. What this means is that although these projects may contribute to basic knowledge, they may or may not be so important for the commercial success of Japanese firms.

As for "technology" pull-through demand, MITI has had relatively weak procurement power. In addition, Japan lacks massive funding on military-related research and development. However, as an example, the Japanese do procure some of their own military aircraft under contract from United States companies—at two times the price of buying them directly from the United States. Obviously, if the Japanese are more interested in dynamic competition in the long run and feel the aircraft industry is important, then producing the plane within the country at an economic loss today—with government money—still provides knowledge and skills in the long run. What is bad economic reasoning

Table 10.2

Percentage of Government Funds in Industry Research and Development Expenditures

	Japan	United States	Germany	France
Year	1984	1985	1984	1983
Percentage	2.0	32.7	17.4	22.4

Source: Odagiri and Goto 1989, Table 11.1.

in the short run may be very good in the long run, especially as regards technology.

Government action in many fields—science and technology policy, industrial policy, the patent system,[20] antimonopoly laws—are all important factors creating a framework for economic activities. The government can also play a crucial role in encouraging companies to produce certain types of technology, but without spending much money or directly intervening in "market failure." The organization of these different activities, especially their role in influencing behavior decisions, and the interaction in relation to technological change and diffusion have been important in the Japanese economic success.

Conclusion

This chapter has shown that the organization of different parts of the Japanese society has important implications for the workings of the Japanese market system, particularly in relation to technological development and diffusion. Capitalism is a general name for a flexible and changing mode of regulation of production and of society, with the market at the center. The market and the processes of technological change are not separate subsystems working with abstract mechanical and universal laws and motion; instead, the economy is an integral part of every society and of the multitude of routinized interactions that occur there. The national structure of incentives and disincentives for technological development and diffusion needs to be understood because of the importance of product and process technologies for economic change, competitiveness, and productivity growth.

This chapter has analyzed the Japanese economy with reference to societal organization for the Japanese national system of innovation. The underlying argument is that each national capitalist economy must provide a framework for developing and diffusing technology but that some specific manifestations of capitalism provide more (or better) incentives for producing, commercializing, and reinvesting in technological change than others. National specificity in research is necessary once a researcher drops the assumption of reversible time and attempts to bring forward the path dependency of decisions made in the past (Hodgson 1991). National historical developments are therefore important. Some readers might want to argue that the Japanese case is so dependent on the past and its own peculiarities that we should not compare it with other industrialized countries. However, each nation has followed its own specific historical path of economic development (Senghaas 1985), and in any case, generalizations are a necessary part of social science research.

The Japanese system, as manifested in different spheres of society such as their labor market and organization of industry, is able to combine two attributes. On the one hand, there is a repeated pattern of long-term decision making and planning, which enables stable relations, possibly even rigid ones, to thrive. On the other hand, there are those aspects that are more affected by short-term fluctuations and that enable quick adjustment to change. This combination of rigidity and flexibility provides both stability to enable a carryover of previous knowledge and success—in addition to the longer time horizon—as well as flexibility to enable a rapid change. This dual type of interaction in Japan seems to have been particularly important in the area of technological change because modern technology usually requires much knowledge (which is necessarily gained through previous experience, production, or education) but which also changes rapidly, sometimes radically.

Notes

1. The countries included in the Nelson book are Argentina, Australia, Brazil, Denmark, Canada, France, Germany, Israel, Italy, Japan, South Korea, Sweden, Taiwan, the United States, and the United Kingdom. A more theoretical book on national systems of innovations is forthcoming from the Institute for Production at Aalborg University, Denmark (Lundvall 1992).

2. Even a consultant for multinational companies like Ohmae implicitly agrees. On the one hand, in "Triad Power," Ohmae argues that United States–Japan–Europe form a relatively homogeneous Triad market of 630 million wealthy consumers with similar tastes—which implies a common consumption culture. On the other hand, in "Beyond National Borders," he discusses (at a superficial level at least) and exemplifies Japanese cultural differences that affect company and political agreements.

3. Some of the bizarre explanations "include the idea that the Japanese have about thirty more feet of intestines than other people and that the Japanese brain performs its functions in different areas than the brains of other nationalities" (Prestowitz 1988, p.

81). This perception of the Japanese extreme uniqueness even extends to physical objects such as meat and medicine. Arguments that have been seriously presented by the Japanese in official discussion include examples such as this: American beef is not suitable for Japanese intestines, and foreign medicines must first be tested on Japanese, because their bodies function differently (from the rest of humanity!) (Wizelius 1990). Of course, such arguments can also be interpreted as strategic to protect the domestic market.

4. This group orientation is supported by a number of other characteristics of Japanese culture such as the emphasis on harmony, the concern with conformity, the necessity of both group ethics and careful monitoring, and the importance of these personal relationships (Prestowitz 1988, p. 83).

5. This sort of argument cannot be supported by quantifying cultural factors or weighing their relative importance.

6. An additional aim of this section, however, is to address some widespread myths about the absolute "uniqueness" of the Japanese system.

7. In Japan, lifetime agreements are upheld and reinforced by the seniority-based (*nenko-jorestsu*) system of wages and fringe benefits. Wages increase with age of the worker and with length of service in a company. Obviously, the Japanese wage and benefits system directly reinforces people's tendency to stay with one company—thus reinforcing lifetime employment—because moving horizontally into a similar job in another company means losing pay and benefits. In addition, the second company would think twice about hiring that person for a permanent position because of (his/her) questionable loyalty.

8. Whether or not these workers are content with this situation in a male-dominated society is a different question.

9. The greatest contrast is with a country sometimes said to share many characteristics with Japan—that is, Sweden; in Sweden, universities are free, students receive guaranteed grants and loans to study, and other types of labor-market training are fully paid by the state, including lost wages.

10. In addition, in-firm training gives firms control over their supply of labor because it enables firms to shape workers for an occupation rather than seeking workers to fill a job.

11. Obviously this dual large-small structure creates a system of dependency, where the large one can force the small supplier to take risks and bankruptcies that the large corporation, tied by a permanent labor force and high debts cannot take—just as there are trade-offs between permanent and temporary workers in the labor market. However, there are mutual advantages and disadvantages and common attempts to mitigate damages (cf. Okimoto 1989, p. 130).

12. A declining long-run average cost curve means that as more and more units are produced the cost per unit decreases as production becomes more efficient.

13. Thus a higher price paid by Japanese consumers and businesses could underwrite lower prices on the same goods exported to other countries.

14. Much of the following is based on Okimoto (1989, ch. 3 and ch. 4).

15. In other words, politics in Japan is like politics in Europe and the United States in that political juggling and thinking—and not rational economic thinking—often dominates.

16. Okimoto (1989) argues that seven factors can account for MITI's latitude for action:

(1) The capacity of MITI and industry to reach consensus;
(2) The wide scope of MITI's authority over the manufacturing sectors . . . ;
(3) MITI's emphasis on promotional rather than regulatory policies . . . ;
(4) MITI's minimal reliance on formal legislation . . . ;
(5) MITI's capacity to use informal persuasion and administrative discretion instead;
(6) MITI's relatively small budget for public procurement . . . which limits opportunities for pork-barrel politicking; and
(7) The electoral importance of labor-intensive groups in the LDP's grand coalition. (p. 181).

17. Indirect support in the form of forgone tax revenues (to write off investment in technology, etc.) and subsidies through reduced interest rates on loans.

18. Both the United States and France have large government expenditures for military research to promote technological projects considered necessary for national prestige or defense. It is an interesting question why West Germany has such a high proportion of government support to private research and development expenditure, given it does not have the high defense-related expenditure.

19. The Bicycle Racing Fund funnels proceeds from betting on bicycle racing to MITI, which then has full discretion over their use.

20. From the United States there has been criticism of the complicated and slow patent system in Japan. As an example, Texas Instruments filed a patent in 1960 that covers essentially all manufacturing of semiconductors; in 1989, Texas Instruments was finally awarded the patent. To emphasize the importance of this patent, which took twenty-nine years to process, people estimate that Japanese companies will have to pay $500–700 million dollars per year to Texas Instruments (*Rubrik Teknik* 26 [March 1990], p. 12).

Bibliography

Edquist, Charles, and Maureen McKelvey. 1991. "Högteknologiska produkter och produktivitet i svensk industri." [The Diffusion of New Product Technologies and Productivity Growth in Swedish Industry: A Study for the Swedish Productivity Delegation.] (English version available from authors.) In SOU 1991:82, *Drivkrafter för produktivitet och välstånd*, Bilaga Expertrapport 10 "Forskning, teknikspridning och produktivitet." Stockholm: Norstedts.

Edquist, Charles, and Bengt-Åke Lundvall. 1991. "Comparing the Danish and Swedish National Systems of Innovation" in Nelson. Also published as a Tema T Working Paper, no. 77, Linhöping, Sweden.

Ergas, Henry. 1987. "Does Technology Policy Matter?" in Bruce Guile and Harvey Brooks, eds. *Technology and Global Industry: Companies and Nations in the World Economy*. Washington, D.C.: National Academy Press.

Freeman, Christopher. 1987. *Technology Policy and Economic Performance: Lessons from Japan* London and New York: Pinter.

Freeman, Christopher, and Carlotta Perez. 1988. "Structural Crises of Adjustment: Business Cycle and Investment Behavior." In *Technical Change and Economic Theory*, ed. Giovanni Dosi, Christopher Freeman, Richard Nelson, Gerald Silverberg, and Luc Soete. London: Pinter.

Hodgson, Geoff. 1988. *Economics and Institutions: A Manifesto for a Modern Institu-*

tional Economics. Cambridge: Polity Press.

―――. 1991. "The Evolution of Economies and the Temporal Dimension: Is Neloclassical Theory a Limiting Case?". Paper presented at the Conference for the Society for the Advancement of Socio-Economics, Stockholm, June 16–19.

Kawashima, Yoko. 1987. "The Place and Role of Female Workers in the Japanese Labor Market." *Women's Studies International* 10, 6: 599–611.

Koike Kazuo. 1987. "Human Resource Development and Labor–Management Relations." *The Political Economy of Japan*, ed. Yozo Yamamura and Yasukichi Yasubu. Stanford: Stanford University Press.

Komiya, Ryutaro. 1988. "Introduction." *Industrial Policy of Japan*, ed. Ryutaro Komiya, Okuno Mashiro, and Kotaro Suzumura Tokyo: Academic Press, Harcourt Brace Jovanovich.

Komiya, Ryutaro; Okuno Masahiro; and Kotaro Suzumura, eds. 1988. In *Industrial Policy of Japan*, ed. Ryutaro Komiya, Okuno Masahiro, and Kotaro Suzumara. Tokyo: Academic Press, Harcourt Brace Jovanovich.

Lundvall, Bengt-Åke. 1988. "Innovation as an Interactive Process: From User-Producer Interaction to the National System of Innovation." In *Technical Change and Economic Theory*, ed. Giovanni Dosi, Christopher Freeman, Richard Nelson, Gerald Silverberg, and Luc Soete. London: Pinter.

―――. 1992. *National Systems of Innovation: An Analytical Framework*. London: Pinter.

McKelvey, Maureen. 1991. "How Do National Systems of Innovation Differ? A Critical Analysis of Porter, Freeman, Lundvall and Nelson." In *Rethinking Economics: Markets, Technology and Economic Evolution*, ed. Geoff Hodgson and Ernesto Screpanti. London: Edward Elgar Publishing. Also published as a Tema T Working Paper, no. 79, Linköping, Sweden.

Nelson, Richard. 1990. "Capitalism as an Engine of Progress." *Research Policy* 19: 193–214.

―――. 1992. *National Systems of Innovation: A Comparative Study*. Oxford: Oxford University Press.

Odagiri, Hiroyuki, and Akira Goto. 1989. "National Systems Supporting Technical Advance in Japan." Paper presented at the National Systems Supporting Technical Advance in Industry Conference, November.

Ohmae, Kenichi. 1985. *Triad Power: The Coming Shape of Global Competition*. New York: Free Press.

―――. 1987. *Beyond National Borders: Reflections on Japan and the World*. Homewood, Ill.: Dow Jones–Irwin.

Okimoto, Daniel. 1989. *Between MITI and the Market: Japanese Industrial Policy for High Technology*. Stanford, Calif.: Stanford University Press.

Polanyi, Michael. 1967. *The Tacit Dimension*. London: Routledge and Kegan Paul.

Porter, Michael. 1990. *The Competitive Advantage of Nations*. London: Macmillan.

Prestowitz, Clyde, Jr. 1988. *Trading Places: How America Allowed Japan to Take the Lead*. Tokyo: Charles E. Tuttle.

Rosenberg, Nathan. 1982. *Inside the Black Box: Technology and Economics*. Cambridge: Cambridge University Press.

Rubrik Teknik. 1990. "Patent klart efter 29 år," Måndag 26 mars.

Schein, Edgar. 1985. "How Culture Forms, Develops and Changes." In *Gaining Control of the Corporation Culture*, ed. Ralph Kilmann, Mary Saxton, and Roy Serpa, 17–43. San Francisco and London: Jossey-Bass.

Senghaas, Dieter. 1985. *The European Experience: A Historical Critique of Development Theory*. Leamington Spa/Dover, New Hampshire: Berg Publishers.

Sigurdson, Jon, and Yael Tågerud. 1989. *Globala Trender inför 90-talet*. Stockholm: STU.

Spero, Joan Edelman. 1985. *The Politics of International Economic Relations*. 3d ed. London: George Allen and Unwin.

Tachibanki, T. 1984. "Labour Mobility and Job Tenure." In *The Economic Analysis of the Japanese Firm*, ed. Masahiko Aoki. Amsterdam: North-Holland.

von Wolferen, Karel. 1990. *The Enigma of Japanese Power*. London and New York: Macmillan.

Wizelius, Tore. 1990. "Maktens gåta i Japan: Den unika kulturen som ingen riktigt kan förstå." *Dagens Nyheter*, August, 29, p. B3.

Yamamura, Kozo. 1988. "Caveat Emptor: The Industrial Policy of Japan." In *Strategic Trade Policy and the New International Economics*, ed. Paul Krugman, 118–41. Cambridge: MIT Press.

Yamamura, Kozo, and Yasukichi Yasuba, eds. 1987. *The Political Economy of Japan*. Vol. 1. *The Domestic Transformation*. Stanford, Calif.: Stanford University Press.

11. Structural Competitiveness and Strategic Capacities: Rethinking the State and International Capital

Bob Jessop
Klaus Nielsen
Ove K. Pedersen

This chapter explores some of the changing forms of competition in an increasingly global economy and the associated reorientation of state activities to secure national competitiveness. Although we try to introduce some order into the confusing and often contradictory political economy literature on competition and competitiveness, the most distinctive feature of our account is its particular approach to the state and the official discourse about competition. We therefore examine the state's structural selectivity and strategic capacities and relate these to shifts in official discourse about competitiveness.

In particular, we examine the changing role of the state (broadly defined) in industrial policy in a period marked by a significant redefinition of conditions making for international competitiveness. We explore the nature, preconditions, and dynamic of structural competitiveness (which involves not only nationally specific comparative advantages as well as firm-specific capacities but also the competitive implications of a wide range of institutional externalities) and also consider the politically mediated capacities to pursue national accumulation strategies. Our concern in both cases is dynamic rather than static. Thus, we also explore how the factors making for competitiveness are being redefined through emergent trends in the global economy and their associated economic discourses and how the very form of the state itself (still broadly defined) is being reorganized in response to these changes.

We proceed in five steps: first, by reviewing four crucial economic shifts that have affected the nature of economic competition in the world economy; second, by reviewing the nature of market forces, competition, and competitiveness; third, by reflecting on the nature of the state and its strategic capacities; fourth, and this is the major part of the article, by presenting three case studies about state and competition—dealing with Denmark, Sweden, and Britain; and fifth, by drawing some general conclusions.

New Challenges to International Competitiveness

Among the many tendencies and trends discernible in contemporary capitalism there are four that are often cited as having major implications for international competitiveness. These are the increasing impact of new technologies, the growing internationalization of the world economy, the alleged transition from Fordism to post-Fordism, and the increasingly triadic nature (United States–European Communities–Japan) of the world economy. No such identification of tendencies and trends can be entirely innocent, of course; this is particularly clear for the last two tendencies. For these trends are also likely to cause contention among active participants in the internationalization process itself but may well become self-fulfilling prophecies if enough economic and political forces base their action on them.

1. One of the four trends having major implications for international competitiveness is the rise of new core technologies as the motive and carrier forces of economic expansion and the increasing integration of different technologies in producing a given range of products as well as their application across different sectors. New core technologies relevant to the current competitive struggle include microelectronics, telecommunications, data processing, optical technologies, robotics, new materials, renewable energy sources, and biotechnology. Their mastery is held to be critical to continued growth and structural competitiveness, yet few firms are likely to have the skills, capital, and knowledge needed both for basic research and for product and process development on their own. Indeed, many are so knowledge-and-capital intensive that they require collaboration (especially at precompetitive stages) across many interests (firms, university, public and private research labs, venture capital, public finance, etc.), drawing on resources at different points on the globe. Such cooperation reduces competitive and technological uncertainties and helps internalize the spillover of research benefits (cf. Hughes 1989). Thus, there is a clear trend toward technological cooperation among firms within each part of the triad and among distant competitors in different parts of the triad (cf. Ohmae 1985; Hughes 1989).

The dynamics of technology flows, shifts in comparative advantage, and competitiveness will depend on the diffusion and absorption of new technologies, and there is increasing concern about how best to transfer technology in this context. Transnational companies clearly play a key role here (and are increasingly collaborating in various forms of strategic alliance (see especially Contractor and Lorange 1988; Hughes 1989; Vonortas 1990), but there is also growing interest in most economies in state sponsorship of technology transfer and diffusion. For, as Hughes notes, ''international technological competition is seen to have intensified firstly because medium or high technology industries are the main areas where the advanced industrial economies can expect or hope to have a competitive advantage, given the pressures of competition from the newly industrializing countries in less technology intensive products'' (Hughes 1989, p. 276). This can be a key element in strategies for economic growth in the light of changing forms of competitiveness—with Japan being particularly advanced in its Schumpeterian and quite explicit "knowledge-intensive industrialization" strategy. The four Asian Tigers (South Korea, Taiwan, Hong Kong, and Singapore) are also moving into new technologies to counteract protectionism and the threat from second-tier Newly Industrialized Countries (NICs) (cf. Ernst and O'Connor 1989). But "sunrise industry" policies are crucial to many advanced capitalist societies, too, and have also been taken up at the European Community (EC) level.

2. A second trend having major implications is the massive internationalization of financial and industrial flows involving more firms, more markets, and more countries. This tendentially homogenizes economic space as leading-edge technologies are diffused, foreign direct investment is undertaken by all metropolitan powers, a small but increasing number of NICs develop their own multinational companies (MNCs) and transnational businesses (TNBs), and markets become international. Thus MNCs no longer operate in a multidomestic economy where foreign operations are run with minimal cross-national coordination via subsidiaries with their own managements, via acquisitions and mergers with limited global integration, or through cooperation agreements among otherwise independent enterprises. Instead, they operate in a global economy in which operations are integrated across national borders in relation to an overall global accumulation strategy, and it is hard to ascribe the firm any specific "territoriality" owing to the complexity of its interrelationships and the global spread of share ownership with active trading in different stock markets worldwide (cf. Hood and Vahlne 1988; Petrella 1990).

A reinforcing factor here is the spread of world markets (or markets that eventually will become such) regulated by universal standards (Petrella 1990, p. 99). Clearly this does not mean that the operations of global firms are identical from country to country or that they are (or will ever become) equally dispersed across the globe; it does mean that they are subject to an overall strategic plan that is formulated on a global scale. In turn, this has major implications for the role of the nation-state and for the concept of the "national" economy as a natural unit of the world economic order. One crucial effect is that national economic space is no longer the most obvious starting point for pursuing economic growth, technological innovation, or structural competitiveness. This is increasingly reflected in the transnational strategies of firms and states alike. It is in this context that Petrella notes how "the success of the national enterprises on the world scene is a prerequisite for the achievement and preservation of the country's technological and economic autonomy" (Petrella 1990, p. 102). This holds not only for advanced capitalist economies but also for the four Asian Tigers and other latecomer industrializing nations.

3. A third trend is a transition from Fordism to post-Fordism as the dominant

model of development shaping economic and political strategies. This involves a paradigmatic shift from a growth model concerned with mass production, scale economies, and mass consumption (cf. Jessop 1990a). This shift in the dominant technoeconomic paradigm has major implications for enterprise and sectoral strategies even where Fordism (economies of scale, division of work/specialization, and standardization of goods and services) was not as such previously dominant in particular branches or national economies. For it provides an interpretative framework within which to make sense of the current crisis and its disruptions to the circuit of capital and to impose some coherence on the search for routes out of the crisis. This transition is associated with a crisis of United States economic hegemony (with which the Fordist paradigm is especially associated) and an emerging struggle among the United States, Germany, and Japan to define a hegemonic post-Fordist paradigm. This, in turn, radically undermines strategies based on the 1970s wisdom that internationalization was essentially driven by United States multinationals and that the state's task was to find an appropriate response to this American challenge.

At stake today in international competition is the competitive struggle to switch quickly and smoothly among innovative products and processes with each new product offering better functional qualities and improved efficiency in production. It is no longer a question of competing through economies of scale in the production of standardized goods and services using dedicated production systems but of competing through the capacity to introduce flexible manufacturing or service delivery systems and to exploit the resulting economies of scope. This explains why Best can describe the ''new competition'' as being led by business enterprises based upon new production and organizational concepts. ''At the centre of the new competition as being led by business enterprises based upon new production and organizational concepts, is the entrepreneurial firm, an enterprise that is organized from top to bottom to pursue continuous improvements in methods, products, and processes'' (Best 1990, p. 2). And this explains in turn why Mytelka (1987, p. 32) can justifiably claim that ''the key to longevity has become an ability to control the transformation of the market rather than respond to changes in it'' (cited in Vonortas 1990, p. 205).

4. A fourth tendency is a redefinition of the macroeconomic global hierarchy, a redefinition in which concepts such as European Economic Space and the Pacific Rim Economic Community are promoted to challenge the economic dominance of the United States sphere of economic influence. It is far from clear that these concepts correspond to real trends independently of their identification and active promotion in official discourses, but insofar as a range of official institutions and business strategies are premised on them, they can become self-fulfilling. Certainly they have come to play a key role in discussions of competitiveness. For our purposes the most important of these new regional concepts is the accelerated economic integration of the EC, which was begun as a deliberate move to overcome ''euro-sclerosis'' and to reinforce Western Europe as a

"triad power" (Ohmae 1985). The end of the cold war and the marketization of Eastern Europe are still highly uncertain new trends and will be not considered here; nor will we discuss the emergence of the Pacific Rim economic region. But it is worth noting here our opinion that the growing advocacy of triad power ignores significant countertendencies toward the reemergence of regional economies as well as toward a growing interpretation of the so-called triad powers.

Each of these factors has crucial implications for the dynamics of competition and the state's role in securing competitive advantage. We approach these in two steps. We begin by presenting some basic conceptual distinctions regarding competition, competitiveness, and competitive strategies; then we will discuss some of the implications of these trends for state functions and accumulation strategies. It is no part of our argument that competition is always and everywhere recognized as such and that those involved in competition have clear strategies toward it. For not all the conditions affecting competition are acknowledged, and it operates *ex post* in unanticipated ways. But we do insist that competition and competitive strategy have become more and more reflexive and that there is growing concern with issues of competition. This simply reflects the truism that social agents are capable of choice and strategizing. Thus we must examine how self-conscious and reflective economic and political agents involved in these processes have become and also examine the modes of calculation they employ to this end. It is also important to explore how far this involves second-order strategizing about how to enhance competitiveness as well as how to engage in competition with existing levels of competitiveness.

Competition, Competitiveness, and Strategies

Competition occurs on a stratified terrain rather than a level playing field. As the hierarchy of forms of competition and competitive players alters, the dynamics of competition also changes. We can approach competitive hierarchies from several directions: changes in the relative importance of different markets in setting the parameters of competition, changes in the relative super- and subordination of different forms of competition, and changes in the corporate forms associated with advantages in given fields of competition.

The first hierarchy concerns the relation among four types of markets: financial, industrial, and commercial markets together with emerging "metamarkets" in the increasingly important field of intellectual property rights. These can be considered both within national economies (e.g., the dominance of City interests in Britain) and across national economies (e.g., the emergence of an "international intellectual property regime" as part of the high-tech neomercantilist strategies pursued by the United States and Japan). Financial market transactions prompted by short-term money-making opportunities have grown at the expense of long-term industrial (or producer) interests and have engineered massive restructuring of firms through new financial instruments. Likewise, as technologies become more knowledge-intensive, access to markets in technological know-how (licenses, databases, patents, technology transfer, etc.) become crucial to effective competition, and the appropriation of knowledge becomes a key factor in competitive success (Colombo 1988; Ernst and O'Connor 1989).

The second hierarchy is more complex and concerns the relation among different forms and/or bases of competition. Thus, as well as the conventional neoclassical distinctions among the number of agents in markets (perfect, imperfect, monopolistic, etc.), we can also cite other, supposedly less "pure" forms of economic interaction (such as networks or strategic alliances). To these can be added a concern with the bases on which these different forms of economic interaction operate (e.g., costs and prices, various forms of rent, state subsidies, etc.). This is not simply relative sub- and superordination. Thus, even where liberal competition survives in current capitalism, it is often subordinate to monopolistic competition (e.g., suppliers to retail chains, subcontracting to monopolies). Conversely, as new technologies and processes or product innovations become more widespread, technological rents will diminish and allocative efficiency will become more significant.

The third hierarchy concerns the corporate form assumed by the competition setters in different markets and/or forms of competition. The peak of the global corporate hierarchy is currently occupied by denationalized transnational banks and "stateless" multinational firms (cf. Grou 1985). The leading banks now offer a full range of financial services, and the leading MNCs now specialize in high-tech, high-value-added groups of products (e.g., specialty chemicals, advanced transport, energy resources). Combining these hierarchies, we can say that the dominant competitive forces are those that set the terms of competition in the most important market. And, as the forms of competition and competitive strategy shift, patterns of competitive advantage will also alter. In turn, this implies that the state's capacity to promote competitiveness depends on its ability to pursue competitive strategies adapted to the position of the national economy and its key economic actors within the changing hierarchy.

The idea of competitiveness is conceptually ambiguous and politically controversial. Even a cursory review of the literature reveals many ways of defining and measuring it; even the briefest acquaintance with current policy debates will indicate the political issues at stake. These points are related. For competitiveness is a discursively constructed notion with obvious strategic implications both economically and politically. Different notions entail different forms of political action with different effects on the competitive positioning of firms, sectors, regions, and nations, as well as on the balance of political forces within and beyond the state. The role of politics is indicated in a recent claim that worries and proposals about European competitiveness expressed by the European Commission derive more from French than German experience, for it is French rather than German industry that is uncompetitive and it is France that has neomer-

cantilist and dirigiste traditions (Grahl and Teague 1990, pp. 159–60). Conversely, the 1992 "internal market" strategy tends to reflect more the weight of
neoconservative national governments within the European Community during
the 1980s insofar as it is more neoliberal in approach. Despite such conceptual
ambiguities and political controversies, however, we now present some
elementary distinctions about competitiveness at the micro- and macrolevels.

Microeconomic competitiveness concerns firms and is measured through
market share, profits, and growth. Different strategies correspond to these different indicators and will also vary with the forms of competition. Where liberal
competition prevails, for example, competitiveness mainly depends on prices
and cost inputs. In many branches and sectors, however, competitiveness cannot
be reduced to relative costs and prices. Together with data on market share,
employment levels, profits, or exports, these are now often seen more as symptoms rather than causes of competitiveness. Thus, research shows that price differences are weighed against differences in product quality, after-sales service,
and so forth. Likewise both managerial and industrial economics claim that
"firm-specific advantages," that is, factor(s) unavailable in the short-term to
competitors, are the key basis for competitiveness (Casson 1983; Dunning
1988). Such advantages are essential where monopolistic competition prevails.
They might originate in production (patent rights, know-how, research and development capacity) or in marketing (design, image, knowledge of likely
demand, sales networks). This has led, in turn, to increasing concern about
input-side criteria for assessing competitiveness. The U.S. Congress established
an Office of Technology Assessment in 1978 to assess the competitiveness of
U.S. industries, and this examines industry and market structures, the nature of
work forces, availability of materials and components, supporting infrastructures, the environment for innovation and technology diffusion, business and
economic conditions, government policies and interactions with the private sector, and international trade relations (Alic 1987, pp. 8–9). Similar ideas have
been expressed in Porter's concept of the *national diamond* of factors affecting
the competitiveness of specific firms or sectors (1990). Many other studies could
be cited as well to illustrate the growing recognition of the many factors that influence a firm's competitiveness.

The multidimensional character of competitiveness is even more strongly pronounced at the macroeconomic level. The concept of macroeconomic competitiveness is controversial since some critics deny that "economies" can function
as units of competition. They are right insofar as "economies" are not real
agents or subjects but wrong insofar as real agents or subjects do identify
"economies" as engaged in competition and act on this perception. This could
occur for political or military as well as for economic reasons and is closely connected to the organization of world society in and through nation-states. In this
context, definitions of competitiveness and their associated discourses are liable
to change. Mercantilist notions from the seventeenth century can be contrasted

with the imperialism of the 1890s or recent worries about structural competitiveness. Key indicators in recent years have been factor endowments; relative prices, costs, and exchange rates; and shares in world exports or ratios of foreign penetration of home markets. Given these concerns, real subjects may seek to enhance macroeconomic competitiveness either because of its perceived impact on the overall competitiveness of individual firms operating in a given national economic space or because of the repercussions of macroeconomic competitiveness on other objectives—whether economic (such as electoral consequences) or military capacities. Such concerns will be reflected, in turn, in different types of strategy to enhance competitiveness.

The dominant theoretical perceptions of macroeconomic competitiveness have stressed the exclusive importance of relative prices and/or comparative advantages. Traditional international trade theory has related competitiveness to comparative advantages as shaped by factor endowments. Another approach distinguishes between comparative advantages as shaped by microeconomic factors and competitiveness as being a macroeconomic problem associated with the development of prices, costs, and exchange rates. Empirical studies have questioned these simplistic perceptions. Thus, Kaldor (1978) has shown a "perverse" (positive) relation between export performance and growth in relative prices or costs; Leontief (1953) has shown that the United States had net exports of labor-intensive products and net imports of capital-intensive manufactured goods. Various studies have shown other factors explaining the development of competitiveness. For example, Fagerberg (1988) has shown that the development of market shares at home and abroad for fifteen Organization for Economic Cooperation and Development (OECD) countries from 1961 to 1983 is strongly related to the ability to compete in delivery (capacity) while price- and cost-competitiveness played rather a limited role.

The macroeconomic aspect of competitiveness includes not only prices, costs, and exchange rates but also the structures that influence the capacities of firms to compete in technology, delivery, after-sales service and to develop other forms of firm-specific advantages. A useful concept here is *structural competitiveness*. The OECD sees this as "a way of expressing the fact that while the competitiveness of firms will obviously reflect successful management practice by entrepreneurs or corporate executives, it will also stem from the strength and efficiency of a national economy's productive structure, its technical infrastructure, and other factors determining the 'externalities' which firms build on, that is, the economic, social, and institutional frameworks and phenomena which can substantially stimulate or hamper both the productive and competitive thrust of domestic firms" (Science, Technology and Information [STI] Review 1986, pp. 86–87).

The multidimensional character of this perception of macroeconomic competitiveness is evident from a summary of the aspects of economic structure relevant to structural competitiveness. These include "the size of domestic markets, the structure of domestic production, relationships between different sectors and industries . . ., the distribution and market power of supplier firms . . ., the characteristics and size distribution of buyers, and the efficiency of non-market relations between firms and production units.'' It might further depend on ''no exaggerated conflict in the field of income distribution, price stability, flexibility, and the adaptability of all participants in the market . . . a balanced economic structure based on new technology, favorable scientific and technological infrastructure and realistic requirements for risk containment and environmental protection'' (STI Review 1986, pp. 91–92).

Once macroeconomic competitiveness is deemed relevant, it can be targeted for action, but the definition of competitiveness, the target variables, and the strategies adopted are all discursively constituted and will vary from case to case. In some cases, extraeconomic factors can prove crucial (e.g., tariff and nontariff barriers to trade, access to state subsidies); but, insofar as competition is mediated through market forces, it will depend on the struggle to increase efficiency. In the latter context, it is useful to distinguish three forms of efficiency that bear on the competitive strength of economic agents: (1) Ricardian or allocative efficiency, (2) Kaldorian or growth efficiency, and (3) Schumpeterian or innovative efficiency.

Ricardian competitiveness depends on efficiency in the allocation of resources to minimize production costs with a given technical division of labor and on the assumption that current economic conditions will continue. Kaldorian competitiveness depends on efficiency in the allocation of resources among available processes and products in terms of the likely impact of (re)allocation on economic growth. And Schumpeterian competitiveness depends on efficiency in allocating resources to promote technical, product, and organizations innovations that will alter the pace and direction of economic growth (cf. Dosi et al. 1989; Hagedoorn 1989). Clearly the movement from one to another involves higher degrees of reflection; this is not just a question of cognitive powers but also of the organization of economic and political forces for reflection. Each strategic step toward a Schumpeterian competitive strategy requires a more radical approach to competitiveness: If allocative efficiency takes the technical labor process for granted, growth efficiency is oriented to alternative production techniques, and innovative efficiency is concerned with innovation in products, processes, and organization.

We suggest that there is an increasing concern with Schumpeterian competitiveness and that this is now reflected in the debate over structural competitiveness. Whereas the dominant macroeconomic perceptions of competitiveness were until recently based on Ricardian or Kaldorian efficiency, the newly introduced concept of structural competitiveness points toward a Schumpeterian understanding of efficiency. This is now incorporated into OECD analyses, has become central to recent EC industrial policy, has long played a crucial role in the industrial policies of Japan, South Korea, and Taiwan, and is an integral part of

West German policy. Even in the United States, where allocative and growth efficiency have long been hegemonic perspectives, there is now a concerted effort to reorient industrial policy toward structural competitiveness (Dertouzos et al. 1988). Similarly, from a corporate strategy viewpoint, Porter's contribution can also be seen as an attempt to redirect industrial and governmental efforts from short-term, Ricardian efficiency to longer-term, dynamic, Schumpeterian concerns.

The State and Accumulation Strategies

Earlier we briefly mentioned four emergent trends in the global economy. These have clear implications for possible state functions in securing structural competitiveness, and it is to these that we now turn. For ease of presentation, we now deal with the four trends in the same order as they were introduced earlier in this chapter and note some possible implications. But it is no part of our argument that there is any necessary, objectively determined link between the individual trends that we happen to have identified and specific features of the current political reorganization and rearticulation of different levels of the state. Nor do we claim that these trends in themselves guarantee that states will develop the capacities to perform such functions. Indeed, we have already noted that these trends can be (and are) integrated and expressed in quite different discourses and linked to contrasting strategic conclusions as different forces seek to make sense of the conflicting tendencies and countertendencies at work in the global economy. Given these cautionary remarks, however, we review some of the more obvious implications of the current restructuring.

Globalization and State Functions

First, given the growing competitive pressures from NICs on low-cost, low-tech production and, indeed, on simple high-tech products, the advanced capitalist economies must move up the technological hierarchy and specialize in the new core technologies if they are to maintain employment and growth. States have a key role here in promoting innovative capacities, technical competence, and technology transfer so that as many firms and sectors as possible benefit from the new technological opportunities created by research and development activities undertaken in specific parts of the economy (STI Review 1986, p. 86). Conversely, as the budgetary and fiscal pressures on states as national economies become more open, states must shift industrial support away from efforts to maintain declining sectors and toward promoting new sectors. Alternatively, given that the new core technologies are generic and applicable to many different fields of production, states should at least intervene to restructure declining sectors so that they can apply new processes, upgrade existing products, and launch new ones. In all cases, the crucial point at issue is state action to encourage the development of new core technologies and their application to as wide a range of activities as possible in order to promote competitiveness.

Second, as internationalization proceeds apace, states can no longer act as if national economies were effectively closed and as if their growth dynamic were autocentric. Small open economies, such as those of Sweden and Denmark, had already faced this problem during the postwar boom, of course; now even large, relatively closed economies have been integrated into the global circuits of capital. Nowhere has this become more evident in the last decade than in the United States. For the increasing concern over United States competitiveness and the associated debate about the need for an explicit national industrial policy reflect the increasing exposure of a quasi-continental, broad-based, highly productive economy to the pressures of competition in the global system.

In particular, many macroeconomic policy instruments associated with the Keynesian welfare state lose their efficacy with growing internationalization and must be replaced or buttressed by other measures if postwar policy objectives such as full employment, economic growth, stable prices, and a sound balance of payments are still to be secured. In some cases, these policy objectives were abandoned by state managers as they placed their faith in market forces. In others, new measures were taken to secure the old objectives in changed circumstances. In almost all cases, states have become more involved in managing the process of internationalization itself in the hope of minimizing its harmful domestic repercussions and/or of securing maximum benefit to their own home-based transnational firms and banks. In turn, this means that states must get involved in managing the process of internationalization and creating the most appropriate frameworks for it to proceed. Among the many activities included here are introducing new legal forms for cross-national cooperation and strategic alliances, reforming the international currency and credit systems, promoting technology transfer, managing trade disputes, developing a new international intellectual property regime, and developing new forms of regulation for labor migration. This leads to the paradox that as states lose control over the national economy they are forced to enter the fray on behalf of their own multinationals.

Third, as the dominant technoeconomic paradigm shifts from Fordism to post-Fordism, the primary economic functions of states are defined. Fordism was typically associated with a primary concern with demand management within national economies and with the generalization of mass-consumption norms. This reflected the belief that Fordist mass production was demand driven and could only be profitable when high levels of demand were maintained and markets for mass consumer durables expanded. The class compromise supporting the Fordist Keynesian welfare state also encouraged this pattern of economic intervention. But the transition to post-Fordism is prompting a reorientation of the primary economic function of the state. The combination of the late Fordist trend toward internationalization and the post-Fordist stress on flexible production has encouraged states to focus on the supply-side problem of international competitiveness and to attempt to subordinate welfare policy to the demands of flexibility. In this sense, we can speak of a shift from the Keynesian welfare state to the Schumpeterian "workfare" state (cf. Jessop 1990c). This does not mean that the motley diversity of political regimes will disappear with the transition to post-Fordism. For the Schumpeterian workfare state can take neoliberal, neocorporatist, and neostatist forms, depending on institutional legacies and the balance of political forces. But a general trend does seem to be emerging both in official discourse and in the *de facto* shifts in forms of state intervention.

Fourth, as the forms of internationalization become more contentious and conflictual and competing strategies evolve around the triad powers, nation-states must tackle not only the domestic repercussions of global restructuring but also the domestic problems emerging from the changing international balance of forces. There is a complex dialectic at work here. Alongside the trends toward globalization and the formation of supraregional triad economies, we can see a reemergence of regional and local economies within the nation-state. In certain respects this is associated with a "hollowing out" of the nation-state as powers are delegated upward to supraregional or international bodies or downward to regional or local states or among local states with complementary interests (on these trends, see, for example, Bell 1987; Dyson 1989; Sabel 1989; and Jessop 1991b). But this structural transformation is also associated with a continuing role for the nation-state in managing the changing balance of political forces entailed in the complex and contradictory process of globalization. For the nation-state is still the most significant site of struggle among competing global, triadic, supranational, national, regional, and local forces; social cohesion still depends on the state's capacities to manage these conflicts.

The State and Competitiveness

In approaching the state's role in relation to competitiveness in a changing world economy we could logically address five issues:

1. What is the extent to which such changes derive from prior state activities and discourses and are reinforced by current actions and discourses?

2. What are the repercussions of such changes on the state as an institutional ensemble endowed with a specific structural selectivity, with specific strategic capacities, and with a specific social and material basis?

3. What are the state's capacities—both cognitive and organizational—to monitor and model these changes and to assess their implications for its activities and objectives?

4. What are the state's capacities to guide these changes and promote them in the interests of structural competitiveness?

5. What is the official discourse that expresses the state's understanding of these other issues and reorients its activities in the light of such changes?

In dealing with the final issue, of course, we examine how the state itself would answer the preceding questions as well as the strategic conclusions it draws from its answers.

In so framing these questions, we assume that the state is best analyzed as a complex institutional ensemble whose capacities derive not only from its internal articulation but also from its linkages to forces beyond its boundaries. In contrast to many other accounts of state action, ours problemizes the boundaries and unity of the state as an apparatus endowed with capacities to act. We do not believe that state formation is a once-and-for-all process but argue that the state apparatus must be continually reconstituted in and through practices that endow its various (and changing) elements with a sufficient degree of internal cohesion and that orient them to a common set of purposes. We relate such practices to a dominant state strategy to impose some coherence on its different parts (internal unity) and/or a dominant project to secure cohesion within the wider society (state project). In considering both aspects, our approach also involves examining how state capacities are projected beyond their formal boundaries by connecting them to the "microphysics" of power rooted in institutions, organizations, and interactions outside the state. State power is always and inevitably related to this microphysics, but there are clearly wide variations in the extent to which the state can reflexively monitor and coordinate this dependence.

It is in this context that the changing conditions of global competition are important, for it is a crucial part of our argument that the conditions of competition have changed in ways that require a radical reorientation of state capacities and their coordination with the microphysics of power within the economy and civil society. This can be undertaken in different ways since there is no single state form or state strategy that is always and uniquely associated with successful competition. Thus liberal, corporatist, and *dirigiste* strategies have all worked in some conditions and failed in others; strategies must be developed and adapted in relation to strategic capacities (a relation) and to changed conditions of competition. Moreover, strategies that worked in the past may not work currently or may not be readily transferred to other cases or countries. Nonetheless, although there is a wide variety of possible strategies, a state's success in this regard depends on its having the appropriate form and capacities for a given strategy. This holds even for the apparently counterintuitive case of the liberal, nightwatchman state. A successful noninterventionist strategy depends on the state's capacity to insulate itself from external pressures to intervene and to restrict its own actions to those that maintain the general external conditions for free-market forces. The fact that liberal strategies do not always succeed and can fail because of the incapacity of a state to refrain from ad hoc and politically motivated interventions is exemplified by the British case presented later in this chapter.

Returning now to the main thrust of our argument, we add that state capacities to advance an accumulation strategy depend, in turn, on the state's second-order capacity to reflect upon and manage its capacities and to pursue strategies that secure its own internal unity. This is what gives the political sphere its relative autonomy, with the result that one cannot treat politics simply as "concentrated economics." Indeed, the need to establish apparatus unity might well lead to policies that appear irrelevant or contradictory in relation to accumulation strategies. But without a modicum of apparatus unity (which does not become so great as to inhibit a degree of flexibility), the state could not realize the political conditions needed to implement an accumulation strategy.

The State and Strategy

Given our frequent references to strategy and strategic capacity, we should briefly define our terms. Our preferred definition of strategy involves more than purposeful action. In general, it involves an overall vision of a desirable future state of affairs and a programmed path of actions to realize it. The more the pursuit of the strategy involves monitoring progress toward objectives and corresponding amendments to goals and/or means, the more reflexive it will be—especially where such reflexivity involves coordinating actions over different time horizons and in relation to different fields of action. In this sense, it is possible for collective actors (e.g., firms, unions, states) as well as individuals to pursue strategies. The key requirement is the capacity to formulate a vision, to pursue actions related to it, and to monitor the results. Strategic capacity is nothing more (but also nothing less) than the ability to formulate and implement strategies. This can also be a property of societal systems (such as the economic or political system) as well as of individuals or collective actors; for, although systems as such are incapable of strategic calculation, they can be more or less conducive to effective strategizing among the individual and collective agents operating on their terrain. Indeed, strategic capacity involves more than qualities of the agent considered in isolation insofar as such a capacity also reflects how agents are inserted into a wider action context.

The strategic capacity of a firm therefore depends on the institutional and extra-institutional preconditions that enable the various agents within it to coordinate short-term incentives with long-term calculations and to subordinate their immediate self-interest to common objectives implied in the strategy. Likewise, as we have already noted, the strategic capacities of the state depend on its ability to project its power beyond its boundaries through linking up with the microphysics of power in economy and society. And in both cases strategies must be adapted to the specific vulnerabilities of agents, systems, or other objects of action. It is in considering this adaptation that strategic capacity can be related to the ability to monitor changes in the environment and the conditions of strategic success and to learn from prior attempts to realize strategic objectives. It is also here that one can assess how conducive different societal systems are to strategies to promote structural competitiveness.

There is a rich literature on corporate strategy, but its practitioners have not extended their concepts to the state and its capacities. Our aim is to develop concepts of state strategy bearing on competitiveness and to introduce our conclusions into a discussion on corporate strategy. We are well aware that strategic capacity is not reducible to state capacity—even where the state has the primary role in strategy formation. One way to approach this is through the strategic selectivity of the state system. This can be defined in terms of the ways in which the specific organization of the state differentially privileges the access of some forces (representation) to formulate specific policies and secure their support within the state apparatus (internal articulation) and then to effectively implement these policies (intervention) in relation to a specific microphysics of power (social and material bases of the state). All of these aspects must be related, of course, to the more general vulnerabilities of the targets of intervention. At stake in analyzing strategic selectivity is not only the specific institutional and organizational forms that characterize the state but also their strategic repercussions with regard to the access of specific forces pursuing specific strategies to secure access to the state and also with regard to the strategies pursued in and through that access in relation to the wider society (see Jessop 1990b).

Rather than pursue these issues further through what would inevitably be an excessively abstract and formalistic analysis, we prefer to illustrate our arguments in this regard from the case study material. Thus, we return to these issues in our concluding remarks. Meanwhile, we will specify a crucial concept for a strategic-relational analysis of structural competitiveness, namely, *accumulation strategies,* and consider the implications of such strategies for the state's role in accumulation. Just as firms may formulate and follow their own economic strategies alone or in concert with other firms, so too can states develop and pursue such strategies in relation to the national economy. Whereas the former strategies are usually analyzed in terms of forms of enterprise calculation and/or corporate strategy, the latter have been discussed elsewhere in terms of accumulation strategies. It is to these that we now briefly turn.

An accumulation strategy "defines a specific economic 'growth model' complete with its various extra-economic preconditions and also outlines a general strategy appropriate to its realization" (Jessop 1983). Thus, the growth model envisaged therein must start out from the existing mode of growth and then specify how to consolidate that mode of growth and/or move to a different mode of growth. To avoid possible confusion here it should be noted that, while a growth model is essentially a strategic concept, a mode of growth is more structural. For the latter term refers to the specific configuration of firms and industries in a given economic space and the modalities of their insertion into a broader (ultimately global) division of labor. In this sense, the mode of growth reflects the competitive positioning (comparative and competitive advantages) of firms and sectors in the changing international division of labor and hence the position of national economies in the international hierarchy.

This affects the changing balance between functional complementarities and antagonistic relations among the various economies involved in any given plurinational productive system, i.e., how far their respective cyclical behaviors, structural crises, and general growth dynamics mesh to generate rather than block long-run growth in these national economies (cf. Aglietta 1982; Mistral 1986). For obvious reasons, it also affects the prospects for domestic growth.

At any given time the mode of growth will reflect complex patterns of decline (owing to competitive disadvantage), growth (owing to competitive advantage), and recovery (owing to effective restructuring of uncompetitive sectors). Whereas these issues are determined in the first instance by the productive circuit of capital (firm-level factors), the macroeconomic context is also important. It is here that the concept of structural competitiveness is so central to our understanding of growth dynamics. This, in turn, points to the potential significance of state capacities and state action in promoting an accumulation strategy that enhances competitive advantage and thereby transforms the mode of growth. Indeed, as internationalization becomes an increasingly dominant feature of capitalism, it is vital that accumulation strategies take account of the conditions making for structural competitiveness if they are to be successful. This is not to suggest a purely voluntaristic or decisionistic view of the state's role in accumulation—we have already noted how any strategy is conditioned by both the existing mode of growth and the capacities of the state. It is to be noted that states can intervene to modify growth trajectories through skillful attention to the various social preconditions that lead to competitiveness.

Three Case Studies

We now present three case studies on these issues. The countries chosen are Denmark, Sweden, and Britain. All three have open economies that grew more slowly than the OECD average after the first oil shock and that have been especially hard hit by the global economic trends noted earlier in this chapter. Although the three countries share this rather poor economic growth record, they differ significantly in the causes for this. To explore these issues, we must examine the specific interaction among the three sets of variables already listed: changes in the mode of growth, the specific structural selectivity of state forms and their implications for strategic capacities, and the changing forms of competition. Limited space precludes any extended discussion of these cases, and our arguments here simply involve a shortened, integrated version of the three separate studies presented by Jessop, Nielsen, and Pedersen (1992).[1]

Modes of Growth and Regulation

We could typify the Swedish mode of growth as based on a small and open Fordism, the Danish as based on a small and open non-Fordist niche economy, and the British as based on a large and open flawed Fordism that has matured and entered into crisis. We examine how the four changes noted earlier in the chapter have begun to reorder the global economy and its division of labor. We deal with each economy in turn.

Sweden

Sweden exports refined and processed raw materials as well as products of its giant multinational engineering firms. The latter produce capital goods and mass consumer durables and are notable for their commitment to research and development at home and direct investment abroad. At the same time, Sweden's policy of neutrality has encouraged selective self-sufficiency in energy, alimentary goods, and military equipment. This mode of growth has been sustained and reinforced by a mode of regulation initiated by the Social Democrats that combines commitment to equality and social welfare with concern for economic efficiency and development. The core elements of this mode of regulation were a solidaristic wage policy, an active labor-market policy, expansion of public welfare services, a stabilization policy for wages and prices, a policy for regional development, an active role for public capital formation, and control over financial markets. Its precondition was the high degree of organization and centralization on the Swedish labor market.

From 1952 until 1983 collective wage agreements on the private labor market were negotiated and agreed upon in full sovereignty by the LO (Swedish national blue-collar union) and the SAF (Swedish national employees federation). The government never once intervened in their negotiations. Wage differentials were managed through a very complex system that combined minimum wages, automatic indexation, and negotiated wage differentials across branches, skills, and jobs. The policy facilitated continuous upgrading of Swedish industry and high concentrations of capital. Whereas this policy implied a continuous layoff of workers, it was also tied to an active labor-market policy to upgrade skills and promote labor mobility. In important respects the postwar Swedish model resembles the ideal-type image of Fordism: an accumulation regime based on a virtuous cycle of mass production and mass consumption and a mode of regulation in which productivity-based collective wage formation, extension of wage relations, Keynesianism, and the welfare state play key roles. Certainly, until the mid-1970s, these features seem to have guaranteed a continuous improvement in the industrial structure and the reskilling of labor, just as the high research and development investments seem to have ensured Sweden a leading position in technological development.

Denmark

Denmark's mode of growth is rather more peculiar. On the supply side of the economy—the original referent of the concept—Fordist structures are by no means predominant. The labor process involves the predominance of craft organizations and a large number of highly adaptable, flexibly specialized small and medium-sized enterprises (SMEs). There are few giant firms and relatively little foreign direct investment. It is not surprising, then, that Denmark's accumulation regime lacked a virtuous, autocentric circle of mass production and mass consumption. Instead, as Fordist norms of consumption spread, they were met by extremely high imports of consumer durables. Domestic mass production remained largely absent, and imported mass consumer durables were financed through non-Fordist exports and a growing mountain of foreign debt. The exports came chiefly from the sizable (and highly competitive) agricultural and agro-industrial sector and from other industrial sectors that produced high-quality consumer and capital goods for unstable niche markets.

Conversely, as already implied, the demand side does fit the Fordist model. In the 1960s, the Danish economic takeoff began in earnest and growing prosperity saw the rapid adoption of Fordist demand patterns. As well as mass private consumption of standardized consumer durables, there developed mass collective consumption of welfare services, an institutional framework that served to generalize Fordist consumption norms, and a pattern of state-sponsored urban growth that strongly favored Fordist consumption. Rapid expansion of the house-building and construction sector that accompanied fast urbanization and the spread of Fordist life-styles gave a strong boost to domestic production and absorbed significant amounts of capital and labor. The growth of the public sector was particularly remarkable and reinforced domestic demand. In 1960 public spending in relation to gross domestic product (GDP) was lower in Denmark than the OECD average. However, as a result of comprehensive reforms in education, health, and social welfare, the share of GDP rose from 25 percent in 1960 to 40 percent in 1970 and then to 60 percent in 1982. In short, if we attempt to characterize the Danish model of growth in relation to the ideal type, we could label it demand-side Fordism with a rather typical Keynesian welfare statist mode of regulation.

Britain

Britain's economy did not move successfully into a Fordist trajectory nor did it manage to find expanding non-Fordist niches in an expanding global Fordism. In this respect, it corresponds neither to the Swedish case (Fordism) nor the Danish case (flexible industrial production). Although the mass-production industries, their suppliers, and their distributors did grow at the expense of traditional staple industries in the 1950s, they did not fully secure the fruits of the Fordist revolution. British-owned industry based at home rarely got the same returns from the new techniques of mass production as its overseas competitors did or, indeed, as foreign-owned firms in Britain did. Among the factors behind this productivity gap were the slow growth rate in Britain, the impact of

Britain's distinctive form of union organization, and the inadequate managerial skills of British entrepreneurs.

Among its consequences, given the government's commitment to maintaining full employment levels of demand and an expanding social wage, was increasing satisfaction of mass-consumption demand through imported goods rather than domestic output. Moreover, insofar as the British economy was non-Fordist, the way it was inserted into the emerging world economy pushed it down the international hierarchy. Among the many factors shaping this negative dynamic were the City's position in the global economy and industry's continuing commitment to slow-growing (former) imperial markets rather than to the dynamic Fordist economies of Europe and North America. The problems involved in this "flawed Fordist" mode of growth grew serious in the 1960s as its competitive weakness across most markets became more evident. Despite this double failure on the supply side, however, Britain's mode of regulation showed a precocious commitment to the Keynesian welfare state. But even this proved to be flawed because of the structural incapacity of the British state to operate this mode of regulation effectively through liberal, corporatist, or *dirigiste* channels.

Strategic Capacities

That strategic capacities are crucial to the successful realization of a given accumulation regime can be seen in each case because the relative success of the Swedish model, the rapid "second industrialization" of Denmark, and the intermittent decline of the British economy are all related to the distinctive strategic capacities of their respective states as well as to their industrial profiles and insertion into the world economy. Let us explore this further.

The Swedish and Danish states have some common features in their strategic capacities and in this context can both be described as "negotiated economies" (Nielsen and Pedersen 1991). In such cases, state capacities do not hinge on its ability to steer or coordinate behavior through legal administrative means. Instead, the behavior of autonomous social agents is coordinated through discursive and institutional means that enforce compromises and mobilize consensus. Coordinated decision making is typically based on discursive political and moral incentives rather than threats and economic incentives. Such decision making depends, in turn, on a multitude of institutions with different functions. Some try to mobilize mutual understanding among the social partners around an ideological (normative) framework for actual decision making. Others provide forums to evolve compromises on themes and procedures for later negotiations, which occur in yet other institutions.

The preconditions for such strategic capacities have evolved only slowly. Central to this process was recognition of the coordination problems caused by the polycenteredness of societal power and state authority accompanying the delegation of autonomy to the organizations of the labor market and the rise of a segmented and decentralized welfare state. Also central are the need for compromise caused by a certain symmetry of power among the major societal agents and the potential for consensus in these culturally and technically extremely homogenous countries.

In both Sweden and Denmark the capacity for developing strategies mainly depends on the capacity for mobilizing mutual understanding among autonomous agents and coordination behavior through compromises. This capacity depends, in turn, on the whole institutional setup rather than on the discretionary powers of the state in a narrow sense. However, as the next sections of this chapter show, the strategic capacities of the Swedish and Danish states (broadly defined) are also very different.

The strategic capacity of the *Swedish* state derives mainly from a stable "historical compromise" between the major societal forces and from established forms of policymaking and implementation. There is close cooperation between the elites representing the major societal actors as well as comprehensive and stable corporative links between private interests and the state. Since the 1940s and 1950s, policymaking has been run by a small, interwoven elite of experts with close links to either the Social Democratic movement (including leading civil servants) or to big, export-oriented, capital-intensive companies, which became increasingly multinational in scope. These links were enforced in the 1950s and 1960s by comprehensive and stable corporatist ties among private interest associations, Parliament, and the central state apparatus. In the heyday of the Swedish model, this form of integral state seemed capable of guaranteeing continuous adaptation of the supply side and even of concerning itself with Schumpeterian efficiency in some respects. More recently, however, sharp ideological confrontations have emerged as the model has been denounced outright by major business interests and the Social Democrats have grown weaker. This shift can be partly explained by the growing internationalization of Swedish capital and the increasing integration of Sweden into European economic space.

The capacities of the *Danish* state are quite different. The historic importance of the farmers' movement and small owners as well as the fragmentation of labor (and the decisive absence of semiskilled Fordist mass workers employed in large firms) meant that the basic conditions for stable, long-term compromises between big capital and big labor never existed. This obliged the two classes to make unstable compromises with other social groups. Capital and labor also lacked the autonomy from government control enjoyed by their peers in Sweden and had no equivalent formalized role in government decision making. Danish parliamentary politics were also problematic because of the fragmentation of political parties. Indeed, since 1973, the political scene has been marked by permanent instability, successive weak minority governments, and a pattern of decision making dominated by short-term political calculation.

Consequently, the Danish state lacks an effective means of microeconomic intervention and the historical achievements of Danish social democratic governments have been restricted to building a generous welfare state with only negligible "socialization of investments." Even so, it has been possible in the Danish context to formulate and implement relatively coherent national long-term policies through nonauthoritative means of coordinating policy among a multitude of social agents. This is due to an institutional setup that is quite different from the Swedish version of the negotiated economy. The Danish case is to a much higher degree based on broad and even popular acceptance of policies and on discursive coordination and mutual understanding in one rather coherent and independent elite group representing various interests, and to a much lesser degree based on stable institutions for developing compromises among elites connected to the (two) major societal groups as in Sweden.

The *British* state is marked by chronic incapacity. This is evident in the differential access of political forces to the state system, the internal articulation of the state, and its capacities for intervention. The British state is not readily accessible to forces demanding intervention; the internal articulation of the state means that apparatuses inclined toward intervention are low in the state hierarchy; the capacities for intervention are weak. When attempts have been made to go beyond the liberal approach, the strategies have often been crisis driven, ad hoc, and temporary. Liberal strategies were tried within a Keynesian framework based on simple demand management. But the operation of market forces was weakened by various market imperfections and, even when market forces might have worked effectively, by a stream of politically motivated state interventions.

Corporatist solutions largely failed because their organizational preconditions were missing (cf. previous sections in this chapter). There were clear divisions of interest between industrial and financial capital; industry had no strong peak organization and was fragmented; and the City preferred a liberal strategy based on an open economy, minimal intervention, and overseas investment and enjoyed a measure of economic dominance even when its views were not accepted. Organized labor was also weak, fragmented, and decentralized. On the political front, two parties with different programmatic commitments alternated in office, and major economic policy U-turns often occurred in the lifetime of a given government.

Finally, *dirigiste* solutions failed because of the state's incapacity to influence the microlevel of the economy and the resulting need to rely on the relatively blunt instruments of money, law, and moral persuasion. Even such efforts as it made were often ill-formed, ad hoc, poorly coordinated (if not downright contradictory), short-term in orientation, and often narrowly political in motivation. Commitment to *dirigisme* was also weak because economic intervention was dominated by a Treasury-Bank axis, whose primary concerns were restraining public spending, defending sterling, and short-term economic crisis management. Whatever their long-term benefits to the economy might have been, active structural policies were inconsistent with such aims in the short term. Thus,

Britain has suffered from market forces prone to market failures rather than spontaneous self-expansion, corporatist strategies without the corporatist structures and the commitments needed to sustain them, and state intervention without an interventionist state able to steer an open economy dominated by monopoly capital.

The Forms of Economic Crisis

The 1970s were troublesome for all three economies—but for Britain more than the others. This obviously reflects their respective modes of growth, changes in the world economy, and the capacities to respond to the resulting crisis tendencies. Paradoxical as it might seem, it was not the most Fordist economy that experienced the worst crisis: this honor was reserved for Britain with its doubly flawed insertion into the world economy. Denmark suffered less at first, since its flexibly specialized industry and ability to serve unstable niche markets provided some initial protection; but the more general discontinuities in global economic organization made it ever harder for its industry to adapt. These contrasting experiences were reflected, in turn, as is discussed later in this chapter, in the types of economic and political responses favored in each case.

Swedish industry in the 1970s suffered from declining world demand and increased international competition in markets for most of its internationally competitive products. Its bigger plants also faced the sociotechnical limits of Fordism caused by the rigidities of traditional mass-production technologies earlier than many competitors: the technical problems of coordinating long and complex production lines and absenteeism, high labor turnover, and more direct forms of working-class resistance.

Denmark, thanks to its industrial structure, was not so much affected by these problems. Indeed, its flexible specialized industry was well placed to adapt in the short term to stagnant total demand, differentiated consumer demand, and comprehensive technological restructuring. But, in the long run, the delay and temporal concentration of Denmark's postwar "second industrialization" precluded it from winning significant market shares in the large, fast-growing markets dominated by international firms. This suggests a longer-term problem of competitiveness in the Danish export sectors. Certainly, with the onset of the crisis in 1973, Denmark has grown especially slowly. This is reflected in massive macroeconomic imbalance with continuous deficits on balance of payments, high unemployment, and political instability.

Britain was very hard hit by the emerging crisis of global Fordism. This reinforced its secular economic decline and the problems created by the failure to move a successful Fordist growth path in the postwar period. The 1970s witnessed progressive deindustrialization and rising unemployment. This was due to the combined impact of decline in Britain's established industries as increasing global competition revealed their underlying weakness and of an inability to secure sustained takeoff in sunrise industries. The resulting vacuum was partially filled at first by further expansion in the public sector and later by a neoliberal engineered expansion in private-sector services. In neither case did this do much to boost the long-run competitiveness of the United Kingdom economy. As the unraveling of the Thatcher boom suggests, the profligate expansion of the service sector may have proved counterproductive here.

Discourses and Strategies of Competitiveness

It is well known that the initial reaction to the emerging crisis in the 1970s was to blame the oil shocks. Later attention turned to problems of stagflation and the search for ways to relieve cost-push and demand-pull pressures within increasingly open economies. Wage restraint and monetarism became key items on the policy agenda. As these, too, proved ineffective, attention turned to deeper causes of the crisis. The search for greater flexibility (especially in labor markets) and for less regulation and state control was proclaimed. Even more recently there has been increasing concern with the issue of structural competitiveness—requiring attention not merely to economic variables of factors but also to a whole series of social, political, cultural, educational, and institutional factors that bear on the capacities of different societies to compete and innovate in an increasingly global economy. It is these changing orientations toward competitiveness and the required policy responses that concern us here.

Sweden

Concern with structural competitiveness is not unknown in the postwar era. The selective openness of the Swedish economy, its tradition for neutrality in international politics, its powerful multinationals and its interventionist state had in the 1940s already laid the ground for political debates about Sweden's integration into the international economy. The 1960s also saw strategies developed for a major regional restructuring of the whole country (moving industries and parts of the population from the north to the south), for building an energy sector mainly based on nuclear power, and for constructing new towns, roads, harbors, airports, and so forth, to promote Sweden's physical integration into Western Europe.

However, beginning only in the second half of the 1970s has the competitiveness of the Swedish economy been regarded as an urgent problem. This occurred because of high deficits on the balance of payments and a sharp fall in world market shares. Since this crisis was preceded by significant increases in relative unit labor costs (RULC) and an industrial profits squeeze, the crisis was initially interpreted as a "cost crisis" (Erixon 1989). This opinion was not confined to employers and the bourgeois parties; it was also shared by the Social Democrats and informed the "Third Way" they pioneered on regaining power in 1982. High growth and full employment were to be achieved without balance of payment problems by improving the competitiveness and aggregate profitability of exports through lower wage costs. This marked a decisive break with traditional postwar policies that aimed to restructure industry through the differential profitability of firms and sectors caused by the solidaristic wage policy. The Third Way combined wage restraint first with openly declared, and then indirectly engineered, devaluations. After 1987–88 this policy seemed less successful as wage formation became more conflictual, inflation continued, and market shares continued to decline. Thus, ideas about competitiveness changed again. Attention turned now to the unfavorable product and market mix of Swedish exports. Sweden has actually gained market shares in stagnating traditional sectors while losing market share in fast-growing high-tech sectors such as electronics (Horwitz 1988). Improved profitability did promote innovation and investment in new technology, but it also locked resources into mature industries and reduced the pressure to adapt. As these results became clearer, concern grew about measures to secure structural competitiveness rather than just cost competitiveness.

This reorientation was prompted by growing internationalization of Swedish capital. There has been a massive shift of Swedish investment into the EC and into mergers, acquisitions, and strategic alliances. This has destroyed jobs, investment, and research and development at home; it has also undermined the effectiveness of measures to stabilize demand at home through Keynesian fine-tuning, financial regulation, public capital formation, and related policies. Indeed, the inherent features and effects of such policies are now seen as obstacles to structural competitiveness: the tax system, high wage costs, excessive regulation of capital markets, an overblown public sector, and so forth. (Industrins Utredningsinstitut [IUI] et al. 1990, pp. 205–52). It is now claimed that Sweden must join the global trend toward liberalization and deregulation in order to compete. Some changes have already been made; a tax reform in line with contemporary wisdom (decreasing the marginal tax rate, broadening the tax base, and reducing rights to offset expenses against tax), abolition of foreign-exchange controls, and harmonizing technical standards and norms. Indeed, Swedish legislation has adapted to the ''internal market'' process faster and more thoroughly than most EC member states.

More recently still, in October 1990, the Social Democratic government stated its intention to join the EC. And, by December 1990, all of the major political parties had agreed upon the terms for membership application. The decisive turn toward the EC is not unrelated, of course, to the exit of Swedish multinationals. It is accompanied by other measures that will also undermine the traditional Swedish commitment to self-sufficiency and national autonomy. As a result, nuclear energy production will disappear (although recent Social Democratic statements question the wisdom of the earlier decision to gradually dismantle the nuclear power plants) and Sweden will be integrated into a European energy system. Likewise, autonomy in monetary policy has been abandoned with the recent liberalization of financial markets. Even the legal constraints on the foreign ownership of Swedish property and takeovers of Swedish firms have been relaxed.

But economic factors alone cannot explain these changes. The basic causes for the breakdown of the Swedish model lie elsewhere—in the long-term erosion of some of its preconditions. First, the autonomy of the organizations in collective wage formation has been shattered. This is partly due to the growth of organizational conflicts and the trend toward decentralization that accompany the rise of the new technoeconomic paradigm of post-Fordism with its emphasis on flexibility and its fragmentation of the labor force. Wages are (industrywide and national) agreements. In turn, this has limited the prospects of a solidaristic wage policy for egalitarian and macroeconomic ends. At the same time the economic crisis and concern over cost competitiveness prompted the government to intervene in 1990 for the first time in wage negotiations to impose wage controls and to control strike activity.

Second, the "historic compromise" between the Social Democrat movement and big business came under challenge. The Social Democrats initiated this with the 1975 law on codetermination and the 1983 proposal of wage-earner funds intended to socialize investment and ownership of capital. In response, capital stepped up its own activities to resist the perceived threats to its autonomy, and there was a general polarization and ideological conflict. In particular, from the late 1970s, representatives of big and medium-sized industry began to build a large number of institutions (including newspapers, radio and TV stations, publishing houses, research centers, etc.) to counteract and openly contest the Social Democratic elite's positions in the central and local state system (Ekdahl 1990).

While the Social Democratic elite was defending the universal welfare state and the full-employment policy, the elite representing big capital was calling for labor market deregulation, privatization, and commercialization of the public sector.

Third, corporatist links have been badly weakened. The Swedish Federation of Employers' Organizations decided in 1990, for example, to resign from its formal positions in public bodies and to limit its policymaking activities to lobbying. Fourth, the state's capacities to intervene at the microeconomic level and promote structural competitiveness have been radically recomposed. It no longer depends entirely on formal and organized interaction among privileged societal actors as big business seeks to develop alternative channels of influence and an independent voice and as rank-and-file unions and Social Democrat party members reject calls for wage restraint. But, fifth, as old patterns wither away, new forms of concerted action are emerging elsewhere in the Swedish political economy. At plant level, for instance, labor and capital have developed new forms of cooperation allowing increased flexibility in accordance with a new consensual vision of democracy, flexibility, and upgrading of qualifications (Elam and Börjesson 1990). The present strains might be interpreted as part of an adaptation process instead of an outright abolition of the negotiated economy.

Denmark

Economic policy debates in Denmark have focused for some decades on measures needed to improve the competitiveness of Danish industry as the key to removing macroeconomic imbalances and promoting economic growth. Because of the balance of payments deficits the need to improve competitiveness became urgent in Denmark much earlier than in Sweden. Even in the early 1970s it was already widely agreed that resources should be shifted from the public sector and other sheltered branches to the internationally competitive sector to remove the seemingly permanent deficit. Recession delayed the implementation of this program, but public-expenditure policy still became a key instrument of economic management by the end of the decade. Remarkably this policy—aided by a short-lived period of above average OECD growth—transformed an enormous public-finance deficit in 1982 (10 percent of GNP) into a surplus (3 percent of GNP) only three years later. Wage policy was the other main instrument in Danish efforts to improve international competitiveness during this period. Although it originated in attempts to improve the trade-offs between inflation and unemployment, it was reinterpreted in the 1970s in terms of the need to improve competitiveness. Since 1979 wage policy has become accepted by all the main actors as an instrument not only for reducing RULC but also for long-term redistribution of income from wages to profits (Pedersen 1991). This was supported by successive devaluation while the Social Democrats still held power.

In the period 1979–82, Danish international competitiveness as measured by RULC improved by around 20 percent because of wage-restraint and exchange-rate adjustments. Although competitiveness was then generally still perceived as equivalent to RULC, heated debates did occur among various institutions over the concept. During 1984–86, a consensus emerged around an extended formulation. Product innovation and productivity, technology content, marketing, and flexibility on labor markets and in industrial organization were included in the concept of international competitiveness. A key sector here was the Technology Board, which is a corporatist policy and campaign institution for promoting technological progress. It successfully argued that technological development and restructuring have a strong impact on the competitiveness of Danish industry. Reports from the OECD and the Danish government also played a role, since they revealed serious industrial backwardness on several of these newly identified aspects of competitiveness.

On international markets Denmark had increasingly become specialized in standardized goods with low-technology content. Other evidence showed that

Denmark had net total imports in research-intensive and high-tech goods. The decisive formulation of the new consensus was produced by the Danish Ministry of Finance and elaborated in contemporary documents from other public agencies and peak organizations. They identified a series of structural problems and concluded that a structural policy should be applied to increase the level of technology, education, and research and to change the composition of exports as far as products and markets are concerned. Among the specific obstacles identified were the absence of large firms able to conduct extensive, quality research and development and the additional weakness of small and medium-sized enterprises (SMEs) regarding managerial and financial capacity. The cure was to be the formation of "industrial locomotives" through mergers and interfirm networks among the SMEs. Other obstacles were said to be insufficient cooperation between public research and commercial application and overrigid legal barriers between public agencies and private firms. Finally, attention was drawn to excessive regulation of Danish capital markets and the limited mobility and the training of the labor force. In all these areas a consensus emerged on steps to take, and some reforms have followed.

Of particular interest in relation to state capacities is that the objectives for wages and public spending were largely met in the period 1982–86. This was achieved through the existing mechanisms of policy coordination. But some severe macroeconomic balances remained, and the balance of payments worsened. To cope with these problems, new instruments were needed. Even the bourgeois government abandoned its hostility to measures that intervene directly on the supply side. Not only were the problems serious, but internationalization, the liberalization of financial markets, and the move toward the internal market meant that traditional general instruments had become less effective. Conversely, structural intervention and supply-side measures would become more important. Technical considerations apart, the structural policy had also been blocked in 1988–89 by the reemergence of more traditional conflicts in Danish politics (Nielsen and Pedersen 1989). This involved a clash between export-oriented industry and big business and finance (big by Danish standards at least), and smaller companies oriented to the domestic market. The first group favored the "locomotive strategy," whereas the second has united behind a so-called tax strategy based on tax and spending cuts whose combined effect should be to reduce production costs.

The Social Democrats favor full steam ahead in pursuit of the locomotive strategy. However, the bourgeois government is split between representatives from each strategy. The Liberal party advocates the tax strategy and a more confrontational attitude to the Social Democrats, while a dominant group in the Conservative People's party favors the locomotive strategy and more consensual parliamentary policies. This strategic split was sharpened when the Liberal minister of taxes and duties from 1988 challenged the position of the minister of finance as the dominant governmental campaign institution. High marginal taxes are alleged to be the main problem on the grounds that they reduce the supply of labor, savings, and risk taking; create pressure for higher wages; and distort investments, including decisions on plant location.

Since 1988, election results and opinion polls have strengthened the Liberal Party at the expense of its more center-oriented partner(s), and government policy has drifted rightward in a period of extreme minority parliamentarism. In 1989, the bourgeois government launched its "grand plan" for economic recovery. This involved little but a set of tax reductions and other measures to counteract the loss of revenue; no structural policy measures were mentioned. But it did signify that the neoliberal supply-side approach had at least temporarily become dominant in the bourgeois government. Despite lengthy negotiations, no compromise was reached. The implementation of structural policy suffered accordingly with only meager funds being allocated to new programs and savage cuts imposed on the main industrial programs. While continuing lip service is still paid by government to the need for structural policy and enhanced support for research and development and labor-market reforms, the neoliberal approach remains dominant. But so far, more radical neoliberal measures to reform the welfare state have been blocked. Meanwhile, other more pressing structural reforms (such as promoting organic links between technology enclaves and small firms) are neglected both in the heat and paralysis of party battle and in an intensifying struggle within the central state itself between agencies with different interests in the locomotive and tax strategies.

Into this policy vacuum have stepped private institutions. A wave of mergers among "big" Danish firms and, to a much lesser degree, acquisitions and strategic alliances involving foreign capital have taken place. The decision to resort to this locomotive strategy was initiated by a group of big banks and insurance companies, wage-earner funds and (collective) pension funds, trade unions, and representatives of Danish big industry. This group has not just initiated mergers. It has also, among other things, made important investments in venture capital and basic research, attempted to force through a major restructuring of the Danish agro-industrial complex, and prevented hostile foreign takeovers of Danish firms. Furthermore, all these initiatives have been coordinated by common institutions that analyze and decide on issues that are normally the area of industrial policy. It might actually be designated a private industrial policy, formulated, propagated, and implemented within the institutions of the negotiated economy as usual—apart from the absence of direct government or political involvement (Petersen 1989).

In this sense the negotiated economy remains vital for all actors. Besides the emergence of the negotiated "private industrial policy," the bourgeois government has leaned heavily on its customary practices and has also introduced several new practices and procedures along the same lines. In particular, we should note the establishment of quadripartite negotiation among labor, capital, the central government, and the organization for local municipalities (Pedersen

1991). In at least one case, such negotiations have led to an agreement about issues that were hitherto blocked in Parliament. These innovations are all the more remarkable because the bourgeois parties in government have expressed a dislike in principle of many of the institutions of the negotiated economy. This system of coordination has been reorganized and reinforced rather than weakened through the 1980s. Contrary to the situation in Sweden, the strategic capacities inherent in the Danish model have been preserved.

Britain

The failure of corporatist and *dirigiste* strategies in the 1970s reduced faith in state steering capacities and renewed the belief in market forces. Thus, it was the neoliberal forces that secured the dominance of their interpretation of economic decline and the reasons for Britain's lack of competitiveness. They attributed failure to the weakness of free-market forces. Management was not free to manage; workers had too many restrictive practices and/or were prevented by union power from offering themselves for work at market-clearing wages; and the state was overburdening capital and labor alike with its fiscal demands, its inflationary policies, and its willful intervention. The solution was simple. The state should limit itself to securing the monetary and legal conditions for the free market and policing social order. In turn, this implied a commitment to rolling back the frontiers of the state in order to liberate market forces. The neoliberal strategy for competitiveness therefore includes privatization, deregulation, liberalization, introducing market proxies and commercial criteria into the residual public sector, tax cuts to free capital and households to spend their income in the marketplace, and measures to promote internationalization. Clearly this approach does not exclude state intervention and even welcomes it in some instances. But it does limit such intervention to macroeconomic measures to control inflation and supply-side microeconomic measures to reinforce free markets.

Against this dominant neoliberal current, we can find four others:

1. A neo-Schumpeterian approach directly concerned with the conditions for structural competitiveness in manufacturing industry in the light of the growing internationalization of trade and investment;
2. A neo-Schumpeterian approach more concerned with the impact of deindustrialization on local employment and regional prosperity and placing its faith for the revival of both in a state-sponsored shift toward flexible specialization of post-Fordism;
3. A neo-corporatist approach calling for active concertation between a new Labour government and the trade unions to modernize the national economy for the British people in the light of changing global economic conditions;
4. A neomercantilist approach in which Europe rather than the national economy becomes the key unit in the competitive struggle among triad powers and at-

tention is paid not just to manufacturing but to the full range of competition.

These four approaches by no means exhaust the available alternatives, but they are the most significant in recent political discourse in Britain. They are informed by different perceptions of the four global trends noted at the beginning of this chapter, and they also assess them from different economic and political viewpoints. In the first two cases considered, the approach turns mainly on the perception of competitiveness; in the second two cases, it hinges more on the political perspective. But there are other links; thus the first and third involve restructuring for manufacturing capital and organized labor, respectively; the second and fourth for local and "Euro-nationalist" interests.

Each of these accounts is associated with a particular institutional redesign of the state, a specific role for the social partners, and a specific interpretation of the factors making for competitiveness. But their most significant common feature is movement away from a Ricardian account of market forces to one that recognizes the importance of innovation and growth. The neoliberal approach is oriented to the activities of individual firms and to cost and price competitiveness. Its aim is to remove restrictions on the free movement of market forces and to extend their scope.

Neo-Schumpeterian views clearly adopt an account of structural competitiveness informed by shifts in technoeconomic paradigms and long-wave theories of capitalist accumulation. Such approaches aim to secure competitiveness through a mixture of technology and industrial policies that try to win a leading role for national firms in the technological race for modernization. Flexible specialization strategists seem to depend more on growth efficiency and a more modest neo-Schumpeterian view oriented more to continual product and process innovation by small and medium-sized firms. They are less interested in big science and technology and also neglect the problems involved in some of the knowledge-intensive and capital-intensive technologies. Theirs would be a world of competitive, niche-market software houses rather than a world of competitive global information technology transnational corporations (TNCs). And the neocorporatist position seems attached to a neomercantilist, even late Fordist, understanding of competition. If tripartite institutions can be secured, then the interests of national capital and labor can be protected.

These views have had limited impact on the central state under Thatcherism. But they have been tried at the level of the local state and/or are being promoted in and through the EC. A number of local authorities have experimented with a flexible specialization restructuring strategy for labor (e.g., Greater London Enterprise Board); others have been particularly active in the field of technology transfer and venture capital to promote neo-Schumpeterian market forces. The European Community is pursuing a Technological Community strategy alongside its neoliberal 1992 policies and is active in this regard at both the federal and local levels.

It is at the local and the EC levels that we can find the political and economic forces committed to the Schumpeterian approach as well as a political space (however constricted at the local level or overarching at the EC level) that permits such interventionist forces to press their demands and strategies. Indeed, in order to mobilize support behind the strategy, local states are being reorganized to secure effective participation of local venture capital, local research and educational institutions; local manufacturing capital, trades councils, chambers of commerce; and the press. Measures are being taken to marginalize old corporatist, municipal socialist, or liberal conservative forces. The limits of the local state are nonetheless evident in the failure of such policies where conditions are least favorable (contrast Merseyside with London) and central state support is lacking. Likewise, the EC level poses problems in that the neoconservative governments of the 1980s in Germany, Britain, Denmark, and the Netherlands have opposed too much public expenditure on the technology community and have favored the neoliberal 1992 strategy. Overall then, while a discourse of structural competitiveness and Schumpeterian efficiency has been developed, few effective steps have been taken to implement it. Yet again we find that state incapacity is contributing to economic decline in Britain.

Conclusions

This chapter has examined some theoretical and empirical problems in the field of globalization, structural competitiveness, and state policies. Readers probably have noted that we include concepts in the theoretical section that are not deployed in our empirical analyses and that we have also introduced some concepts in the case studies that are not mentioned in our theoretical introduction. This reflects the nature of the two exercises as well as limited space. Nevertheless, we hope that our theoretical remarks have provided a heuristic framework and some working hypotheses for studies of competitiveness in more countries than we have been able to analyze here (or, indeed, would be able to analyze anywhere). Conversely, some concepts needed to analyze a given empirical case are relatively specific and would be misplaced in the general introduction. The important point to note is that all the concepts, wherever they first appear, should be mutually consistent; for they derive from the same broad theoretical perspective with its strategic-relational approach to the political economy of the state as well as to the political economy of the economy. This said we can now draw some more general conclusions about the case studies.

The contrasting patterns disclosed in the case studies are best understood in terms of the complex interaction of three sets of variables:

1. The changing modes of growth characteristic of the three national economies
2. The emerging discourses and strategies concerned with competition and competitiveness

3. The strategic selectivity of the state and its capacities for guiding efforts to enhance competitiveness

In this context the Swedish case involves a dynamic, export-oriented, high Fordist economy with some large TNCs engaged not only in foreign trade but also in overseas production and concerned with the adoption of flexible production techniques to enhance their competitiveness. The Danish case involves a late-developing, export-oriented, non-Fordist flexible craft production economy with many interconnected small and medium-sized enterprises committed to foreign trade but less inclined to invest abroad; the capacity to innovate products and processes in existing fields of production is good but it is proving hard to shift into knowledge- and capital-intensive technology because of the absence hitherto of suitable industrial locomotives. The British case is one of flawed Fordism: a declining, import-oriented, weak Fordist domestic economy with many TNCs busily engaged in moving investment, jobs, and production abroad and a dominant international financial center whose immediate interests are in further internationalization rather than economic regeneration.

Thus, the three cases clearly involve quite different patterns of competitive positioning in relation to the four trends identified near the beginning of this chapter, and this, in turn, indicates a need for different strategic responses in order to maintain or restore structural competitiveness. Yet, while the dominant discourse in Britain is stubbornly neoliberal and neo-Ricardian in its approach to reversing industrial decline and places an ill-judged, blind faith in the capacity of market forces to steer investment into profitable, export-oriented activities, the institutional and organizational properties of the negotiated economy in Sweden and in Denmark have permitted more balanced discourses and strategies to emerge. The two Scandinavian cases are clearly not identical in all respects. This reflects not only the different modes of growth but also the differential strength of the social partners, their commitment to negotiation over the appropriate response, and the stability of the social compromise that helps to sustain the negotiated economy.

Even where there is a broad consensus on the appropriate strategic response to the crisis of competitiveness, however, it does not follow that this can be effectively implemented. This reflects not only the adequacy of the strategies in relation to strategies being pursued in other productive systems but also the capacities of the state and the social partners to implement the strategy. In this regard, too, we find Britain disadvantaged. It has a central state with weak state capacities and is unable to compensate for this through effective organization of the economic forces needed to support a central state initiative. Neoliberal policies have failed just as surely as neocorporatist and neo-*dirigiste* strategies to reverse the long-term decline of Britain's economy.

The Swedish case provides a neat contrast. It had traditionally had an effective central state with good links to the social partners and a relatively stable social compromise. And its position in the global economy provides a sound competitive base from which to launch a strategy for enhanced competitiveness. The very changes that require such a reorientation of accumulation strategy and so fundamental a redefinition of the Swedish state project (with the decision to apply for EC membership only the most radical revision) have paradoxically helped to create the conditions needed for this reorientation. This is because the changes progressively eroded the preconditions of the Swedish model and made it possible for capital and politic for labor and the Social Democrats to shift their ground in the light of changing perceptions of competitiveness. What is interesting is the extent to which the Social Democrats themselves have accepted the apparent logic of internationalization and reoriented their own accumulation strategy toward a more Schumpeterian workfare approach. How far this will be thrown into chaos by the recent election debacle remains to be seen.

The Danish case is intermediate. Its liberal tradition, its unstable social compromise, and its uncertain social partnership make it harder to secure effective support for a new structural competitiveness initiative and to implement it when (or if) it is agreed. At the same time the manner of its insertion into the emerging global economy is more problematic, but there is still much to play for—especially with Denmark's strategic geopolitical location between Sweden and the European mainland and the recent developments in the Baltic region and former Soviet Union. Moreover, despite the apparent paralysis or immobility in the parliamentary and party systems, there is still sufficient flexibility and strategic capacity to provide greater prospects for recovery than is true of the British case. This is readily apparent in the concerted pursuit of a private industrial strategy and the central state's capacity to bypass party fractionalism and in fighting with the development of quadripartite bargaining. The Danish crisis is mainly attributable to the inadequacy of Denmark's insertion into the world economy. The continued vitality of its negotiated economy mode of regulation has meant, however, that a response has been possible within existing institutional forms.

Whether or not the substitution of Major for Thatcher at the head of a weak British state will fundamentally transform the British case is doubtful to say the least. Thatcherism was certainly a major contributory factor to the aggravation of the British crisis—and certainly no solution. Some overdue improvements were undoubtedly made but the long-standing institutional weakness of the state in its integral sense in Britain remains, and the accelerated internationalization of the British economy under Thatcherism has done little to enhance its structural competitiveness.

Note

1. For further documentation we refer to Nielsen (1991) and Pedersen (1991) on Denmark; SOU (1990) on Sweden; and Jessop et al. (1991) on the British case.

Bibliography

Aglietta, M. 1982. "World Capitalism in the Eighties." *New Left Review* 136: 25–35.

Alic, J. A. 1987. "Evaluating Industrial Competitiveness at the Office of Technology Assessment." *Technology in Society* 9, 1: 1–17.

Bell, D. 1987. "The World and the United States in 2013." *Daedalus* 26 (Summer): 1–33.

Best, Michael H. 1990. *The New Competition: Institutions of Industrial Restructuring.* Cambridge: Polity Press.

Casson, A., ed. 1983. *The Growth of International Business.* London: Allen and Unwin.

Colombo, U. 1988. "The Technology Revolution and the Restructuring of the Global Economy." In *Globalization of Technology: International Perspective,* eds. J. H. Muroyama and H. G. Steve. Washington, D.C.: National Academy Press.

Contractor, F. J., and P. Lorange. 1988. *Cooperative Strategies in International Business.* Lexington, Mass.: D. C. Heath.

Dertouzos, M., R. K. Lester, and R. M. Solow. 1988. *Made in America.* Cambridge: MIT Press.

Dosi, G.; L. A. Tyson; and J. Zysman. 1989. "Trade, Technologies, and Development: A Framework for Discussing Japan." In *Politics and Productivity: The Real Story of Why Japan Works,* C. Johnson, L. A. Tyson, and J. Zysman. New York: Ballinger, 3–38.

Dunning, J. H. 1988. *Multinationals, Technology and Competitiveness.* London: Unwin Hyman.

Dyson, K., ed. 1989. *Local Authorities and New Technologies: The European Dimension.* London: Croom Helm.

Ekdahl, Å. 1990. "Högerhrafferna till offensiv." *Dagens Nyheter,* December 30, p. 3.

Elam, M., and M. Börjesson. 1991. "Workplace Reform and the Stabilization of Flexible Production in Sweden." In *The Politics of Flexibility, Restructuring State and Industry in Britain, Germany and Scandinavia,* ed. B. Jessop, H. Kastendiek, K. Nielsen, and O. K. Pedersen, 314–36. Cheltenham, England: Edward Elgar.

Erixon, L. 1989. "Den tredje vägen—inlåsning eller fornyelse," *Ekonomisk debatt* 17: 181–95.

Ernst, D., and D. O'Connor. 1989. "Technology and Global Competition: The Challenge for Newly Industrializing Economies." Paris: OECD.

Fagerberg, J. 1988. "International Competitiveness." *Economic Journal* 98 (June): 355–74.

Grahl, J., and P. Teague. 1990. *1992: The Big Market, The Future of the European Community.* London: Lawrence & Wishart.

Grou, Pierre. 1985. *The Financial Structure of Multinational Capitalism.* Leamington Spa: Berg Publishers.

Hagedoorn, J. 1989. *The Dynamic Analysis of Innovation and Diffusion: A Study in Process Control.* London: Pinter.

Hood, N., and J. E. Vahlne, eds. 1988. *Strategies in Global Competition.* London: Croom Helm.

Horwitz, E. C. 1988. "Marknadsandelar för svensk export 1978–84." *Arbetsrapport*, no. 15. Stockholm: Kommerskollegiet.

Hughes, K. S. 1989. "The Changing Dynamics of International Technological Competition." In *The Convergence of International and Domestic Markets*, ed. D. B. Audretsch, L. Sleuwaegen, and H. Yamawaki, 269–94. Amsterdam: North-Holland.

IUI, ETLA, IFF & N/OI. 1990. "Growth and Integration in a Nordic Perspective." Stockholm: The Industrial Institute for Economic and Social Research.

Jessop, B. 1983. "Fordism and Post-Fordism: A Critical Reformulation." COS Working Paper. Copenhagen: Copenhagen Business School.

———. 1990a. "Fordism and Post-Fordism: A Critical Reformulaton." COS Working Paper. Copenhagen: Copenhagen Business School.

———. 1990b. *State Theory: Putting Capitalist States in their Place.* Cambridge: Polity Press.

———. 1990c. "After Thatcher." *New Statesman and Society* (November):

———. 1991a. "Thatcherism: The British Road to Post-Fordism." In *The Politics of Flexibility*, ed. B. Jessop, H. Kastendiek, K. Nielsen, and O. K. Pedersen. Cheltenham, England: Edward Elgar.

———. 1991b. "Verenderte Staatlichkeit: Changes in Statehood and State Projects." In *Staatsaufgaben*, ed. D. Grimm. Baden-Baden, Germany: Nomos Verlag.

Jessop, B., K. Nielsen, and O. K. Pedersen. 1992. "Structural Competitiveness and Strategic Capacities: Rethinking State and International Capital." "Case Studies: Sweden, Denmark and Britain," COS Research Report, Center for Public Organization and Management. Copenhagen: Copenhagen Business School.

Kaldor, N. 1978. "The Effects of Devaluations on Trade in Manufacturers." In *Further Essays in Applied Economics*, ed. N. Kaldor. London: Duckworth.

Leontief, Wassily. 1953. "Domestic Production and Foreign Trade: The American Capital Position Reexamined." In *Proceedings of the American Philosophical Society*, 332–49. New York.

Mistral, J. 1986. "Regime international et trajectoires nationales." In *Capitalismes fin de siecle*, 167–202. Paris: PUF.

Nielsen, K. 1991. "Learning to Manage the Supply–Side. Flexibility and Stability in Denmark." In *The Politics of Flexibility. Restructuring State and Industry in Britain, Germany and Scandinavia*, ed. B. Jessop, K. Nielsen, and O. Pedersen. Cheltenham, England: Edward Elgar.

Nielsen, K. and O. K. Pedersen. 1989. "Is Small Still Flexible—An Evaluation of Recent Trends in Danish Politics." *Scandinavian Political Studies* no. 4.

———. 1991. "From the Mixed Economy to the Negotiated Economy—The Scandinavian Countries." In *Morality, Rationality and Efficiency: Perspectives on Socio-Economics 1990*, ed. R. M. Coughlin. New York: M. E. Sharpe.

Ohmae, K. 1985. *Triad Power: The Coming Shape of Global Competition.* New York: Free Press.

———. 1990. *The Borderless World.* New York: Harper and Row.

Pedersen, O. K. 1991. "The Institutional History of the Danish Polity. From a Government Centered to a Center Drifting From of State." COS Research Report (May). Center for Public Organization and Management. Copenhagen: Copenhagen Business School.

Petersen, J. 1989. "Pensionskapital i erhvervslivet. Historiske forudsaetningar og in-
    stitutionelle konsekvenser." Roskilde: Institut for Samfundsökonomi og Planlaeg-
    ning, Roskilde Universitetscenter.
Petrella, Riccardo. 1990. "Technology and the Firm." *Technology Analysis and
    Strategic Management* 2, 2: 99–110.
Porter, M. 1990. *The Competitive Advantage of Nations*. London: Macmillan.
Science, Technology and Information (STI) Review. 1986. "Science, Technology and
    Competitiveness." *STI Review* 1 (Autumn):86–129.
Sabel, C. F. 1989. "The Re-emergence of Regional Economies." Discussion Paper FS I
    89 : 3. Berlin: WZB.
SOU. 1990. "Maktutredningens slutrapport." SOU 1990: 4. Stockholm.
Vonortas, Nicholas S. 1990. "Emerging Patterns of Multinational Enterprise Operations
    in Developed Market Economies: Evidence and Policy." *Review of Political Econo-
    my* 2, 2: 188–220.

12. Size, Integration, and Unemployment: The Nordic Countries Facing the European Single Market

Jan Otto Andersson

Introduction

One of the fatal problems of "economic man" economies is their inaptitude to handle problems that have a strong collective or social aspect. This stands out in theories concerned with international economic relations. A consistent "economic man" approach ends up by looking upon the nation-states as "clubs" distorting the optimal market solutions. Another way of trying to solve the puzzle of the nation-states is to see them as analogs to "economic men," as solid units trying to maximize their welfare in a world consisting of several competing "economic man–nations." The first approach is an ultraindividualist (and often ultracosmopolitan) view, the second an ultranationalist view, each of which leads to extremist positions loaded with pernicious political consequences. It has fallen on the shoulders of different heterodox, and in a broad sense institutionalist, theorists to try to elaborate a position that is less abstract and less prejudiced.

In this chapter I study the relationship between internationalization and unemployment. Is it an accident that the rate of unemployment grew much faster in the countries of the European Community (EC) in comparison with the countries of the European Free Trade Association (EFTA) during the 1970s and that the unemployment rate remained much higher during the 1980s? Is there an optimal size of the economy or an optimal degree of dependence on foreign trade and inward investments (investments by foreigners/foreign companies in the country) in order for a country to maintain a high rate of employment? Will the EFTA countries, especially the Nordic ones, be able to avoid the EC rates of unemployment if they are incorporated into the "single market"? In the theoretical argumentation, I use concepts elaborated by the French regulation school, especially from Gérard de Bernis.

How Unemployment Varies Between Countries

Let us start by looking at one central indicator of economic performance: the rate of unemployment during the 1980s.

Compare the average rates of unemployment 1980–89 and the increase in these rates since 1970–74 in the OECD (Organization for Economic Cooperation and Development) countries, arranged according to population size in 1985. Looking at Table 12.1, several interesting observations concerning the relationship between unemployment on the one hand and size, EEC membership, and the degree of *inward internationalization* of the economy[1] on the other hand, can be made:

1. In the three largest economic units (EEC, the United States, and Japan), the rate of unemployment is positively related to both the size of the economy and to the ratio of imports of goods to gross domestic product (GDP). In 1986 the imports/GDP ratio was 8.8 percent in the United States and 6.5 percent in Japan. (*OECD in Figures.* Supplement to the OECD Observer 1988, pp. 30–31). According to my rough calculations, the import share of the EEC, taken as one unit, was more than 11 percent in 1986. As to dependence on inward investments, this is nil in Japan and lower in the United States compared with the EC (Office for Official Publications p. 92).

2. The "lilliputian" countries, Iceland and Luxembourg (together with Switzerland), stand out because of their very low unemployment rates.

3. The countries inside the EC all (except Luxembourg) have higher rates of unemployment than those remaining outside (the six EFTA countries). There were no observable differences between the Netherlands, Belgium, and Denmark on the one hand and the EFTA countries on the other in the beginning of the 1970s. All had very low rates of unemployment. Among the Nordic countries, Denmark, the only member of the EEC, clearly has the highest rate of unemployment.

4. Small countries with the largest unemployment rates, Belgium and Ireland, are probably inwardly the most internationalized economies.[2] Among the OECD countries, the ratio of imports to GDP was the highest in Belgium (58.6 percent), Ireland (47.3 percent), and the Netherlands (43.0 percent) in 1986.[3]

5. The rates of unemployment in Canada, Australia, and New Zealand are in line with their size. The ratio of imports to GDP is also highest in Canada (22.3 percent in 1986). New Zealand is, however, more dependent on imports (22.2 percent) than is Australia (14.3 percent). As to the dependence on inward investments, Canada comes first and New Zealand last.

6. The unemployment ranking of the poorest OECD countries, Turkey, Portugal, and Greece, corresponds to their size. Portugal, which is about the same size as Greece, is somewhat more dependent on imports (32.6 percent and 28.5 percent, respectively, in 1986) and has a somewhat higher rate of unemployment.

Table 12.1

Unemployment in Different Countries, 1970–74

Country	Population (millions)	Unemployment (percent of labor force)	Change in unemployment rate 1970–74
USA	239	7.3	+ 1.9
Japan	121	2.5	+ 1.2
Turkey	51	11.1	+ 3.2
Canada	25	9.3	+ 3.5
Australia	16	7.5	+ 5.3
Sweden	8	2.1	+ 0.3
Austria	8	3.2	+ 2.2
Switzerland	7	0.6	+ 0.6
Finland	5	4.9	+ 3.5
Norway	4	2.8	+ 1.3
New Zealand	3	4.4	+ 4.2
Iceland	0.2	0.8	+ 0.2
EEC member countries:			
Germany	61	5.6	+ 4.8
Italy	57	10.3	+ 4.2
UK	57	9.6	+ 7.1
France	55	9.1	+ 6.4
Spain	39	18.0	+17.2
Netherlands	14	8.5	+ 7.0
Portugal	10	7.5	+ 5.1
Greece	10	6.3	+ 3.6
Belgium	10	11.1	+ 8.9
Denmark	5	8.9	+ 7.3
Ireland	4	14.3	+ 8.6
Luxembourg	0.4	1.4	+ 1.4
EEC (total)	322.4	9.5	+ 7.0

Source: OECD Economic Outlook 48, December 1990, Table R 19.

A Surprisingly Strong Correlation

It is not possible to use the OECD sample in order to calculate reliable regression estimates between unemployment and different indicators like country size, dependence on trade, and inward investments. The observations are too few, especially when we leave out the poorest OECD countries. Instead, I have constructed two variables, one indicating the unemployment performance during the

1980s and the other being a rough measure of the combination of size and internationalization.

The first variable is the sum of the average rate of unemployment during the 1980s and the increase in this rate since the early 1970s. The second part of this variable enables us to measure performance not only in relation to other countries, but also in relation to the earlier performance of the country. The international economic problems starting in 1973 affected all countries, but some were more able than others to avoid a rise in long-run mass unemployment.

The second variable is a sum of four variables: size, dependence on imports, dependence on foreign direct investments, and membership in the EC.

Size was measured by population. Entities with more than 100 million inhabitants (EC, United States, and Japan) got three points; countries with ten to one hundred million inhabitants (Germany, Italy, United Kingdom, France, Canada, Australia, the Netherlands, and Belgium) got two points; countries with 1 to 10 million inhabitants (Sweden, Austria, Switzerland, Denmark, Finland, Ireland, Norway, and New Zealand) got one point; Luxembourg and Iceland got zero points.

Dependence on imports was measured by the rate of imports of goods to GDP in 1986. Countries with a rate over 30 percent (Luxembourg, Ireland, Belgium, the Netherlands, and Switzerland) got three points; countries with a rate between 20 and 30 percent (Norway, Iceland, Austria, Sweden, United Kingdom, Canada, New Zealand, Finland, and Germany) got two points; entities with a rate of 10 to 20 percent (Australia, Italy, and EC) got one point; the United States and Japan, with rates below 10 percent got zero points.

Dependence on inward investments was judged by the help of different sources. I estimated the rank of the countries as follows: Ireland. Belgium, the Netherlands, the United Kingdom, and Canada—three points; Luxembourg, Denmark, France, Australia, the United States, and EC—two points; all others (except Japan, which got nil)—one point.

Every member of the EC, and the EC itself got one point—the rest nil, indicating internationalization through formal integration.

Figure 12.1 shows the graphical connection between the two sum variables. The construction of the variables is of course somewhat arbitrary, but the positive connection stands out very clearly, and minor changes in the estimates would not destroy it.[4] One change that would even strengthen the relationship would be to take account of unemployed guest workers in Switzerland and Luxembourg.

Unemployment, Productive Systems, and Modes of Regulation

Are all these observations due to chance? Or is there any reason to believe that countries that are large or are "inwardly internationalized" are less willing or able to maintain high levels of employment? Challenging the traditional view

Figure 12.1. **Unemployment Level and Integration**

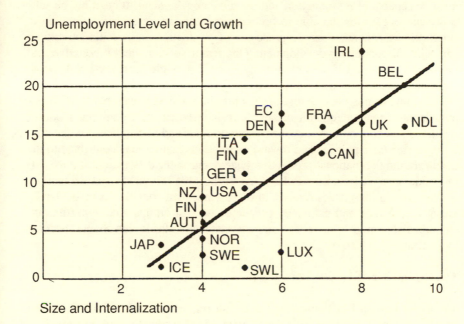

Unemployment Level and Growth

Size and Internalization

that large country size and inward internationalization are economically advantageous, I propose the following theses:

1. The ability and the willingness of a country to maintain a high level of employment depend on the internal coherence of the national productive system and on the existence of a corresponding national mode of economic regulation.

2. Inward internationalization, that is, a stronger dependence on imports of goods and foreign capital, tends to break up the coherence of the national productive system.

3. The ability of a country to establish and maintain a national mode of economic regulation, corresponding to the productive system, depends on the coherence of the productive system and on the ability of the economic groups to articulate their interests on a national level.

4. It is generally easier for economic interest groups in small countries to organize and to articulate their interests nationally. On the other hand, a small country is generally more dependent on imports and foreign capital. Thus, it is easier to try to establish a suitable national mode of regulation in a small country, but the mode of regulation may be more vulnerable because of stronger inward internationalization.

The terms *productive system* and *mode of regulation* have been elaborated by de Bernis (1987), a French economist in the tradition of Marx and Perroux. He understands integration as the establishment of a coherent productive system, sustained by a set of institutions, a mode of regulation. The productive system must be capable of reproduction and of stable development. It need not be self-sufficient, but it must be able to procure necessary imports, without having to surrender the coherence of the processes of production and circulation and its capability of continuous development. One feature of a modern productive system is the existence of a "union of payment," a single currency valid for all economic transactions within the territory.

According to this view, *integration* is not the same as "open borders" or internationalization. Integration means the establishment of a common mode of regulation, a common currency, and common rules and institutions. On the contrary, *laissez-faire* policies and inward internationalization may contribute to the disintegration of a national productive system and to the dislocation of the existing mode of regulation. Like Polanyi, de Bernis (1987) believes that the market, in order not to be self-destructive, must be embedded socially, in particular by means of the state and nationally organized interest groups. Following this institutionalist approach, the observations registered so far in this chapter become more clear.

The EC, the United States, and Japan

The EC is not yet functioning as a coherent productive system with a distinct mode of regulation. There exist no economic policy routines and no organized interest groups, the task of which would be to regulate the economy in times of economic disturbances. To the extent that common policies exist, their application will primarily be geared to the situation of the leading economies, in particular Germany. This, rather than the alleged "eurosclerosis," can explain the dismal experience during the 1970s and 1980s.

The United States has an established productive system and a national mode of regulation, but its interest groups are relatively fragmented and weak in relation to those in Japan, which is the only large economy with a compact national system of production and innovation.[5] Japan is also a country with strong corporatist traditions, which give support to a national mode of regulation.

We can interpret the project of constructing a single market in the EC of 1992 as an effort to establish a new productive system with a new multinational mode of regulation, i.e., as a more or less conscious protective movement in Polanyi's sense.[6] It can, however, also be formulated as a deregulation project, undermining both the national states and the EC bureaucracy.[7] If the first option is prevalent, the EC will possibly get a mode of regulation that in the future may be conducive to a reduction of the high rates of unemployment. But, because of the largeness and fragmentation of the EC productive system, it is probable that the rate of unemployment will remain higher there than in Japan and the United States. If the second option is the dominant one, the prediction is that the economic instability and unemployment levels will increase further in the area.

The "Lilliputians"

The very low unemployment levels in Luxembourg and Switzerland are slightly misleading, since the proportion of immigrant workers is high. They are the first who have to adapt to changes in the demand for labor. However, the permanent inhabitants of the two countries have been able—thanks to the relative smallness of their countries—to arrange their economic situation in a way that ensures their own economic security and well-being. Whether they will be able to maintain their national modes of regulation after being fully integrated into a European single market remains to be seen.

Iceland does not depend on immigrant workers but has maintained an extraordinarily high level of employment. The main reason for this is the existence of a peculiar Icelandic mode of economic regulation. This mode is adapted to the main exporting sector, fishing, which dominates the economy. Both the catches and the prices of fish fluctuate widely, but through a system of profitability guarantee, of income sharing within the fishing industry, and of income equalization among all sectors of the economy, the Icelandic model has provided full employment and a relatively high standard of living. One necessary element of the model has been the possibility to devaluate the *kronur* quite often.[8] The different institutions (the funds, the forms of ownership, the indexation of agricultural prices, and wages, etc.) correspond to the particular needs of the economy and constitute a coherent system. It would have to be completely rearranged if some element (e.g., the possibility to devaluate) was to be abolished. This explains the reluctance of Iceland to accept the single-market project unconditionally.

The EFTA Countries as Exemplified by Finland

The Nordic countries and the other two EFTA countries—Switzerland and Austria—are all relatively small economies with high standards of living, low protection of imports of nonagricultural goods, national productive systems, and institutions particularly suited to their conditions. Thus, there is not one Nordic or EFTA model, but one for each country. I illustrate the different countries by using Finland as an example and reference point:

1. There exist strong linkages between the economic sectors and complete vertical chains from research and development through the production of means of production to the production of sophisticated final products. The Finnish forest industry is linked to forestry in the peasant economy; to transportation on both land and sea; to the production of forestry machinery; to paper and sawmill equipment; to the packaging, chemical, and graphic industries; to building components and furniture.

2. Foreign control over natural resources, industries, and financial institutions is marginal. The proportion of the industrial labor force employed by foreign-

owned firms, most of which are Swedish, was only 3 percent in Finland in 1983. In comparison to nationalistic France, where the share of foreign-owned firms in industrial employment has been some 20 percent, this proportion is very low. The activities of foreign banks in the Finnish credit market have been restricted, and foreign ownership of natural resources has been regulated.

3. The proportion of the final demand going to imports is not as high as one would expect from the openness and the small size of the economies. Despite rather unfavorable climates, the EFTA countries have a high degree of national self-sufficiency in the production of food. The Finnish import of goods as a percentage of GDP was 21.8 percent in 1986. In the Finnish case, the necessity to import crude oil is the most important lack of self-sufficiency. The oil and gas have mostly been bought from the Soviet Union in exchange for different manufactured goods. However, Sweden, the United Kingdom, and Germany have been of roughly the same importance to Finnish trade as the Soviet Union. Among the EFTA countries, Austria is in a special position by being economically oriented toward only one major power, West Germany, from which more than 40 percent of Austria's imports originate.

4. The EFTA countries are all characterized by a high degree of inclusive corporatism and national economic coordination. If we disregard Switzerland, only Denmark has a level of unionization that comes close to that of the EFTA countries, but even Denmark's unions are not as vertically organized as those of the other Nordic countries. The business interests are organized in a centralized way in the EFTA countries, especially in Switzerland (Katzenstein 1985, p. 90). Because of "democratic corporatism" of these countries, economic policies have typically been easy to coordinate on a national level. Finland, for example, belongs to those countries in which adjustments in wages and employment take place rapidly thanks to the high degree of unionization and centralized income policies (Tyrväinen 1988; Pohjola 1988).

5. The EFTA countries have (until recently) maintained relative independence regarding monetary policies. Finland, Norway, and Sweden used to operate systems in which their national currencies were tied to a basket of currencies. The proportions in the basket were determined on the basis of the (changing) importance of different currencies in the foreign trade of each country. Such a system reduces the swings that would follow from being linked to only one of the major currencies. They also used devaluations (e.g., Finland 1977–78, Sweden 1982, Norway 1986) and revaluations (e.g., Finland 1989) in order to restore competitiveness or to contain inflation. The monetary independence was strengthened by exchange controls.

In all three countries, exchange regulations have recently been abolished, international capital movements liberalized, and the national currency linked to the European Currency Unit (ECU). Thus, the former autonomy of monetary policies has been seriously undercut, the consequences of which have been high interest rates and growing rates of unemployment.

Thus, it seems, we have come across a group of industrialized countries, which despite their smallness and openness to foreign trade, have been able to preserve a certain autonomy of economic policy and to avoid the high rates of unemployment typical of the 1980s in Europe as a whole.[9] Integration into the Single European Market, either through a European Economic Area (EEC and EFTA) agreement or through full membership in the EC, could mean a dis-integration of the particular national productive systems and modes of regula-tion.

Many elements of the traditional Swedish model, as formulated by Rehn and Meidner in the 1940s, have already been given up, although the stress on active labor market policies still remains. One major reason has been the internation-alization of the Swedish firms and, in particular, the abolition of exchange controls. If more economic policy instruments are relinquished and if the tax systems are harmonized, the ability to maintain a broad national consensus concerning industrial and incomes policies is reduced. There is the paradoxical possibility that an integration of the Swedish economy into a large European market may reduce economic openness by finally destroying the old mode of regulation, which was an important prerequisite for this openness.[10]

Today, in 1991, the Finnish economy is in a deeper crisis than ever before in peacetime. One obvious reason is the collapse of trade with the Soviet Union. But as a consequence of the deregulation of international capital movements and the linking of the Finnish *markka* to the ECU, the government has lost two pow-erful instruments to regulate the economy: exchange controls and the exchange rate. As Finland is also adapting its economy to the single market, the pos-sibilities to design and raise taxes have diminished. The risk that unemployment will rise to ''European'' levels and remain there for a long time is imminent.

Conclusions

The standard theory of economic integration does not take into account the need to institutionalize markets and the role of nation-states in the creation of in-tegrated and adaptable systems of production and regulation. It overlooks the cultural and social element in economic transactions. It therefore underestimates the costs of national disintegration that follow the establishment of a multina-tional ''internal market'' for commodities and factors of production.

Despite the standard theoretical disadvantages of a small-size economy, many small nation-states have been able to perform relatively well in the world economy not only when the international economy has been expanding and liberalized, but also in times characterized by international depression and disintegration.[11] One reason for this has been their ability to maintain a coherent productive system and to adapt their mode of regulation in response to new—often external—challenges. It is very difficult to describe the necessary conditions for the maintenance of autonomy in a particular national economy and to pinpoint the optimal level of internationalization/integration. Although it is possible to point out extreme cases (Albania and Ireland), the Nordic countries seem to have been able to find a favorable balance in most situations. They have represented what I have described as "peninsular democratic corporativism."

The creation of a large internal European market once again forces the Nordic countries to scrutinize this balance. Are the standard economic welfare arguments for international liberalization so strong in this case that it is worth risking the disruption of national modes of regulation in the smaller countries? Contrary to the situation when the free-trade areas were established, they now have to decide whether to transfer important parts of the decision making to European institutions. The choice has to be made in a situation where the future of these institutions is still open. On the one hand, the new institutions would have to be effective and democratic, and on the other hand, the small countries are afraid of losing their political influence to the large ones. These two goals are very difficult to advance at the same time.

Notes

1. The degree of *inward internationalization* of an economy is indicated by factors such as the share of imports of GDP, the share of foreign-owned companies in total output, and the money market's dependence on international loans.

2. In relation to their populations, Ireland and Belgium are the two European countries that are most dependent on foreign inward investments. The accumulated value of the stock of U.S. investments in Ireland is twice the size of the Irish GDP, and that in Belgium is about half the size of the Belgian GDP. There is a concentration of Japanese industrial investments in Ireland, Belgium, the Netherlands, and the United Kingdom. On the other hand, such investments are very small in Norway, Finland, and Switzerland (Office for Official Publications 1990, pp. 83–108). The relative dependence on inward investments of different countries can also be found in "Direct Investment Flows: Share of Major Countries in Area Flows 1971–1989," in *OECD Economic Outlook* 48 (OECD 1990), table 4, p. 6.

Total Imports of Goods as Percentage of GDP, 1986

EFTA		EEC	
Austria	28.5	Belgium	58.6
Finland	21.8	Denmark	27.7
Iceland	28.9	Germany	21.3
Norway	29.1	Ireland	47.3
Sweden	24.8	Netherlands	43.0
Switzerland	30.3	UK	23.0

Source: OECD in Figures, 1988.

3. The above table indicates the degree to which the EFTA countries, despite their smallness, have relatively low import dependence ratios:

4. The coefficient of correlation is +0.79, which is significant at the .001-level.

5. The term *national system of innovation* has been coined by Christopher Freeman (1988). He stresses the close links between users and producers in the Japanese economy.

6. This is the interpretation of Björn Johnson (1990).

7. "This is indeed an exciting prospect: governments submitting to market competition in this way will be a sight to see. And the beauty of it is that there is no need for tedious negotiations in Brussels, no need for ponderous majority voting, no need for a nanny Commission to oversee it all. It is a matter of free choice—governments, parliaments, industrial pressure groups, trade unions and 'public opinion' can choose either to move with the market or live masochistically with self-inflicted wounds. In a word, the principles of free competition based on differences do away with the necessity for a whole layer of bureaucracy. Instead of abandoning sovereignty to Brussels, our governments have, in principle agreed to share it with consumers—yet another instance of the federal principle of devolution at work" (Curzon Price 1988, p. 17).

8. The Icelandic model is described in Mjöset et al. 1986, pp. 97–103.

9. The percentage change in total civilian employment between 1979 and 1986 was as follows in some European countries (*OECD in Figures* 1988, pp. 12–13):

Percentage Change in Total Civilian Employment, 1979–86

EFTA		EEC	
Austria	−0.8	Belgium	−2.6
Finland	7.8	France	−1.6
Iceland	15.8	Germany	−1.0
Norway	11.4	Ireland	−5.4
Sweden	2.1	Netherlands	6.5
Switzerland	3.8	United Kingdom	−3.4

Source: OECD in Figures, 1988, pp. 12–13.

10. For a good discussion of the Swedish position in relation to the process of internationalization and European integration see the article by Göte Hansson (1990).

11. The Nordic countries and Switzerland succeeded relatively well in overcoming the crisis of the 1930s and strengthened their democracies during those difficult years.

Bibliography

Andersson, Jan Otto. 1988. "Scandinavie sans chômage." *Projet* 214 (November–December).

Bernis, Gérard Destanne de. 1987. *Relation économiques internationales*. 5th ed. Paris: Dalloz.

Curzon Price, Victoria. 1988. *1992: Europe's Last Chance? From Common Market to*

Single Market. London: IEA.

Freeman, Christopher. 1988. "Japan: A New National System of Production." In *Technical Change and Economic Theory*, ed. Giovanni Dosi et al., 330–48. London: Pinter.

Hansson, Göte. 1990. "Den internationaliserade ekonomins autonomi." In *Makt och internationalisering*, ed. Göte Hansson and Lars-Göran Stenelo. Stockholm: Carlssons.

Johnson, Björn. 1990. "Project 1992 or 'The Empire Strikes Back.'" *Nordisk Tidskrift för Politisk Ekonomi* 25/26: 18–33.

Katzenstein, Peter. 1985. *Small States in World Markets*. Ithaca and London: Cornell University Press.

Lundvall, Bengt-Åke. 1988. "Innovation as an Interactive Process: From User Producer Interaction to the National System of Innovation." In *Technical Change and Economic Theory*, ed. Giovanni Dosi et al., 349–69. London: Pinter.

Mjöset, Lars, ed. 1986. "Norden dagen derpâ. De nordiske økonomisk-politiske modellen og deras problemer på 70- and 80-tallet" Oslo: Universitetsforlaget.

OECD in Figures. 1988. Supplement to the OECD Observer. June/July.

OECD. 1989. *Economic Outlook* 46 (December).

———. 1990. *Economic Outlook* 48 (December).

Office for Official Publications of the European Communities and Commission of the European Communities. 1990. "Panorama of EC Industry 1990," Luxembourg.

Pohjola, Matti. 1988. "Työehtosopimusjärjestelmän tulevaisuus." [The Future of the Collective Bargaining System.] *TTT-Katsaus* 4: 8–23.

Simon, E. D. 1939. *The Smaller Democracies*. London: Victor Gollancz.

Tyrväinen, Timo. 1988. "Palkat ja työllisyys järjestäytyneillä työmarkkinoilla." [Wages and Employment on Organised Labor Markets.] Helsinki: Suomen Pankki.

Part III.

**Changing Institutions:
Focussing on Experiences in
Northern and Eastern Europe**

13. The Institutional History of the Danish Polity: From a Market and Mixed Economy to a Negotiated Economy

Ove K. Pedersen

Introduction

While Denmark in economic terms often is characterized as a mixed economy, in political terms it is probably better seen as an example of a country with a highly differentiated and, in functional terms, very complex institutional structure.

Compared with other countries (except for other Nordic and a few small mid-European countries), Danish political history is characterized by a number of distinct traits: a small and open economy, a stable political system, a high proportion of organized wage earners, a political culture marked by social partnership, and a long tradition of institutionalized class cooperation (Katzenstein 1985).

Because of this political history, the institutional structure is "impure." It contradicts most principles of how a liberal market-oriented economy ought to be institutionalized. Institutions stemming from a market economy are blended with institutions both from a mixed and from a negotiated economy (Nielsen and Pedersen 1991). Market power and state authority are mixed in corporate bodies, decentralized state organs, and private and semipublic institutions. Public authority is delegated to a high number of private and semipublic institutions, and decisions are taken in negotiations among mutually autonomous and collectively organized partners.

In this chapter I identify several types of institutional structures. The purpose is to show how three institutional structures are mixed: one pertaining to a market economy, one to a mixed economy, and one to a negotiated economy.

Structures—A Preliminary Review

The history of institutionalized class cooperation in Denmark goes far back in history (Pedersen 1985, 1989). The long-lasting tradition of cooperative links among social partners (state, capital, and labor) has developed into a multi-layered and policy-centric institutional structure. Links among social partners have become institutionalized; institutions have clustered, and clusters have been ordered to form a system of generalized political cooperation.

The purpose of this chapter is to identify aspects of institutionalization, of clustering, and of systemic relations among social partners in a composite political order. Three levels of analysis are presented: (1) the level of single institutions, (2) the level of institutions clustered, and (3) the level of clusters ordered to form a system.

This typology alone should point to the fact that there is no simple description of how the polity is organized and resources allocated in Denmark. The long-lasting tradition of institutionalized class cooperation has developed into a complex institutional structure mixing institutions and clusters of institutions.

Emphasis is on how institutional preconditions for a market economy, a mixed economy, and a negotiated economy have been created. This chapter concludes by describing how the parts of a complex and variable set of clusters are coordinated by the use of new techniques of coordination creating possibilities for a negotiated economy. The institutional preconditions for a negotiated economy are connected to the generation of a contingent and emergent system of generalized political cooperation among social partners: labor, capital, and the state.

In the Danish case, therefore, we are not dealing with only one set of institutions creating possibilities for only one way of allocating resources. We are dealing with many sets and ways.

In the following two sections, I describe the institutional history of the wage relation and of the welfare state. The purpose is not only to describe the distinctive institutionalization of the two policy fields but also to see how this had led to a mixture of institutions pertaining to a market and a mixed economy.

Institutional History—Market Economy

In spite of governmental intervention as many as twenty-eight times in pay negotiations since the 1930s, it became hardly possible during the 1970s to draw a distinct line between wage- or incomes-policy interventions and indirect guidance and control of the formation of wages. A peculiar institutional arrangement of the labor market made it possible for governments and peak organizations (federation of other organizations or umbrella organizations) in common to manage the wage formation by consensus mobilization, bi- and tripartite negotiations, and external as well as internal control of members (Pedersen 1989, 1991b). Indirect guidance and control of the formation of wages rather than discretionary intervention by the government was increasingly used to adjust nominal wages to ever-changing macroeconomic conditions.

The flexibility acquired by this lack of any clear-cut distinction between state intervention and self-regulation originates from the established Danish tradition of mixing collective with individual wage agreements. This tradition goes back to the turn of the century and has been characterized by increasing problems of coordination over the years.

In institutional terms, labor-market relations in Denmark were established by the individualization of workers and capital owners as legal subjects and by the constitution of a certain government-centered order of autonomy among labor, capital, and the state. In this chapter, we examine how the individualization and the creation of a structural order became linked.

During nearly two hundred years of struggle (from the late seventeenth century to the beginning of the twentieth century), four institutional features came to characterize labor-market relations in Denmark: juridification, universalism, economic individualism, and commodification.

1. *Juridification* was one of the institutional features that characterized labor-market relations. The making of the "Danish worker" occurred by legal and administrative means. Even if multifarious economic and political struggles paved the way for individual freedom "to possess and to alienate the capacity of labor," both absolutist kings and democratic parliaments were always able to set the pace and the direction for the deregulation of customary rules bestowing guilds, towns, nobles, masters, and husbands with the right to decide the use of the capacities of labor in their possession. The individual right for "all and everyone" to exclusively possess labor was constituted by formal acts according to general principles of constitutional law. The constitution of market relations came to be government-centered. During absolutist regimes as well as democratic ones the right to possess labor was enacted by generally accepted rules for policymaking (Pedersen 1991b).

2. *Universalism* was a second institutional feature. The making of the "Danish worker" followed different timetables. While restrictions in accordance with social status and property were deregulated beginning in the mid-nineteenth century, regulation pursuant to residence (town or countryside) was removed beginning in the late nineteenth century. Yet, it was not before the beginning of the twentieth century that restrictions according to sex, age, and matrimony were eased. Skilled men were the first to be entitled to enter markets with personal and economic rights, married women the last. Economic individualism became universal from the mid-twentieth century (Pedersen 1991b).

3. A third institutional feature that characterized Danish labor-market relations was *economic individualism*. The exclusive right to possess the capacity of labor was assigned to individuals both as a personal right (the right to enter—or to refuse to enter—a labor contract according to one's own free will) and as an economic right (the right to enter a labor contract at conditions agreed upon). The capacity of labor became the monopoly of individuals and not of guilds, towns, nobles, masters, or husbands. In terms of competence and conduct, individuals were assigned the right of self-regulation or the freedom to enter (or to

refuse to enter) self-interested relations with other individuals. The individual became the nexus of economic relations, and economic individualism became the constituent element of the labor market.

4. A fourth institutional features was *commodification*. Labor was commodified. By economic individualism, opportunities were created for a commodity exchange of labor. The legal interpellation of individuals made it possible for them to possess, alienate, and use their capacity to labor as "a thing." Yet the capacity to labor only came to be accepted as a peculiar commodity. In legal terms, it can be possessed, alienated, and used, but always within limits defined by maxims of law. The personal right, *stricto jure*, excludes any indefinite, unlimited, or unlawful alienation of the capacity to labor (Larsen 1857–58; Lassen 1882; Gram and Vogt 1887–88).

Accordingly, economic individualism came to assume a particular form of state. While individuals were endowed with autonomy (exclusive rights of capacity to labor) by the state, the authority to protect this autonomy and to define how far and with what purpose the self-regulation can be used was centered in the government. A government-centered form of state was constituted. (See Figure 13.1.)

This "government-centered form of state" was never fully universalized before the first element of structural transformation was introduced. A long list of restrictions was still attached to the right to possess the capacity to labor (especially for married women, young people, criminals, and social clients) when workers and employers alike in the late nineteenth century began to organize themselves into collective entities.

Unions were organized as early as the 1870s and 1880s, but they were twice dismantled when the state judged them to be subversive (socialist) organizations, and they were fought by employers refusing to enter into legal agreements with organizations on behalf of individuals. From 1870 to the turn of the century, the Danish labor movement then fought two interrelated battles: one for the right to organize in economic and political associations; the other one for the right as a union to enter into legally binding collective agreements with employers. Both struggles were finally settled 1899–1900.

Beginning in 1890, the state lifted its ban on unions as well as on socialist parties. From 1896 to 1898 employees and employers alike were organized in nationwide peak organizations, and in 1899 the two peak organizations signed the so-called September Agreement (*Hovedaftalen*). This agreement laid down procedural rules concerning industrial action. It also paved the way for the Parliament to accept the right of workers to associate in economic organizations. The September Agreement still applies today and embodies the legal relations between employers and employees. This is done in three ways.

First, the two organizations mutually accept each other as equal and free legal subjects according to private law. The right of the workers to unionize was recognized by the confederation of employers as the managerial prerogative of

Figure 13.1. **The Institutional Boundary Between State and Market Was Defined by Maxims of Law**

Constitutional law *stricto jure* prevented (and prevents) the state from invalidating the personal right (Haarløv 1958; Zahle 1986). The individual was assigned exclusive control of his own capacity. In market relations, though, this autonomy came to be relative. The state was enabled to intervene in the economic right, setting conditions and limits for what can be agreed upon. State and market, accordingly, became formally separated but also interdependent. Economic individualism was both delegated and protected. The autonomy was both absolute and relative. State and market came to be two distinct yet mutually dependent institutional arrangements constituting a particular order of autonomy.

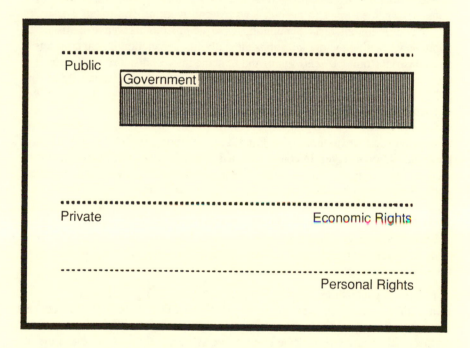

the confederation of trade unions. The right to generate monopolies without intervention by the adversary was agreed upon according to private law.

Second, organizations are assigned the right of action. Trade unions have the right to legal strikes, while employers obtained the right to lockouts. Both measures are only to be enforced in the case of conflicting interests—that is, after an agreement has expired and in connection with renegotiations.

Third, the organizations accept an "obligation to peace." No agreement can be revoked by conflict and no "legal" conflict can take place during the period of agreement.

According to the September Agreement, then, three features of interest came to characterize the system of collective bargaining on the private labor market:

1. *Juridification.* The right to organize, to hire and fire, to strike, and to lock out was agreed upon according to private law. On the other hand, in 1900 the Parliament granted the two peak organizations autonomy to generate a position of monopoly on the labor market and to negotiate working conditions according to rules agreed upon in the September Agreement. In consequence, organizations were granted autonomy to generate monopoly positions and to self-regulate the economic rights of their members.

2. *Institutionalization.* In the period from 1890 to 1910, private and semi-public institutions were developed on the labor market. Private bipartite institutions were agreed upon to negotiate wages and working conditions and to arbitrate conflicting interests. Semipublic tripartite institutions were established by public law granting the organizations the authority to sanction illegal conflicts in the Industrial Court (*Arbejdsretten*) and to settle interest disputes in the Board of Conciliation (*Forligsinstitutionen*). Organizations were granted authority to conciliate and sanction conflicts. Organizations were delegated "public authority" to control their members by external institutional means.

3. *Centralization.* During the 1920s, collective bargaining became centralized, first at the sectoral (industry) level and later on during the 1950s and 1960s at the peak (national) level. In contrast, conflict initiation and control stayed at the sectoral level. An internal hierarchy, then, was erected between the organizations. Peak organizations could negotiate general agreements, while sub-organizations could negotiate specific agreements in a "hierarchy of functions." Internal means of control were generated.

The Basic Agreement, then, had a number of radical consequences for relations between labor and capital as well as for the overall structure of the Danish form of state:

1. The organizations were assigned independent rights and obligations. Hence, the relationships between the organization and its members—or between the legal subject (the organization) and the legal person (the member)—became divided. Labor agreements came to have two subjects : the collective and the individual. A particular mixture of collective and individual rights and obligations was established (Hasselbalch 1979). Over the years the organizations were increasingly made competent and responsible in relation to economic rights, while the individual stayed competent and responsible in relation to personal rights:

• The individual still had the right to enter (or to refuse to enter) a wage agreement. Neither the state nor the individual's organization could (or can) force him or her to work.
• The individual, too, had the right to enter agreement bringing him or her conditions better than the ones agreed upon by collective agreement. The individual's

personal right to search for better conditions was (and is) untouched.
• Finally, wages and other disbursements are the individual's personal property. Neither the state nor the individual's organization could (or can) confiscate his or her payments without authority granted by public law.

Thus, the first significant consequence of the Basic Agreement was the constitution of a specific organizational structure. The structure came to be based on a distinction between the organization as an independent legal subject with authority to sign and enforce collective agreements and the member as an independent legal person with autonomy to enter (or to refuse to enter) any agreement. This distinction has since constituted the basis for the development of an internal hierarchy inside organizations between leadership and members, whose respective rights and obligations are regulated by organizational statutes.

2. The industrial class conflict was institutionally isolated. An industrial arena was established, delimited by the statutory regulations embedded in the Basic Agreement. Hence, another important consequence of the Basic Agreement was the constitution of a certain social system. This system came to be based on the separation of the industrial arena from the political arena. An independent arena pertaining to labor legislation was generated for how to enter, terminate, and maintain agreements just as for how to distinguish between industrial (legal) and political (illegal) conflicts.

3. Finally, authority was delegated from the state to the labor-market organizations. Through the Parliament's acceptance of the organizations as autonomous parties, the state delegated parts of its sovereignty to regulate, to judge, and to sanction the relations between employers and employees. A third significant consequence of the Basic Agreement, then, was the constitution of a new form of state. A multicentered form of state was constituted. (See Figure 13.2.)

Besides transforming the structure of the Danish form of state, the Basic Agreement also transformed the relation between labor and capital. This relation became institutionalized, and institutions became clustered in a functional network (FuncNet). Mutually autonomous organizations as well as mutually autonomous industrial and political institutions were coordinated by nonauthoritative, negotiated principles commonly agreed upon. Cooperative institutions negotiated, conciliated, mediated, and sanctioned private agreements and did so from different positions of competence in an interinstitutional division of labor among private, semipublic, and public bi- and tripartite institutions.

However, it was not before the end of the 1950s that the unintended consequences of this institutional cocktail of individual and collective arrangements and of industrial and political institutions became evident. From then on and for more than thirty-five years, two interrelated yet seemingly irreconcilable and still more accentuated problems of coordination came to play a decisive role in macroeconomic policymaking.

Figure 13.2. **The State Form Changed from a Government-centered to a Multicentered One**

The individual autonomy was split in two: one pertaining to personal rights, which remained in the hands of the individual; and one pertaining to economic rights (for members) delegated to the organization. Individuals could (and still can) decide to prefer their own well-being to that of others, while organizations could (and still can) regulate market relations by collective agreement. This regulation, on the other hand, was depoliticized. Collective actions with any political purpose were deemed illegal according to agreements between the peak organizations. A division of labor, then, was institutionalized between organizations and the political system. Organizations could (and can) regulate wage and working conditions; the state could (and still can) intervene when possible in political terms. The labor market, then, came to establish not merely a single authoritative decision-making center, but a multicentered structure within which mutually autonomous (individual and organizational) actors as well as mutually autonomous (industrial and political) institutions could function.

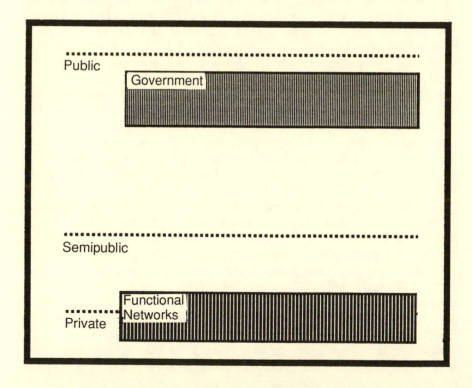

The first was articulated in the 1950s and formulated as follows: Organizations are unable to control members and suborganizations so far as they are free to enter agreements bringing them better conditions than agreed upon in collective agreements (Blueprint 154 1956). The second problem was articulated in the 1970s and was finally formulated in the 1980s: Organizations have gained too much authority restricting the freedom of members and suborganizations to prefer their own well-being to that of others (Pedersen 1991b).

During the 1970s, then, it became increasingly clear that the problem of coordination had changed from too little to too much collective authority and from too much to too little individual self-reliance. It became evident that the organization of industrial relations was somehow unable both to control the formation of wages and to secure individual mobility and flexibility. However, it was not before the late 1970s that more subtle guidance and control of wages was introduced in the search for a more balanced mix of individual incentives and collective solidarity and control. From 1985 interventions by the state were deemed inefficient as were centralized negotiations between peak organizations. From 1987 decentralized negotiations became mixed with mechanisms for centralized coordination. Finally, from 1989 there was an attempt to blend local as well as individual agreements with wage-steering mechanisms in the hands of the organizations (Pedersen 1991b).

This search for a finely tuned mixture of individual autonomy and collective solidarity and control has so far (from 1987 to 1991) probably led to the most effective control of the entire wage formation ever to be seen in Denmark (Sónderriis 1990).

Yet, despite the successful application of wage policy measures, severe macroeconomic problems remained. Reports from the government and OECD (Organization for Economic Cooperation and Development) during the 1980s show that Denmark on international markets increasingly had become specialized in goods with low-technology content and that productivity both in absolute and relative terms has continued to fall in the same period (Finansministeriet 1986). Accordingly, the flexibility of the labor force was severely hampered by the successful application of the wage policy.

Institutional History—Mixed Economy

Having discussed the development of institutions of wage formation we now turn attention to the organization of the welfare state. The organization of the welfare-state policies took place between 1950 and 1975 through gradual compromises among social-liberal, conservative, and social democratic parties. The welfare state was never developed on the basis of a comprehensive plan. It developed through an ongoing pragmatic policy process of negotiations, deals, and eventually compromises among political parties, private interests, and social and economic experts. Five features of interest came to characterize the organization of the welfare state:

1. *Co-optation of private interests*. Private interest organizations—mainly those representing the two parties on the labor market as well as the welfare

professions—were granted a monopoly by the government to influence or directly to participate in decision-making processes in the public administration. A vast number of normally tripartite policymaking and decision-making bodies (councils, boards, and commissions) were established inside the public administration. Thus, private interests were co-opted in public administration, and an "open administration" in contrast to a "closed bureaucracy" was established.

2. *Delegation of policy authority.* The administration—together with tripartite boards and councils—was delegated authority to make discretionary decisions, and by administrative rule making to develop standards for state interventions. The relationship between the legislative and the executive power was reformulated. Parliament was increasingly in charge of staking out overriding objectives, whereas the administration was assigned the task of implementing these through compromises among multiple interests in cooperative bodies. A "political administration" in contrast to a "neutral bureaucracy" was thus established.

3. *Segmentation in policy fields.* The overall administration and control was handled by policy segments. Five important segments were developed: the labor-market, the agricultural, the educational, the social, and the health-care segments. These segments were only gradually generated as policy communities where representatives from political parties, interest organizations, public administration, and municipalities—from different positions in a hierarchy of competencies—could formulate public policies and make decisions through negotiations and agreements. A "segmented" in contrast to a "unitary" administration was thus developed.

4. *Decentralization of welfare tasks.* Welfare functions were transferred from the central state to either the municipalities or the organizations. Welfare programs were pursued under broad statutory statements of general purpose decided by Parliament and implemented through the delegation of policymaking and discretionary decision-making powers to the municipalities or to the organizations. The majority of welfare-state functions became financed and handled by municipalities. Thus a "local" in contrast to a "centralized" welfare state was established.

5. *Coordination of dispersed authority.* From the mid-1970s attempts were made to coordinate this comprehensive dispersion of public authority to tripartite bodies, municipalities, and organizations. Cross-boundary institutions were formed to coordinate and control public expenditures, thereby integrating multiple public and private organizations. The municipalities became permanent partners in implementing a public-expenditure policy represented by their proper private interest organizations, KL (*Kommunernes Landsforening* [The National Association of Local Authorities in Denmark]) and AR (*Amtsrådsforeningen* [The Association of City Councils in Denmark]). A "negotiated" in contrast to a "hierarchic" coordination of budget and expenditures was attempted.

Important differences came to characterize these segments. Institutions were clustered differently, establishing different types of segments. In Hierarchical

Segments (HieraSegs) institutions were ordered in a hierarchy of competences with the minister (i.e. the government) "at the top" in a delicate interplay with formally competent but not autonomous tri-partite bodies. In Horizontal Segments (HoriSegs), on the other hand, institutions were ordered by a hierarchical distribution of autonomies between mutually autonomous hierarchical segments with the central government "at the top." A policy-centered form of state was thus constituted. (See Figure 13.3.)

However, it was not before the beginning of the 1970s that the unintended consequences of the uncontrolled development of welfare-state policies and the organization of an open, political, local, and segmented welfare-state administration became evident.

In 1960 Danish public expenditures were lower in relation to gross national product (GNP) than the average level within OECD (24.6 percent vs. 26.0 percent). In 1982 the picture had changed: Denmark 60.2 percent, OECD 48.5 percent. Again, it was not before the mid-1970s that the need to curtail internal cost and external demand was transformed into a policy for public expenditures and not until 1982 that this policy achieved rather remarkable results. In 1982 Denmark had an enormous public finance deficit (10 percent of GNP). Within four years, however, this had been transformed into a surplus (3 percent of GNP) (Nielsen 1988).

Despite the successful application of austerity measures, severe macroeconomic problems remained. The growth of the competitive industrial sector was never sufficient to finance imports and growing welfare expenses. From 1963 to 1989, Denmark as a consequence had a permanent deficit on its balance of payments, just as from the 1960s and onward it accumulated a foreign debt (almost 40 percent of GNP in 1988), experienced a constantly rising tax burden, and saw a steady increase in the public deficit (almost 10 percent of GNP in 1982).

In Search of New Instruments

Then, in the period from 1982 to 1991, both wage and public expenditure policies began to demonstrate effectiveness in coordinating the functional network (the FuncNet) and the segments (HieraSegs and HoriSegs). Objectives were met as far as wages and public expenditures were concerned.

However, severe macroeconomic imbalances remained. Austerity measures created a high and stable level of unemployment (1980: 7.0 percent; 1983: 10.5 percent; 1986: 7.9 percent; 1988: 8.7 percent). New and growing pressures were put on welfare-state services (public expenditures as a percentage of GNP—1980: 56.9 percent; 1983: 62.0 percent; 1988: 59.8 percent). Productivity continued to fall (factor input and productivity in the business sector, annual growth rate: 1973–79: 1.19 percent and 1978–89: 0.92 percent).

Consequently, new means were needed if the government was to repair the

Figure 13.3. **The State Form Was Changed from a Multicentered to a Poly-Centered Distribution of Autonomy**

Organizations were co-opted and delegated public authority to formulate, decide, and in some cases even to implement public policies. Universal social (welfare) rights were distributed to individuals, while tripartite bodies and municipalities were granted authority to perfect and to elaborate these through discretionary decision making. Vertical and horizontal segments were generated to coordinate dispersed public authority by concerted actions between multiple actors and institutions. Thus a policy-centered structure of authority and autonomy was established within which mutually autonomous (individual and organizational) actors, as well as mutually autonomous (central and local) institutions and mutually autonomous (vertical and horizontal) segments could function.

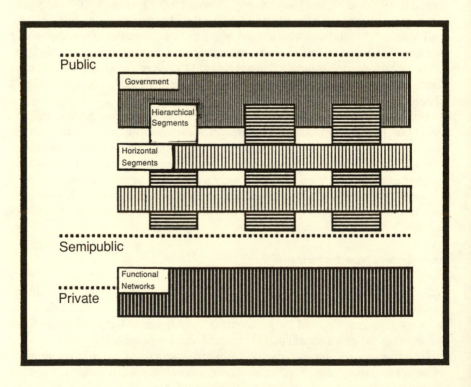

macroeconomic imbalances. This need was further strengthened by a growing awareness that the days of a fine-tuning stabilization policy were over and that the mechanisms for gradual adjustments of industrial relations and public expenditures had been pushed toward their limits. The relative importance of a structural policy and supply-side measures was increased, and the need for a change in the reservoir of macroeconomic instruments was formulated.

This change in the reservoir of instruments took place between 1976 and 1986. Measures for a structural policy (Nielsen and Pedersen 1989) were created, on the one hand, through the development of an active industrial policy and, on the other, from a reformulation of macroeconomic problems and objectives for the country as such.

By the end of the 1970s a new set of macroeconomic problems and instruments was initiated by a shift in the understanding of international competitiveness. New socio-economic objectives were highlighted, and the need for new means was realized. A structural policy was formulated that emphasized supply-side measures, for example, technological renewal and industrial restructuring. These changes in the collective views of international competitiveness disclosed a capacity to formulate macrostrategies for a national economy as such.

In the following part of this chapter, I describe how this strategic capacity was generated through a very complex institutional transformation in bi-, tri-, and even quadripartite cooperation and consultations. Emphasis is on how social partners have contributed to the formulation and implementation of a national strategy through changes in collective orientations and in the existing setup of institutions.

To understand how it has been possible to formulate and even propagate a national strategy (the structural policy) in a polycentered form of state, we have to distinguish between at least three different policymaking processes in the 1980s:

1. A structural policy was formulated, and all the major political actors were mobilized around a mutual understanding of structural competitiveness as the primary objective of societal changes and adjustments.

2. A stalemate among political parties, organizations, and municipalities, however, has blocked a coordinated and controlled participation of the state in the implementation of a structural policy.

3. However, single processes have been unfolded within newly established but also preestablished institutions and clusters of these. In combination with the preestablished distribution of autonomy a new form of state has been generated creating possibilities for a systemic ordering of the actual institutional arrangements in a policy and its patchwork implementation.

Changes in Cooperative Institutions: Part One

From an overall view of the institutional history on (and in connection with) the labor market, I now move to a more detailed study of how new institutions and clusters of institutions have been established following the shift from demand- to supply-side measures in macroeconomic policymaking.

The description introduces two new clusters of institutions and shows how these came to be coordinated through a generalized system for political cooperation. It is shown that a systemic order has been created for the coordination of a polycentered form of state and that this has taken place through the formulation and implementation of a national strategy for structural change.

At first I describe how multipartite communicative actions from the mid-1970s have developed into a Communicative Arena (ComArena). The formation of the arena is closely connected to the generation of a socio-economic ideology.

This ideology was originally formulated by a tripartite "Labor-Market Commission" (1949–57). Later on, it was developed into communicative actions among social partners circumscribed by a socio-economic ideology defining the field of policy intervention and the range of proper policies. A whole series of institutions was created in an ongoing process of institutionalization and policy constitution (Pedersen 1985, 1989).

One of the single most important institutions in this connection was founded in 1955. The purpose was to study if and how macroeconomic imbalances could be explained by the lack of any coordination between economic and social organizations and institutions. In 1956 the committee submitted Blueprint 154, describing for the first time not only the need to coordinate the formation of wages with socio-economic objectives, but also suggesting the establishment of the Economic Council (*Det/Ökonomiske Råd*).

The purpose of the Economic Council was clear. By law it was obliged to "contribute to the coordination of economic interests," pointing out socio-economic problems and proposing macroeconomic means. It should describe economic and social problems, while at the same time transforming the socio-economic ideology into policy measures capable of achieving broad acceptance among the major interests on the labor market and throughout the political system.

The Economic Council has done precisely this for almost thirty years. In slightly fewer than one hundred reports it has pointed at ever-changing socio-economic problems and solutions and in this way (over the years) transformed what were originally some very broad socio-economic ideals into an ever more wide-ranging socio-economic ideology, thus reshaping the fundamental conceptual grasp of reality on the part of the general public and policymakers alike.

Yet, in spite of the Economic Council's contribution to the formulation and propagation of the socio-economic ideology (Pedersen 1985, 1991b), it is much more important to point to the fact that the role of the Economic Council has been copied.

From the early 1970s, policy institutions began to call attention to the fact that welfare-state expenditures had grown out of control (*Perspektivplan I and II* 1971 and 1973). Later on, institutions were established within the Treasury to transform this warning signal not only into a public expenditure discourse but also to integrate this with the socio-economic ideology propagated by the Economic Council. A conceptual link was established between public expenditures and socio-economic objectives and imbalances (Nielsen and Pedersen 1989).

In a first phase (1960–75), a socio-economic ideology was formulated and propagated. Wage and expenditure policy measures became dominant in a demand-side oriented socio-economic ideology. From 1973 a shift in the socio-economic ideology was undertaken. A new institution was set up. The Technology Board (*Teknologirådet*) was assigned the tasks to follow and to survey technical and industrial developments here and abroad and to take or guide action in order to promote technological development. The Technology Board was expected to formulate and propagate a new technological policy, to design new institutions, and to conduct experimental implementation. The long-term objective was to modernize the Danish economy and to eliminate the macroeconomic imbalances through the promotion of technological progress.

A vital step was taken in 1983, when the Program for Technological Development (*Det Teknologiske Udviklingsprogram*) was proposed by the Technology Board and followed by Parliament. The program laid the groundwork for an active industrial policy and for a break with nearly thirty years of demand-side-oriented macroeconomic policy measures. The Program for Technological Development covered promotion, development, and internationalization of technology, financial support for research and development, and technological service.

One of the reasons for this political consensus in 1983 was the simultaneous reformulation of socio-economic problems and objectives for the country as a whole. A long-lasting debate among various institutions and organizations started around 1980 about the content of the concept of international competitiveness.

In the 1960s and 1970s international competitiveness was generally perceived as equivalent to relative unit costs of labor. The dominant perceptions stressed the exclusive importance of relative prices. International competitiveness was understood as wage competitiveness managed by demand-side policies (i.e., wage, incomes, and public-expenditure policies).

Already in the early 1980s, a revised version of this formulation was applied by the Economic Council. Competitiveness was now measured by a composite index including relative unit cost of labor, capital costs, productivity, and exchange-rate development. During the years from 1984 to 1986, a broad political consensus was established around an extended version of this formulation. The dominant perception stressed the importance of a national economy's productive structure, the technology content and marketing of its products, and the degree of flexibility in its labor markets and in its industrial organization.

International competitiveness came to be understood as structural competitiveness. Product innovation and productivity, technology content, marketing, and flexibility in the labor market were made part of the concept. This reformulation was primarily promoted by the Technology Board and by the Labor Movement Trade Council (*Arbejderbevægelsens Erhvervsråd*). They both successfully noted that technological development and industrial restructuring could have an important impact on the competitiveness of Danish industry.

The decisive formulation of the new consensus, however, was produced by the Ministry of Finance (*Finansministeriet*) in 1986. Employing a broad conception of competitiveness it called attention to the fact that Denmark suffered from a structural problem. Export products had an insufficient content of technology and Danish export markets have declining shares of international demand. The conclusion was clear: a structural policy had to be applied to increase the level of technology, education, and research and to change the composition of exports as far as products and markets were concerned.

In a second phase (1976–86), the content of the socio-economic ideology was changed. Active industry and labor-market policies became dominant in a supply-side oriented socio-economic ideology. Nevertheless, even if the institutions mentioned came to contribute both to the propagation of a socio-economic ideology and to a shift in its content, it is much more important—once again—to point to the fact that the role of these institutions was also copied.

Institutions with the function of taking part in the formulation and propagation of the socio-economic ideology (i.e., campaign institutions) were established by the government, the municipalities, the Central Bank, and the interest organizations, and even by the bigger banks and insurance companies.

None of these second-generation campaign institutions became tripartite bodies—as had the Economic Council. They were established as economic secretariats for trade unions, for employers' organizations, and for municipalities and governments. There are many examples of such campaign institutions. However, rather than discussing examples, it is of greater importance here to underline the existence of a certain form of communicative action (a verbalized "multipartite dialogue") among capital, labor, and municipalities and government through the roles played by campaign institutions.

To point at communicative actions as a type of social partnership is no doubt uncommon. However, in defending my thesis, I want to emphasize these three facts:

1. All the institutions mentioned actually were (and still are) formulating social and economic problems in terms of the socio-economic ideology—they are "talking" within the same discourse, making common outlooks possible.

2. The institutions take part in communicative actions where they comment on and criticize the models, the data, the formulated problems, and the proposed solutions put forward by the other participants—they "talk" to each other in an ongoing debate, creating common knowledge and making common understandings of problems and solutions possible.

3. The institutions have shown themselves to be able to pass this debate on to the social partners in particular and to the public in general—they have mobilized the majority of the Danish population to form an opinion on these posi-

tions, making a popular consensus around national problems and solutions possible (Petersen et al. 1989).

Accordingly, my understanding of a ComArena (or of multipartite consultation and coordination through communication) is as follows: A ComArena exists when the social partners through a series of institutions have constructed a common ideology and in ongoing communicative actions among their campaign institutions formulate common knowledge, common outlooks, and common understandings of problems and solutions.

In this way the social partners in Denmark have proved to be capable of verbalizing experiences and constructing perceptions of changing macroeconomic situations. Also, they have proven themselves to be capable of formulating a strategy for structural change and technological renewal and of achieving broad acceptance of this among the major interests on the labor market and in the political system.

Changes in Cooperative Institutions: Part Two

Since 1987 politics in Denmark have run into two paradoxes. One paradox has arisen as a national strategy has been formulated and a structural policy has been initiated. All social partners have come to identify international competitiveness with structural competitiveness. Yet only a patchwork implementation of the strategy has been possible. A consistent, overall, and coordinated implementation has been blocked by a political stalemate.

Another paradox has arisen despite the fact that opinion polls show clear acceptance in the population of the socio-economic ideology; the polls show a prevailing agreement on the gravity of the national debt problem and even a readiness to make ''great sacrifices (decreases in real wages, etc.) to take the nation out of the crisis'' (Pedersen et al. 1989). This popular consensus, however, has not resulted in electoral support for a stable party system enabling a majority in Parliament to agree upon economic policy measures governed by the guidelines of a structural policy.

After 1973, a situation of extreme minority parliamentarism dominated every corner of Danish politics. Extreme minority parliamentarism is characterized by at least four different features (Rasmussen 1989):

• Minority governments without permanent majority coalitions
• Shifting majorities behind economic policies
• No guarantee for majority to support the yearly Budget Bill (*Finansloven*)
• No guarantee that a minority government will step down when outvoted by a majority in Parliament

Denmark has undergone two periods of extreme minority parliamentarism. The first was the period from 1973 to 1983. The second started in 1987. The lack of majority behind a stable economic policy in 1987 forced the bourgeois government to enter into consultations and negotiations with political parties, organizations, and municipalities. A MegaArena was created compounding political parties, municipalities, and organizations in ongoing consultations and negotiations across boundaries between politics in Parliament and bi- or tripartite cooperation in segments and networks.

In the MegaArena, social partners coordinate policies through "grand bargains," "political pacts," or "political packages," combining aspects of different policy fields—that is, wage, expenditure, industry, labor-market, tax, and social policies.

A MegaArena has existed in Denmark for many years. Examples of grand bargainings across boundaries between politics in Parliament and bi- and tripartite cooperation can be found since the 1930s, especially in times of economic crisis. However, prior to the 1980s it was not possible to coordinate a polycentered form of state through negotiations in a MegaArena circumscribed by a commonly accepted macroeconomic strategy. In 1987 a cluster of institutions was constructed outside (but also integrating) politics in Parliament and outside (but also integrating) bi- and tripartitism in segments and networks. This cluster I call a MegaArena not only because it mixes politics between social partners and politics in Parliament but also because it does so with a given purpose: to implement a given and commonly accepted strategy.

In 1987 the prime minister for the first time invited the Danish workers association (*Landsorganisasjonen*) and the Danish federation of employers associations (*Dansk Arbejdsgiverforening*) to join the government in tripartite consultations. A common headline for consultations soon came to be "Structural Problems in the Labor Market." But even if the headline stayed the same during the following three years, a number of different subtopics were negotiated. Every single subtopic, however, stemmed from failed negotiations in HieraSegs of FuncNets. Unsolved problems spilled over into the MegaArena and became mixed with questions related either to wage formation or to public expenditure and revenues.

During four years of continuous negotiations, policy adjustments and changes in the labor-market structure have been agreed upon by quadripartite bodies in the MegaArena. The prime results are the following: a common agreement that the labor force has to be restructured through pre-job and on-the-job training programs and that employment programs have to be used accordingly; and the decision to implement two programs for restructuring the labor force.

Today three clusters of institutions for policymaking are in operation: segments inside the bureaucracy, networks outside direct political influence, and the arenas integrating a new set of actors in a new set of functions (ComArena and

MegaArena). A Center-Drifting Form of State has been constituted. (See Fig. 13.4).

Conclusion—Negotiated Economy

I maintain that a national strategy (the structural policy) has been formulated. I also maintain that profound changes in attitudes have occurred (structural competitiveness) and that new policy instruments and institutions have been created. These achievements, however, ought not to divert attention from the problems and ambiguities. The emergence of a structural policy is a very new phenomenon, and severe questions remain as to its implementation. Only a patchwork quilt of policies has been implemented.

The most decisive factor in explaining how Denmark during the last ten to fifteen years has coped with problems of adaptation and development is to answer this question: How have social partners been able to govern national changes through joint policymaking in a world of multiple actors and institutions? We have to look at how a system for generalized political cooperation has been developed enabling social partners to formulate and implement a change in national strategy.

In doing so I use elements from the theory of negotiated economy (Pedersen 1985, 1986, 1991a; Nielsen and Pedersen 1989, 1991; Berrefjord, Nielsen, and Pedersen 1989). In the ideal-type negotiated economy, allocation of resources is determined neither by individual agents adapting to market changes nor by public authorities through autonomous decision making. Instead, an essential characteristic of a negotiated economy is the interconnections of discursive and institutional features enforcing compromise and mobilizing consensus among a multitude of actors acting from different positions in a multilayered and polycentered institutional setting. In a negotiated economy, decisions are made through institutionalized negotiations among agents who reach binding decisions based on discursive, political, and moral imperatives rather than through formal contracts, legal sanctions, or organizational hierarchies.

To understand how it has become possible to coordinate a multitude of actors by enforcing compromise and mobilizing consensus, we have to understand the way in which institutions or clusters of institutions have been ordered to form a contingent and emergent system for generalized political cooperation. While a system for generalized political cooperation is the institutional prerequisite for a negotiated economy, the system itself can only be identified by pointing at mechanisms and bodies able to establish interactions between otherwise closed subsystems (Jessop 1987). Four such mechanisms have been identified so far:

1. Institutions and clusters alike have become part of a general field of communication. They are innovators of the ComArena and participants in its common orientations. As participants, they are bound to accept the logic of

Figure 13.4. The State Form Changed from a Poly-Centered to a Center-Drifting Form of State

On the one hand, decision making in three clusters was compounded within a Mega-Arena. On the other, the formulation of (wage, labor-market, expenditure, and industry policies) was compounded within thematically defined limits of the socio-economic ideology. Organizations were co-opted in multipartite decision-making processes in the MegaArena. Institutional prerequisites for communicative cooperation were developed by the ComArena. Policy processes could drift from one cluster to another, from one center of authority to another. Possibilities were created for synchronized and temporally timed actions within clusters but also across boundaries. The plurality of different clusters each of which performs crucial functions and none of which can claim unchallenged supremacy over the other, were coordinated by quadripartite negotiations and inter-associational communicative actions. A contingent and emergent system for generalized political cooperation was established.

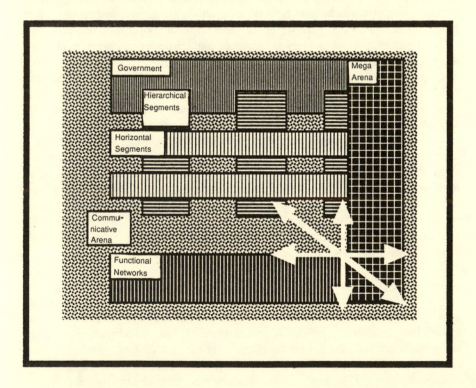

argumentation (Pedersen 1989; Nielsen and Pedersen 1991). This logic, then, provides the first mechanism linking otherwise closed subsystems together in a system for generalized political cooperation.

2. Institutions and clusters alike have been equipped with internal discursive structures representing the socio-economic ideology as such. The construction of a series of discursive subfields (wage, expenditure, industry, and labor-market discourses) and the gradual integration of these into the overall ideology of socio-economics provide the second mechanism coupling subsystems with their environment. This mechanism permits subsystems to reflect on the identity of the system and their proper role and function in its reproduction.

3. Policymaking and decision-making processes in institutions and clusters alike have been interlocked by the synchronization of events. The MegaArena provides means for the timing of policy processes and for the temporal ordering of choice and opportunities. Events in institutions can spill over into clusters just as events in clusters can spill over into the MegaArena. The synchronization of events, then, provides the third mechanism for coupling subsystems to their environment. This mechanism permits agents to reflect on how to coordinate short-term incentives with long-term calculations and to subordinate their ego preferences to the possible outcome at the systemic level (Pizzorno 1978; Marin 1985; March and Olsen 1989).

4. Direct linkages between institutions and clusters have been secured through single agents (persons and organizations alike) with roles in several clusters and arenas. There are only a small number of organizations at the top level, across boundaries, and in the MegaArena. They provide the fourth mechanism for bridging otherwise closed subsystems and contribute to the possibilities of systemic cooperation.

These and other mechanisms will have to be studied further. Only additional research can provide a full description of the system for generalized political cooperation. A full identification, however, will have to take into consideration how these four mechanisms have been institutionalized in a special set of bodies.

In the theory of a negotiated economy five such complementary bodies have been described (Pedersen 1985, 1986, 1991a; Nielsen and Pedersen 1991; Berrefjord, Nielsen, and Pedersen 1989):

• *Policy bodies*. Policy bodies aim at formulating economic and social problems and at identifying political measures necessary to solve them. They are usually erected by the government or the Parliament. The Technology Board mentioned earlier is an example.

• *Campaign bodies*. The aim of campaign bodies is to describe societal problems in socio-economic terms, while at the same time transforming the socio-economic ideology into a rationale capable of achieving broad acceptance throughout the political system and by the entire population. The Economic Council is an example.

• *Discourse bodies*. Discourse bodies aim at transforming the dominant perceptions of socio-economic problems into systematically structured, analytically justified, internally coherent, and externally verifiable language codes. An example is the role played by the Department of Economics at the University of Copenhagen in developing socio-economic theories, which reflect the dominant perceptions of the socio-economic ideology between social partners.

• *Negotiating bodies*. Negotiating bodies draw up timetables and outline frameworks for forthcoming negotiations. They negotiate rules for conjoining and voting, mediate specific and general demands, and sign agreements. Examples are bipartite roundtable negotiations between peak organizations on the labor market.

• *Conciliating and sanctioning bodies*. These are normally semipublic, that is, created by law but governed by bi- or tripartite representatives with the purpose of conciliating and sanctioning breaches of agreements. Examples are the Industrial Court and the Board of Conciliation.

The system for generalized political cooperation is much more than an instrument for decision making and coordination of a multilayered and policy-centered set of institutions. The overall system of generalized political cooperation can be seen as the institutional prerequisite for a negotiated economy.

Bibliography

Berrefjord, O., K. Nielsen, and O.K. Pedersen. 1989. "Forhandlingsökonomi i Norden—en indledning." In *Forhandlingsökonomi i Norden*, ed. K. Nielsen and O.K. Pedersen. Copenhagen and Oslo.

Blueprint 154. 1956. "*Samarbejdsproblemer i den danske ökonomiske politik*. Copenhagen: Ministry of Finance.

Finansministeriet. 1986. Finansredogörelsen 1987. Copenhagen: The Ministry of Finance.

Gram. G.W., and H. H. Vogt. 1887–88. *Den Nordiske Obligationsret. Almindelig Del*. Copenhagen: Nordisk Retsencyklopædi.

Haarløv, T. 1958. "Retten til arbejde—og pligten. In *Festskrift til Poul Andersen*, ed. E.A. Abitz et al., 215-30. Copenhagen: Nyt Nordisk Förlag.

Hasselbalch, O. 1979. *Arbejdsretlige Funktioner*. Copenhagen: Copenhagen School of Economics.

Jessop, B. 1987. "Economy, State and Law in Autopoietic Theory." Essex Papers in Politics and Government, no. 42. Colchester, England: University of Essex.

Katzenstein, P.J. 1985. *Small States in World Markets. Industrial Policy in Europe*. Ithaca: Cornell University Press.

Larsen. 1857–58. *Samlede Skrifte*. Bind (volume) 1–2. Copenhagen: Gyldendal.

Lassen, J. 1882. *Den Danske Obligationsrets Almindelig Del*. Copenhagen: Gyldendal.

March, J.G. and J.P. Olsen. 1989. *Rediscovering Institutions. The Organizational Basis of Politics*. New York: Free Press.

Marin, B. 1985. "Generalized Political Exchange: Preliminary Considerations." EUI Working Paper, no. 85/190. Florence: European University.

Meier Carlsen, E. 1990. "En kegle ad gangen." In *Det Fri Aktuelt*, October 15.

Nielsen, K. 1988. "Den borgelige regeringens styring af den offentlige sektors økonomi." In *Fra vækst til omstilling—og Modernisering af den Offentlige sektor*, ed. K.H. Bentzon, 295–332. Copenhagen: Nyt fra Samfundsvidenskaperne.

Nielsen, K., and O.K. Pedersen. 1989. "Is Small Still Flexible?—An Evaluation of Recent Trends in Danish Politics." *Scandinavian Political Studies*, no. 4. Oslo.

————1991. "From the Mixed Economy to the Negotiated Economy: The Scaninavian Countries." In *Morality, Rationality, and Efficiency, New Perspectives in Socio-Economics*, ed. R.M. Coughlin, 185–205. Armonk, New York: M. E. Sharpe.

Pedersen, O.K. 1985. *Institutionel Historie*. Roskilde

————.1986. "Forhandlingsøkonomi og Samfundsøkonomi." In *Scandinavian Political Studies*, no. 3, 187–99.

————. 1989. "Laerprocesser og Forhandlingsspil. On løndannelse og forhandlingsôkonomi i Danmark." [Learning Processes and the Game of Negotiation.] In *Forhandlingsôkonomi i Norden*, eds. K. Nielsen and O. K. Pedersen. Copenhagen: Jurist-og Økonomforbundets Forlag.

————. 1991a. "At First They Were Two, Then Three and Now Four. Generalized Political Co-Operation in Modern Danish Political History." Kassalow, E. M. *Tripartite Consultation and Cooperation in the Making of National Economic and Social Policy*, ILO—report. Geneva:

————. 1991b. *Arbejdets institutionelle historie. Ôkonomisk individualisme i Danmark 1550–1800*. Copenhagen: Center for Organized Studies (COS).

————. 1992. "Stabilitet og forandring i overenskomstsystsystemet på det private arbejdsmarked 1985–91." In *Økonomi og Politik*, Jurist- og Økonomforbundets Forlag, Vol. 65, no. 1: 30–41.

Perspektivplan I and II. 1971 and 1973. "Økonomi—og Budgetministeriet." Copenhagen: Ministry of Finance.

Petersen, Eggert, et al. 1989. "*De krisebevidste og offervillige danskere. Den politisk-psykologisk udvikling 1982–86–88*." Aarhus Universitet: Psykologisk Institut.

Pizzorno, A. 1978. "Political Exchange and Collective Identity in Industrial Conflict." In *The Resurgence of Class Conflict in Western Europe since 1968*, vol. 2, ed. Colin Crouch and Alessandro Pizzorno 192-226. New York: Free Press.

Rasmussen, E. 1989. "Partiernes adfaerd ved den endelige afstemning on finansloven: Stilfaerdig jordfaestelse af en parlamentarisk norm." *Politica* 1, 2: 165–73.

Skow, Larsen L. 1989 "De gråhårede skal redde dansk økonomi." In *Weekendavisen* 1, October 13, pg. 10.

Sønderriis, E. 1990. "Industriens Arbejdsgivere: Vores lønstyring redder landet." In *Information* 1, November 29, 26–39.

Zahle, H. 1986. *Dansk forfatningsret. Menneskerettigheder*. Vol. 5. Copenhagen: Christian Ejlers Forlag.

14. Devolution of the Negotiated Economy? Sweden's 1990 Food Policy Reform

David Vail

In June 1990, after several years of tinkering around the margins of agricultural policy, the Riksdag, the Swedish parliament, enacted a fundamental market-oriented reform. Its core elements are the following:

• Phased deregulation of domestic markets over a five-year period, eliminating price supports as the principal means of assisting farmers.
• Substitution of fixed—and lower—tariffs for variable import levies, which has insulated producers from international competition.
• Termination of export subsidies for any surpluses produced at a cost above international market prices.
• A series of measures directly targeted to agriculture's noncommodity or "public goods" benefits.

If the new Food Policy is vigorously implemented, it will end over half a century of heavy state intervention in farm and food markets. It will put Sweden in a vanguard role among the advanced capitalist nations, whose politicians have talked much in recent years about the need for market-oriented agricultural policy but have done little to bring it into being.[1]

Several plausible interpretations of the political-economic motives behind the reform have been offered. A mix of growing overproduction, depressed world food prices, and fiscal constraints made the budgetary cost of dumping food surpluses untenable. The Social Democratic government sought to strengthen its

I am indebted to colleagues in Sweden, Denmark, and the United States for their comments on earlier essays from which this chapter is distilled. I especially appreciate the generous tutoring of Lars Drake, Knut Per Hasund, Louis Johnston, Michele Micheletti, Klaus Nielsen, Ove Pedersen, Ewa Rabinowicz, and Peter Söderbaum. Since none of them agrees fully with the interpretation presented here, the responsibility for any errors or omissions is clearly my own.

support among voters fed up (no pun intended) with double-digit food-price inflation. Readiness to phase out import protection and export subsidies was in reality a Swedish bargaining chip in the current trade negotiations of General Agreement on Tariffs and Trade (GATT). Swedish citizens' willingness to pay for an expensive farm policy was eroded by evidence of the negative social and environmental impacts of industrialized farming methods. And farmers' political clout had eroded along with their numbers and economic importance. In a multiparty political system like Sweden's, with a minority Social Democratic government forced to engineer coalitions issue by issue, each of these factors probably had some influence. In sum, momentum for policy change in the late 1980s, like the policy inertia of the preceding half century, was overdetermined by the convergence of multiple forces.

This chapter interprets the 1990 Food Policy legislation at a somewhat more systematic level as one of many signs that core institutions and relationships of Sweden's governance regime—the "negotiated economy"—are unraveling and that the country's distinction as a "middle way" between unfettered capitalism and bureaucratic centralism may be waning along with the twentieth century. The puzzle is that, although Social Democratic Sweden has generally lagged behind the neoliberal shift that is sweeping the capitalist world, it is out front in deregulating agriculture (Gunn 1989).

The Negotiated Economy: A Working Definition

Nielsen and Pedersen (1990) have presented a synopsis of the negotiated economy. (See also Pestoff [1989] and the chapters in this book written by Berrefjord and Heum and by Jessop, Nielsen, and Pedersen.) At the present stage of capitalist development they interpret resource allocation and income distribution as outcomes of a dialectical interaction between negotiation processes and three other core institutions—markets, voting procedures (i.e., democracy), and administrative rules (i.e., bureaucracy). Models of the mixed economy tend to stress only the latter three mechanisms. The mix and relative influence of these institutions are subject to change, and Nielsen and Pedersen (1990) associate the ascendance of negotiation in governance of twentieth-century Scandinavian economies with their "homogenous populations, relative symmetry of power in the labor-capital relationship, and long history of compromising, integrating and mediating" (1990, p. 3). In other words, the negotiated economy is embedded in specific historically evolved class relations and sociocultural conditions. Nielsen and Pedersen (1990) stress the following:

> The decisionmaking process is conducted via institutionalized negotiations between the relevant interested agents, who reach binding decisions typically based on discursive, political or moral imperatives rather than threats and economic in-

centives, even if such threats and rewards . . . might be essential elements of the framework around the negotiations. (p. 3)

To borrow from Hirschman (1971), the centrality of "voice," articulated through interest organizations, and of "loyalty," developed through stable, long-term negotiated relationships, is reinforced by the practical impossibility of "exiting" from those relationships. Competitive market pressures, electoral politics, and regulatory structures can be viewed as imposing boundary conditions on negotiations.

Since the state plays an integral role in negotiations between economic agents, much negotiation can be viewed as a dimension of the complex corporatist relationship between the state and interest organizations. In a parliamentary democracy, corporatism puts the state in contradictory roles: It articulates and represents the "public interest" while simultaneously mediating conflicting private interests. Indeed, Swedish corporatism antedates full democratization. In the late nineteenth century, a relatively autonomous state administration "invented" several corporatist structures to carry out its dual roles (Rothstein 1988). In several cases, the state essentially created "encompassing" national organizations to represent economic interests so that negotiation could proceed. In agriculture, these included the Federation of Swedish Farmers (LRF) and the Consumer Delegation. Micheletti (1990a) calls this process "sponsored pluralism."[2]

A central proposition of corporatist theory is that neither the state nor interest organizations are fully independent actors. "The state delegates powers and participates in decisionmaking processes without full authority," and interest organizations are "integrated in the political process in a stable, long term manner" through a web of moral, cultural, discursive, and institutional ties. A basic premise is thus that self-interest becomes "tamed," though not purged, through these socializing processes (Nielsen and Pedersen 1990, pp. 7, 13). This behavioral interpretation stands in sharp contrast to "public choice" theory, the preferred interpretation of neoclassical economists. Public choice posits rational self-interested ("rent seeking") behavior on the part of political actors, including politicians and bureaucrats, and interprets negotiations as strategic games. (In the context of Swedish agricultural policy, this view is forcefully argued by Bolin et al. [1986] and Rabinowicz [1990].)

The purpose of this chapter is not to engage in debate about the theoretical coherence of the concepts *negotiated economy* and *democratic corporatism* or to test their empirical validity as applied to modern Sweden. Rather, I accept that "negotiated economy" is a useful description of the hybrid mode of production that took shape in piecemeal fashion in Sweden over a period of several decades following the Social Democratic party's ascent to power in 1932. Specifically, the term captures one of the principal mechanisms used to constrain market forces and bureaucratic authority and to mediate conflicting economic interests in the Swedish agro-industrial system. The term also hints at the nontrivial differences that distinguish Sweden's version of capitalism from the mixed economies of, say, Great Britain or the United States.

Where this analysis parts ways with Nielsen and Pedersen (ibid.) is in their assertion that "the Scandinavian countries are increasingly assuming the character of a negotiated economy." To the contrary, recent evidence from agriculture and, *a fortiori*, other aspects of Swedish political economy seems to support the opposite hypothesis: Negotiation is losing its hegemonic role, most importantly . to market forces but also to new bureaucratic rule-making procedures and, in the present period of fluid political party affiliations, to party and electoral politics. My contention actually rests on a Nielsen and Pedersen proposition, namely that the four core instruments governing the economy (negotiation, voting, administrative rules, and market mechanisms) "compete, disturb, and eventually supersede each other" (ibid., p. 3). The tempo of change in Sweden's economic governance regime appears to have accelerated in recent years, and in the concluding section, I explore briefly the probable agricultural-policy impact of Sweden's application for membership in the European Economic Community in 1991.

Agriculture's Privileged Position in Advanced Capitalism

A discussion of the forces impelling agricultural policy reform should begin with a description of the preexisting policy regime. In this context, it is worth noting that Swedish agricultural policy has been generically similar to that of many other nations and to the European Community (EC). Farm import protection and domestic price supports are prominent exceptions to the growing dominance of market forces at the current juncture in international capitalist development. The policy measures that insulate farmers from domestic and international competition take several forms. The European Community variant, like Sweden's, centers on internal price supports backed by variable import levies (this was, in fact, Sweden's innovation in the 1940s). In the Swedish case, farm prices and first-stage processed-food prices are negotiated semiannually through a corporatist process described later in this chapter.

Artificially high prices and a range of "rationalization" measures promoting structural and technological transformation have stimulated high levels of input intensity and output. These policies are deeply implicated in the tendency toward chronic excess farm production over the past fifteen years. In the face of well-organized political resistance to a fundamental farm policy reform, the EC, the United States, and others have coped with their "butter mountains," "wine lakes," and "grain gluts" by tacking additional costly measures onto already complex policy regimes: export subsidies, acreage set-asides, "extensification" schemes, milk quotas, dairy herd buyouts, and so on. This reaction contrasts with the trend toward market-oriented deregulation of other economic sectors.

In the meantime, widespread export dumping has depressed world prices for food and feed grains below the break-even level for most farmers in most countries. Notwithstanding the existence of nearly a billion chronically malnourished people in the third world, chaos in the food system of the former Soviet Union, and ominous signs of global climate change, most agricultural economists predict that glut—not scarcity—will continue to plague capitalist agriculture at least for the remainder of this century (Berlan 1990; Goodman and Redclift 1989).

The 1980s agricultural crisis, with its tangible symptoms of chronic surpluses, growing fiscal burdens, farm financial distress, environmental pollution, and rural socio-economic decay, made news all across Western Europe, North America, and Oceania. National debates over what to do about farm policy have taken place in a setting of fiscal disarray, broad economic deregulation, and ascendent neoliberal ideology. At the international level, the United States and the Cairns Group of agricultural exporters (fourteen nations including, e.g., Argentina, Brazil, Canada, New Zealand, Thailand, and the United States) made the dismantling of agricultural protectionism (and by implication domestic price supports) a priority objective in the current round of GATT trade negotiations. Indeed, the Uruguay Round, which began in 1986, has repeatedly been set back by agricultural disputes. It stalled out in December 1990, when agreement could not be reached on a compromise timetable for gradual deregulation submitted by Sweden's agriculture minister.

Most nations—and the EC—have temporized, reacting piecemeal to their food gluts and farm budget burdens, while politicians posture rhetorically about the need for a more thorough policy overhaul. Sweden, in the meantime, enacted just such an overhaul in June 1990, without great international fanfare. Sweden's farm policy, unlike its innovative macroeconomic, social-welfare, and labor-market policies, has not been widely studied outside Scandinavia. Yet the 1990 reform should be instructive to agriculturalists elsewhere as an experiment with the type of adjustment that may soon prove more widely necessary. It should also interest socio-economists, as a signpost on a new political-economic course being charted by the Social Democratic party, which shaped Sweden's negotiated economy over a sixty-year span and is now modifying, if not dismantling, it.

Democratic Corporatism in the "Swedish Model"

Sweden's postwar social structure of capital accumulation and sustained economic growth was grounded in a classic labor-capital accord. It is commonly traced to the 1938 Saltsjöbaden Agreement, which legitimated centralized wage negotiations between the Swedish Employers's Federation and the major trade union federations. The state mediated labor–capital conflicts and articulated a collective interest that centered on restraining aggregate wage increases, minimizing production losses caused by strikes and lockouts, and fostering distributional equity. The state's legitimacy in this tripartite relationship was cemented by its commitment to maintain full employment and its avoidance of intrusion into corporate management and investment decisions. The accord was given weight by the fact that trade union federations represented nearly all wage earners and were the Social Democratic party's core supporters. One indication of the success of centralized wage bargaining at restraining the market's "invisible hand" was the introduction of *wage solidarity*: compressing wage differentials generally and equalizing the pay of workers in comparable occupations, regardless of differences in their employers' productivity and profitability (Esping-Anderssen 1985; Lundberg 1985; Milner 1989).

In the 1960s, trade union and Social Democratic intellectuals breathed new life into the venerable democratic socialist vision of an "economic democracy" that transcended full employment, universal entitlements, and equitable distribution. A series of laws mandating workplace codetermination was enacted in the 1970s, adding further layers of negotiation and consultation to the corporatist labor–capital relation. In 1984, legislation was also passed promoting the gradual socialization of capital through wage–earner funds governed by representative boards.

Democratic corporatist institutions and negotiation processes have governed many other collective actions in addition to the core labor-capital relation. In Micheletti's terms, Sweden is "organizationally saturated," with "encompassing interest organizations" acting as agents for groups as diverse as housing tenants, forest owners, parents of disabled children, performing artists—and, of course, farmers. The great majority of citizens approve the formal incorporation of these organizations into policy design and implementation, since the result is perceived to be an improvement in the quality of social life (Micheletti 1990a).

Interest organizations are typically represented on the state commissions that develop legislation affecting their members' interests. Corporatist negotiations often substitute for free markets or individual contracts, as when local housing authorities join with landlord and tenant representatives to establish rent ceilings and related rights and responsibilities. Interest organizations also have formal and informal roles in ground-level policy implementation. Rothstein terms this *administrative corporatism* and stresses the relatively minor authority of state ministries and the major role of national boards and agencies in policy execution.[3] They and their numerous subcommittees and advisory councils include substantial, often majority, interest-group representation (Rothstein 1988). Finally, the discursive dimension of corporatism centers on a dense communication network of conferences, interest-group publications, and mass media reportage.

Analysts who are ideologically attracted to democratic corporatism contend that socialized, state-mediated economic decision making counteracts the anarchy and the inequities of the market. It instills an ethic of social responsibility in participants—a willingness to compromise and seek consensus—that facilitates more efficient decision making and socially superior outcomes (Micheletti 1990b; Milner 1989; Pestoff 1989). Critics, particularly the public-choice economists, contend that corporatism perpetuates an illusion that the common good prevails. In reality, private interests "capture" parliamentary committees and state agencies and employ negotiation mechanisms to gain, protect, and legitimate economic rents. In contrast, the "public interest" (read: the aggregate of consumers' and taxpayers' individual interests) is diffuse, poorly represented, and overwhelmed (Bolin, Meyerson, and Ståhl 1986; Rabinowicz 1990). This interpretational dispute has important consequences that are explored further later in this chapter, in the case of agricultural policy.

The Agricultural Policy Regime

The Social Democrats (SAP) came to power in 1932 in a "Red-Green" coalition with the Agrarian party that continued off and on for a quarter of a century. In the 1930s, Swedish farmers were mired in a severe economic depression; they also represented over 30 percent of the voters, which gave them an electoral clout that could not be ignored. The two parties negotiated a "cattle trade" whereby farm interests accepted the Social Democrats' antidepression fiscal measures while the SAP tolerated farm price supports and import protection to revive agriculture. A long line of Social Democratic economists, notably Myrdal in the 1930s and Lindbeck[4] in the 1960s, have been outspoken critics of permanently insulating farmers from competition and subsidizing them via the mechanism of high food prices. Import protection and price supports cause static economic inefficiencies, inhibit the dynamic flow of labor to higher productivity employment, and have regressive distributional effects via inflation of staple food prices. These economic costs and equity contradictions were tolerated, however, because Agrarian party support was strategically necessary for the Social Democrats' continued governance and for the success of their large socioeconomic agenda (Vail et al. forthcoming).[5]

A half century of intervention in the market should not be interpreted simply as political expediency, however. For one thing, collective memories of hunger during the World War I naval blockade and the need to secure Sweden's diplomatic neutrality justified measures to maintain food self-sufficiency and some production capacity in sparsely populated, economically submarginal farming regions. Further, late industrializing Sweden had a tradition of worker–peasant solidarity. Wage earners, most of them a generation or less removed from the farm, empathized with yeoman family farmers. The policy objective of income parity between efficient farms and skilled industrial workers (set in 1947) was consistent with the labor unions' commitment to "wage solidarity."[6] Citizens' willingness to pay for costly farm supports was cemented by cultural ties. Regardless of their class, urban Swedes had—and still have—a place in the heart for these ancestral villages and agrarian landscapes. Farmers were recognized as the stewards of this heritage. In sum, the "moral dimension" of political culture underlay the creation and persistence of farm supports, as it does in most industrial capitalist nations. Finally, for three decades steadily rising consumer (voter) incomes and steadily increasing farm productivity kept food price increases within politically tolerable bounds (Frykman and Löfgren 1979; Vail et al. forthcoming).

The encompassing interest organization that came to represent nearly all farmers is the Federation of Swedish Farmers (LRF). Because its member cooperatives own most of the capital in farm input and primary food-processing industries, LRF has also come to represent unionized workers in these sectors in its lobbying activities and negotiations. There is thus a direct link between farmers and a sizable fraction of the trade union movement. Today, LRF is the dominant agro-industrial interest organization, but the interventionist farm policy did not result from political pressure brought to bear by any centralized farm pressure group. On the contrary, LRF's prominence derived from the creation of an interventionist policy regime. In particular, centralized price negotiations under the auspices of the National Agricultural Marketing Board effectively forced Sweden's dispersed farm organizations to consolidate.[7]

Once established, the LRF became an encompassing, highly structured, and by all accounts extremely effective interest organization. It heavily influenced the legislative bodies and executive agencies that make, interpret, and execute farm policy. LRF members have been prominent in the Agrarian party (later renamed Center party) and well represented in the Parliament. Until 1970, farmers made up over three-fourths of the Parliament's permanent agriculture committee (the current figure is around 40 percent) (Micheletti 1990b, p. 111). Indeed, a Center party sheep farmer served as Sweden's Prime Minister for part of the short period of nonsocialist coalition governments, from 1976 to 1982. The LRF has been formally represented on commissions designing farm legislation (along with consumer and labor delegates). Its officers and technical experts sit on various advisory commissions and have been routinely consulted by administrative agencies and the agricultural research establishment. As is common in other nations, the agricultural bureaucracy is largely staffed with people from farm backgrounds. At the local level, farmers dominate most of the County Agricultural Boards. The LRF's influence has persisted despite the steady contraction of agriculture's share of economic activity and of farm people as a fraction of the electorate. (Fewer than 3 percent of the economically active population are now engaged in agriculture.)

Viewing this dense web of state-private interactions, critics of the democratic corporatist theory of the state reject the hypothesis that LRF has somehow been "tamed" by its multiform involvement in the policy apparatus. Rather, they view the nexus of LRF, the Parliament's permanent agriculture committee, and the farm bureaucracy as a classic "iron triangle" that largely shapes the policy agenda and runs the administrative apparatus with a high degree of autonomy (Bolin et al. 1986; Rabinowicz 1990).

Semiannual price negotiations for farm commodities and semiprocessed foods have been a site of direct encounter between the Federation of Swedish Farmers and the so-called Consumer Delegation. This relationship was yet another product of the state's social engineering, since the Consumer Delegation was a legislative creation in 1963. Most observers agree that producer interests have nearly always prevailed over consumer interests in price setting. Indeed, for much of the postwar period, substantive negotiation was largely preempted by a legislated formula requiring that rising input costs be automatically passed through to farm prices in order to maintain parity income for "efficient family farms." This effectively deprived the consumers of a collective voice. Furthermore, the LRF's well-financed media campaigns, playing on emotional themes like "national preparedness" and protection of the "living countryside," helped maintain a favorable climate of public opinion toward farmers, at least until the mid-1980s when the cost of farm supports to taxpayers and consumers soared to nearly 2 percent of household income (Micheletti 1990b; Rabinowicz 1990).

Economic Crisis and the Erosion
of Social Democratic Governance

Swedish agricultural policy is complexly related to an unfolding crisis in the larger economy and to change in economic governance that has been precipitated by it. These "preconditions" for the 1990 food-policy legislation can be presented in only a synoptic and stylized form here (see chapter 11 in this book written by Jessop, Nielsen, and Pedersen, but also Pestoff [1991] and Vail et al. forthcoming, for a more thorough discussion).

Sweden's long wave of stable economic expansion ended in the mid-1970s, as external pressures mounted and the class accord undergirding the postwar expansion began to unravel. The economy was caught up in capitalism's global industrial and financial restructuring. Heavily dependent on energy imports and industrial exports, Sweden was particularly vulnerable to the two oil shocks and the Japanese/Newly Industrializing Countries (NIC) challenge to its traditional heavy-industry exports. Internal contradictions were amplified by the combination of "imported" stagflation and a secular productivity slowdown. The Social Democratic government's attempt to maintain full employment via expansionary macroeconomic policy intensified a serious "wage drift" above the centrally negotiated norms. The breakdown of collective wage restraint, in turn, compounded the loss of international competitiveness, squeezed corporate profits, and reinforced the "cost disease" of the public sector.

The coincidence of economic stagnation and expansionary fiscal policy precipitated a severe budget crisis. The deficit peaked at 12 percent of gross domestic product (GDP) in the early 1980s when unemployment reached the unprecedented level of 4 percent. The profit squeeze was a joint consequence of labor and energy costs. It led to a contraction in domestic capital accumulation and a sharp increase in capital flight, with ominous long-term implications for employment and productivity growth[8] (Bosworth and Rivkin 1987; Lundberg 1985; Svenska Handelsbanken 1990).

The twists and turns of Swedish politics since 1973 have been heavily influenced by the unfolding and still unresolved economic crisis. After more than four decades in power, the Social Democrats were voted out in 1976. However, economic conditions went from bad to worse under a succession of bourgeois coalition governments, and the voters returned a minority SAP government in 1982. This situation was perpetuated by the 1985 and 1988 election results. The economy, meanwhile, made a brief surge during the 1983–85 period and then settled into a uniquely Swedish full-employment stagnation, with unemployment below 2 percent for several years but GDP growth averaging only 2 percent per year from 1986 to 1989, falling to 1 percent in 1990, and turning close to zero in 1991. Mounting wage pressure and sluggish productivity growth pushed inflation back to double digits in 1990. That induced a restrictive macroeconomic policy response that raised unemployment to 3 percent by mid-1991, with expectations of still higher unemployment to come.

The Social Democrats' internal splits, both strategic and ideological, have been brought to a head by the lack of effective tools in the traditional policy kit to fix simultaneous economic stagnation, wage-push inflation, and corporate blackmail (the threat of capital flight). The position of the party's neoliberals has been strengthened by several factors: the chronic low-level economic malaise, the necessity of making repeated compromises with the (centrist) Liberal party to pass economic legislation,[9] a distinct rightward drift in voter sentiment, and public anxieties about the corporate exodus and Sweden's relationship to the European Community. The political climate has also been influenced by several years of sophisticated and aggressive free-market propaganda underwritten by the Conservative party and the Swedish Employers Federation; this has further eroded public confidence in the old corporatist remedies of negotiation, compromise, and bureaucratic intervention (Pestoff 1991).

The Social Democratic government's response is revealed in a series of recent shifts in policy and in institutional arrangements:

1. A pronounced movement away from centralized regulations and negotiations and toward "market-oriented" policies, particularly deregulation of financial markets and *de facto* abandonment of centralized wage bargaining and the wage solidarity principle.

2. Benign neglect of "pension fund socialism" (the wage-earner funds) through curtailment of dedicated tax revenues.

3. A "supply-side" tax reform that sharply reduced top end income tax rates and increased reliance on excise taxes; in practice, if not intent, the tax package is regressive.

4. Creeping privatization of core public services such as health and child care, to cope with the public sector's "sclerosis."

5. A partial shift of responsibility for the sick pay system from the state to employers.

6. Abandonment of the commitment to (over)full employment.

These policies point to a detour from Sweden's "middle way" that does not appear to be either marginal or temporary. It is not simply that the "economic democracy" project has been sidetracked but that policies that long symbolized the commitment to social equality and economic equity have been sharply curtailed. Out of economic crisis and political contention, a new governance regime, based on a new admixture of negotiations, market forces, electoral procedures, and bureaucratic regulations may be taking shape. Ironically, despite the SAP's neoliberal maneuvering, the probability that it can keep its hold on power after the 1991 election is low. The government has already resigned briefly, in early 1990, when its "crisis package" to cope with the wage-price spiral was rejected by parties to the left and the right. Opinion surveys from 1988 to mid-1991 showed voters abandoning the Social Democrats in growing numbers.[10] As the 1991 election approaches, the probable gainers are the Conservatives, who for the first time drew even with the SAP in early 1991 polls; the center-right Christian Democrats, who seem likely to surpass with ease the 4 percent vote that they need to win Riksdag seats for the first time; and the New Democracy party, a right-wing populist insurgency that has attracted an extraordinarily large number of frustrated young working-class voters. The nonsocialist parties are currently trying to iron out a common-front strategy for the September 1991 election, but there is a distinct probability that no stable majority coalition can be formed. [11] (Bergström 1991; Wickbom 1991).

These, in a nutshell, are the broad political-economic conditions that brought agricultural policy to the center of the political agenda at the end of the 1980s.

External Crisis and Internal Contradictions
Undermine Agricultural Corporatism

Sweden's agricultural policy crisis stems partly from the systemic forces just described and partly from the food system's own maturing contradictions. Three of these—related to economics, environment, and national security—warrant brief discussion.

The long history of artificially high farm prices and "rationalization measures" to promote technological and managerial transformation bred chronic and growing excess production by the late 1970s. By 1984 the gap between production and domestic demand reached 65 percent for wheat, 27 percent for milk, and 23 percent for pork. Similar policies with similar results in the EC, the United States, and other nations flooded international markets and depressed prices. As a result, Sweden's budgetary cost of financing export dumping quadrupled. From 1980 to 1984, rising farm input costs, passed on to consumers via the parity pricing formula, pushed retail food prices up 66 percent.[12] Popular skepticism about the archaic agricultural policy was kindled by media attention to the evidence of deteriorating goal attainment and cost-effectiveness (an attention encouraged by the Social Democrats) (Rabinowicz 1990; Vail et al. forthcoming).

Popular disillusionment was also connected to a spreading "Green consciousness" in Sweden, coupled with mounting evidence of industrialized agriculture's adverse impact on water quality, rural landscape, wildlife habitat, and animal well-being. Polls conducted during the 1988 election campaign showed that environmental concerns were the top political priority of Swedish voters. In reaction, every political party stepped up its efforts to convey an environmentally friendly image, and the Greens became the first new party in seventy years to win seats in the Riksdag.[13] Economic interest organizations like the Federation of Swedish Farmers also scrambled to "clean up their image," while farmers and agricultural policy were increasingly held accountable for the spread of monotonous monoculture landscapes, nitrogen leaching into ground and surface waters, perceived chemical threats to food safety, and inhumane treatment of farm livestock. Opponents of the old farm policy whose motives were primarily political and economic did not hesitate to play upon these Green concerns.

As cold war tensions waned in the late 1980s, old notions of national security, including food self-sufficiency, also came into question. Profound changes in the nature of warfare provoked doubts about the relevance of maintaining capacity for a year or more of food self-sufficiency in wartime, especially as Swedish food production is heavily dependent on imported fuel and chemical inputs. Social Democratic leaders—and many others—saw no justification for a policy that causes excess food production at costs far above world market prices, using technology that required inputs whose supply would presumably be disrupted in an international crisis.

Of course long-standing policy regimes, popularly legitimated and backed by well-organized vested interests, are not eliminated overnight. But the Social Democrats and their *(pro tempore)* allies in the bourgeois parties had their sights set on an archaic agricultural policy. It was an obvious target in the SAP's larger struggles to contain the budget deficit, reduce inflationary pressure, promote intersectoral labor mobility, encourage efficiency through "market-oriented" deregulation, and project a Green image to voters. Centrist and Conservative political parties agreed with the SAP about the means—agricultural policy reform—if not the end: maintaining Social Democratic power.

In the later 1980s, both the substance of agricultural policy and its corporatist decision-making procedures came under siege; LRF and the farm bureaucracy found themselves outflanked on several fronts:

1. Legislation eliminated the parity pricing formula 1985, which had automatically passed higher farm costs through to farm prices. This breathed new life into price negotiations by empowering the Consumer Delegation to make its voice heard as the consumers' advocate. More than once in recent years, it broke off (exited from) negotiations without reaching a resolution on prices.

2. Largely bypassing the agricultural establishment, the government redefined national food security, emphasizing larger stockpiles of food and critical farm inputs and de-emphasizing highly subsidized peacetime production.

3. The Environment Protection Board and the Ministry of Environment and Energy, rather than the agricultural agencies, were assigned to investigate agro-environmental problems and formulate policy responses on issues ranging from nitrogen leaching to landscape preservation.

4. In 1988 the government proposed a complete overhaul of farm policy but shunned the traditional corporatist method of setting up a state commission with interest-group representation. Instead, it formed a small "working group" consisting only of members of the Parliament from each party and a staff recruited from nonagricultural ministries. To accentuate the increased priority of consumers' interests, the working group's charge was to propose a food policy, not a farm policy.

Much could be said about the Food Policy enacted by the Parliament in June 1990 and its likely social, economic, and environmental consequences. Supported by all parties except the Greens, the new policy reflects Swedish politicians' mastery of the art of compromise.[14] It is predictably generous to thousands of farm operators who will suffer reduced revenues, decapitalization of assets, and pressure to exit from agriculture. The new policy is also innovative in a number of ways, for example, in its direct compensation of farmers for their "production" of "public goods" like wildlife habitat and landscape amenities; its measures to integrate part-time farming more closely into rural development strategy; and its support for experiments in farm production of renewable biomass energy (Vail et al. forthcoming).

For this essay, however, the key features of the Food Policy are its economic liberalism and diminished use of corporatist mechanisms. After a five-year transition, farm commodity markets will freely reflect domestic demand and supply forces. Price negotiations, central to the corporatist regime, will disappear. Fixed tariffs will replace the variable import levies that in the past automatically insulated domestic prices from international fluctuations. Furthermore, the government has declared its willingness to cut agricultural tariffs deeply as part of a GATT resolution. By implication, the political contest over levels of farm price support will shift from a corporatist arena—the Agricultural Marketing Board—to the tariff-setting process of the Parliament.

Thousands of marginal farms are likely to "disappear" as tariff protection is reduced and prices fall to market-clearing levels. As taxpayers, citizens will pay a sizable bill in the short run to compensate farmers for their capital losses and to assist their transition to new occupations; but as consumers, citizens will benefit from lower food prices (or at least slower inflation). Since farm sales account for less than 30 percent of retail food expenditure in Sweden, the consumer gains from deregulation depend critically on measures to inject greater price competition into the heretofore protected and highly concentrated food-processing and distribution sectors. The Social Democrats have made this a high-profile issue in the 1991 election campaign, and just as they had hoped, the cost of a typical "market basket" of food has begun to decline in recent months. Finally, national resource allocation and general economic welfare are expected to be marginally improved by a more rapid flow of labor and capital from agriculture into higher productivity uses (Vail et al. forthcoming).[15]

Evolution or Devolution of the Negotiated Economy?

The negotiated economy has been described as a dialectical interaction among markets, democratic processes, bureaucracy, and negotiations. The intended message of the preceding sections is that in two distinct ways the agricultural policy regime is shifting away from the institutional configuration that prevailed for over half a century. In the policymaking process, the influence of democratic mechanisms (legislation, interparty collaboration, election campaigning) has increased relative to negotiations directly involving interest organizations. In policy substance, market forces are intended to assume a much more prominent role, as farmers and agro-industry are edged out of their secure corporatist niches.

Despite these changes, it would be incorrect to infer that Sweden's negotiated economy is dead, either in agriculture or in the economy at large. Many elements of the new agricultural policy regime are not yet in place, and many details have yet to be decided. A wide range of low-profile negotiations continue as various state and private actors attempt to shape the policy's details and administration. The LRF's continued prominence is evident, for example, in legislative discussions about future farm tariff levels as well as the magnitude and form of state support for biomass energy crops. The new Food Policy calls for decentralization of many programmatic decisions, and farmers' agents dominate the County Agricultural Boards that will allocate public funds for such programs as landscape preservation and rural development.

The evidence presented in this chapter suggests that overall, the Nielsen and Pedersen assertion (1990) about the increasing prevalence of negotiations in resource allocation and income distribution is not persuasive in the Swedish case. Yet their most recent observations—stressing the evolution of new forms of interaction between negotiation and other governance mechanisms and a shift in locus from centralized toward decentralized negotiations—are consistent with what we observe in Swedish agriculture. In sum, ambiguities in the present situation make it premature to conclude whether the 1990 Food Policy represents the devolution, or simply an evolution, of the negotiated economy (cf. chapter 11 written by Jessop, Nielsen, and Pedersen).

From a narrow economistic perspective, focusing on allocative efficiency and consumers' welfare, the partial decorporatization of Swedish agriculture can be considered a progressive measure. Yet, viewed as a moment in the degeneration of Sweden's sixty-year-old Social Democratic project—and considering the environmental and cultural-historical values that may be threatened by market-driven "rationalization" of the farm economy—it is problematic whether the neoliberal policy regime will prove socially progressive or regressive.

On top of these ambiguities, the prognosis has been complicated by a parliamentary resolution—just six months after passage of the new Food Policy legislation—to reverse Sweden's long-standing position and seek membership in the European Economic Community. (The resolution is yet another instance of Social Democratic collaboration with the major nonsocialist parties.) The formal membership application is being prepared as this is written. It seems certain that EC membership would sharply constrict the relative autonomy that allowed Sweden's negotiated economy to take and flourish as a distinctive "middle way." For Swedish agriculture specifically, incorporation into the EC's Common Agricultural Policy would mean a quick and dramatic reversal of the market-oriented reform of 1990 and a return to agrarian corporatism of a sort. This would not be the familiar Swedish agrarian corporatism, but the unique multinational corporatism that puts the Common Agricultural Policy so much at odds with the free-market principles that will shape the "Single Europe," which is due to come into existence just one year from now.[15]

Notes

1. A few advanced capitalist nations, most prominently Australia and New Zealand, had already established market-oriented farm policies before the mid-1980s.

2. Private interest organizations face a problem analogous to that of the state in aggregating their constituents' interests and mediating internal conflicts. Micheletti presents an intriguing history of this process in the case of the Federation of Swedish Farmers (Micheletti 1990b).

3. The central responsibility of ministries is to formulate policy rather than to administer it.

4. Lindbeck subsequently left the Social Democrats and became one of their most vocal critics on social and economic policies.

5. After SAP–Agrarian coalition governments ceased in the mid-1950s, the SAP's tactical reason for tolerating an unappealing agricultural policy was to help deter an Agrarian alliance with the bourgeois parties. By the way, the steady contraction of farm numbers and rural voter support led the Agrarians to take the name Center party and seek a broader constituency—while remaining a voice for farm interests.

6. Since assured income parity inhibited the exodus from farming, agricultural policy was in perpetual conflict with the macroeconomic goal of transferring resources to more productive industries.

7. Until 1971, two national farm organizations, a farmers' union and a federation of cooperatives, coexisted. They were consolidated into LRF with active encouragement from the state.

8. Swedish corporations have invested abroad for decades, but in the 1980s direct foreign investment increased almost tenfold to about $18 billion in 1990. The corresponding inflow of foreign capital grew slowly until 1988 and covered less than 20 percent of the outflow (Svenska Handelsbanken 1990: 14).

9. The Social Democrats' traditional economic policy ally, the Left party, was not willing to sign on to many of the government's neoliberal reform proposals in the 1980s, forcing the SAP to build bridges to the bourgeois parties.

10. A caveat: One should not prejudge Swedish elections. A similar decline in Social Democratic voter support occurred in the run-up to the 1988 election, but the party emerged with its fragile government intact.

11. The Social Democratic party lost its power in the 1991 election. The new government is a minority coalition of four bourgeois parties.

12. Budgetary pressures also led to a phase-out of consumer subsidies on several staple foods during this period. This action undoubtedly contributed to citizens' skepticism about agricultural policy.

13. Once in the Parliament, the Green party did not impress voters with its legislative program. Defects in its strategy for practicable change and the dominance of economic issues in the 1991 political debate are likely to reduce voter support for the Greens below the 4 percent threshold needed for continued Riksdag representation.

14. The Green party withheld support primarily because the proposed policy measures were not sufficiently aggressive in discouraging agricultural use of fossil fuel and chemicals.

15. Exiting farmers will be compensated for capital losses, and those who convert arable land to energy crops or forest will also receive financial assistance. Older farmers will be given pension options. The past success of Sweden's active labor-market policy and the economy's shortage of skilled labor suggest that younger farmers, as well as workers in the agro-industrial complex, will be able to find productive employment elsewhere.

The longer-term cost of the policy reform will depend on how heavily the state subsidizes development of biomass energy from farmland. At current oil prices, the subsidy element would have to be very large; thus either consumers (via higher energy prices) or taxpayers would have to foot the bill.

Bibliography

Berrefjord, Ole, and Per Heum. 1991. "Non-Market Governance of Business in a Market-Based Economy." Paper presented at the Society for Advancement of Socio-Economics Conference, Stockholm, June.

Bergström, Hans. 1991. "Election Year '91: Social Democracy in Crisis." *Current Sweden*, no. 381. Stockholm: The Swedish Institute.

Berlan, Jean-Pierre. 1990. "Capital Accumulation, Transformation of Agriculture and the Agricultural Crisis." In *Instability and Change in the World Economy*, ed. Arthur MacEwan and William Tabb, 205–24. New York: Monthly Review Press.

Bolin, Olof, Per-Martin Meyerson, and Ingemar Ståhl. 1986. *The Political Economy of* the Food Sector. Stockholm: SNS Förlag.

Bosworth, Barry, and Alice Rivkin, eds. 1987. *The Swedish Economy*. Washington, D.C.: Brookings Institution.

Drake, Lars. 1987. "The Value of Preserving the Agricultural Landscape." Fifth European Congress of Agricultural Economists. Balatoaszeplak, Hungary.

Esping-Andersen, Gøsta. 1985. *Politics Against Markets: The Social Democratic Road to Power*. Princeton: Princeton University Press.

Frykman, Jonas, and Orvar Löfgren. 1979. *Culture Builders*. New Brunswick, N.J.: Rutgers University Press.

Goodman, David. 1991. "Some Recent Tendencies in the Industrial Reorganization of the Agri-food System." In *Towards a New Political Economy of Agriculture*, ed. Williams Friedland et al., 37–64. Boulder, Colo.: Westview Press.

Goodman, David, and Michael Redclift, eds. 1989. *The International Farm Crisis*. New York: St. Martin's Press.

Hirschman, Albert. 1971. *Exit, Voice and Loyalty*. Cambridge: Harvard University Press.

Lundberg, Erik. 1985. "The Rise and Fall of the Swedish Model." *Journal of Economic Literature* 23, 2: 1–36.

Micheletti, Michele. 1990a. "Interest Groups in Post-Industrial Sweden." *Jahrbuch zur Staats- und Verwaltungswissenschaft 1990*. Berlin: Max Planck Institute.

———. 1990b. *The Swedish Farmers' Movement and Government Agricultural Policy*. New York: Praeger.

Milner, Henry. 1989. *Sweden: Social Democracy in Practice*. New York: Oxford University Press.

Nielsen, Klaus, and Ove Pedersen. 1990. "From the Mixed Economy to the Negotiated Economy." In *Morality, Rationality and Efficiency: Perspectives in Socio-Economics*, ed. R. Coughlin. Armonk, N.Y.: M. E. Sharpe.

Pestoff, Victor, ed. 1989. "Organizations in Negotiated Economies." Report 1989, no. 2. University of Stockholm, Department of Business Administration.

———, 1991. "The Demise of the Swedish Model and the Rise of Organized Business as a Major Political Actor." Paper presented at the Society for Advancement of Socio-Economics Conference, Stockholm.

Rabinowicz, Ewa. 1990. "Agricultural Policy: Old Wine in New Bottles." Report 32, *The Study of Power and Democracy in Sweden* (series), Uppsala: University of Uppsala.

Rothstein, Bo. 1988. "Social Classes and Political Institutions: The Roots of Swedish Corporatism." Report 24, *The Study of Power and Democracy in Sweden* (series), Uppsala: University of Uppsala.

Svenska Handelsbanken. 1990. "Sweden in the World Economy." Stockholm.

Vail, David, et al. 1993 (forthcoming). *The Greening of Agricultural Policy in Industrial Nations: Swedish Innovations in a Comparative Perspective*. Ithaca: Cornell University Press.

Wickbom, Ulf. 1991. "Election Year '91: The Most Important Issue in Sweden: Can Anyone Form a Government This Fall?" *Current Sweden*, no. 380. Stockholm: The Swedish Institute.

15. Non-Market Governance of Business in a Market-Based Economy: The Case of Norway

Ole Berrefjord
Per Heum

The Organization of Economic Activity

Two Utopias: Perfect Competition and Central Planning

The institutional framework constituting the contrasting models of perfect competition and of central planning is frequently applied as a point of departure when studying the organization of economic activity. The model of perfect competition assumes a large number of consumers with their own preferences. Consumers express their preferences through their decisions to buy, signaling to producers what they should produce. Producers are also assumed to be small and large in number, so that neither is able to influence prices. By allowing producers to keep their profit, and assuming that they try to maximize it, the model describes how producers have to adapt to the consumers' sovereign will. The necessary information is contained in prices that clear the markets. Competition and the profit incentive assure that resources are allocated to produce goods and services that serve people's interests. No conscious coordination or explicit gov-

This chapter summarizes the perspective that was applied to the study of business corporations in the Norwegian Power Study in the 1970s. It is an updated and revised version of a summary article from this Power Study project, originally written in Norwegian (Berrefjord and Hernes 1989). The continuation and extension of this work is now organized in the research program "Large Industrial Corporations—Industrial Transformation and Economic Growth" at the Center for Research in Economics and Business Administration (SNF). The Norwegian Research Council for Applied Social Science (NORAS) and SNF are its major financial supporters.

ernance is needed. It is all taken care of by the famous "invisible hand."

On the other hand, the model of central planning requires a powerful con-ductor. The state apparatus is seen as the center of command, and producers get directives to produce according to needs that are ascribed to them from the cen-tral political authority. The model assumes that the state has the capability to collect, to interpret, and to articulate the real preferences of its citizens; that it possesses the required information on production resources and opportunities; and that it can order efficient production of goods and services through adminis-trative measures to satisfy the needs in society.

The economic efficiency that both these ideal models claim to obtain does not hold when they are confronted with the real world. Most obviously, the model of central planning is challenged by the collapse of the economic systems of Cen-tral and East European nations. However, the model of perfect competition is also challenged—by monopolization in production, by low utilization of produc-tion factors, and by social costs.

Neither of the models seems to grasp the complex set of institutional frame-works that are obviously at work in a modern economy. Their institutional as-sumptions are too narrow or restricted. Even in a market-based economy, the governance of business may be considered as some sort of compromise between the two model extremes. Markets are an important means through which prefer-ences are expressed and production resources allocated. Nevertheless, compared with the model of perfect competition, markets are modified in several respects—partly by the companies themselves, for instance through corporate growth and strategic alliances, which provide companies with market power; partly by the state, for instance through regulations on new business entries, which directly affect business operations (Berrefjord and Heum 1990a and 1990b), or through redistributive measures.

Furthermore, markets are not only instruments through which preferences are expressed and through which production factors are allocated. Preferences are also expressed through the political system, leading to rather extensive public planning in several areas within the society. Planning is also an important part of the operations of large corporations and, in several instances, of coordinating operations of several producers. In short, neither the model of perfect competi-tion nor the model of central planning captures the organization of the economy in current industrial societies.

Three Dimensions in Focus: Corporate Growth, Intercorporate Relations, and Business-Government Interactions

The research issue we face is to examine the molds in which the compromises between market competition and planning, that is, the actual organization of economic activities in industrialized countries, have been cast. What is the actual organizational pattern? What characterizes the processes through which it has been developed, and how does this mixture of governance mechanisms affect economic performance?

It is not enough simply to state that capitalists unilaterally have opposed state intervention, whereas socialists have always been skeptical in applying the market mechanism. In reality, different groups at different times and on their own initiative have tried to mobilize, to strengthen, and to limit the influence of the state. Businesses may in some instances oppose state intervention, while in others they might claim that the state ought to get involved. Thus, the struggle is not about whether the state shall take part in governing economic activity but about how it ought to take part and for what purposes and in favor of whom. In other words, in this context there is room for a significant ideological mix.

In the 1970s, a major study took place that analyzed power in Norwegian society. In the project on the governance of large corporations, we assumed that a base was formed by market forces, which were modified by corporate growth, by joint actions within the business community, and by political rivalry and cooperation between business and public authorities. Thus, we could relate our work to discussions about ideal governance models—markets, democracy, and bureaucracy—described in the social sciences: the logic of these models, how they may become perverted, and how their application in practice may disturb the functioning of each other (Hernes 1978). Negotiations were then considered as a fourth governance system, which was not so neatly modeled as the other three but which in several respects functioned as oil in the machinery of society.

Theoretically and empirically we attempted a microbased approach to institutional economics, considering corporations as the key agents in our analysis of the economy. Thus, one important dimension in the institutional and organizational outcome of the compromises already spelled out in this chapter should be company size. Companies could be ranked along a small-to-large scale. Two other dimensions were also applied to illustrate the institutional complexity governing business operations: intercorporate relations and business–government interactions. Here we thought companies should ideally be measured along a loose-to-tight scale. This is illustrated in Figure 15.1.

Different industries or the whole economy can in principle move in different directions within this three-dimensional space. The number of new companies may increase, or the number of corporations may be reduced. Organized relations between companies may increase or decrease in number and intensity. And the companies' interactions with government may become tighter or looser.

In an institutional approach to the organization of business, however, we are concerned not only with the development along these three dimensions separately but also with ways in which the scores correlate along the dimensions

Figure 15.1. **Three Dimensions in Analyzing the Organization of Economic Activity**

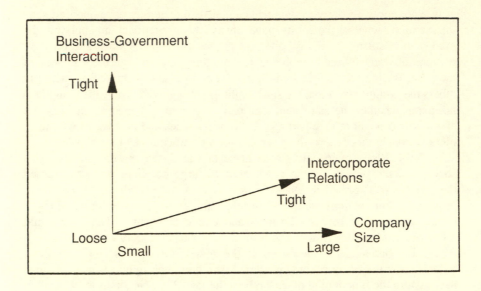

given. We may, for instance, ask whether corporate growth and a small number of dominant corporations within the national economy at large promote cross-ownership, interlocking directorates, high activity within trade associations, and tight relations with government. Or is it so that the larger and more dominant a corporation becomes within its sphere of production, the less it will orient itself directly toward other companies, trade associations, or the government?

Data and Definitions

The questions raised in the previous paragraph concern in principle all industries. In this paper, however, we limit this scope by focusing on manufacturing, mining, oil and gas, construction, and electricity production. Despite this limitation, these industries are significant in the Norwegian context:

• Their combined value makes up more than 40 percent of Norway's gross domestic product (GDP) less public administration.
• They cover all production of goods except for that which takes place in farming and in fisheries.

• They account for more than 70 percent of Norway's exports.

Thus, they may in some sense be regarded as a strategic core concerning the economic development and welfare of the nation as a whole.

The data we employ in this paper are collected in connection with two projects. One project is the Power Study from the 1970s; the other is our ongoing project on "Large Corporations in the Mixed Economy—Industrial Transformation and Economic Growth." To a certain extent, we make use of information from our data base on the largest industrial corporations in Norway. However, our most extensively used data come mainly from a survey among a sample of top executives in corporations operating in Norway in 1976 and 1988, in particular concerning intercorporate and business–government relations. This is not a random sample, but it embraces all larger corporations. Large, however, here refers to a small-nation standard, that is, the samples include corporations with more than 200 employees and up to almost 40,000 (as the largest in 1988).

As data are available from the mid-1970s and late 1980s, we are also in the position to examine changes in the pattern of governance regarding business in Norway. In the period between the surveys, a number of events took place that may have affected this governance pattern or the institutional structure surrounding business operations in Norway. One such event is the emergence of oil and gas extraction in Norway's economy (Berrefjord and Heum 1987 and 1990b). Another is the international recession in the late 1970s and early 1980s. A third could be the renaissance politically of trusting the market.

In this paper, however, only to some extent are we able to address such questions as these: Which changes have actually taken place? What might be the causes behind the observed changes? Our work is still in progress. We need to advocate caution regarding the simple figures that we present here, even though we find no reason to believe that more sophisticated analyses will alter the overall picture envisaged in this paper.

More work is needed, however, until we can decide on which samples from the two years we can apply to make reasonable comparisons. Corporations change by conducting mergers and divestments, by moving into new businesses, and by applying the new technology. Thus, we do not have identical units to compare for the two survey years, even though the names of companies in many instances are unchanged. To justify comparisons, we have chosen to consider corporations that, taken together, account for about the same share of industrial activities within the industries we focus on, both in 1976 and 1988. The samples we make use of in this chapter account for roughly 40 percent of all employment in Norway within the industries in question. This means that from the 1976 survey we had to include 215 corporations, of which well above 70 percent answered the questionnaire. In 1988, the number of corporations was reduced to 194, of which a little more than 60 percent responded.

Corporate Growth

Corporations and their management may have different motives that all tend to corporate growth and intercorporate coordination. The basic target, however, is to reduce uncertainty imposed on the corporations from the outside and to strengthen their control in matters, issues, and events of great interest to them.

In Norway, studies show that domestic production has become more concentrated during the post–World War II period. The average size of industrial corporations has also increased. For instance, in our 1976 sample, the corporations on average employed 1,000 persons; in the 1988 sample, almost 1,350. Another illustration is the average size of the thirty largest industrial corporations: In 1936 they employed some 1,400 on average (Walderhaug 1991); in 1971 and 1989 the averages were 3,100 and 5,600, respectively (Heum 1991).

Corporate growth in the 1980s particularly concerned the largest of Norway's large corporations. Takeovers and mergers significantly contributed to their growth. Including all their worldwide operations, Figure 15.2 shows how the value added of the ten largest corporations in particular increased when compared with domestic production in manufacturing and oil and gas. As these largest corporations increasingly conducted production abroad, the figure overrates their position in terms of production taking place in Norway. However, they beyond doubt also strengthened their position significantly in this respect over the period considered. This concentration of production can partly be analyzed in the context of industrial restructuring, which may accompany an international recession. However, the introduction of oil and gas in Norway's economy has also demanded more large-scale operations. Besides, the liberalization of markets has probably played a role in the sense that larger strategic business corporations have been considered as useful in strengthening the international competitiveness of Norway's business. International competitive forces may have caused domestic production to become more concentrated.

In this national context, these processes of concentration imply that the governance of production is increasingly conducted through administrative measures. More and more transactions take place within the corporations' own administrative borders. Market governance is to some extent replaced by hierarchical governance and control within corporations (cf. Coase 1937; Williamson 1975).

Intercorporate Relations

A study of corporate development should also consider how corporations organize their external relations. Thus, one empirical issue is to investigate how the trend toward concentration in production is linked to the level of intercompany coordination. Does the hierarchical control over production coincide with an increase or decrease in the companies' joint efforts to administer markets?

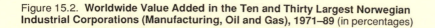

Figure 15.2. **Worldwide Value Added in the Ten and Thirty Largest Norwegian Industrial Corporations (Manufacturing, Oil and Gas), 1971–89** (in percentages)

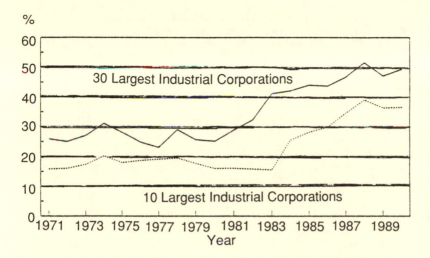

When a few corporations operate in the same markets, not only do they adapt to all unanimous market forces, but they also act and react vis-á-vis each other. As any action taken by one of them may affect the opportunities of the 9 others, they all develop an interest in influencing the disposition of others to their own advantage. Mutual dependency ignites initiatives and reactions, which may lead to rivalry and conflicts as well as to cooperation and coordination.

Our point of departure has been that a corporation will tend to enter into cooperation with others when it feels that this will put it in a better position to handle external uncertainty (cf. Thompson 1967) or, to put it differently, when it serves its interest (Coleman 1973; Hernes 1975). The relevance of this is supported by much empirical evidence. For instance, the harder a company finds it to replace deliveries from one supplier with those of another, the more it is inclined to enter into a long-term agreement with the supplier to secure its supplies (Berrefjord and Heum 1982). This illustrates how mutual dependency may forward a more permanent exchange of control than what is generally assumed for pure market transactions.

Interesting questions are, In which areas do corporations cooperate and what are the trends that can be traced in this respect? Corporate growth could imply that the need for external cooperation is being reduced: As more are brought within the borders of a corporation's authority, there may be less to coordinate with other corporations. On the other hand, corporate growth may also promote more cooperation within the business community. When some corporations grow, the others may have to coordinate more to counteract that growth. Or, when companies grow, they also become more visible as poten-

Table 15.1

Percentage of Top Executives Who Reported an Increase in Permanent Cooperation Between Their Corporation and Other Companies in Different Areas of Cooperation

Areas of Cooperation	1976 percentages ($N = 154$)	1988 percentages ($N = 117$)
Production	39.9	34.2
Product development	37.9	33.3
Computer technology	39.9	28.2
Sales, marketing, exports	29.4	32.5
Supplies	30.7	26.5
Versus public authorities	30.7	24.8
Horizontally in purchasing	18.3	23.1
Horizontally on sales terms	11.1	6.0
Horizontally on prices	8.5	3.4
Vertically on terms and prices	2.0	8.5

Sources: The Power Study and SNF.

tial cooperating partners.

The top executives in our surveys were asked if the level of permanent cooperation with other companies had increased, decreased, or stayed unchanged. Table 15.1 shows the share who answered that it had been increasing for different areas of cooperation. Hardly anyone reported that it was decreasing.

Both in the mid-1970s and in the late 1980s, the top executives reported that the corporation's direct and permanent cooperation with other companies was increasing rather than declining. The areas in which most executives reported an increase are the same for both years. These areas are connected directly to their production or to basic functions regarding their operations. Direct cooperation between corporations to strengthen their market power does not seem to have been the subject of extensive change. However, this is also in general prohibited, so other answers should hardly have been expected. Several top executives report that direct intercorporate cooperation is on the increase only regarding efforts to influence the government.

Another form of linkage between corporations is expressed through the composition of their board of directors. Table 15.2 shows that in 1988 about 70 percent of the top executives in the surveys hold at least one such position in another company. In 1988, a larger share, compared with the mid-1970s, held such a position in at least three companies. Here we also have to bear in mind that these figures underrate the extent of such coordination between companies because they do not include representatives of a corporation other than the executive.

Intercorporate coordination may also be more indirect than expressed so far.

Table 15.2

Percentage of Top Executives with Board Membership in Other Companies, 1976 and 1988

Number of positions	1976 percentages (*N* = 154)	1988 percentages (*N* = 117)
0	30.1	27.4
1	20.9	12.7
2	21.5	18.8
3 and 3+	27.5	41.1

Sources: The Power Study and SNF.

Membership in interest organizations, such as trade associations or an organization for employers, may serve as an illustration. This also has to be crucial in evaluating the importance of intercorporate relations for the functioning of markets and of the economy.

The top executives were asked to what extent the corporation depended on their interest organizations in different areas. The answer categories were "to a great extent," "to some extent," "to a small extent," and "not at all." Table 15.3 presents the share who answered to a great extent or to some extent for each of the areas that were included in the question.

The corporations' dependency on their interest organizations seems to be most extensive regarding their relations to the public sector and public debate. To a much smaller extent, this dependency seems to exist regarding services connected to the business operations of the corporations. However, a study on a sample of companies with fewer than twenty employees (Schjelderup 1980) showed that these relied more heavily—and in particular—on their organizations in this respect.

A factor analysis of the 1976 data further envisages two dependency dimensions. The first consists mainly of the areas A-to-C, indicating that interest organizations serve a purpose of influencing public decisions and public debate. The second captures areas E-to-G in particular, indicating that they also serve the purpose of being a service producer for its members. The relevance of corporate membership in such interest organizations is further reflected by the activities of the top management toward these associations. In 1976, as in 1988, more than three out of four top executives in the survey were, or had been, serving a position of trust in at least one of the trade associations in which their corporation was a member. The top management also interacts frequently with the corporation's most important interest organizations.

Table 15.3

Percentage of Top Executives Who Considered Their Corporation to Be Dependent on Its Interest Organizations, 1976 and 1988

Areas of Dependence on Interest Organizations	1976 percentages (N = 154)	1988 percentages (N = 117)
A. Ability to influence public decisions of great importance to the corporation	82.4[a]	72.6
B. Ability to forward its corporate interest in the public debate	78.4	65.0
C. Knowledge of public regulations of importance to the corporation	81.7	65.0
D. Education and seminars	60.1	55.6
E. Information on markets and industrial development	48.4	44.4
F. Knowledge of technology	30.0	33.3
G. Influencing dispositions of competitors	30.0	17.9

Sources: The Power Study and SNF.

Note: [a] All percentages represent the share of top executives who categorized the extent of their corporation's dependence on their interest group as "to a great extent" or "to some extent" as opposed to "to a small extent" and "not at all."

In 1976, 80 percent reported that they did so on at least a monthly basis; in 1988, 62 percent said they did the same.

Table 15.3, as well as the frequency of contacts between top management and trade associations, indicates that the role of such interest organizations may be subject to change. More work, however, is needed to document whether the importance of trade associations really is on the decline and, if so, to explain why this change has occurred. One reason might be that the large corporations do not consider these organizations as important as before, for instance, because the increase in concentration of production means that in some industries there is now only one major corporation in operation, which in some sense may replace the interest organization. Interest organizations may also have become more selective about whom they frequently interact with.

In summary, our findings clearly indicate that different forms of administrative control within markets are increasing. The corporations have grown significantly, and they are to a large and increasing extent controlled by institutional owners (Berrefjord and Dahl 1988). Furthermore, cooperation between corporations seems to be extensive—and on the increase. Consequently, power relations within the business community, and between business and consumers, depend largely on how these administrative mechanisms work and on their distributional effects.

These trends of concentration in production and more administrative governance mechanisms concerning market transactions also raise the question of the relation between business and politics. How, and to what extent, do the large corporations apply their strength and collaborative tools to influence public decisions?

Business–Government Interactions

Microeconomic textbooks discuss the behavior of consumers and producers within different market contexts. In macroeconomic textbooks, the means of the state to govern the development of a national economy are among the topics that are addressed. In textbooks on marketing, students learn how to influence consumers, and in law school the legal framework within which companies operate is taught.

All these descriptions, however, neglect the point that not only are the corporations economic agents in a market, they are also political agents. They devote resources to change and influence market conditions and political ramifications to their own advantage. In doing so, they will also make use of political means.

The increasing growth and specialization of the public sector, also in areas that directly affect business, mean that the companies must hold an interest in the outcome of public decisions. These changes in the magnitude and scope of the public sector have probably increased the rate of return that companies can expect from their political actions designed to promote corporate initiatives in that direction.

Similarly, public authorities hold an interest in how corporations operate. The state of a nation's business forms an important base for the realization of several of the welfare ambitions that are expressed through the political system. Hence, business and government share a mutual desire to interact, but not always for the same purpose.

Our surveys contribute to mapping these interactions between business and government. In Table 15.4, we refer to the share of corporations where the top management more than once during the previous year was reported to have been in touch with government institutions on behalf of the corporation or industries in which the corporation operates.

The frequency of interaction is more extensive with local than with central government. It is also more extensive toward the public administration than toward publicly elected representatives. These differences can to a large extent be explained, in different matters concerning business, by the delegation of public authority from politicians to the administration and from the central to the local level.

It is evident, however, that interactions with publicly elected representatives are reported to have become more extensive between the mid-1970s and the late 1980s. We will have to look further into this matter to explain why. In a way, it contradicts what we might expect from the general interpretation of political

Table 15.4

Percentage of Corporations Where the Top Management Had Been in Contact with Different Government Bodies More Than Once During the Previous Year, 1976 and 1988

Government bodies	1976 percentages ($N = 154$)	1988 percentages ($N = 117$)
Central government:		
The storting; local representatives to the parliament	36.6	55.6
Central administration	76.4	69.3
Local government:		
Publicly elected representatives	51.0	67.0
Local administration	88.9	85.5

Sources: The Power Study and SNF.

trends: that politicians are losing power to the administration. At the central level, however, at least two explanations seem likely. One is that the government no longer has a firm majority base in the *Storting,* the parliament, meaning that more is unsettled when a proposition is forwarded to the Storting. The other is that the administration may have become more reluctant in dealing with lobbyists and that politicians increasingly serve as an outlet for such corporate actions.

The top executives were also asked whether the frequency of such interactions between the top management of the corporation and government had been increasing or decreasing or had stayed at the same level over the last five years. Hardly anyone reported that it had been decreasing, whereas according to Table 15.5 a significant number claimed that it had been increasing. The more extensive interactions with the Storting representatives are reflected in these trend considerations. On the other hand, the frequency of interactions with the central administration and local government seems to be leveling out.

Similarly, the top executives were asked whether such interactions with government had become more important for the corporation over the last five years. Also here, hardly anyone reported that the importance of such contacts had been decreasing. In fact, as Table 15.6 spells out, a larger share than those who reported an increase in frequency thought these interactions had become more important for the corporation. No wonder they also reported that the top management now spent more time on such relations than before.

The top management is not necessarily the only one to represent the corpora-

Table 15.5

Percentage of Corporations Where the Frequency of Interactions with the Government Bodies Is Reported to Have Increased During the Previous Five Years, 1976 and 1988

Government bodies	1976 percentages ($N = 154$)	1988 percentages ($N = 117$)
The Storting	17.6	29.1
Central administration	51.5	38.5
Local government	54.9	38.5

Sources: The Power Study and SNF.

tion in its external relations. On several occasions, different groups within the corporation may cooperate for the corporation's purpose. Such coordinated actions may, for instance, be that the top management deals with those they are attached to politically, whereas the blue-collar representatives deal with the political opponent, that is with the Labor party. Or it may be that both the top management and employees are jointly represented in meetings with government officials.

Such coordinated actions are not just rare incidents. Their composition also coheres with important features of the structure underlying the concept of a negotiated economy (Berrefjord, Nielsen, and Pedersen 1989). However, even though this representation of a negotiated economy applies to Norway, Table 15.7 shows that this cannot be the most common way to handle the corporation's external relations in Norwegian business. Nevertheless, a closer look is still required into the occasions when such joint operations are considered to be the most beneficial for the corporation.

Regardless of the form these interactions between business and government take, it is evident that they must have different causes. Some interactions are probably more or less procedural according to public regulations, but through these interactions the corporations naturally try to pursue their interests. Some are intended to influence the outcome of ordinary day-to-day decisions within the public sector or more *ad hoc* matters that affect the operations of the corporation. Some may concern business projects where the government might play a role. Others may influence and change general ramifications and regulations to the advantage of the corporation. We will try to dig deeper into this material

Table 15.6

Percentage of Top Executives Who Reported That the Relations with Government Have Become More Important for the Corporation During the Previous Five Years, 1976 and 1988

Government bodies	1976 percentages (N = 154)	1988 percentages (N = 117)
The Storting	19.6	35.9
Central administration	56.2	47.0
Local government	58.2	43.6

Sources: The Power Study and SNF.

Table 15.7

Percentage of Corporations That Reported at Least One Joint Action of Top Management and Employees with Government Institutions on Behalf of the Corporation During the Previous Five Years, 1976 and 1988

Government bodies	1976 percentages (N = 154)	1988 percentages (N = 117)
The Storting	26.8	29.9
Central administration	49.7	37.6
Local government	43.1	48.7

Sources: The Power Study and SNF.

later on in our project work.

Corporations, however, are not the only initiating source of such interactions. As we have already stated, the government also holds an interest in dealing directly with corporations. It may be on specific issues or in order to get general information or judgments from business agents on different matters. The breadth and extent of such initiatives are reflected in Table 15.8. Here the top executives have noted areas where the central government has directed a special inquiry to their corporation during the previous three years.

Table 15.8

Percentage of Top Executives Who Reported That Their Corporations Received a Special Inquiry from the Central Government During the Previous Three Years, by Different Areas, 1976 and 1988

Area where central government directed inquiry	1976 percentages (N = 154)	1988 percentages (N = 117)
Product development	15.7	20.5
Localizing business operation	41.8	41.9
Financial issues	22.8	24.8
Production and employment	37.3	37.6
Environmental issues	51.6	49.6
Coordination between corporations	15.1	28.2
Structural rationalization	20.2	27.3
Deliveries of goods and services	20.9	22.2
Exports and foreign trade issues	33.7	30.0
Preparation of public regulations	26.2	38.5

Sources: The Power Study and SNF.

In this paper, we do not discuss the detailed content of these interactions. It is worth mentioning, however, that the interactions we talk about do not have the features of direct state intervention. They take place in a rather cooperative context and are aimed at increasing the competitive strength of domestic business while trying to ensure national welfare. Hence, in principle, business does not have any doubts about dealing with the government, even though it does not agree with everything the government does. Rather, business is quite positively disposed toward such cooperation. At least, that is what is revealed from Table 15.9, which shows the attitudes of the top executives toward further development of the cooperation between business and government in different areas. The answer categories in the questionnaire were "very positive," "quite positive," "quite negative," and "very negative." Table 15.9 comprises those who answered "very positive" and "quite positive."

To summarize, we have shown that interactions between business and government have become more extensive through the 1970s and 1980s and that these relations are of increasing importance according to the judgments of the top business executives of large Norwegian corporations. This also has to play a role when interpreting operations within a small, open economy like Norway. Administrative control of markets, owing to corporate growth and inter-

Table 15.9

Percentage of Top Executives Who Are Positive Toward the Development of Further Cooperation Between Business and Government in Different Areas, 1976 and 1988

Areas of cooperation	1976 percentages (N = 154)	1988 percentages (N = 117)
Developing and upgrading product and technology	61.2[a]	64.9
Localization of production facilities and offices	59.5	47.0
Public support, guarantees, and financial arrangements for business investments	76.5	70.1
Public support, guarantees, and financial arrangements for business operations	54.2	36.8
Export financing	71.2	65.8
Industry structure	52.9	46.2
Preparation of public regulations	73.2	85.5

Sources: The Power Study and SNF.

Note: [a] All percentages represent the share of top executives who categorized their attitude toward further development of the cooperation between business and government as "very positive" or "quite positive" as opposed to "quite negative" and "very negative."

corporate coordination, underlines the necessity of linking organizational theory and market theory to an understanding of how such an economy operates. According to the preceding discussion on business–government relations, we also add the need to include political theory. The key to grasping developments within such economies is in the interface of theories concerning economics, politics, and organization.

Structure and Trends in the Governance of Norway's Business

In closing the chapter, it is necessary to investigate how the three dimensions—corporate growth, intercorporate relations, and business-government interactions—are linked together. Can we trace a pattern so that a certain score for a corporation on one of the dimensions also indicates how it scores on the other two? For instance, does frequent interaction between a corporation and the government coincide with a high degree of internal administration and external coordination of transactions? Or are the activities that a corporation engages in along one of these dimensions independent of the activities it chooses along the other?

In the Power Study we made a comprehensive correlation analysis of the 1976 data; we have not yet done so with the 1988 data. Altogether, thirteen indicators were grouped to illustrate the three dimensions underlying our analysis (cf. Figure 15.1). However, as the data we have presented on business–government interactions indicate, we are not able to test how firm these relations are. Our information is on their frequency; companies are measured on this dimension along a rare-to-frequent scale.

All indicators we applied correlated positively, although at varying strengths. Nevertheless, this means that the more "actively" a corporation operates along one of the dimensions, the more it also tends to be "active" along the other two: The larger the corporation, the more extensive are its relations with other companies and with the government.

Even though correlation analysis in itself does not provide us with any cutting point, the pattern that this revealed generated an idea of duality within Norway's business community. This idea of connections between the dimensions we have applied is illustrated in Figure 15.3.

Even though similar analysis of the 1988 data has not been conducted in detail so far, we expect it will support this notion of duality. We also think that the observed concentration of production implies that a larger share of Norway's production is now taking place within the context provided for by the upper right box in Figure 15.3. If so, we increasingly face a challenge regarding our understanding of how the economy functions and regarding the competence and capability requirements for the agents at work—firms, interest organizations, and public institutions—to have the economy operate efficiently. In particular, the government should be aware of the danger that business may try to involve the state in their projects in a way that leaves the downside risk to the state while business keeps the upside potential to itself (Berrefjord 1990). The short-term interests of business might then easily undermine the long-term interests of society.

This does not mean, however, that we do not think that the government has any role to play regarding the development of domestic business. Rather, it means that we advocate caution and a need to improve our understanding as to how this kind of an economy really functions. Neither the causes behind the development of nonmarket governance measures nor their effects on the economic and social performance of business are easily spotted by our current cognitive glasses.

The pure existence of an "upper right box" challenges our current analytical tools. If such a context should now prevail for more of Norway's production than in the mid-1970s, this challenge simply becomes more urgent. What is needed is not only a revision of the statistical data on which we base our economic analysis, but also a reconsideration of the models underlying economic politics. Information on the largest corporations ought to be improved, and it

Figure 15.3. **The Duality of Norway's Business Community**

should allow for linkages to more macroeconomic as well as political-administrative theories and models. In short, this challenge may be summarized as the need for a more coherent theory of institutional economics.

Bibliography

Berrefjord, Ole. 1990. "Public Projects and Corporate Behavior—A Negotiated Economy in Norway." Paper to the Second Annual International Conference on Socio-Economics, Washington, D.C., March 16–18.

Berrefjord, Ole, and SvennÅge Dahl. 1988. "Shareholders in Norway's Business" (in Norwegian). In *Bilaga 9 Ågande och inflytande i svenskt näringsliv.* Stockholm: Statens offentliga utredningar nr. 38.

Berrefjord, Ole, and Gudmund Hernes. 1989. "Large Corporations, Markets and Bureaucracy" (in Norwegian). In *Forhandlingsøkonomi i Norden,* ed. Klaus Nielsen and Ove K. Pedersen 171–90. København: Jurist-og Økonomiforbundets Forlag.

Berrefjord, Ole, and Per Heum. 1982. "Economic Power Groups" (in Norwegian). In *Maktutredningen,* Slutrapport. Oslo: Norges Offentlige Utredningar nr. 3.

———. 1984a. "Offshore Petroleum Activities and the Development of the Political Economy in Norway." *Peuples méditerranéns* 26: 203–10.

———. 1984b. "Norway: Vulnerable Wealth." In *Economic Growth in a Nordic Per-*

NORWAY'S GOVERNANCE OF BUSINESS 337

spective. ETLA/IFF/IUI/IØI. Report no. 40. Bergen: Institute of Industrial Economics.

————. 1990a. "Political Governance of the Petroleum Industry—The Norwegian Case." In *Naive Newcomer or Shrewd Salesman? Norway—A Major Oil and Gas Exporter*, ed. H. O. Bergesen and A. K. Sydnes, 6–27. Oslo: Fridtjof Nansen Institute.

————. 1990b. *Natural Resource-Based Industries: Big Business and the Role of the State—The Case of Norway's Oil and Gas*. Working Paper no. 26. Bergen: Institute of Industrial Economics.

————. 1990c. "Political Governance of the Petroleum Industry—The Norwegian Case." In *Naive Newcomer or Shrewd Salesman? Norway—A Major Oil and Gas Exporter*, ed. H. O. Bergesen and A. K. Sydnes, 28–48. Oslo: Fridtjof Nansen Institute.

Berrefjord, Ole, et al. 1987. "Norway: On the Brink of Recession." In *Growth Policies in a Nordic Perspective*. ETLA/IFF/IUI/IØI. Report no. 88. Bergen: Institute of Industrial Economics.

————. 1990 "Norway: On the Track of Long-Term Balanced Growth?" In *Growth and Integration in a Nordic Perspective*. ETLA/IFF/IUI/NÖI. Report no. 125. Bergen: Institute of Industrial Economics.

Berrefjord, Ole, Klaus Nielsen, and Ove K. Pedersen. 1989. "Negotiated Economy in the Nordic Countries—An Introduction" (in Danish). In *Forhandlingsøkonomi i Norden*, ed. Klaus Nielsen and Ove K. Pedersen. København: Jurist-og Økonomiforbundets Forlag.

Coase, Ronald. 1937. "The Nature of the Firm." *Economica* 4 (November): 386–405.

Coleman, James S. 1973. *The Mathematics of Collective Action*. London: Heineman Educational Books.

Hernes, Gudmund. 1975. *Power and Powerlessness* (in Norwegian). Oslo: Universitetsforlaget.

————. 1978. "Power, Mixed Economy and Mixed Administration" (in Norwegian). In *Forhandlingsøkonomi og blandingsadministrasjon*, ed. G. Hernes. Oslo: Universitetsforlaget.

Heum, Per. 1991. *The Macro-Relevance of Large Industrial Corporations*. Working paper. Bergen: SNF.

Schjelderup, Liv. 1980. *Small Business in a Large-Scale Society* (in Norwegian). Oslo: Universitetsforlaget.

Thompson, James D. 1967. *Organizations in Action*. New York: McGraw-Hill.

Walderhaug, Klaus. 1991. *The Largest Corporations in Norway's Manufacturing. A Comparison of 1936 and 1988*. Working Paper. Bergen: SNF.

Williamson, Oliver E. 1975. *Markets and Hierarchies: Analysis and Antitrust Implications*. New York: Free Press.

16. Evolution of Interest Representation in Poland

Jerzy Hausner
Andrzej Wojtyna

The Representation of Interests
in Traditional Socialist Systems

Given the basic tenets of socialism, one might expect that group interests should manifest themselves mainly in the planning process, which should provide a mechanism for their coordination. In reality, however, the planned economy does not create conditions for the free expression of particular group interests. This is due, in Józefiak's opinion, to the monocentric character of the non-economic social order (Józefiak 1984, p. 145).

Formally, those taking part in the socio-economic planning are, apart from the state administration, various political bodies (representative organs, Communist party, political organizations) and social bodies (trade unions, associations, self-government organs). In practice, however, the role of those political and social organs is mostly nominal. In view of their position in the system of power, they are for the most part unable to express social interests.

The dominant position of organs of economic state administration in the system of power makes them the most efficient channels for the articulation of interests. The fact that the organs in question articulate group interests has a number of consequences for the management of the economy and society. We would like to draw attention to some of them:

1. The fact that the state organs are concerned with the transmission of interests means, of course, that this is not done by other political and social bodies. And just from this point of view, criticism is leveled at the way various socio-occupational and self-government organizations fulfill their functions. Yet it would be wrong to think that the role of those bodies in the articulation of interests is completely nonessential. In fact, some of them do play in that process an active, though not fully independent, role. It consists in

an indirect expression of interests to the state organs or in a strengthening of the articulation already taken up by those organs. As a result, the bodies under discussion must adjust their organizational structure and activity to the activities of the administration, the best example of which is the way trade unions have functioned.

2. The subordination of planning to the administration and the articulation of group interests by the latter lead to the situation in which socio-economic planning and then the realization of the plans become an area in which social interests do clash, but only those in the form of organizational (branch) interests. So the interests of social groups influence the planning in an indirect way. At the same time, competition within the economic administration over the formulation and realization of plans is being strengthened.

3. The weakness of the nonadministrative channels of interest articulation results in the situation in which social aspirations that are in conflict with the interests of the administration apparatus are "pushed" below the level of articulation. That leads to the discontent and opposition of some social groups or to the articulation of their interests outside the legal system of authority.

4. The articulation of group interests through the administrative organs transforms a system of management into an area of many types of social conflict and as a consequence leads to the institutionalization of conflicts within this system.

The last observation provides a good starting point for discussing a system of coordination solving social conflicts in socialism. The fact that social conflicts become institutionalized within the administration system obviously leads to their resolution being determined by the way the administrative organs function. In this case, the hierarchical and centralized structure of the administration creates a situation of "the upward transmission of social conflicts": They are not solved at the lower levels of the system in which they originally emerged but are moved up to the central level. In this process, the particular units of the administration not only shake off the responsibility for the resolution of conflicts but present them in a light favorable to them. That means that they define grievances from the point of view of their own interests. Consequently, by the time the conflicts have reached the central level, they have been gradually distorted. Therefore, it is really very difficult, if not impossible, to get a clear picture of that conflict in central organs. This, of course, reduces the possibility of reaching a viable solution.

Many writers have stated that central decision makers perceive conflicts in a technocratic manner and thus prefer solutions in harmony with that perception (Staniszkis 1976). It seems that this is the result of, among other things, a complex system of identifying, defining, and transmitting a conflict situation through the structure of state administration. It leads to the political authorities getting entangled in conflict situations without having at their disposal—as a rule—any possibility of acquiring unbiased information about the situation. Moreover, the steps they take are not likely to solve the conflict by removing its social causes, and will merely neutralize its effects. A typical example of this is the granting of additional benefits and privileges to the groups revealing tension, without real attempts at identifying the roots of the conflict.

The institutionalization and technocratization of the resolution of social conflicts under the socialist system has its repercussions in the sphere of social consciousness. The most important of these is a vertical perception of conflicts in so far as they are perceived as a clash between the arguments of a given group and the action taken by the authorities. The opposition ''us'' (social group, society) versus ''them'' (authorities) reflects the way in which people perceive the methods of solving social conflicts. Another consequence is the ideological rationalization of the technocratic practice resulting in a myth of all the interests in socialist society being uniform. According to conventional wisdom, the decision makers represent the long-term interests of the whole society. They competently identify the real needs of society, and on this basis they formulate a rational strategy of the socio-economic development that takes into account objective limitations in the possibility of meeting an excessive number of just demands. The particular activities of various groups, owing to their ignorance of those objective limitations, disrupt the realization of the accepted strategy. That is why—in Pajestka's opinion—such disruptions should be removed by means of proper education aimed at creating a social unity of goals (Pajestka 1980). According to his opinion, restrictions imposed on the flow of information, and attempts to manipulate it, are fully justified sociotechnical measures.

New Areas of Conflict in the Polish Postsocialist Economy and Evolution of Institutional Forms of Interest Representation

Along with the traditional areas of conflicting interest that are characteristic of a socialist economy, new ones are also emerging. Their appearance is undoubtedly a result of changes in the economy, although—and this is very significant—they are closely linked to the state's activities. The state administration is seldom an arbiter in those conflicts since it is usually a party to them. So the conflicts that prevail in a traditional socialist economy are still vertical ones. These new areas of conflict concern such questions as the following:

- privatization of state property
- government's policy toward various economic sectors
- restructuring and demonopolization of the economy
- continuing with the commitments assumed by the previous authorities and observing the privileges granted
- foreign economic cooperation

In this chapter there is a focus on one issue, the government's policy toward different ownership sectors.

At first, "equality of the sectors" was the main slogan of the advocates of economic transformation. They kept indicating that once equal rights were given to all enterprises, the private ones would prove more effective than the state ones, and the private sector would consequently develop more dynamically than the state one, which would bring about a favorable change in the structure of ownership. But in 1990 the arguments for the necessity of a preferential treatment of the private sector became increasingly stronger, and one could already notice symptoms of such a policy on the part of the government.

In the second part of 1990, voices opting for the equal treatment of the sectors became much more insistent, and the suggestions were no longer concerned only with the question of taxes. Some liberal experts (also those close to Wałesa), as well as the Center Alliance, the influential political group that was at the head of Wałesa's presidential campaign, have come out with the idea of protecting the private sector at the expense of the state sector. The bottom line of this concept is as follows: "Private economy was destroyed in Poland by the state. It is the state therefore which should rebuild it now by strengthening it with funds taken over from the state sector and using them for the development of the private sector" (Oblicki 1990). This would, in fact, be an undertaking of the "primitive accumulation of capital" like that carried out during the forced introduction of the socialist economy. Obviously, this kind of undertaking would immediately generate tremendous tension and social conflicts, whereas its consequences for the system seem to be rather incompatible with the idea of a market economy and democratic order. The shortcuts to capitalism, as suggested by some, would probably lead to state capitalism and not to the liberal version, with all the consequences of such a development, because it would be Asian rather than European capitalism.

The state's policy toward various sectors is also discussed in view of the very dynamic growth of the informal sector in the Polish economy, mostly seen in the street trade. Representatives of registered private business, while defending the rules of equal competition, demand that the state administration and local authorities ban this sort of informal trade.

At the same time, some liberal economic circles are asking for a curb on the "black market" and have also requested a tax "amnesty" and the legalizing of undeclared incomes intended for investments. This might, in their opinion, raise additional capital for the purchase of state enterprises.

Another sphere of conflicts emerges as a result of the government's policy toward state enterprises. No matter how fast the process of privatization is, for quite a long time the state sector will prevail in the Polish economy. Any changes in it will continue to be of the greatest importance for the economy. The government's policy toward that sector will probably be aimed at starting three processes: commercialization, restructuring, and demonopolization. In 1990 the government came forward with a proposal of commercialization for the state enterprises, which was meant to be an "introductory privatization." According to this proposal, the state enterprises would be transformed into joint-stock companies with the government Treasury as the sole owner. The companies would be controlled by the supervisory boards appointed mainly by the Ministry of Ownership Transformation. The governmental experts also assumed that the government could bring about an *ex officio* commercialization of the enterprises and thus exclude them from the regulations of the State Enterprises Act.

This proposal was strongly criticized and opposed by the Economic Council. The members of the Economic Council, which is an advisory body to the Cabinet, noticed among other things that the government's proposal does not set a clear goal for the proposed commercialization. Its implementation would therefore not open any long-term prospects for the enterprises transformed into companies. They also acknowledged that such commercialization would lead to a bureaucratic recentralization of management and to a concentration of power in ministerial hands. The Economic Council took an official view that "the commercialization of enterprises should orient their activity towards the maximization of economic surplus (profit) and the value of assets as well as to make the decision-making processes independent from the political and bureaucratic pressures." In order to achieve this aim, it is necessary, above all, to create a competitive market environment around the state enterprises and to allocate property rights. In the Economic Council's opinion, weaknesses of the government's proposals are due to shortfalls in the government's attitude toward such fundamental questions as the role of the state sector, the position of workers' self-management, and the level of uniformity of rules and conditions for various economic sectors. The Economic Council did not acknowledge that the only possible form of commercialization is the transformation of enterprises into joint-stock companies with the Treasury as a sole owner and proposed on its part other forms of state enterprises such as managerial-oriented and workers' self-management-oriented enterprises based on leasing.[1]

This commercialization must entail a clash of interests because it relates to the very functioning of state enterprises, their organizational structures, and their management. Particularly conflict-prone appears to be the establishment of a new management system and a position of personnel representatives in it—the employees' councils and the representation of trade unions, as well as the setting up in those commercialized enterprises of their boards, which would replace the former upper organs and would in the first instance be responsible for the "sanitation" of the enterprise and for adapting it to the new circumstances. This will upset both the traditional balance of power in the enterprise and numerous formal and informal workers' rights and privileges.

Together with the changing interests of particular social groups, the organizations representing those interests are changing too. Many of the already existing organizations have been compelled to adapt themselves to current changes—or are just trying to do so—both at the level of the set of interests and at the level of authority. Some of them are losing their capacity of representation in the new circumstances. In addition, quite new organizations are emerging.

In order to highlight some phenomena emerging in this area, we would like to take Solidarity as an example. We are speaking here of Solidarity as a trade union, not as a social movement and a political group. While these are inter-linked, they must be considered separately. The dilemma Solidarity is currently facing is the question of whether it should be a union taking part in decision making or one concerned solely with defending workers' rights. The first approach consists in the treatment of Solidarity as a force cogoverning the country and responsible for its systemic transformation. Its advocates are to be found primarily among activists at the regional and central levels who combine their trade unionist work with politics. But the sharing of power means that the union must also share the government's responsibility for its policies, especially economic policy. This policy, because of its drastic consequences for the majority of the citizens as regards their living standards, has increasingly become the object of criticism. That is why the activists at the enterprise level opted for the union to be concerned with demands and fiercely attacked the government and administration.

The dispute between the advocates of the two approaches appeared distinctly during the outbreak of strikes. A characteristic example of this was the attitude of various Solidarity bodies toward the railway workers' strike (May 1990), which paralyzed rail transport over a vast area of the country. As a result of differences in attitude toward that strike, the position of the National Solidarity Commission was far from clear. On the one hand, it did support the railway workers' demands and expected the government to meet them instead; on the other hand, it disapproved of the very form of the protest, accusing the organizers and their supporters of acting for political reasons and of trying to hamper the reforms. The Solidarity leadership, including Wałesa himself, made an otherwise successful attempt to stop the strike at the cost of support for the strikers, and the government promised to meet their demands. This type of strikebreaking did not resolve the dilemma of whether to be with the government or against it—it merely neutralized the situation and removed the tension. Apparently Solidarity assumed the traditional role of a union (expressing demands) but, in fact, by effectively replacing the government, it did accept the responsibility for the latter's activities.

The tension arising from that dilemma keeps growing as the process of privatization is becoming more intensive with all its consequences and as the mass layoffs of state-enterprise workers are becoming a reality. At the Sejm (the lower house of the Polish parliament), the majority of Solidarity deputies and the union's official representatives supported the government's proposal of shares being distributed among all citizens instead of being transferred to the enterprises' workers. This drew a protest from the representatives of the enterprise commissions of the state's largest enterprises who have set up the National Agreement of Enterprises commissions. They came out with a demand for privatization bills to be amended so as to reconsider the previously rejected solutions of employees' shareholding. This network agreement demands a strong emphasis on workers' interests and opposes the union's sharing responsibility with the government for the latter's policy so as not to involve the union in political conflicts. The agreement involves close cooperation with a group of self-government activists who have called into being the Union of Workers Ownership and who are fighting for the idea of employees' shareholding while declaring themselves opposed to the government's privatization proposals and to the bills adopted by the Sejm.

The enterprise activists have also fought against mass layoffs, which are an inevitable consequence of the state sector's restructuring and the growing commercialization of its units. They demanded amendments to be introduced into the bill on employment and group layoffs, and should this demand be met, it would restrict the capacity of state enterprises to adapt themselves to the requirements of market competition.

All these developments reveal basic contradictions in the evolution of Solidarity. It came into being as a social movement protesting against the economic inefficiency, social injustice, and autocracy of the previous system. It was born in major state enterprises, and its leading cadres came from their staffs. By bringing about the fall of the Communist system, the movement opened the possibility of far-reaching systemic transformation. But the inevitable consequence of this transformation is the elimination of the state socialist sector and of the rules that guided its operation. The costs of that process will be borne largely by the staffs of the big enterprises, that is, by those people who gave Solidarity its power when it was born.[2]

This contradiction provokes splits and tensions within Solidarity itself. It gives rise to a strong tendency to re-create and activate the branch structures of Solidarity. Indeed, their influence has been growing, and they have gradually seized the right to negotiate with the government over the economic conditions of their respective branches. Their philosophy is quite simple and very characteristic: What is now required are negotiations between the Solidarity government and the Solidarity branch organizations. If these negotiations became an important factor in resolving socio-economic conflicts, then it would give a very strong impulse to the re-creation of strong branch corporations in the Polish economy, with all the consequences of such a development.

A question of independent protest actions taken by the branch sections became so serious at the end of 1990 and beginning of 1991 that it provoked the firm intervention of the National Commission (the highest authority of Solidarity), which decided to plan and centrally supervise a course of branch negotiations with the government. It was announced that the proper statutory sanctions would be used against those activists, organizations, and sections that did not subordinate their activities.

The Political Dimension of Interest Representation

The ongoing systemic transformation causing the increase of interest conflicts will be an important factor activating of various social groups and, as a consequence, pluralizing the political system. The impact of this factor has so far not appeared in its full extent. For at the early stage of systemic transformation, economic divisions and respective political divisions have not yet manifested themselves clearly. Most important, they still appear in a form from the past epoch. Hence, the structure of the political system is not yet adjusted to the set of economic interests. While the latter are still expressed mostly through the branch corporations, and their articulation mirrors a corporate level of social consciousness, the political activity—anyway weaker and weaker—is mobilized first of all through the values and symbols appealing either to nationalism or to the moral reasons understood in a fundamentalist way (Staniszkis 1989).

Some social groups find no political representation of their interests. Consequently, they are inclined to articulate their demands through spontaneous protests. One can expect that in the transitional period from the previous system to a market economy there will be a growing tendency among those groups to stage wildcat strikes, organized mostly by young workers. It would appear that such behavior can only be curbed by introducing more restrictive legislation.

An effective response to the needs and expectations of various social groups calls for a network of suitable communication feedback between those groups and political decision makers. The lack of such feedback results in a very vague recognition by the authorities of the entire spectrum of economic interests.

The characteristic feature of the Polish economy (and of every postsocialist economy) shaping the system of interest representation is the domination of the state sector. In such a situation, the government inevitably becomes, sometimes against its will, a party to any conflicts of interest instead of being an arbiter helping in their settlement as it would like to be. Of course, the perception of the government as an employer and as the subject responsible for the economic situation of particular enterprises and of their staffs is a deep-rooted feeling. It is a transposition to the present circumstances of a long-lasting experience from previous years and decades, and it also had a material aspect resulting from the fact that the government is a sort of board of directors for the enterprises in the state sector.

So all expectations and postulates of the enterprises' workers and the enterprises' managements are addressed to the government. This attitude is strengthened by the trade unions, which charge the government with the task of solving particular conflict problems and situations. The economic recession and the immense difficulties producers now have in coping with adapting to new circumstances favor this attitude. Consequently, there is pressure upon the government from below to intervene in common processes that some economists blame on the market's weakness.

The government's enforced intervention has two major consequences. First, it makes it easier for producers to survive and thus contributes to the blocking of structural changes in the economy. Second, it provokes similar pressure on the part of other producers who demand similar support. In this way, the government becomes a party to conflicts while objectively sustaining the conditions that have made it a party in the first place.

The domination of the state sector and the government's intervention enforced from below into material processes are the two essential factors that lead to the reemergence of the corporatist representation of interests. Specific points of this process can be summarized as follows:

• The role of branch structures in economic conflicts is increasing.
• The economic conflicts have a mainly vertical direction, and the government is a party to these conflicts.
• Particular enterprises and branches of the state sector strive to slow down or block restructuring that will affect their employees.
• The basic reference point and so the source of conflicts is the average wage in the sphere of production.
• Social consciousness is dominated by the conviction that economic protests of various occupational groups are justified and that it is the government's duty to undertake negotiations and to respond to strikers' demands.

An observed increase in the corporatist system's importance in the sphere of interest representation became apparent soon after the wave of protest actions that took place in the middle of 1990. The model sequence of events looked as follows: The systemic and personnel changes carried out by the government brought about in the previous period a paralysis of corporatist structures; the corporatist articulation in the defense of interests became rather ineffective; in this situation, the growing discontent with the sharp decrease in incomes expressed itself in spontaneous protest actions; the government did not wish to enter into direct negotiations with the protesters and refused to make any concessions at all; Solidarity's leaders joined the protests, by which they tried to save their prestige and position in the system of power; the government was forced to become a party to the negotiations and hence reinforced the corporatist character of the conflict. So what did appear in practice was the absence of institutional safeguards against a similar string of developments.

This precarious situation is strengthened by the political rivalry that is now taking place. Many political groups try to capitalize on the social dissatisfaction and criticize the government while formulating a vision of the possible improvement of the people's material situation. Criticism of the government's program from the populist position became an immediate weapon in the fight for influence, this becoming acute with the approach of parliamentary elections in Poland. This is the line of procedure adopted in particular by the two trade union organizations competing with Solidarity—the once official trade union OPZZ[3] and Solidarity 80.[4]

Hence, there is a growing awareness in government and parliamentary circles of the need for a transformation in the economy that would create the ways of interest articulation and negotiation that are characteristic of a market economy. Currently, three bills are the object of legislative work: on trade unions, on employers' organizations, and on the settlement of labor disputes. The introduction of those bills will certainly lay the foundations for a new system of interest representation. Yet it seems to be an illusion on the part of many experts and politicians that their enforcement would mark a turning point in this area. This could be regarded only as a starting point on the path to a really new system of interest representation, with progress in this field depending on the actual change in economic and political relations.

The creation of an efficient mechanism of negotiations is one of the main tasks that has been undertaken by the government led by Bielecki. This process develops through the active participation of government representatives in relieving the protests and conflicts that continue to erupt. On this point, this government is apparently behaving in a manner different from that of the former government, which was prepared to negotiate only with the representatives of central trade union bodies. By doing this, the government tried to enforce the infeasible rules of the trade union act then in effect.

In the course of many disputes and negotiations in which the present government has been involved, the Ministry of Labor and Social Affairs elaborated the coherent proposals of the conduct of negotiations. The submitted proposal defines precisely the principles, conditions, parties, and procedures of the negotiations. Undoubtedly, this interesting proposal admitted the necessity of setting a proper material and professional framework for the negotiations, which in the Polish circumstances is an absolute novelty and in sharp contrast with the completely implicit mechanism of corporatist bargaining. It can be easily foreseen that the implementation of this proposal will encounter serious difficulties and might even be impossible in the short run.

Among many barriers, one should mention the attitude and behavior of the trade unions. The organizational structure and role of Solidarity are unclear and not fully developed. Hence, demands articulated toward the authorities by the representatives of different levels of the union are very often incoherent and even contradictory. Moreover, the relations between central bodies of particular trade unions are so tense that one can hardly imagine the possibility of their joint participation in negotiations.

The second barrier to implementation of the proposed system of negotiations is a lack of the crystallized representation of employers. As for the interests of the majority of employees, a model of their joint representation by the state enterprises' managements and trade unions still prevails. There are thus conflicts with experts from the central administrative organs, which are caused by more than their increasingly frequent Solidarity membership.

An efficient mechanism of negotiations requires the stable relationships between various representative and decision-making bodies. The practical situation, however, is far removed from this assumption. Strong clashes between different social groups and their formal representatives in Parliament mean that the government is permanently under multilateral pressure and that none of the particular representatives want to recognize the agreements reached with another. The complexity of the situation also results from the fact that the Sejm does not constitute a political base for the government, because the balance of power in the Sejm is unstable and was not reflected in the government's structure. Therefore, the particular Sejm's commissions often limit their role to criticism of the government's policy and do not attempt to shape and strengthen this policy by intermediating between the given social groups and the government.

The idea of a social contract is sometimes expressed as an immediate remedy for existing weaknesses of the interest representation. Entering into a contract should guarantee a possibly fast and conflict-free way of taking the Polish economy through a transitional period. Regardless of how far this idea could be implemented in the Polish circumstances, it is clear that its content itself is vague. Particularly vague are proposals concerning either the parties or the substance of such a contract. The former government assumed that it should be an agreement between the government and the trade unions regarding fundamental and detailed questions of socio-economic policy. The course of the presidential campaign showed clearly that there are no political and institutional structures in which the framework of such an agreement could be negotiated and recognized.

Now, from a perspective of the coming parliamentary election, the idea of such a social contract comes back in the form of a "Treaty for Poland" proposal, which should be an agreement covering systemic rather than policy questions. Divisions that came into existence during the political struggle for the presidency seemed to be so strong that the conclusion of such a systemic treaty is highly unlikely. But if the systemic vacuum would not be filled by negotiations, then this could only be done by some social force being able to force its hegemony upon remaining groups.

Notes

1. "Stanowisko w sprawie komercjalizacji przedsiebiorstw panstwowych" (An Opinion on the Commercialization of State Enterprises), *Zycie Gospodarcze* 1990, no. 42.

2. Interesting remarks on this subject were expressed by W. Modzelewski in his paper "Lad demokratyczny a formy walki" (The Democratic Order and the Forms of Struggle). In *Studia nad ladem spolecznym*, W. Nieciunski and T. Zukowski, eds. Vol. 2, 101–2.(Warsaw University, 1990.)

3. OPZZ is All Poland Alliance of Trade Unions, the government-sponsored trade union confederation established during the martial law (1983) when Solidarity was banned.

4. Solidarity 80 is the trade union formed by a group of Walesa's opponents within Solidarity who did not accept the idea of roundtable negotiations with Communist rulers in 1989.

Bibliography

Józefiak, C. 1984. Tradycyjny system planwania centralnego i kierunki jego ewolucji [The Traditional System of Central Planning and the Lines of Its Evolution] in: Funkcjonowanie gospodarki polskiej. Doswiadczenia, problemy, tendencje, ed. J. Mujzel and Sz. Jakubowicz, Warsaw. Polish Economic Publishers.

Pajestka, J. 1980. Swiadome ksztal towanie procesow spol eczno-gospodarczych w gospodarce scojalistycznei (The Conscious Shaping of Socio-Economic Processes in the Socialist Economy) in: Racjonalnosc gospodarowania w socjalizmie, B. Kaminski and A. Lukaszewicz eds., Warsaw. "Polish Economic Publishers".

Oblicki, J. 1990. Przyspieszenie w gospodarce (Acceleration in the Economy) "Tygodnik Solidarnosc", no. 28.

Staniszkis, J. 1976. Antynomie organizacji (The Antinomies of Organization) (typescript). Warsaw: Warsaw University.

——————— 1989. Ontologia socjalizmu (Ontology of Socialism), Warsaw. "Polish Economic Publishers".

17. Transforming a Centrally Planned Economy into a Market Economy: The Case of Czechoslovakia

Otakar Chaloupka
Miroslav Klusák
Eva Mašková
Pavel Mertlík

Introduction

Privatization can be recognized more and more as the critical aspect of economic reforms in the countries of Central and Eastern Europe. This trend has its roots in the very concepts of the economic reforms implemented within the framework of which the creation of the private sector assumes the essential role in creating the new system. The delicate nature of the present economic situation follows from the measures implemented by the designers of the economic reform from the higher echelons of the political forces now in power, especially with respect to their degree of radicalism. Radicalism of political subjects—especially in case these wield political power—is bound to aggravate problems in processes of reproduction of the sociopolitical consensus, negotiation, and coordination.

This situation results in increased social tensions in consequence of which the political subject in question is tempted to modify the original political idiom, as well as the structure of purpose and means considered originally, the political subject finally being in danger of losing his initiative and position alike. The growth of social tension corresponds to the resistance of the "partners" of the power structure pursuing the reform—both individual and group subjects of everyday economic life. This resistance (be it passive or active) follows from their perception and understanding of, interpretation of, and attitudes toward the measures of the state executive bodies. The accomplishment of any centrally conceived intentions requires mutual matching of the rationality of the privatization process on the one hand (considered here as the objective and central component of the system in question) and on the other hand the executive component (considered as the subjective, "microeconomical" component in the given case). Therefore, the subjective dimension of the feasibility of the privatization process is understood to be the acceptability of a specific privatization project for its addressees.[1]

The Czechoslovak Privatization Project

The basic framework of the Czechoslovak economic reform achieved the form of a relatively comprehensive project in the course of 1990. On the theoretical level, the principles of the contemporary neoconservative economics have been claimed to constitute the basis of the reform by its designers, whereas in terms of values, the project claims to be based upon the principle of enhanced economic effectiveness alongside those of political democracy and the ethical aspects of ownership. The core of the reform can be expressed in three areas of reform steps: (1) privatization, (2) liberalization of markets, and (3) restrictive macroeconomical policies of the state.

The general liberalization of markets with the exception of that of labor was implemented from January 1, 1991. By this date, the past system of direct governmental adjustment of both wholesale and retail prices, interest rates, and foreign exchange rates by the state was abolished. Only a very limited set of prices of selected commodities (rents; railway tariffs; communications fees and charges; prices of water, heat, fuels, electricity, and some selected basic raw materials and agricultural products) remained under the direct control of the government. The correlation between the wholesale and retail prices is set by the turnover tax at a percentage rate. The rates of interest follow from the discount rate of the State Bank of Czechoslovakia (which remained under government control, the monetary policies of the State Bank having thus remained those of the government both *de facto* and *de jure*) and the maximum deviation set by the State Bank of the trade interest rates from the discount rate. The rates of exchange between the Czechoslovak and foreign currencies and bills of exchange follow from the balance between supply and demand at the Czechoslovak foreign exchange, the State Bank interventions being aimed at maintaining these rates near the official exchange rates set by the government. The Czechoslovak foreign exchange is accessible to registered Czechoslovak residents only (i.e., legal persons registered in Czechoslovakia as businesses) under the mediation of the Trade Banks (this being the so-called limited internal convertibility system of the Czechoslovak crown).

The situation in the area of wages and salaries is a different one. Wages have been liberalized only for private enterprises and for joint ventures. Czechoslovak state enterprises, cooperatives, and all other employers (institutions, schools, medical facilities, the military and security forces, etc.) are still obliged to comply with the wage-control regulations in force from the era of the centrally planned economy. This wage system means a virtual freezing of wages and salaries.[2]

The increase in prices witnessed so far has been caused by demand-pull inflation by 50 percent at least (the transformation of repressed inflation into an open one together with the closing of the inflationary gap inherited from the centrally planned economy). The retail price index is going to increase further, especially because of the effect of the cost-push inflation. The full effect of the increases in the wholesale prices of raw materials, heat, electricity, and fuels executed by January 1, 1991, is going to be reflected in the retail prices of consumption goods in the second half of 1991 only, because of the extreme level of production inventories characteristic of the Czechoslovak economy owing to which companies still use in part the stock purchased last year at lower prices. Therefore, the gradual reflection of the increased prices of the primary inputs in the prices of products of final consumption is going to constitute a mighty source of cost-push inflation.[3]

The macreconomic policies of the government have been based upon the monetaristic concept of equilibrium growth of the money supply and upon the principle of a balanced state budget. Hence, a slight surplus was approved for the state budget for 1991.[4]

By January 1, 1991, the state sector together with cooperatives had still been producing around 98 percent of the gross national product (GNP). The liberalization of markets and the implementation of the macroeconomic restrictions were commenced before the privatization process was started, and there had been no structural changes in the individual fields of the economy. The extreme measure of concentration in the individual industries and the monopolization of the economy following this has resulted in a dramatic increase in the measure of monopoly by Czechoslovak companies—a measure unparalleled in the market economies of Western countries. In the current situation, the key to further progress of the reform is seen in a change of the ownership relations structure.

The designers of the privatization project intend to transfer about 75 percent of the state enterprises into private hands at a fast pace. The privatization of cooperatives has also been discussed.[5]

Two methods have been selected by the designers of the privatization process to constitute the basis of the process of transformation: sale of the present state enterprises to foreign subjects (be it by takeover by the foreign partner or by establishment of a joint venture in which the capital share by the Czechoslovak side is represented by the production capacities of the existing state enterprises) and the "voucher method" (a nontraditional privatization technique based upon free distribution of the state enterprises' shares to the Czechoslovak population). A third basic method has been added to these two by the Parliament—the natural restitution, that is, the restitution of the nationalized property to the original owners of the heirs thereof according to the property rights as of February 25, 1948 (the date of appointment of the government by which the process of transformation of the economy was commenced into a centrally planned economy of the Soviet type). The framework for the course of privatization, therefore, has been defined by the privatization and restitution acts according to which some steps already have been accomplished.[6]

According to the Small Privatization Act, the property involved is sold at auction to physical persons or private enterprises with no foreign capital participation (nor participation by cooperatives) for Czechoslovak crowns. The auctions started at the beginning of 1991. As indicated by the initial experience, the business units are sold without the real property pertaining, i.e., the business units with their premises located within the so-called nonresidential rooms of buildings remaining under the ownership of the state, municipal, and/or cooperative organizations. No global analyses of data on the course of auctions have been available to the authors so far. Besides small enterprises (shops, small business units rendering services, etc.), companies with several hundred employees were intended to be sold in the small privatization process.

The so-called large privatization process was intended to commence in autumn 1991. The organization of this process should be based upon individual privatization projects to be prepared by the state enterprises. The manner of privatization should also be included in these projects. The projects are subject to approval by the government or by the appropriate central state administration body. Besides this preferential method, sale of Czechoslovak currency and leasing are also possible under the provisions of the Large Privatization Act. However, the latter two forms are to be employed in a minimum number of cases only.

The investment voucher issues are intended to be denominated in nominal units, so-called investment points, each Czechoslovak citizen being entitled to receive an equal number of these investment points free of charge or at a minimum fee covering the administrative costs. Simultaneously, the option of purchase of additional investment vouchers against Czechoslovak currency has been considered at a price set by the government. The investment vouchers shall be subsequently used to "purchase" shares of the companies being privatized according to individual choice. The investment vouchers shall be issued to a name and shall not be transferable; their validity shall be limited in time.

The large privatization process (as well as the small privatization process) should be accomplished within the next two-year period, that is, basically by the end of 1993. The fundamental barrier in the area of our interest was defined by the reform designers as the illusions surviving about social and corporate ownership, about self-government, and about democracy penetrating the entire economic structure in addition to social life—and about the dominant and sufficient role of managers and corporate personnel bodies in strategic decision making.

The Privatization Project: The
General Orientation of Attitudes

The development of public opinion has shown certain positive tendencies in view of the project objectives.[7] By the end of 1989, the ordinary person can be assumed to have considered the economic situation of the society to be a very problematic one, without seeing the solution to its problems in a speedy reintroduction of the capitalist economic conditions (at the minimum "likelihood" of 89 percent).

During the year from November 1989, a shift in the perception of private enterprise can be sensed. At first, private enterprise was correlated with negative perception of black-market practices, illegal foreign exchange in the streets, and other forms of the so-called gray economy. Its perception of it as a productive activity beneficial to both the citizen and society at large has increasingly been gaining ground.[8]

Of course, this change of attitudes among the population, which is generally favorable toward privatization, is internally differentiated as far as both the population itself and the subject and forms of the privatization process are concerned.[9]

When the available data are used to analyze the degree of coexistence of concepts at the individual level, some individuals expect private enterprise to develop concurrently with the maintenance of at least the current life standard over the next five-year horizon (at the minimum "likelihood" of 69 percent) or expect private enterprise to develop with concurrent deterioration of morals and human relations (at the minimum "likelihood" of 63 percent).

This data can be used to support the following conclusions on the shift of the general orientation of the attitudes among the population relevant to the privatization process: Although a considerable shift away from a decidedly anticapitalist orientation has occurred since December 1989, this shift does not seem to be supported significantly by correlating private enterprise with the ethical aspect of ownership, which has been claimed by some of the designers of the privatization project. Privatization as a part of the economic reform can be viewed—more or less implicitly—as the necessary route to take, a measure required to be adopted to prevent complete economic collapse. The fact—positive for the privatization project—that the expected development of private enterprise is not unequivocally accompanied by an expectation of permanent decrease in the standard of living (the expectations being rather to the contrary) keeps this issue open: Can the development of private enterprise and its acceleration by the privatization process be understood as an invitation to individual initiative or does it lead to passive tolerance with possible reversal to an action of refusal?

Unfortunately, in seeking an answer to this problem no complex empirical analyses of the social and psychological aspects of the formative process of the orientation of attitudes of the citizenry are available. A few general considerations, however, can be made.

The relatively fast decline of the resistance to the "capitalist route" can be assumed to indicate that such resistance has not constituted a consistent component of the orientation of these attitudes, nor has its intensity been too strong. On the one hand, this could be seen as an indication that the likelihood of its restoration is not too high either. On the other hand, this aspect must be taken into consideration, as has already been mentioned by Hayek (1944/1990) among others. The change in question is a psychological one, a change of the character of the individual in the process of a lengthy and complex state regulation. It is a case of a manifested effect of the mutual interrelation of people's attitudes toward authority and their political ideas on the one hand and the political institutions under which they live on the other (Hayek 1944/1990, pp. 14–15).

In the above case, Hayek highlights the effect of directives issued from a position of authority—prescriptions—upon the deterioration of individual responsibility and decision-making ability, spontaneous planning, and enterprise in the sphere of self-realization.

The above phenomenon, or the psychological consequences of political and economic prescription, have been described in much more detail by Freire (1972) utilizing the experience of colonialistic practices as encountered in the developing countries (Freire 1972).

The prescriptor as the personification of power of which the oppressed have been forcefully deprived or which has used violence to shed its responsibility towards the human individual has a tremendous identification appeal for the oppressed as the personification of all that the oppressed individual is lacking. Freire uses the term "internalized oppressor" and refers to dependencies in issues related to the formation of the value orientation and to subsequent distortions of the interpretation practices of the oppressed, serving to enhance their contradictory life experience. The resulting stress is subsequently channeled into aggressive and/or passive strategies of self-realization.

In our condition, the phenomena in question have been classified by Petrusek (1991) formulating some of the elements of the so-called protocommunist syndrome during his polemics with Dahrendorf.[10] The effect of transition toward market economy implemented from the above and the bureaucratization of this process represents a key moment to the restoration of the old mental stereotypes. Subsequently, the concepts of market economy can easily assume the place of state ownership and planned economy in union with the "ideal of paradise," which was the fundamental pivotal point of the preceding political regimes. The explicit resistance to private ownership leaves "envy" entirely intact as its heritage. Faith in the omnipotence of impersonal "mechanisms" is embodied by the principle of central planning in the form of the Smithsonian invisible hand of "market economy" which teaches us to work, to enterprise, and to make decisions, offering the possibility to avoid personal responsibility.

The Privatization Project:
The Restructuring of Society

The solution to the problem areas is likely to be searched for in the two determinants of formation and transformation of attitudes—the identification with a specific social group and the "scope of view" on the subject of personal attitudes (the broader the scope, the more durable the attitude toward a particular change is likely to be).

Obviously, a situation of discontinuous development of the social structure makes it difficult to operate with empirical data on the orientation of attitudes as assumed by the individual social groups or on the trends of their development.[11]

Sociologists have found a solution to such situations by formulating structural types of individual reactions to the economic reform based upon statistical analysis of opinion polls in order to be able to quantify population groups corresponding to the individual types as well as to estimate the potential development of activities and pressures of these groups within society.[12] The specification of the problematic aspects of the assumed activities of the individual type groups serves as the basis upon which the alternative scenarios of development of the reform process can be conceived.[13]

The following assumptions are involved in the present case:

1. Inconsistencies in the process of forming the space for vigorous progress of the private sector shall impact negatively *handicapped tradesmen* (cf. type 4 in note 12), who then join the outspoken and aggressive enemies of the reform of *socialists* (cf. type 3 in note 12). *Entrepreneurs* (cf. type 2 in note 12) would be likely to reposition themselves to the gray zone of the parallel market, contributing to enormous growth of social tension by the "illegitimate" contrast with the material and social hardships of the remaining population. All delays in the implementation of an essential change in the entire sphere of labor toward meritocratic principles would neutralize the otherwise potentially positive influence of *employees* (type 5 in note 12) who would subsequently become more or less passive allies of the "socialists."

2. Consistent implementation of all the fundamental objectives of the reform can create space and opportunity alike for the realization of the problem associated with "handicapped tradesmen" and "employees" and for integration of the activities of "entrepreneurs" in the process and accomplishment of the system changes. Systematic creation of the social infrastructure of the market should be another precondition for this goal—advisory services and requalification and investment programs for the private sector. The resistance of "socialists" is to be neutralized by a credible social security network.

Without attempting any systematic appraisal of either these conclusions or the procedures whereby these were deduced, we can attempt to utilize these results to formulate a few guidelines for our consideration. In this chapter, we try to analyze in more detail the issue of "space and opportunity" for the realization of individual activity. Before doing that, however, other facets of the structuralization of society are examined: age-related factors.

The Privatization Project: Generations

The specific position of the age-groups—or generation strata—within society is undoubtedly bound to affect the forming and reforming of the social attitudes and the values orientation of its members. Although the age-groups or generation strata of a population represent one of the levels of its social structure bound to avoid discontinuities in its biological dimension, the process of social reinterpretation of identification with a specific generation and of relations among the individual generations is certain to proceed. Nevertheless, this level of the social structure promises at least a kind of internal cohesion of common claims, expectations, and inherent "life" activities within the turmoil of external circumstances including the economic situation.[14]

Available data come mostly from surveys made by the end of 1990 when the "reality" of the reform processes was not perceived in the specific context of their impacts for the population. According to findings of the IVVM (Institute for Public Opinion Research; before December 1989 abbreviated UVVM), fragile optimism could be mentioned as far as attitude orientation of the "younger" age-group toward the privatization project is concerned. Their interest in privatization declined once they discovered that the buyers will consist exclusively of the well-to-do, the go-getters, and those acting on behalf of someone behind the scenes.

The meager data that have been available for the analysis give no grounds to state whether any or which generation is going to become "the generation of privatization" (i.e., that generation related strongly to the process). But the most pronounced tendencies can be said to be those of the middle generation to become the "privatized generation" and those of the younger generation to refuse the role of the "privatizing generation" (which has tended to be assigned to it by some of the designers of the privatization project).

Intermezzo

Returning now to our attempt to formulate the guidelines, the following conclusions can be drawn: The problem involved is primarily one of unequivocal involvement of the "anxiety of the future" phenomenon as related to the active/passive orientation. As indicated by results of the Independent Social Analysis Group (AISA—a group for independent sociological analysis formed in Czechoslovakia), this phenomenon could be interpreted as reflecting the dominance of both the structuralization of the prevailing value orientation and the definition of the economic situation within the time period at least coinciding with the commencement of the privatization process. The relation between the active/passive orientation and the privatization process is neither entirely unique nor clear. Finally, knowledge of the objective structuralization of bonds and interactions of the given groups of typically oriented individuals within the society is insufficient when seeking to consider the effect of identification with a specific group. This is with respect the forming of the attitudes orientation of an individual or the manner of his/her definition of the individual economic situation.

In the following, therefore, we attempt to break down the privatization process into several separate issues significant for the forming of the mobilizing definition of the economic situation. At the same time, we strive to comply with the requirement to discuss the identification of the individual with the institutional relationships of one of the following three most significant groups: the newly constituted private entrepreneurs, employees, and management.[15]

Anxieties in the "Entrepreneur" Situation

Anxieties or existent pressures represent an essential component of the entrepreneur situation. An individual assumes the role of an entrepreneur once he or she transforms his or her concept of modifying reality into an actual economic activity that yields private profit—the single source of income of the entrepreneur. In an economic sense, therefore, the entrepreneur's motivation is based upon the share in profit, that is, the raise of income in the case of success and—symmetrically—upon his/her share in the losses, that is, the threat to the entrepreneur's existence in the case of failure.

To a certain extent, both the loss of social security and the anxiety of potentially losing an accustomed standard of living are already present in our economic climate. Additionally, the privatization process has been declared to be aimed at creating space for profit-oriented activities. (Therefore, it is of interest to review the perceived slowdowns to these activities.)[16]

The prevailing flight from uncertainty by means of fixation to the existing corporate structures reproducing the Taylorian paternalistic corporate culture and founded in the paternalism of the state administration stands in complete contradiction to the objective logic of the privatization process at the organizational level of institutional authority. Privatization is logically linked with antiprotectionism, liberalization process, and democratization of the political and economic life, in other words, with de-hierarchization of economic life in favor of horizontal market relations, and so in favor of the authority of the market. The key economic principles implemented by the process of de-hierarchization are the "our customer is our master" principle (i.e., the transition from the criteria-setting role of the higher-ranking bureaucrats to focusing on the end user of the products and services) and the principle of economic autonomy in the accomplishment of the entrepreneurial objectives (i.e., the transition to the so-called external path upwards principle or the encouragement of founding activities of new business units and new market subjects).

The social significance of the economic concept in these principles can be specified more closely. The process involved is that of depolitization of economic life by the dismantling of the dependence of the economic subjects upon the central and, predominantly, political directives. The process of suppression of bureaucracy as such significantly reduces the likelihood of tendencies aimed toward restoration of the centralistic planning and direct control. Reproduction of bureaucratic mannerism in the corporate sphere is restricted by abolition of nonproductive functions and activities within the structure of organization, by radical reduction of management costs, and by the creation of an environment conducive to the development of a democratic corporate structure. In reducing the significance and entrenchment of political influences, the process acts against economic monopolization and in support of economic competition. We have thus disclosed the most significant characteristic of the said process—it constitutes a significant precondition of a "natural" or gradual restructuring of the national economy.

In constituting the actual individual meaning of the said process, that is, from the viewpoint of its significance for the individual activity, inhibitions have been perceived in the following areas. Besides the fear of losing security that the state enterprise—and a large state corporation especially—seems to provide, the other anxieties include the following: those of decreased turnover with the reduction of the organization and the subsequent drop in the volume of profit, those related to the loss of position and prestige of the company and of its employees in the social and political environments, those of coping with reduced income due to the reduction in the number of subordinates, and those resulting from lack of confidence in one's own capacities to cope with the altered work conditions (applying to managerial jobs especially).

The complex of anxieties in the business sphere is comprehensively expressed in the pressure at the prices level, while anxieties of the consumer are expressed in increased economy measures—but not in savings oriented at long-term investments. The anxieties of consumers as employees result in additional pressure toward wage and salary increases. On the other hand, anxieties of the state are expressed in the pressure toward increased taxation, restriction of expenditures, and intensification of administrative measures.

The point in question is not only that increased measure of uncertainty of the economic environment increases the burden placed upon the individual willingness to bear business risks. A graver aspect of the situation must be addressed once the environment of the potential entrepreneur—instead of offering outlines of new market-oriented adaptation practices designed to handle the uncertainty (cultivation of market relations, improvement of the corporate culture, development of democratic negotiation institutions)—continues to offer more or less innovated bureaucratic practices of the past. This phenomenon can result from, among other causes, incorrect definition by the designers of the privatization project of the barriers to its implementation as seen from the standpoint of subjective individual acceptability, resulting ultimately from the designers' insufficient understanding of the psychological correlations of economic behavior.

The Entrepreneurship: The Two Logics of Privatization

Therefore, the vicious circle of anxieties is not likely to be resolved by the formal administrative transfer of state property and its distribution outside the market. The fundamental logic of the so-called Transformation Act seems to be aimed at this transfer by which the institutional implementation of the privatization process in the narrower sense is to be expressed. (The issue of "rationality of the centralistic measure" mentioned in the introduction to the presentation is already recurring.)[17]

The individual confronted with the logic of the state property distribution to new owners by other than market mechanisms has to cope with a more extensive set of relations, the said logic being only a partial result of these. The logic of bankruptcy of the state economy—any responsibility for which has been spontaneously disclaimed by the present leaders of the state institutions—is the starting point from which the logic has been formed. The said logic was subsequently explicitly allowed to take its effect in the corporate sphere (where its full implementation is prevented from taking place—as far as the formal viewpoint is concerned—by the absence of the company bankruptcy legislation together with the political anxieties of the state administration on the practical side). Privatization thus assumes the role of a legislation of the disclaimer of responsibility of the state bodies for the condition of companies of which they are the founders. According to a statement by one of the designers of the reform, "the sale of enterprises to foreign business is not a sale of the national wealth but that of national problems."

From the practical viewpoint, the individual is to be "addressed" by the so-called voucher privatization. The voucher privatization addresses the individual in his or her role as a citizen. The acquisition of a capital share by the individual in a company with an unclear history and future, without him having even the elementary experience and competence in the areas of forming, implementation, and control of an entrepreneurial project, tends to transform the individual potentially into a passive receptor of annuity—"rentier"—(in the better case) than into an active entrepreneur. Moreover, the only asset the individual actually invests in the above situation is his/her faith in the company, its employees and managers especially. Our citizen in this case is nothing more than a mere consumer lucky enough to be given the chance to increase his/her consumption by selling the capital shares given to him/her by the state or even to "credit a corporation" to be able to increase consumption in the future or to at least maintain the substance of it.

In view of the three possible basic variants of the interest strategies of the state administration in the privatization process (1. sell the company to a foreign party for fiscal reasons; 2. maintain control over the company for strategic reasons; 3. dispose of the company at any price), there exists a very real chance of a reverse transformation of our "rentier" into a simple citizen-consumer at the moment the company in question shatters its credibility or goes bankrupt. The identity of an individual as an employee, manager, or private entrepreneur is virtually irrelevant, since experience and competence in real business activities cannot be articulated socially or implemented in the real time given by the life perspective of a company managed in the said manner.

As far as the presently considered problem areas are concerned, the most significant factor is that the individual in the position of our "rentier," described earlier, shall be given, together with the property ownership rights, the responsibility both for the fate of the company of which he/she owns the shares and for the fulfillment of the hopes of about 70 percent of the population that the current standard of living will be obtained within five years—or for the fulfillment of the hopes of about 50 percent of the population—that it will increase.[18]

There seems to be no other single, safer way to activate the mental stereotypes of the "protocommunist syndrome" than the said radical measure of the state administration. The mass of the new "private property owners," who acquired their property through no merits or character qualities of their own, and the mass of their employees therefore appear to be in a situation of "existence uncertainty" to extort assistance from the state administration—be it by "extorting" their passive dependence and/or by aggressive reaction.

There is another alternative logic contained potentially in the privatization concept as it has been reflected in the structure of the so-called Transformation Act. This logic is based upon the state's acceptance of its share of responsibility in the condition of the corporate sphere as well as in the implementation of the economic function of the privatization process. The economic function follows from the enhancement of performance of the privatized economic activities by means of increasing the level of motivation of the subjects involved (managers and staff alike, employees and employers) and by creating better organizational preconditions for the implementation of these activities. The fetishism of property rights concerned with ownership is negated in favor of those concerned with share in the profit and with control of the business activities. In other words, instead of transfer of assets, the transfer stressed in the present case is the transfer to autonomous economic subjects of activities and functions performed at high cost and low efficiency by the state bureaucracy. This logic would not seek subjects willing to accept donated assets of the state enterprises. Those searched for and formed in the process would be the individuals able to conceive of business objectives, through which economically effective and socially acceptable utilization of the corporate capacities could be guaranteed. The individual in such a case would be addressed as the potential bearer of entrepreneurial abilities, that is, of the ability to initiate, innovate, and develop production, to accept risks and responsibility, and to capitalize his/her income. The state would assume two separate functions in relation to the individual: as the central administration acting in its administrative, economic, and political capacities in a measure standard in countries with developed market economies on the one hand, and as the property owner on the other, using market principles in the process of allocation of its assets to the most agile entrepreneurial subjects, that is, in the process of their privatization.

However, the most important factor from our viewpoint is that the said logic addresses the individual by an offer directed toward his/her positively and spontaneously motivated initiative, one being far from a prescription, though benevolently and condescendingly presented. This forward approach is in its own stead a precondition of a more competent and hence broader interest in the entrepreneurial activity as the subject itself of privatization (and consequently also a more permanent attitude orientation). At the same time, preconditions are created to form a more durable relation of responsibility of the individual in regard to his own entrepreneurial activities (in both the economic and broader social contexts), than is conceivable at the platform of the social role of our "rentier," described earlier; the concept constitutes a path and does away with the burden of the past in the area of deformed thinking and practical behavior of the individual as an economically acceptable one which provides support for the positively motivated response of the subject to the privatization process analyzed as the voucher privatization.

Notes

1. By defining the scope of our interest and its social importance, the data amenable to analysis are also actually defined. These include, in particular, the attitudes and interpretations of the privatization process as conceived by the economic subjects—in both real public discussions of official negotiations and model situations like sociological public opinion polls and similar surveys.

2. While the retail prices of consumer goods and services have grown by at least 35 percent during the first three months of 1991 as compared with the price level at the end of December 1990, wages and salaries have grown by less than 2 percent during the same period.

3. As of May 1, 1991, the government has prepared the retail prices of fuels, heat, and electricity to grow by about 300 percent (the process in question is one reflecting the discontinuation of subsidies of household consumption from the state budget). Apartment rents are going to grow by thousands of percent.

4. The discount rate exceeded 13 percent, resulting in trade interest rates on bank credits reaching as much as 24 percent (the figures being from the end of March 1991). The money supply in the economy has risen by only 2 percent; the GNP declined by at least 3 percent during the same period (both figures have been obtained by comparison with the end of December 1990). The rate of unemployment has risen from less than 1 percent to close to 3 percent during the period considered.

5. The scope of the task can be clarified a little by the following data. According to the official statistics, the overall value of state property (fixed capital in productive and nonproductive industries audited at purchase factor costs) as of January 1, 1988, amounted to Kcs 3.6 thousand billion (30 Kcs = $1). The proportion of it to be privatized within a relatively short period has been assumed to amount to about Kcs 2.8 thousand billion. Assuming about 50 percent of this sum to have been subject to capital consumption in recent years, the remaining value of property to be privatized still amounts to Kcs 1.4 thousand billion (in nominal account evaluation at balance factor costs—i.e., after

depreciation). Of course, the market price of this capital obtained using standard pricing methods common in developed market economies would exceed these figures many times.

The only domestic "private" capital to counterbalance the property available is the household savings, amounting to Kcs 360 billion deposited in Czechoslovak banks (nominal GNP representing Kcs 800 billion, the tendency to save being currently undermined by both the present and the feared inflation). To comprehend the complexity of the whole project, it is sufficient to compare the Kcs 360 billion with the property value estimated (providing even for the fact there exist extensive shadow savings and shadow capital in the hands of our economic subjects deposited abroad).

6. Of the volume of the state property to be privatized as stated above, the government estimates assume about Kcs 300 billion to be restituted to the original owners and their heirs as of 1948. This reprivatization process has been expected to stretch over many years because the number of legal disputes expected to arise between the heirs will far exceed the (insufficient) capacity of the Czechoslovak courts of law. The property subject to reprivatization has been exempted from all the other forms of privatization available. The remaining property—assuming the property in question amounts to Kcs 1.1 thousand billion at balance factor costs—shall be privatized according to either the Small or the Large Privatization Acts. The rating of specific assets under one or the other is under governmental jurisdiction.

7. The criticism of the economy had been growing over a long-term period (December 1987: 70 percent, May 1988: 80 percent, October 1988: 87 percent, December 1989: 92 percent; percentages based on participants in the opinion polls [UVVM—Sondy—the Institute for Public Opinion Surveys, Prague, fall 1989]). In November and December of 1989, however, the support for the individual concepts of the future development in Czechoslovakia was distributed for both months as follows: socialist path—45 percent/41 percent; capitalist path—3 percent/3 percent; "something in between"—47 percent/52 percent; no idea—5 percent/4 percent (UVVM—Sondy). (Of the people supporting "Civic Forum" and VPN "Public Against Violence," one-third were for the socialist variant.) The subject of neither privatization nor production means was raised in November 1989 for the first time. Public opinion was surveyed on the issue as early as May 1989. The May results were confirmed by a December 1989 survey, the respondents of which responded to the proposal "not only small businesses and pubs should be returned to private owners, but large production plants as well" in the following pattern: decidedly yes—8 percent; rather yes—14 percent; rather no—33 percent; decidedly no—40 percent; no idea—5 percent.

8. The development of private enterprise was considered important by as many as four-fifths of the survey participants (Ecoma, Prague, fall 1990). From May to November (November 1990), for instance, the number of those stating they were private entrepreneurs rose from 2 percent to 4 percent, and of those claiming intentions of doing so, from 13 percent to 19 percent (AISA—the Independent Social Analysis Group, Czechoslovakia, November 1990). According to the same source, 27 percent of citizens considered investing their money in private enterprise, 41 percent intending to invest in private enterprise in privatization.

9. Almost 90 percent of respondents approve of turning small businesses and shops over to private hands; 20 percent approve of privatization of all companies excepting

mines. Almost one-fifth agree with selling factory property to foreign investors, and over one-fourth would prefer to see it in the hands of labor-managed firms. But less than one-tenth would leave it to the former owners and almost one-third of respondents have expressed no opinion.

On considering the context in which expectations concerning the development of private enterprise are related to those concerning complex economic reform, the following pattern is obtained: 95 percent of the population expected the reform to open opportunity for private enterprise, 67 percent expected substantial decline in the standard of living, 73 percent expected considerable decline in social benefits, 59 percent expected huge social injustice, 94 percent expected the gap in property ownership to broaden, 67 percent expected a decline in morals and relations among people, and 31 percent expected the economy to assume a wrong direction of development. However, 70 percent expected the reform to prevent complete economic collapse from occurring, and 53 percent expected their family's standard of living to increase within the five-year horizon, while 74 percent hoped for it not to be worse (AISA).

10. Petrusek, 1991, pp. 14–15. (Dahrensdorf in his work "The Modern Social Conflict" contends that totalitarianism destroys the conditions for its origination by its mere realization. Petrusek concludes his article by expressing his belief in the possibility of such a reversal in view of the depth of the changes in the mental stereotypes of people.)

11. The empirical sociological survey "The Transformation of the Social Structure of the Czechoslovak Society" is to yield its first results by spring 1992 (coordinated by the Institute of Social and Political Science of the Faculty of Social Sciences of the Charles University, Prague, and the Sociological Institute of the Czechoslovak Academy of Sciences). The dominants of structuring of the value orientation, as well as cultural standards and patterns of specific social groups, can be comprehensively analyzed only on the ground of the analysis of the transformation of the social position of individuals and groups resulting from changes in social relations concerning ownership and right of disposition of the production means; position in the process of division of labor; regional, ethnic, and national identification; property distribution; income and standard of living; power structures; and other aspects of social life. So far, the conflict between the egalitarian bureaucratic social system and the meritocratic system has been examined. In the article mentioned in note 12, Petrusek (1991) presented a few comments on the above subject: "egalitarianism, anti-intellectualism, anti-elitism, and the overvaluation of manual labor—which he finds typical of Czechoslovak public opinion—have jointly created a comprehensive attitude oriented against performance, against individualism, against innovation, social differences, one by which the type of social structure which had formed during the real socialism era is effectively stabilized."

12. Of the sources available, the analysis performed by the end of 1990 by the AISA group appears to be the most comprehensive. The following seven basic types have been described in the "Response 1991" typology of the authors presented therein:

1. *Theoretical liberals*—liberal orientation and passive support of the economic reform and of the political development (Czech and Slovak Federal Republic [CFSR]: 16 percent; Czech Republic [CR]: 19 percent; Slovak Republic [SR]: 12 percent). The type is characterized by the fundamental conflict between general attitudes on the reform and the actual un-

preparedness to utilize the opportunities the reform is opening in the economic sphere. Not interested in private enterprise.

2. *Entrepreneurs*—activity in the area of private enterprise with positive motivation (CSFR: 7 percent; CR: 8 percent; SR: 6 percent). The type is characterized by their willingness to invest their resources in various economic activities, especially in the field of private enterprise. They see radical reform as an opportunity for individual self-realization. Their intention to enter private business is motivated by their orientation toward supreme performance rather than high consumption.

3. *Socialists*—decided refusal of the reform (CSFR: 24 percent; CR: 21 percent; SR: 31 percent). The type is characterized by the high measure of anxiety connected with the consequences of the reform for the standard of living and by their preparedness to exert their claims by constraint. Regardless of extreme anxiety about the future, passive life-style is the dominating mode of the group, with significant value orientation toward work, education, and performance. They do not consider the option of entering private business.

4. *Handicapped tradesmen*—anxiety-motivated activity compounded with interest in private enterprise (CSFR: 10 percent; CR: 9 percent; SR: 12 percent). The type is characterized by searching for an individual solution to an oppressive life situation in the form of participation in the sphere of private enterprise. High measure of anxiety for the future, high activity compounded with individualistic approaches and rather egoistic value orientation, accompanied by absence of cultural capital.

5. *Employees*—anxiety-motivated activity, without interest in private enterprise (CSFR: 12 percent; CR: 11 percent; SR: 12 percent). The type is characterized by a high measure of anxiety concerning the consequences of the reform process. No intention of involvement in private business activities. Activities focused on attaining the status of a top-ranking employee, high degree of qualification, together with a willingness to increase labor efforts exerted. Capable of exerting their claims by constraint.

6. *Enterprising pensioners*—interested in private enterprise with insufficient opportunity (CFSR: 8 percent; CR: 8 percent; SR: 7 percent). The type is characterized by proreform orientation and an optimistic outlook on the future. Their interest in private enterprise is accompanied by a declaration of insufficient space for these activities. The average age is the highest of all the other types classified—over half of them are older than fifty-five.

7. *Passive individuals*—passivity without any pronounced relation to the economic reform (CSFR: 23 percent; CR: 24 percent; SR: 20 percent). The type is characterized by deep passivity, orientation toward defensive life strategies and avoidance of conflicts. Slightly antireform bias and anxieties about the future are not accompanied by the resolve to participate in labor strife.

13. Reactions of types 1, 2, 3, 6, and 7 (note 12) have been classified as stable and largely independent of the actual course of the reform. For type 2, "entrepreneurs," a certain measure of conflict follows from the productive legal sphere. Type 3, "socialists," as a constant source of problems for the reform can gain support from types 4, "handicapped tradesmen," and 5, "employees" (representing 46 percent of the population overall).

14. According to data, the AISA group (Czechoslovakia, November 1990) opinion polls indicate that 53 percent of the population expect their standard of living in five years to be higher than that experienced today. The distribution over different age categories is as follows: for 18- to 24-year-olds: 62 percent, with the percentages in the next age-groups declining to reach 48 percent and 47 percent in the 45–54 and 55–64 age-groups, respectively, to increase again to 66 percent in the 65-and-over age-group. A

similar pattern can be obtained by analyzing the expectation of a significant drop in the standard of living. Overall, 67 percent of the respondents share this expectation. The differences over the age-groups are as follows: 18–24 years: 57 percent; 45–54 years: 71 percent; 65 and over: 61 percent. A similar correlation can be seen here. Greater optimism and hopes of the younger and the older generations could be mentioned as opposed to the middle-aged group.

As far as the intention of the individual to enter private enterprise on his or her own is concerned, 23 percent of respondents have expressed interest in the effect overall; 27 percent in the 18–24 and 25–44 age-groups alike; with less interest witnessed in the 45–54, 55–64, and 65-and-over age-groups at 16, 14, and 13 percent, respectively. A similar pattern can be traced in answers reflecting the intention to invest money in business activities. The overall percentage is 30, with the following distribution over the age-groups: 18–24 years: 33 percent; 25–34 years: 36 percent; the interest then declines: 35–44 years: 31 percent; 45–54 years: 26 percent; 55–64 years: 20 percent; and 65-and-over: 18 percent.

The mismatch between the figure of 23 percent presented above as the percentage of those willing to enter business activities on their own and the figure mentioned in note 8 of 19 percent is likely to be explained by different numbers of questionnaire items for different specific analyses performed by the AISA group. The mismatch in the case of "willingness to invest money" is likely to be similarly explained.

15. By "decomposing" the privatization process, the issue of the "scope of view" should be examined in its turn, considering in this respect in what pattern the meaning of privatization is revealed in its internal "objective bonds" in the context of the economic reform. By focusing on the "mobilizing definition of the economic situation," the normative aspect of our analysis and interpretation is accounted for and already introduced at the beginning of the treatise by the promise of surveying the "acceptability" of a specific privatization project. In this, not only do the criteria follow from the project itself, with the human individual and his or her capacities in particular being accounted for, as well as the very meaning of the economic reform itself, but this transition to a market economy is also conceivable only by changing the patterns of behavior of the individual and group economic subjects. This change actually is the meaning and criterion of the reform process (both as a whole and of its individual steps). In brief, the "theoretical circle," or the social mediation of human activities, has thus been defined.

Finally, the analysis of "significance of the individual topics (problem issues) for the formation of the mobilizing definition of the economic situation" allows us to proceed in the further explications more strictly from positions of individual complementarity to the sociological or economic study, that is, proceed from the position of reproduction of the social structures. We have not been too concerned with whether an individual is going to be an entrepreneur good enough to develop her or his activity within the space available. The issue we have been concerned with is whether the individual is going to be active enough to take up activity within the space available or, rather, what composition of conflicts between prescriptions and positive motivations is going to limit the individual, restricting her or his subjectivity, defining what the individual identifies with and what is alien to her or him.

16. The "entrepreneurial situation" is interpreted entirely differently in state and private enterprises. While the faith in protectionist measures of the state has still survived in

the state enterprises and while the enterprises are encouraged to harbor hopes of this kind by the lack of clear-cut rules of conduct for the company founders and for other state bodies in relation to "their" enterprises in the transitional period, the process of buildup of uncertainty by private entrepreneurs has proceeded. By March 1991, therefore, more than 80 percent of private entrepreneurs could be said to have their business as a secondary activity.

> 1. The rule of limiting interactions of the central state bodies has been proclaimed in order to promote the development of private enterprise. Instead of de-etatization of the economy, the proliferation of state coaching can be witnessed with a concurrent increase in the unpredictability of state interactions, in the meddling of nonbusiness elements in corporate activities, and in corruption.
>
> 2. The necessary changes of the legislative structure of economic life are perceived as too slow in progress, contradictory in many cases, and/or chaotic. The process of formation of the finance and tax system is perceived in a similar light. The extreme pressures from the financial and taxation spheres, together with the insufficiently clear and just administrative and legal environment and the limited material economic conditions, are interpreted as a justification for reproduction of the practices of the shadow economy in both the state sector and especially in the newly established private sector.
>
> 3. Moreover, the management of state enterprises experiences negatively some of the specificities of the still-surviving remuneration principles based more upon the number of subordinates than upon the profit achieved, as well as the conflicting corporate internal climate together with the instability of their position.
>
> 4. The employees' perception is one of a specific feeling of loss with respect to competencies of the Trade Union bodies and the relevance of their interest in influencing corporate decisions after they were deprived of their rights to participate in the company management—the term *loss* is to be understood in terms of the hopes after November 1989 and not as related to past practice. (cf. especially "Bariéry rozvoje" 1991, p. 7; Khol 1990; Vitečková et al. 1990.)

17. The paradox of this logic is highlighted also when confronted with so-called small privatization, the predominant form of which is that of auctions at which rent of business premises for restricted periods of time is sold by the state. In the majority of cases, the entrepreneur purchases the leasing without any chance to estimate its real value as well as without knowing whether, by whom, and when the capital he or she invested is to be banned from the premises in question.

18. This is a situation that could be considered rather similar to that of the former German Democratic Republic as far as the quantitative parameters are concerned, where the liquidation of only about 20 percent of the enterprises was considered at the beginning of the privatization process and where only about 20 percent of the enterprises were considered not to require liquidation by March 1991.

Bibliography

"Bariéry rozvoje." 1991. (Barriers of Development—An Analysis of the Associations of

Businessmen of the CR and the SR.) *Týdeník Hospodářských nopvin*, no. 13, p. 7.
Československo—listopad 1990. 1990. (Czechoslovakia—November 1990). Prague: AISA.
Devereux, G. 1967. *From Anxiety to Method on Behavioral Sciences*. Hague-Paris: Mouton.
Freire, P. 1972. *Pedagogy of the Oppressed*. Harmondsworth: Penguin Books.
Hayek, F. A. 1944/1990. *Cesta do otroctví* [The Road to Serfdom]. Prague: Academia.
Khol, J. 1990. *Percepce a vnitřiní akceptace východisek a principů ekonomické reformy hospodářskými vedoucími*. (Perceptions and internal acceptance of the starting points and principles of the economic reform by economic management.) Research report paper. Prague: UP ČR.
Kvalitativní setření postojů obyvatelstva k ekonomické reformé a privatizaci. 1990. (Qualitiative survey in the public attitudes to economic reform and privatization.) Prague: Ecoma—Institute of Business Research, August.
Petrusek, M. 1991. "Jsme vážně z klece venku?" (Are We Really Out of the Cage?) *Přítomnost*, no. 3, pp. 14–15.
"Podzim 1989—UVVM." 1990. (The Fall 1989—The Institute for Public Opinion Surveys.) In *Sondy do verejného mínění* (Probing the Public Opinion) pp. 35–67. Prague: Svoboda.
Vitečková, J., et al. 1990. *Nžory na rozvoj soukromého podnikñí*. [Opinions on the Development of Private Enterprise]. Prague: Sociologický ústav ČSAV.

18. Transition and Conversion in a Small, Open, and Formerly Planned Economy: Hungary

Tibor Palankai

Some Characteristics of Transition in Hungary

There is broad agreement that the main strategic directions and lines of transition in Eastern and Central Europe are marketization, privatization, democratization, and the (re)opening or integration into the world economy.

In Hungary marketization had already started in 1968 with the introduction of the so-called New Economic Mechanism, and in this respect, Hungary has been ahead of the other countries of the region. The marketization, however, has been limited basically to common goods, and by maintaining the closed character of the economy, the structure of the market remained monopolistic. This was strengthened greatly by the fact that the decentralization of decisions meant delegation of power to large companies. In this way, these companies were able to dictate prices, quality, and supplies, and most of the anomalies of the previous Stalinistic bureaucratic planning more or less prevailed (low quality, shortages, unreliability of supplies, etc.). The profit motive was recognized; but as far as the profit was basically a function of market position, the efficiency criteria were lost.

In recent years there were breakthroughs toward marketization in several directions. Formerly, the factors of production were mostly excluded from the process. While the labor market did exist even during the period of centralized planning (reward in the form of wages and salaries and relative freedom of choosing and changing jobs), the capital market was declared "alien" from socialism. In Hungary the first steps toward a capital market were made in the beginning of the 1980s (by issuing communal bonds—bonds or stocks issued by municipal companies—gas; water supply; public telephone company, etc.—to private peoples), and concluded in the opening of the Budapest Stock Exchange in July 1990. It was also of strategic importance that by gradual liberalization of imports since 1988, real competitive market conditions have been created in many fields. By 1991 the administrative licensing had been abolished for more than 90 percent of imports, and for Hungarian importers the national currency had become *de facto* convertible. Imports are controlled only by the application of normative tariffs, as in any market economy.

The marketization process is, of course, not yet complete. The emergence of a normally operating capital market takes time, and the same applies to consolidation of competitive market structures. The marketization also has to be extended to public goods, which does not mean elimination of the welfare state or important public services but broader imposition of principles and rules of market and efficiency criteria. From the point of view of completion of marketization process, the introduction of real convertibility of the Hungarian *forint* is a basic condition, and the government is aiming to achieve this by 1992–93.

As in other East European countries the Hungarian government until recently insisted on the hierarchization of ownership relations, which meant prioritization of the public sector and only limited tolerance of private ownership. The private sector was limited to retail trade and small-scale manufacturing and services, and its share was only about 3 percent of capital assets. Because of marketization and gradual liberalization, the forms of quasi-private entrepreneurship have been expanded in many fields since the 1970s, and particularly in agriculture, based on private plots, the share of private production has reached 25 to 40 percent in the market supply of certain goods.

The judgments and views on private ownership radically changed at the end of the 1980s even in Communist party circles. It was recognized by most Hungarian economists that there is no successful and effective marketization without privatization, and this was officially accepted. In 1988–89, the legal limits on privatization were rapidly abolished, and from an economic policy viewpoint, the private and the public sectors were put on an equal basis. The new democratically elected government in 1990 gave absolute priority to privatization, and the process has been accelerating since then. According to the official data, the share of the private sector in assets reached 15 percent in the first months of 1991, but its contribution to the gross national product (GNP) is estimated to be around 30 to 40 percent. The private sector seems to be the dynamizing and stabilizing factor of the economy. This process is still hindered by several legal, political, and financial factors (lack of domestic capital and the reluctance of foreign investors), but according to the government's economic program, its share may increase to 35 percent in coming years. In the long run, the government wants to reduce the public sector to no more than 35 percent.

Though the 1968 reforms have been connected with gradual democratization and liberalization, a radical turn in the process came only after the step-down of János Kádár from the party leadership in May 1988. The legal frameworks for a multiparty system and parliamentary democracy have been established, and individual and human rights have been extended (free travel, freedom of association, etc.). In practice, the transition to democratic structures was completed by the parliamentary and local elections in 1990, and Hungary was accepted as a Western democracy by admission to the Council of Europe in November 1990.

It is broadly held by transition economists that the maintenance of closed and bureaucratic economic systems in Eastern Europe has led to great economic damage and has to a great extent been responsible for the poor economic performance of these countries. Through lack of real external market relations, these countries have expropriated themselves from the tremendous advantages of the international division of labor, which has been one of the most important factors of prosperity and welfare of the Western world since World War II (rapid growth of trade, foreign investments, transnationalization of company structures, etc.). Therefore, externally an organic (re)integration into the world economy is as important as the internal transformation.

This integration into the world economy requires three steps:

1. *Opening the formerly closed national economies*, which means beyond broad import liberalization, the liberalization of foreign capital investments, and attractive joint-venture legislation. There is no opening without convertibility of the national currency. Apart from convertibility, the legal frameworks in Hungary are set, and the inadequacies are mostly due to political and economic factors (political instability in the region, shortages in proper infrastructures, lack of attractive partners, etc.).

2. *Reorientation and marketization of external economic relations*. These affect mainly the former Council of Mutual Economic Assistance (CMEA) relations, which have been responsible for rigidity and obsolescence of economic structures and often inefficient and loss-making ventures.

3. *Entry into the world economic institutions*. Hungary joined the General Agreement on Tariffs and Trade (GATT) in 1972 and the International Monetary Fund (IMF) and the World Bank in 1982. Hungary has negotiated an association treaty with the European Community (EC), and it is broadly held that from the point of view of prosperity and development of the Hungarian economy, the full participation in European integration is of vital interest.

Economic Circumstances of Transition

The new democracies have inherited obsolete economies, which have been struggling with a deep crisis for many years. This crisis is now aggravated by the adjustment costs and the hardships of transition. Therefore, the socio-economic transformation of these countries must be combined with the difficult tasks of reconstruction and consolidation. For Hungary, the main factor of the acute crisis is the indebtedness of the country, which culminated in critical proportions by the second half of the 1980s.

Hungary, like the other countries of the region, had missed the technological revolution of the 1970s and 1980s, which had led to total renewal of industrial-productive bases, revolutionized organization and management practices, and created new information and communication systems. The former "socialist" socio-economic systems were counterinterested in real technological change, and the necessary sources were wasted on ill-conceived "modernizations" and on financing losses because of delayed reforms and lack of adjustment to far-reaching world economic developments from the early 1970s. After a decade-long delay, the technological and structural reconstruction of the economies of the region is a task of utmost importance, because these countries otherwise have no chance to meet the challenges of their external reintegration. Besides the renewal of their productive capacities, they face the difficult task of complex modernization of their infrastructures (for example, telecommunications) and the restoration of huge environmental damage caused by the negligent policies of former governments.

Hungary is one of the most heavily indebted countries in the region. The roughly $22 billion debt means about $2,200 per capita indebtedness, which is far more than the Polish (second to Hungary) per capita debt of $600. More than 80 percent of Hungarian debt is from financial markets, whereas this makes up less than one-third of Poland's debt. The Hungarian annual debt service is about $3.5 billion, which takes more than 5 percent of its national income. Hungary has been in a resource-losing position for many years, which has led to restriction of investments and to a continuous reduction of living standards. Combined with high costs of adjustment and the breakdown of CMEA markets, this resulted in about a 5 percent drop in GNP and about a 35 percent rate of inflation in 1990. With further reduction of CMEA trade and negative consequences of the Gulf War (1991), another 10 percent reduction of GNP occured in 1991. Furthermore, with an inflation rate of 35 percent and—as something new—a rapid acceleration of unemployment, which had reached 150,000 individuals (about 4 percent) in the middle of 1991, the Hungarian economy is facing serious difficulties. A gradual improvement is not expected until 1994.

There are, however, several positive characteristics and factors in the Hungarian economy, which—compared with other countries of the region—are promising at least from the point of view of consolidation.

1. Hungary has been able to maintain the normal operation of its economy and a relatively balanced supply in the domestic market. Traditionally, this has been particularly important; concerning food supply, Hungary not only enjoyed a balanced domestic market, but was able to export substantial amounts. So far the balanced supply has also been maintained for energy. In exchange for Soviet energy, Hungarian food exports have been an important factor. The breakdown of the Soviet market has had far-reaching negative consequences for several Hungarian companies, and particularly for employment. It is still questionable how far the Hungarian companies are able to adjust to the new situation.

2. As a result of a longer history of reforms and marketization, the costs and the difficulties of the transformation are socially and politically far more accept-

able than in any other Eastern European country. This applies to the acceptance of price changes, the income differences, and the consequences of privatization as well. But unemployment is a new phenomenon, and there is no experience of the extent to which society is ready to tolerate it.

3. The transition has been peaceful in Hungary in the sense that the country has—so far—been able to avoid social and political unrest or upheavals. There have been no strikes (except for the taxi blockade) or large-scale political demonstrations, and it seems that there are better conditions for political consensus than in many other Eastern European countries. The extremist political forces have so far been able to attract only limited support, and it seems that the great majority of the population favors political stability and social peace.

4. Hungary, like Poland, is exempt from ethnic-nationalistic conflicts, and the national questions are integrating rather than dividing factors. In many other countries of the region, these have destabilizing effects and, socially and economically, cause huge costs. Hungary, in this respect, is much better placed to overcome the hardships of transition and to consolidate its economy.

Main Characteristics of the Hungarian Military Economy

Several factors have to be mentioned concerning the historical development of the military sector of the Hungarian economy in the previous decade. As a loser of two world wars, the military economy was more delimited (also by international treaties and obligations) than in many other countries, and this has had an enduring impact on development. At the same time, by imposition of a war-communistic type of system, particularly during the Stalinist period, the Hungarian economy was also highly militarized, and these policies have had long-term consequences on the whole economic development and structure of the country (overextended development of the steel industry and energy sectors because of enforced heavy industrialization). Four characteristics of Hungarian military industries have to be particularly stressed:

1. Hungary has never had a closed and independent military industry, and particularly after 1956 by elimination of special control and management of the arms industry, there has been a relatively close integration of military and civilian sectors. From the seventeen main military industrial companies only one can be considered as a 100 percent arms producer (*Magyar Nèphadsereg Gödöllöi Gyára*), and military production is more than 50 percent at only two others (*Mechanikai Labor* and *Finommechanikai Vállalat*). Their share in the military production of the country is, however, about 30 percent (1988).[1] The technological and financial interaction between the two sectors of the economy had both positive and negative effects. The military technologies were more easily transferred to civilian sectors, and the Soviet phenomenon of "internal COCOM" (export or license control on military products) was never known. At

the same time, the high profitability of the military sector had negative effects on civilian production. Management did not care too much about the costs and qualities of their civilian products as long as they could be subsidized by the profits from military production.

2. The Hungarian military industry is mostly military-related, but the direct arms production is modest compared with that of other countries in the region. In 1988, only 10.8 percent of the production of the Hungarian military industry consisted of artillery and infantry weapons with a further 1.8 percent consisting of ammunition. In the same year, two-thirds of the Hungarian military production consisted of telecommunication and electronic instruments and 13.8 percent military vehicles.[2] The military industry in Hungary is highly specialized, which goes back to the specialization agreements of the 1960s in CMEA, delegating and distributing production of the most important industries among the member countries. Particularly in communication and electronics, specialization is in components, subsystems, or parts, and in these fields Hungary has mostly become a subcontractor of the Soviet space and military sector. Therefore, these industries are heavily export-dependent; in fact, only about 10 percent of the Hungarian military production has been sold at home, most of it having been exported to the other CMEA partners.

The bulk of Hungarian military-related production has been concentrated in seventeen large companies, and they have provided about 90 percent of all military industrial products and services. But five of these seventeen companies have a less than 1 percent share each in total military production of the country. The activity of the main Hungarian military industrial companies is shown in Table 18.1.

3. It is already well known that the idea of high technological standards and of efficiency in the military industries of the Eastern European countries was a myth, and this sector has not been exempted from the systemic illnesses of centralized, bureaucratic management. There were, of course, huge efforts toward the creation of modern high-tech industries and military products; but at the same time, the military sectors were only slightly less characterized than the civilian industries by sluggishness of innovation, poor quality of products and service, waste of resources, low efficiency, and unreliability of supply. The same applied to the Hungarian military industries. Although they have some concentrated high-tech sectors (telecommunications and electronics), their general technological level has been far behind that of the West and in many respects even that of the Soviets.

The enforced specialization agreements in CMEA after 1956 had particularly negative impacts on the Hungarian economy. "Connected with the objectives of Warsaw Pact, the specialization of military industries accelerated, and as a result of it, some of the traditional and successfully operating industries of our country were transferred, for example our radio manufacturing to Bulgaria, and some-

Table 18.1

Share of Military-Related Production in Hungarian Industrial Companies, 1988, 1989, and in Total Military Production (MP)

Military-related production	Military-related production (as a percentage of the company's total production)		Military-related production (as a percentage of Hungary's total military production)
	1988	1989	MP
Artillery and infantry weapons			10.8
DIGEP	9.3	18.9	6.7
FEG	17.5	11.2	3.3
Danuvia	14.0	—	0.8
Ammunition			1.8
Bakonymuvek	10.7	—	0.9
Matrafem	8.2	—	0.9
Telecommunications and instruments			66.7
Gamma	26.2	9.8	1.9
MOM	12.2	—	1.2
FMV	79.4	73.9	16.8
Orion	13.1	—	0.4
Videoton	35.3	28.8	34.9
BHG	10.5	—	2.8
Mechanikai Labor	82.2	68.9	6.5
TAKI	42.0	—	1.7
Telefongyar	7.1	—	0.5
Vehicles			13.8
Labor NIM	49.1	—	1.9
Pestvideki geogy	59.7	40.6	4.5
MN Godollo	100.0	—	7.4
Other companies			6.9
Total			100.0

elements of production of telephone centrals to the German Democratic Republic (GDR); the research and development of military technologies were restructured, which led to narrowing down the research fields in our country, and the research activities were limited only to adaptational and operational problems connected with compulsory license buyings."[3] Because of the so-called Sofia Principle (free transfer of technologies), the flow of worthy technologies became limited even in the military fields. Now this makes transformation and conversion more difficult. "The problems of military industry are aggravated by the fact that the bulk of its products are for not the most modern. Most of these products were made—on the basis of licenses and requirements of our partners—for the former socialist (basically Soviet) market. The partners generally demanded not the most modern products, as far as they expropriated the production of them for themselves."[4]

4. The military sectors of the Eastern European countries have been particularly subject to centralized, bureaucratic control, and they have been mostly exempted from the market-oriented reform measures. In this respect, Hungary has been somewhat different from the others in that the special and separated management of military sectors was abolished after 1956. The Hungarian military-related companies were equally subject to post-1968 reform measures, and the reform aims were no less valid in the military sectors than in the others. At the same time, because the great majority of military production was exported and because in the CMEA trade the bureaucratic practices have prevailed until recently, military production "enjoyed" a special status in the management of the economy.

The export production was physically targeted (in other fields the planned targets in Hungary were gradually abolished after 1968), the supply of materials was rationed, and the prices were set centrally and, in fact, very favorably. In foreign trade, the state monopoly has been preserved, and until recently, the special state companies dealing with foreign trade were required to sell and buy these products, and the bilateral balance of trade was strictly practiced. Owing to strategic and political prioritization and behind the "iron curtain" of top-secret activities, the companies enjoyed better lobbying possibilities and economic policy preferences (better access to financial resources and regulatory exemptions). Working under "secure" planned targets and with calculated, monopolistic prices, these companies were in a much more favorable position than the others. Under these circumstances, the military-related companies were mostly opposed to reforms and structural modernization, and they have not felt it necessary to make serious adjustment efforts concerning the challenges of the technological revolution. Those firms were among the most resistant to the previous reform and marketiziation measures. Thus, it is not without reason that many Hungarian economists rightly felt that they were some of the main opponents of reform efforts.

Conversion Problems of the Hungarian Economy

Since the end of the 1980s, Hungary has had to face complex conversion problems. The strategic revision of basic principles of foreign policies and military doctrines had already started during the 1980s, but the revolutionary changes of 1989 created a totally new situation in East–West relations. From the point of view of arms control and reduction proposals, the change of the military doctrine of the Soviet Union and Warsaw Pact was an important turning point (cf. the emergence of the concept of "sufficient defense"). As early as 1988, this brought some unilateral cuts in conventional arms and subsequently in military budgets.

Besides the political changes, the growing economic difficulties played a very important role and were leading to serious budgetary deficits in all the Eastern European countries because of structural weaknesses—the shortcomings of planning and management systems and increasing indebtedness. These countries, therefore, have to make smaller or greater cuts in their military budgets. In 1989 all members of the Warsaw Pact had already reduced their military expenditures.

As a result of the budgetary problems, military expenditures have been restrained in Hungary since 1986. From that time, in fact, the military budget of the country has been frozen. Originally, a gradual increase in military expenditures was foreseen in the five-year plan for 1986–90, but under the worsening budgetary conditions they were postponed each year.

Owing to aggravating budgetary deficits, the Hungarian government was already compelled to make nominal cuts in 1989. In January 1989, the government of Hungary announced a unilateral reduction of 9 percent in military forces and armaments for the years 1989 and 1990. These cuts affected 9,300 soldiers. About 250 tanks, 430 artillery pieces and mine throwers, 9 MIG-21 fighter interceptors, 6 tactical rocket launchers, and 30 armored personnel carriers were withdrawn. As a first step, a tank brigade was disbanded in Szabadszállás in August 1989, and another was transformed into a motorized rifle brigade. In the summer of 1989, the Hungarian government decided on a 5.5 billion forint ($80 mil.) saving for the years 1989–90. In November 1989, a new army reform was announced by the Hungarian government, and further unilateral cuts of 20 to 25 percent were decided. As a result of these measures, the number of the Hungarian troops decreased from 106,000 to 70,000 by the end of 1991. For 1990, Parliament approved a budget of 40.4 billion forint for the military sector, which according to estimates represented about a 30 percent reduction in real terms (as compared with 1989). In August 1990, compulsory military service was reduced from eighteen to twelve months. For 1991, the military budget of Hungary was set for 54.4 billion forint, which in real terms means no effective increase.

In the circumstances just outlined, it seems no exaggeration to state that Hungary is probably facing the greatest transformation of its economy in its peacetime history. This time the question does not arise simply as a result of political goodwill and decisions: the call for conversion is based on deep-rooted and fundamental political, social, and economic changes in the region and in the international environment. For the future, it is connected with the fundamental transformation of society and the economy, and it raises the need for broad adjustments in government policies, institutions, companies, and of course individuals.

In the short run, however, the conversion of the Hungarian military industry has to be implemented under crisis conditions, and it is accompanied with painful consequences. The sudden cancellation of the export contracts for military products by the Warsaw Treaty Organization (WTO) partners (sometimes with fewer than two months' notice) from 1989 and then the "spectacular" collapse of the CMEA markets in 1990–91 led to a catastrophic situation for Hungarian companies. This meant that the conversion measures had to be made in a shock-type way. In fact, the Hungarian military industry had to be cut down to minimum in three years, and even the existence of some of the companies is threatened. "The fact is shocking, that while the production value of the Hungarian military industry was nearly 20 billion forint in 1988, it will be only 2–3 billion in 1991. Three years ago the Hungarian defense economy employed about 30,000 people (in full- or part-time jobs). If the lost defense industrial orders cannot be replaced by civil sales at the affected companies, then the great majority of these people will be forced into other jobs, of course, if they are able to find them."[5] According to the Hungarian Ministry of Industry and Trade, of those companies that had military capacities, at the beginning of 1991, six were bankrupt or under bankruptcy procedures, nine got into difficult situations, and only four were able to successfully convert their capacities by their own efforts.[6] "The reduction of demand for military products was due entirely to exports; the change in demand by the domestic armed forces in general had no effect on our military industry."[7]

Some Economic Consequences of Conversion

Beyond the technical issues, companies' conversion is basically an economic problem. The change in technologies and production structures is mostly a function of finding new markets and partners. As far as this assumes basic renewal of technologies, which can mostly be acquired from Western companies, the conversion is for the most part, therefore, a question of seeking joint ventures. The process, however, is hindered by several legal, political, and economic factors; in general, there is only slow progress in this respect, even in the military-related sectors, which may be more attractive than the others for Western partners. Among the main defense companies, *Videoton* is in negotiation with Thomson, *Telefongyàr* with Siemens, *Finommechanikai Gyàr* with Alcatel, but only with a modest rate of success.

The Western partners and the joint ventures are also needed as sources of capital because the long-delayed reconstructions are highly capital-intensive. This applies to most of the companies, for their conversion problems are complicated by serious financial difficulties. Under the assumption of favorable future market possibilities, most of the companies in the military field between 1982 and 1988 still made substantial investments in research and development and in new production capacities. These investments were based on miscalculations of future needs in arms and were also considered as compensations for bleak market prospects in civilian fields. The ratio of investment of a company's own sources to the state investment subsidies (credits and free transfer of government funds) was about 1 : 2, but a considerable amount of credit was also drawn from commercial banks. The government funds were, for the most part, extended by the State Development Institute, but some commercial banks also found it attractive to join, giving credit for military investments. Now, with shrinking military sales, many companies are facing serious difficulties in servicing these debts, and the financial problems are further aggravated by similar problems in their civilian sectors. Under these circumstances, the funds needed for conversion are not available, and they can be acquired only through new credits, and mostly under unfavorable conditions.

Though the cuts in military expenditures were mostly enforced by budgetary problems, the budgetary implications, particularly in the light of conversion costs, are highly controversial. In a simplified way, the reduction of military expenditures is often analyzed in terms of opportunity costs. According to this approach, a certain number of tanks or submarines are calculated in terms of the number of hospitals or power plants that could be built with the same amount of money, and these productive investments or this consumption is mostly defined as the "peace dividends" of conversion. Of course, it is generally recognized that national security and military defense are important and indispensable public services, but the relation between the actual military potential and the real national security needs of a given country, as a function basically of political factors, usually remains highly controversial and scarcely identifiable. In the case of deficit- and debt-financing cuts, as in Hungary, however, there are serious reservations, particularly because it is assumed that the peace dividend of conversion does not accrue under such circumstances.

The recent cuts in Hungarian military spending were mainly regarded as the least bad solution, in terms of either further possible tax increases or a reduction of expenditures in education or health, which could even endanger the mere functioning of some vital public services. Under the changed political circumstances, there are a great many people who feel that even more radical cuts would be desirable. But it is also widely accepted that the basically outdated Hungarian military capacity to a certain extent should be modernized and the new defense doctrines (territorial or circular defense) also have costly development implications.

It must also be recognized that the direct cuts in military expenditures do not automatically mean equal budgetary savings. In fact, the net savings can be much less in many respects, and here the danger of miscalculation is the greatest. First of all, the state may suffer losses in tax revenues, and because of the relatively high volume and profitability of military production, these may be substantial. According to some expert estimates, about 50 to 60 percent of recent Hungarian military budgetary cuts may be lost because of these tax revenues.[8]

It is also becoming increasingly realized that the costs of conversion are far from negligible, and a certain part of them must be directly financed from the central budget. This problem applies first of all to the destruction of armaments and equipment. Some of the equipment can be used in civilian sectors, and their sale could be a direct contribution to the budget. In other cases, it is difficult to find markets and users for them, because they are usually technically outdated and physically outworn. At best they can be utilized as spare parts or components. Some arms have to be scrapped and at best sold as junk, even when costs may exceed possible revenues. According to Hungarian army sources, for example, the cost of disassembling a tank is about 250,000–750,000 forint, and only after that can they be refunded.[9] The storage of military products or materials may also be costly and must be covered by the budget.

The same applies to the conversion of buildings and other military facilities. Many of them were designed and built for special military functions, and their conversion to some other use is either physically impossible or very expensive. They require functional rebuilding or they have been left in a very bad condition, as is the case with otherwise usable apartments left behind by the Soviets. The costly reconstruction and renovation of these badly needed facilities, however, are in most cases beyond the financial capacity of the local government, to which they have been transferred. There are also tremendous environmental problems caused by the former negligent attitude of the military establishment and the present withdrawal of the Soviet army.

The military cuts raise conversion problems as regards employment both in the army and in the arms industries. The first cuts of 9 percent in the army did not cause substantial employment problems. They mainly affected the conscripts, who can return to their families and their jobs; in the future, fewer people will be drafted. The reduction of military service from eighteen to twelve months will, in any case, further increase the supply of workers in the labor market.

The possibility of conversion has for a long time been taken into account in the training of officers, and therefore in military colleges and academies so-called dual diplomas are issued: these credentials are also accepted in civilian professions (e.g., in engineering, teaching, and economics). In fact, there is a shortage of trained officers in Hungary. Those who want to stay in the army after the cuts are, therefore, simply transferred to other units. Taking into account possible future cuts, the number of persons enrolled in military colleges has already been reduced to about half. This makes it possible to improve the selection and, eventually, the quality of the new students. The new defense doctrines and strategies envisage new concepts in training and the need for retraining the existing army officers. At the same time, a great many officers are near retirement age. In terms of the draft, the fact that the number of border guards will be reduced by 60 percent by 1995 is having a particularly bad effect on the army. Hungary introduced the possibility of alternative military service in the summer of 1989. In 1990, more than 600 persons applied for that alternative, and most of them will be called in for nonmilitary public (mostly social) service. As the Szabadszállás case showed, the employment problems have serious regional implications. In remote places it is particularly difficult to find alternative jobs in nearby areas, and owing to serious housing problems, it is almost impossible to move elsewhere.

For those employed in military industries, the conversion problems are different. In theory, the cuts in military expenditures and the transfer of resources to civilian sectors will not create unemployment. On the contrary, it is generally assumed that the shift of resources to civilian industries may create more jobs because of the higher labor intensity of the latter. With deficit financing budgetary cuts and with factories closing down in a general crisis situation, it is highly probable that the actual results will be different from this project picture. In view of the difficulties in Hungarian defense companies, it is estimated that the jobs of about 5,000 to 6,000 persons are in jeopardy. This number, in itself, does not seem too high, but given the rapidly accelerating rate of unemployment, it cannot be neglected.

Conversion Policies of Hungarian Governments

It is almost axiomatic that conversion must be based on comprehensive advance planning and explicit government policies. The need for conversion policies and planning, however, arose only in recent years, and Hungary was not an exception.

A more or less comprehensive conversion policy emerged and was worked out by the Hungarian government in the summer of 1989. The Economic Consultative Council of the government discussed the possibilities of a conversion program and made several proposals. The government measures concentrated on the financial difficulties of companies, trying to compromise between the defense interests and the economic capacity of the country.

In order to ease financial difficulties, the most important step was that the companies were granted a moratorium for 1989 on repayment of credits drawn from the State Development Institute for military developments, and in some cases, state funds were directly transferred to companies. Similar arrangements were suggested involving the commercial banks. The export-credit schemes promoting hard-currency exports could be extended to these companies. The commercial banks were encouraged to give development credits to those in trouble, but strictly on commercial grounds. In fact, one of the basic principles of these government policies was that the former special preferences to military projects had to be abolished, and the arrangements and the environment, like those in the civilian sector, had to be market-based. As a condition for the above-mentioned financial support, the companies were obliged to work out their own development plans.

In order to ease financial burdens, a part of the cumulated stocks was also allowed to be transferred to central state reserve funds or to be sold. Some stocks could be calculated as costs, reducing the tax obligations of the company. The government decided that the so-called M-capacities (emergency stocks of fuels, food, and spare parts for arms or armed vehicles for a war situation) would be revised and reduced, easing the burdens both on companies and on the central budget. The bureaucratic foreign trade regulations in the sector were abolished, and the liberalization measures, where they did not hurt strategic interests, were extended to these companies.

It was recognized that the close coordination of interests and the cooperation between the partners were also of the utmost importance. In recent years the companies and the government have been blaming each other, and this has proved to be counterproductive and of no benefit to either side. The views and complaints of companies are summarized in an article in the following way: "We have been obliged for production under the defense legislation, we had to draw credits for that and we have substantial stocks and capacities, which can be used only for military ends. We have, therefore, been pushed into this situation by the government and now the budget must bail us out from this mess."[10]

On the other hand, György Doro, the former deputy president of the Planning Office, pointed out that the companies were warned in advance about possible future military cuts. In fact, the first signals about the possible restraints on military spending had already been given in 1984, and the Planning Office tried to caution the companies about their overambitious military development plans and advised them to take steps for adjustment. As Doro noted: "The companies were very content with that centrally steered situation, as it brought secure and substantial profits."[11]

If special efforts were needed to deal with transformation problems, that also became the subject of discussion. According to government views, the size and the character of these problems do not justify special programs and treatments, and the questions can be solved in the general framework of the stabilization policy. This applies not only to the commercially oriented approach toward financial difficulties but also to the problem of unemployment. According to some official views, the central unemployment facilities introduced from 1989 (compensation payments, unemployment benefits, job transmission of retraining schemes) should cope with the problems. As the Finance Ministry is quoted: "The position of companies in military industrial production is no different to the general situation in Hungarian industry, so nothing justifies their special treatment by the government."[12]

According to the government's views about the future, it is important that the decisions about military developments and industry issues be made in the framework of democratic institutions and in harmony with the real defense needs and export possibilities of the country. "The fate of military industrial capacities will be decided according to the requirements of the new defense concept worked out by Defence Ministry, which will be approved by the Parliament. These laws will provide the financial possibilities and scope of development for the military industry."[13]

Notes

1. Kovacs, Attila. 1990. "Disarmament and the Impacts of Conversion of Military Production to Hungarian Military Economy." *Egyetemi Szemle* ("University Review"), Budapest University of Economics, no. 3.

2. *Magyar Hirlap*, June 15, 1989.

3. Cf. note 1.

4. *Figyelo*, March 28, 1991.

5. *Figyelo*, February 14, 1991.

6. Cf. note 5.

7. Cf. note 4.

8. *Figyelo*, April 13, 1989.

9. *Magyar Hirlap*, May 22, 1989.

10. Cf. note 2.

11. *Magyar Hirlap*, June 14, 1989.

12. Cf. note 5.

13. Cf. note 4.

Bibliography

Kovacs, Attila. 1990. "Disarmament and the Impacts of Conversion of Military Production to Hungarian Military Economy." *Journal of Budapest*. School of Economics, no. 3.

19. Psychological Resistance to Market Relations in the Former Soviet Union

Akhmed I. Kitov

Introduction

Research into the resistance to market relations was undertaken by the author at the Academy of National Economy. It was not provoked by a purely theoretical interest, but rather by a practical implication of the problem as reflected in the process of training. In order to make the trainees of the academy, who are practical managers, ready for the advancing market, it is essential to be aware of their doubt, which makes them stick to the old methods and attitudes rather than reject them in management practices once and for all. To be ready for the advancing market means, instead, to wholeheartedly trust the advent and development of market relations.

Our research may be of interest for foreign businesspeople who intend to develop business contacts with entrepreneurs in the former Soviet Union. Once they know what those entrepreneurs apprehend, why they resist establishing and encouraging market relations, it will be easier for the foreign business people to overcome resistance and to develop reliable business contacts.

For a few years now, starting from 1988, managers at enterprises and public administrators at state offices and institutions functioning as economic management authorities—the total group of the respondents exceeded 2,000 people—have been asked two complementary questions: (1) What are the most unpleasant consequences for you in a transition to a market economy? (2) What are the most positive things that a transition to the market can bring to you personally?

The respondents to the survey gave their answers in writing, followed by an oral discussion, thus allowing them to clarify and finalize their answers. The major objective of the research was to reveal a psychological state caused by oncoming market relations. The results of the survey are provided here.

Motives for the Resistance to Market Relations

The following are some of the motives managers have for resisting market relations:

1. A most widely spread feeling about this problem is that of the *uncertainty of the situation*. It is impossible to visualize, even to imagine, even very approximately and roughly, one's personal career in connection with the reform undertaken. Behaviorally this deprives an individual of any ability to orient his or her life toward a definite goal, to make any realistic plans, and to concentrate efforts on their implementation. The abortive coup of August 19–21, 1991, further aggravated the feeling of frustration, causing havoc in people's lives and minds.

2. *A feeling of something unknown, of an information vacuum.* If the uncertainty mentioned in the previous paragraph stems from the contradictory development of events, the feeling of the unknown results from the fact that people either have no information sufficient to assess the perspectives of their own lives and careers or, having access to information of this type, they cannot be easily entrusted with it for a number of reasons. The duration of a transition to a market is not known, nor is the opportunity to determine one's own role in this process, one's own position. Hence, there seems to be the impossibility of predicting and assessing the sequential order of the stages in a market development. Many other factors only add uncertainty, and general scarcity of information further promotes this feeling of desolation and apprehension in planning one's own career and undertaking relevant steps in this direction.

3. Mistrust in the future is caused by the fact that for a long time there had been *no visible improvements of material standards of life, previously promised so willingly and repeatedly*. On the contrary, the situation deteriorates, the money is devalued, goods disappear from the market, criminal offenses grow in numbers, and conflicts of all kinds become ever more dramatic. Moreover, some executives develop the feeling of frustration, a fatal pattern of events only adding to it, and the feeling of a landslide, with an intensive movement to an even worse situation. In a word, uncertainty of every kind prevails, ranging from doubt to the feeling of doom.

4. *The feeling of an instability in the situation, of the fragility of life, of the nonreliability of the surrounding circumstances.* Even those who find themselves more or less adjusted to the situation in the outer environment are not confident that the temporary balance has been reached for a prolonged period of time. The situation reveals some traits of character, frequently far from the best in nature: There is a trend to make "a quick buck and get away with it," to get hold of anything coming one's way, while there is an opportunity to do so, a kind of revival of "carnivorous" intentions and attitudes. Hence, hurt feelings, insults, and distorted human relations give rise to new conflicts. A certain additional source of instability is further enhanced by poorly thought through economic decisions made by agencies of power and authority.

5. *A foreboding about one's own redundance, a feeling of being unclaimed, a loss of social status, when one's experience and abilities are of no interest to anyone, a threat to be thrown out, a danger of losing the job one likes*—here are but a few of the responses that we give in more detail in this chapter. The es-

sence of their apprehensions lies in the fact that their professional experience and their expertise may prove unnecessary under new conditions, when—a line from the Communist International Anthem slightly adjusted—the one who used to be everything will become nothing. This is a more typical feeling among people in higher positions.

6. *The feeling of forlornness* (an existentialist term), implying the feeling of being left to oneself, a lack of any social protection or guarantee that had grown to be a solid habit through the years of Soviet power in this country. People here had been taught to rely on the state—which allegedly would take care of them and would always continue to do so—and to rely upon the strength of the work-force team (a collective), which now in an advancing market economy may leave people to rely only upon their own strengths and abilities and to try to survive through their own endeavors. This is really something people in the former Soviet Union find quite new and unusual.

7. *Nostalgic feelings about management of a planned economy where the situation is always clear and it is evident what is to be done,* where to turn for cash and resources, where to turn for supplies, where to send the ready product, and so on. There was no danger of going bankrupt, even if there was no cash. When such a situation occurred, the enterprise (i.e., its manager) would immediately get the appropriate subsidy. If the manager failed to meet the plan, it would be lowered in retrospect. In market conditions, one will have to provide one's own supplies, to look for potential consumers, with severe competition at one's heels accompanying the search. So, all this taken into account, the life of a manager in the former Soviet Union was in no way worse and in many respects actually better than the one lying ahead. Besides, it was no doubt easier when managers actually had at their disposal all the property entrusted to them according to their own wishes, and they did not have to ask for anyone's permission or advice and did not have to listen to proposals or suggestions.

8. *A necessity to increase drastically labor intensity in market conditions accompanied by higher requirements for professional skills.*

9. *Rejection of the realities of the market for some ideological considerations.* This is what one of the respondents actually wrote in his answer: "The ideology of the market is alien to me. All my life I have been working in a different way." Here are some more examples of the respondents' feelings and attitudes: "There is an apprehension that I'll have to fight for my own place under the sun, fight with the so far unknown but seemingly severe rules of the game." "It all means a major change in the social way of life, which is incompatible with my own approach." "I'll have to go through numerous social and personal shakedowns due to some psychological unpreparedness alongside an emergence of openly and evidently successful entrepreneurs." "The most unpleasant thing here is when they start assessing my worth in rubles as if I were a commodity of some kind," and so forth.

10. *Open hostility of people to each other,* mutual unfriendliness provoked by

the most unexpected reasons and sometimes by the adversely oriented: the rich and the poor, Communists and non-Communists, veterans and the younger generation, natives and the newcomers, and the like. People have an utter concern with their private lot; frustration and mishaps bring them to the edge of emotional breakdown, overexcitement, and depression. They feel ready to take part in any kind of risky or rash events, ready to join mobs, and ready to act as vandals.

11. *A loss of confidence in power,* due to the inconsistent actions of the authorities (as revealed by the decisions of the government, for instance), because their words and deeds never seem to go together and because those at the top attempt to find a way out of a crisis exclusively at the expense of the working people's budgets and the simultaneous maintenance of—and sometimes an evident increase in expenditure for—the army and the bureaucratic management. "You feel a fool, but it is all the politicians' fault," one of the respondents writes. "I disapprove of the prevailing psychology of a show, of a fair," another one continues, "and I am afraid it will all take us a long time, with the kind of leaders we have at our head, before we manage to develop a market, if at all, but the show and the fair are here now, we have them on our hands." "The greatest fear comes from the fact that partocracy blocks any possible way to acquire property, to become an owner of something, and the worst thing here is that the partocracy may interfere at every movement, at every stage and take back everything by force, and, in addition, send the owner to some remote place," one of the respondents believes.

12. *A concern for the family.* "It is difficult to provide for the family, when everything is in short supply, the prices grow, and the real incomes may fall dramatically over an hour—it looks like a task I cannot cope with," one of the respondents confesses. "It is not clear what will happen to my family on the way to the market and later," admits a respondent. Another one states, "I am afraid for the future of my children." A further answer expresses concern in the following way: "I have sick children in my family, my wife is of poor health, too. Shall I be able to provide for their well-being working alone? For twenty years I have been overworking, but I have made no savings whatsoever." In a word, fear for the future of their families is a frequent apprehension managers suffer as the country gropes its way to a market economy.

13. *Awareness of the inequality in the starting conditions existing at the beginning of a transition to a market economy.* This fact does not stimulate the zeal of those who had not managed to provide for a good start in this race. It does not orient them toward participating in the market competition, for they assess their chances of winning as very slim, if feasible at all. It causes distrust against those ahead of them in this race, a feeling of disapproval, of hatred, of a desire to do them some harm. An attitude of peaceful coexistence with a luckier neighbor has so far occurred very rarely among the population at large. Even when the starting conditions are equal, entrepreneurs who made up their minds

to start their own businesses and who achieved some, though very modest, success enjoy nothing but mistrust and disapproval from the majority of their peers. The level-out principle of paupers' socialism has deeply rooted itself in the psychology of Soviet people.

14. *The feeling of being pushed toward market relations against their will*—is another reason for resistance to the economic reform on the part of a significant share of the population. The psychological preparation of the population and of the policymakers in this field is totally inadequate. There is not now, and there has never been, any scientific program worth speaking of that focuses on the psychological adjustment of the population to market relations. Therefore people have the erroneous impression of the market economy's being pushed onto them. Repeated attempts by psychologists in the former Soviet Union to suggest some recommendations elaborating psychological approaches to the economic changes have repeatedly been rejected.

15. *A lack of knowledge about the market and a lack of experience in management* present another stumbling block, though the inner attitude toward market reform is positive. This lack of knowledge is due to the important fact that there are no clear and unambiguous books and manuals available that deal with market relations. Besides, the leading economists of the former Soviet Union do not share a unanimous opinion concerning the best way for a transition to a market economy. Some of them say, for instance, that municipal flats will be sold to those residing in them at present, while others believe that the present tenants ought to get them free, the same being true about land. Some economists support the idea of giving land to people for private ownership, while others are opposed to it. All this cannot but have an unfavorable effect, adding to the havoc reigning in the ideas on the market. Besides, it must be admitted that antimarket propaganda arranged by the Communist-oriented media still works very effectively—more effectively, in fact, than the promotion of market relations advocated by the democrats.

16. *The feeling of destruction, of a break in human relations that has existed in ordinary everyday life, in economic practices, both vertically and horizontally.* Partners of yesterday, who had been reliable all the way through, lose their significance for each other, fail to live up to their promises, and stop cooperating. The changes in this sphere are comparable only to a landslide, burying and crushing both business and human contacts. The results are hurt personal feelings and frustration. A search for new partners turns out to be a very complicated and time-consuming process, as the chaos reigning in economics and politics prevents people from assessing the situation even with approximate accuracy in order to make new decisions that correspond to the adjusted evaluations of the situation and to implement such decisions correctly.

Thus, there are many different motives and attitudes causing resistance to market relations. It should not be felt, however, that the attitudes of the managers are exclusively or overwhelmingly negative. To prove the point, we would like to provide some answers to the second question of the questionnaire: "What are the most positive things that a transition to the market can bring to you personally?"

What Positive Things Do Executives Expect from the Market?

It ought to be emphasized that the majority of the respondents also provided pessimistic answers to the second question. Some of the most upsetting reactions were: "We are facing an age of mafia relations reigning in society, of people who live dishonestly and will try to justify the dishonestly obtained money." "The state and the people are in the hands of the mafia who are hurriedly selling away and wasting the wealth of the nation." Eight percent of the responses to the second question were unambiguously pessimistic, showing that the respondents have no positive expectations about the oncoming market relations in the country.

The positive expectations reflected in the respondents still show some apprehension in connection with the advancing market relations; the respondents are worried by the discomfort and distress the market can cause in their own futures. Let us consider the hopes the managers bestow upon the developing market relations.

1. *Freedom and economic independence.* This would probably look like the most typical characteristic of the first group of answers, where the respondents express their positive expectations from an enhanced economic reform. Here are some of the answers:

"When the laws are streamlined, there will be an opportunity to work independently, not forced by a driving stick, and to feel an equal partner." "The possibility to be a master of one's own life"; "freedom within sensible limits"; "the possibility to do anything at all, to feel a free person, an individual, a personality"; "freedom of entrepreneurship, of economic activities"; "freedom from centralized management and an opportunity to show one's own knowledge and capabilities"; "freedom of choice"; "my enterprise will become free, economically free"; "at last I will have a complete freedom of action and will stop obeying fools." The general message of all these remarks is an appreciation of the possibility of gaining economic freedom and liberation from the incessant pressure of the bureaucratic structure and from the *apparatchiks*, who in the past had arrested creative initiative and the creativity of managers.

It is too early yet to say that the expectations have already come true. The economic freedom of individuals, even after the rout of the *putchists*, is still very moderate, and time will have to pass before radical changes may come through—and it is not a matter of the legislation. In fact, ideal market laws can be elaborated and adopted, but overt and covert resistance to them occurs, sometimes under the demagogic pretext of protecting the interests of the working people. This situation is likely to continue for some time.

2. *A possibility of self-expression, an opportunity to reveal one's capabilities and potentials* is the common idea underlying the answers of the next group: "I will be able to work independently." "There will be an opportunity to express myself in the conditions of a developed market, if the transition to a market does not lead to great bloodshed." "It gives me the possibility for complete self-expression in creating something, making things on my own, and on this basis my moral status will improve, though after fifty, it seems very unlikely." "It's an opportunity to realize one's own potentials." "It's a pressure to mobilize one's own potential." "It's an opportunity to make use of your own enterprise and thus to ensure your own stability." "It offers the possibility of implementing your own economic views, attitudes, and approaches." "I hope to start a business of my own and to implement my own approaches in organizing business and manufacture." "It gives you the possibility of self-assertion." "It's an opportunity to develop one's ability in the field of commerce." "It increases the level of professionalism, expansion of disciplined labor, an improvement of the product quality."

3. *Improvement of material and cultural conditions of life.* Here are some of the answers: "If I find my own place in the system of market relations, I will have opportunity to earn more, to provide better for the family, to lead a different kind of life on a new everyday routine level, more culturally diversified." "There's the hope of improving your own living standard"; "bringing the standard of life closer to a capitalist standard"; "partaking of the culture." "There will be enough goods in the market, and they will grow cheaper, which ought to lead to the stabilization of the situation." "With my profession and level, I will always be able to find a good job, to earn my bread and have some butter on it, too." "There's hope for our country of resurrecting the dignity and respect of a great nation in the fairly distant future."

4. A hope that there will be *a connection between work and level of well-being,* which is completely lacking at present and which has been the case during all the years of Soviet power. We provide the following examples of the answers to this question: "An opportunity to apply one's abilities to one's own advantage"; "an opportunity to get fair pay for fair work"; "an opportunity to earn money in proportion to one's contribution and an adequate compensation for it on a legal basis, and, consequently, to improve one's own life"; "cultural and material improvement of my life." "I will be able to build my own welfare depending on the results of my work only." "To develop your potential and abilities in commerce and to improve your standard of living as a result"; "a chance to sell your brain to a sensible office, to sensible and decent people"; "chatterers will go, as will loafers, so justice will prevail." "I am so eager to reach success through my own efforts and not depend on any subjective factors." "Your price will be as much as you are worth." "The possibility to throw away all the dogmas and start working for yourself, for your own benefit,

for the benefit of your family; everybody will start working much better.''

5. *Hopes for a better lot for one's children.* This is what respondents write on the topic: ''I would like to see my children live much more freely and in a less dogmatized way.'' ''I hope my children's life will improve irrespective of the starting level. My children and I, we'll have an opportunity to live in compliance with our own abilities.'' ''The children's background will not mean much, but their abilities will.''

The respondents enumerate many other positive expectations in connection with the market. Here are some of them: ''The market will revive kindness in the relations between people, for the people's aggressiveness and hostility, envy and other negative attitudes are caused by poverty and lack of rights.'' ''The market will make it possible to do away with some shameful social phenomena—long queues everywhere—in shops and clinics, at bus stops and railroad booking offices.'' ''The market will bring competition, which will encourage everyone to try to live better than their neighbor does and, consequently, to work harder than their neighbor does.'' ''The market will provide a chance to become an owner, to organize one's own business, to be confident that individuals and their families are protected materially.''

Who Is Against the Market?

The central problem of economic reform is the problem of privatization and denationalization. In order to solve the problem, it is first necessary to answer a number of questions including the following: First, who are the actual owners of state property, and who manages and disposes of it in reality? These individuals will then have to be deprived of this property. Second, who will implement the actual deprivation? Who is strong enough to deprive the real owner (since the formal owner is by definition the state) of his or her property? Third, who will the property be transferred to, since there is a threat of damaging the economic interests of the country in disposing of this property incorrectly?

All comparisons are extremely limited and conditional. But today's situation of expropriation of the proprietors reminds one of the days of the Bolsheviks' October Revolution in 1917. Then, back in 1917, however, it was evident from whom the property should be taken. Situations of that period and of today may coincide only with respect to the results of the act: The proprietor will be expropriated. But back in 1917, the property was in the hands of capitalists and landlords (in reality, it was expropriated not only from them, but from a lot of other people, too—from anyone, in fact, who had something to be robbed of, from the church, urban handicraftsmen, the so-called kulaks, wealthy farmers, and so forth). The method applied then was in full compliance with the task: It was an armed suppression of the class enemy, not only an economic suppression, but a physical one as well, up to the point of physical annihilation. The richer part of the population endured extreme suffering and torture and fell victim to regular acts of mass murder. Just one accompaniment to this was that the psychology of the mob—with sadistic vandal's instincts prevailing—was called upon by the Bolsheviks to "rob the one robbed."

But who are now the actual owners of the property that is considered and called state property? It is not so easy to answer this question, but I would nevertheless like to express my analysis. The state property in our country is managed—almost as if it were their private property—by representatives of the following seven groups of the Communist party and the elite of the former Soviet Union (from the very top to the district-link level), managers, especially those of management personnel of the military-industrial complex, higher-ranking military officers, officers of the Ministry of Interior Affairs and the KGB (State Security Committee), officials of the state bodies of authority, personnel in trade and services as a whole, leaders of pseudo-voluntary organizations (including women's groups, veterans, etc.) and bureaucratized science management.

Resistance to a transition to market relations arises among these groups, which have the opportunity to participate in some way in the distribution and consumption of the national wealth. Not all representatives of these groups are completely opposed to economic reforms. There are quite a few supporters of the market economy among them. But it is these very groups that would lose most if state property were privatized, and so, because of their objective situation they are less interested in passing the factories, plants, and land into private hands than are the people who are not allowed to manage such state property.

It is essential to emphasize that all measures undertaken against the Communist party of the former Soviet Union (the CPSU) and its property after suppressing the abortive putch will not be able to radically change the attitude of the representatives of the party and top-echelon people and the other five groups toward state property within the nearest one or two or even three or four years. The older personnel have already adjusted to the new conditions and will continue to stay in power close to their traditional feeder—state property—for a long time, covering their activities with pseudonew forms of economic management.

Of course, in addition to these six groups, there are other categories of people showing resistance to the market. They are not allowed to participate in the fuss over the property, but some portions come their way, too. These four groups include pensioners, families with many children, invalids, and disabled people. Not very happy about the advent of the market are elderly people who are afraid that they will not be able to change and adapt to changes. Even workers and employees of much younger age-groups who are not accustomed to overworking or simply to working hard would rather continue to live the lives they are used to than risk their beggars' earnings, what little they have. There are also quite a few collective farmers—at rank-and-file level—who learned to live from their own individual plots of land and to steal a little from the collective-farm fields, who are quite satisfied with what they have now, and who are not looking for a better life.

There are other population groups even less interested in the market; these people are not just impartial but are almost hostile in their attitudes. The principal resistance, however, comes from those who retain their power over the state property as if it were their own possession, in order to avoid accusations of any bias against the Party–Soviet elite who exhibit such rigid attachment toward economic power. If the power that belongs today to the economic management personnel brought up by the CPSU switched to one of the numerous new political parties, the opposition to the alienation of state property would be less desperate. Their resistance to attempts at shifting economic power by changes in ownership of property is a natural phenomenon, and to raise hell over this problem means to fight windmills, like noble Don Quixote, the Knight of Sadness.

Bibliography

Kovacs, Attila. 1990. "Disarmament and the Impacts of Conversion of Military Production to Hungarian Military Economy." *Journal of Budapest*. School of Economics, no. 3.

Retrospection

20. The Many Faces of Capitalism

Sven-Erik Sjöstrand

The Need for Comparative Studies

In this short concluding chapter to this rather sizable volume, I try to call the attention of the reader to an underlying common theme that seems to be present in most of the chapters. I suggest that this common theme could be summarized in the phrase that gives the title to this book's final chapter: "The Many Faces of Capitalism."

Most of the authors in this volume not only describe and discuss the institutional structures and changes in the focused upon countries or regions, but they also use a comparative approach. When making comparisons, they either analyze several countries for a certain, rather limited period of time or describe the development for a particular country over a longer time period. The former approach is used in the contributions from Perrow (chapter 6); Kaminski and Strzalkowski (chapter 7); Campbell (chapter 8); Orrù (chapter 9); Jessop, Nielsen, and Pedersen (chapter 11); and Andersson (chapter 12); whereas the latter design is offered especially in the contributions from North (chapter 2), Etzioni (chapter 3), Pedersen (chapter 13), Vail (chapter 14), Berrefjord and Heum (chapter 15), Hausner and Wojtyna (chapter 16), Palankai (chapter 18), and Kitov (chapter 19). Some of these researchers emphasize the idea that there are different forms of capitalism, notably Orrù, who compares the German and Japanese institutional structures and changes. But McKelvey; Jessop, Nielsen, and Pedersen; and Andersson also explicitly focus on this important topic.

The idea of analyzing and comparing different forms of capitalism or market economies is, of course, not new at all in the social and economic sciences. It has for a long time been dealt with in economics in the field of comparative analyses of economic systems and in sociology in the field of social theory. Too often, however, at least in the economic sciences, there has been less emphasis on the internal diversity of capitalistic market economies and, instead, a discussion of the characteristics and merits of such systems when compared with other kinds of economies.

But in a recent book, the French economist Michel Albert (1991) actually focuses on the variety of capitalism or market economies present all over the world. Capitalism—or market-based economic systems—has obviously (at least for quite a long time, according to Albert) triumphed, and communism—or centrally planned economic systems—has disintegrated and degenerated. This new situation, Albert continues, creates a renewed interest concerning the possible existence of significant and important differences among the capitalistic market economies of today (and throughout history).

Albert essentially compares two models of capitalism, the "neo-American" and the "Rhein-model" (Germany, France, and Japan as well as the Scandinavian countries belong here). The former represents a neoliberal or neoclassical type of society, which encourages market solutions in almost all sectors. The latter discloses a society with a more regulated, that is, "mixed" economy, which, for example, embodies rather extensive systems for social security.

For the Rhein-model, the institutional arrangements vary a lot. In Japan, for example, Albert describes social security as primarily provided by the large companies, whereas in continental Europe it is guaranteed by autonomous—but obligatory—assurance systems. In the Nordic countries this kind of social security is often provided through the public sector. Albert also discusses, among many other things, the different views on the role of the state that exist, on the one hand, in Europe and Japan and, on the other hand, in the United States. In the former countries, the state as such (i.e., "the state apparatuses") is more appreciated and conspicuous than among countries belonging to the neo-American model, and so are cooperative arrangements.

In a recent book, Alfred Chandler (1990) introduces his second volume explicitly addressing the dynamics of capitalism, and at the same time he outlines some of its many forms. Although in his analysis he very much focuses on the corporation as such, there is also a discussion about the (environmental) institutional differences in the three countries compared. Thus, the capitalism of the United States is described by Chandler as "competitive," whereas the British economy is characterized as a kind of "private" capitalism, and the German form as a "cooperative" one. In comparing these various forms of capitalism, Chandler focuses very much on the roles and relationships among principals (owners) and agents (executives) in the emerging large corporations. Chandler, however, acknowledges the importance of both law and educational institutions as well as the culture and the political system in his analysis of capitalism. But in contrast to most of the authors included in this volume, for example, he pays limited attention to these phenomena when discussing the institutional structures and changes of these countries.

Both Albert and Chandler, as well as a few other researchers approaching this important research field, introduce institutional differences when they try to describe and explain the variations in the economic performances of different economies and societies. Institutional perspectives and analyses are put into focus, and the need for theoretical contributions and improvements in this area is therefore considerable.

The Basic Ingredient in Comparative
Analysis of Economies: The Institution

In this volume the institutional structures and changes of many countries are described and often also compared. These comparisons deal both with Western
economies (including Japan) and with the economies of Eastern Europe (including the former Soviet Union). In the latter case, however, most authors tend to
concentrate their analysis on the prerequisites for the transitions of these countries to capitalistic market systems (some also describe the actual conversion
processes).

Thus, there are two different—but equally important—sources of knowledge
regarding institutional change presented in this volume. First, there are the *comparative* analyses of several capitalistic market economies as presented by,
for example, Perrow (chapter 6); Campbell (chapter 8); Orrù (chapter 9);
McKelvey (chapter 10); Jessop, Nielsen, and Pederson (chapter 11); Andersson
(chapter 12); Pedersen (chapter 13); Vail (chapter 14); and Berrefjord and
Heum (chapter 15). Second, there are the *descriptions of the transition processes*
involving various forms of capitalistic models and ideals emerging in Eastern
Europe and the former Soviet Union (e.g., Etzioni [chapter 3]; Kaminski and
Strzalkowski [chapter 7]; Hausner and Wojtyna [chapter 16]; Chaloupka,
Klusák, Mašková, and Mertlíck [chapter 17]; Palankai [chapter 18]; and Kitov
[chapter 19]). Together these two somewhat different sources of scientific
knowledge provide us with a complex and valuable picture of the many faces of
capitalism.

In almost all the chapters in this volume there is an explicit recognition of the
vital importance of institutions when discussing economic change or transformation processes. In fact the authors—at least implicitly—suggest that
most comparative economic and organizational analyses strongly benefit
from such approaches. Such a position is easily to be found among all the researchers represented in this volume: North (who formulates a theory of institutional change [chapter 3]), Sjöstrand (who describes a theory about the institutional *répertoire* in [Western] societies [chapter 4]), Williamson (who discusses
the "economics of institutions" or the discrete structural alternatives that are
available to organizations [chapter 5]), Perrow (who analyzes the changing institutions for economic organization [chapter 6], Kaminski and Strzalkowski
(who examine different strategies of institutional change [chapter 7]), Campbell
(who relates basic legal conceptions to economic institutions [chapter 8]), Orrù
(who analyzes institutional cooperation [chapter 9]), McKelvey (who describes
institutions supporting innovative change [chapter 10]), Jessop, Nielsen, and
Pedersen (who compare the institutional structures of three countries [chapter
11]), Andersson (who discusses the institutionalization of markets [chapter 12],
Pedersen (who describes the institutional history of a nation [chapter 13]), Vail
(who analyzes changes in institutional "configurations" in a society [chapter
14]), Berrefjord and Heum (who discuss the institutional "framework" of a

nation [chapter 15]), Hausner and Wojtyna (who describe institutions for interest representation [chapter 16]), Chaloupka, Klusák, Mašková, and Mertlík (who discuss various institutional "arrangements" for privatization [chapter 17]), Palankai (who examines the institutional "framework" of a nation [chapter 18]), and Kitov (who explores attitudes toward institutional changes [chapter 19]).

Thus, institutions obviously *do* matter when making comparative analyses and when studying change and transformation processes for organizations as well as for societies. The concept of an institution (cf. chapter 1) refers to those *coherent systems of shared (and enforced) norms that regulate individual interactions in recurrent situations* and that, therefore, characterize the socio-economic system of any society. To frame and describe the vital institutions connected to a problem or a phenomenon then becomes one of the main tasks for researchers involved in comparative analyses of "structures" or changes in organizations, nations, or other "observables."

A Repertoire of Capitalistic Systems

Orrù (chapter 9) is perhaps the contributor to this volume who most explicitly addresses the idea of the repertoire of capitalistic systems. In particular, he analyzes and compares Japan and Germany, the two most successful larger economies of recent decades. But he also mentions a few other types of capitalism in his conclusion; that is, the family entrepreneurship economies of Italy and Taiwan and the state-orchestrated economies of France and India. Orrù writes that too often capitalism is equated with the capitalism of the United States, thus disregarding a wide variation in the economic structures of the Western societies.

If one compares the capitalism of Germany with that of the United States, it is apparent that there is a substantial difference in their respective institutional structures. German capitalism, he continues, differs as much from U.S. capitalism as Japanese capitalism does—and from Orrù's analysis it is obvious that the economies of Japan and Germany closely resemble each other (cf. also the similar conclusions delivered by Albert).

The neoclassical paradigm is embedded in the economic structures of countries like the United States and—to a certain extent—Great Britain, Orrù continues, but it is highly questionable if that theoretical body or paradigm also is embodied in—and relevant for—other types of capitalism such as the one dominating in both Japan and Germany. The institutional structures are what make the economies of these two countries function in a similar way and make them different from the market economies of the Unites States and several other countries, he summarizes. One advantage of the institutional approach is that it makes it possible to describe and understand the logic that characterizes different economies without getting caught in the search for the ultimate causal factor. This will, according to Orrù, advance our understanding of economic systems as socially constructed—and changing—institutional frameworks.

McKelvey (chapter 10) is also well nuanced when she addresses the repertoire of capitalistic systems. She starts her analysis with the hypothesis that capitalist nations usually vitally differ, that is, their market economic systems are seldom equivalent or uniform although they share some basic features. No single idealized type of economic interaction called "a free market" exists as a distinct subsystem of any society, she states. In practice, McKelvey continues, many important differences in the organization of markets and of marked-based relations exist among societies. These dissimilarities are composed of the various institutional structures of the economies of nations or regions.

When discussing different forms of capitalism McKelvey concentrates on the institutional setting of Japan and uses that as her platform or point of reference. She concludes her analysis by indicating that capitalism should be seen as a rather general name for a flexible and changing mode of "regulation" characterizing a society.

Thus, from the contributions of Orrù and McKelvey, as well as from most of the other authors included in this volume—and from many referred researchers—the hypothesis that there are *many faces of capitalism* seems to be both a plausible and a fruitful one. This volume has shed some new light on that phenomenon, and perhaps it will encourage more research efforts in this exciting and vitally important area. Then it is likely that at least some (or most?) of these efforts will be institutionalistic and socio-economic in their character.

Bibliography

Albert, Michel. 1991. *Capitalisme contre capitalisme*. Paris: Éditions du Seuil.
Chandler, Alfred. 1990. *Scale and Scope: The Dynamics of Industrial Capitalism*. Cambridge: Harvard University Press.

Index

Doro, György, 384

East Asian economic miracle, 172, 229
  see also specific countries
Eastern Europe. See Central and Eastern
  Europe; specific countries
East Germany. See Germany
Economic Consultative Council
  (Hungary), 383
Economic Council (Denmark), 290, 291,
  292
Economic Council (Poland), 343
Economic crisis, forms of, 248–49
Economic individualism, Danish, 279–80
"Economic man economies". See Homo
  oeconomicus
Economic organization, adaptability as
  central problem, 85–86
Economic sociology, levels of analysis,
  172
Economy. See Globalization; World
  economy; specific countries; specific
  types of economy, e.g., Market
  economy; specific economic
  approaches, e.g., Neoclassical
  economic theory
EC. See European Community
ECU. See European Currency Unit
Education
  Japanese system of, 206–8
  Swedish free system of, 222n.9
Efficacy
  comparative, 18, 94
  of privatization, 103
Efficiency
  allocative and organizational, 84, 235,
    236
  of deconcentration, 19, 114–16
  innovative, 235
  Schumpeterian, 235, 246, 256–57
  of vertical integration, 179
EFTA. See European Free Trade
  Association
Electricity production, Norwegian,
  322–23
Elites, in Communist society, 144–45
Employees, privatization and reactions of,
  357, 366–67n.12
Employment. See Labor; Unemployment;
  Wages
England. See Great Britain

"Enterprise business work partnerships".
  See VGMs
Enterprise groups, 209
Entrepreneurs and entrepreneurialism
  as agents of change, 37
  clandestine, 163
  Czech reactions to privatization, 357,
    365n.12
  in post-Communist societies, 52
  quasi-private Hungarian, 372
  situation anxieties, 359–60
  see also Small- and medium-size
    enterprises; Small firm networks
"Equality of the sectors", 342
Equilibrium distributions of transactions,
  95–101
Etzioni, Amitai, 66
Europe. See Central and Eastern Europe;
  European Community; Nordic
  countries; specific countries
European Community, 250, 373
  accelerated economic integration of,
    230–31
  agricultural policy, 304, 315
  productive system, 268
  pursuit of Technological Community,
    256
  Swedish membership application, 315
  unemployment in countries of, 22, 23,
    263
European Currency Unit, 270
European Economic Area, 271
European Free Trade Association
  economies, 269–71
  unemployment in countries of, 22, 263,
    264–65
Excessive competition, 210–11
Exchange rate, Czechoslovakian, 352
Excuse doctrine, 99–100
  and neoclassical contract law, 78–80
Expectations, as social-psychological
  variable, 58
Expropriation of property rights, 97–99

Federation of Economic Organizations.
  See Keidanren
Federation of Employers' Association. See
  Nikkeiren
Federation of German Employers'
  Association, 188
Federation of German Industry, 188

About the Authors and the Editor

Jan Otto Andersson (b. 1943) received his Ph.D. in Economics from the Åbo Akademi University (Finland) in 1976. He has been active in research associations concerned with development and future studies, as well as peace studies and human rights. He is a founding member of the European Association for Evolutionary Political Economy. He has written on subjects related to international trade, the world system, and the nation-state, basic income, problems of "post-Fordism," and Nordic economic policies. His writings include *Studies in the Theory of Unequal Exchange Between Nations* (1976), *Den förbryllande nationalstaten* [The Confusing National State] (1982), *Vänsterframtid. Nationalekonomiska studier av fordismens kris och morgondagens alternativ* [Left Future. Economic Studies of the Crisis of Fordism and the Alternatives for Tomorrow] (1988), and *Controlled Restructuring in Finland?* (1990).

Ole Berrefjord (b. 1948) is Associate Professor at the Norwegian School of Economics and Business Administration, Bergen. Currently, he is on leave of absence, having taken up a position at the Prime Minister's Office. He was project manager for the Norwegian Power Study (1972–80), and from 1981 to 1987 he worked at the Institute of Industrial Economics. He is the author of several books and articles, mostly on corporate strategy and the relationships between markets and politics.

John L. Campbell received his Ph.D. in Sociology from the University of Wisconsin at Madison in 1984 and is Associate Professor of Sociology at Harvard University. He is author of *Collapse of an Industry: Nuclear Power and the Contradictions of United States Policy* (1988), an institutional analysis of the political economic performance of the United States, French, Swedish, and West German commercial nuclear energy sectors. He is co-editor of *Governance of the American Economy* (1991), an examination of the institutional development of eight sectors of the U.S. economy. He is currently conducting a historical study of corporate and individual income tax policy reforms in the United States to determine the conditions under which state autonomy varies in advanced capitalism. He is also continuing his work on economic governance.

421

Otakar Chaloupka (b. 1957) received his master's degree in Social Psychology from Charles University in Prague (Czechoslovakia) in 1983. He received his Ph.D. from the Czechoslovak Academy of Sciences in 1988 for his work on relations between generations in work groups. He is recognized for his publication activity in the social psychology of intergenerational relations, social categorization, and sociopsychological aspects of the economic reform. Before his recent engagement with the newly established psychological consultancy services in the framework of Prague's Labour Office, he worked as a head of the Social Psychology Department at the Institute of Psychology of Czechoslovak Academy of Sciences. He is a member of a task group on theoretical and methodological issues of social psychology of the Czechoslovak Association of Psychologists and the European Association of Experimental Social Psychology.

Amitai Etzioni is University Professor at George Washington University and Director of the Center for Policy Research. He is currently working on socioeconomics, a theory of which was published in *The Moral Dimension, Toward a New Economics* (1988). He served for twenty years as Professor of Sociology at Columbia University, was Guest Scholar at the Brookings Institution, served as Senior Advisor at the White House and also served on the Editorial Board of *Science* and on the Council of the American Sociological Association. He was awarded the Guggenheim Fellowship and was a fellow at the Center for Advanced Study in the Behavioral Sciences. He is editor of *The Responsive Community*, a quarterly, and is the founder and first president of the Society for the Advancement of Socio-Economics (SASE).

Jerzy Hausner (b. 1949) received his Ph.D. in Economics from Cracow Academy of Economics in 1980. He has been working at this school since 1972 and was appointed an Associate Professor in 1989. He has been teaching economics and political science. He is a board member of the European Association of Evolutionary Political Economy (EAEPE). His research work concerns relations between economy and polity in the socialist and postsocialist systems. Some of his writings have been published in English: *Towards a Market Economy and a Democratic Order* (1990), *Polish Economy in Transition* (1991), and *In Systematic Vacuum? Dilemmas of the Transformation Process* (1991).

Per Heum (b. 1949) is researcher at the Center for Research in Economics and Business Administration, Bergen. He participated in the Norwegian Study of Power in the 1970s. From 1982 to 1990 he worked at the Institute of Industrial Economics. He is author of several publications on economic, political, and industrial aspects of large corporations in a small, open economy.

Robert (Bob) Jessop (b. 1946) has studied sociology at Exeter and Cambridge universities. He has lectured in sociology, politics, and history at East Anglia,

Cambridge, Essex, and Lancaster universities in Britain and has also spent extended periods as a visiting lecturer in Australia, Denmark, Germany, and the United States. He is currently Professor of Sociology at Lancaster University, England. His principal work has been concerned with state theory, political economy, comparative sociology, and postwar British politics. Among his own books are *The Capitalist State* (1982), *Nicos Poulantzas* (1985), *Thatcherism* (1988 as co-author), and *State Theory* (1990); he has also co-edited *Economic Crisis, Theory, Trade Unions, and the State* (1985), *Technological Change, Rationalization, and Industrial Relations* (1985), and *The Politics of Flexibility* (1991). In addition, he has published seventy journal articles or chapters in books. His current research projects are concerned with marketization in Eastern Europe, Scandinavia, and Britain and with the role of the state in promoting international structural competitiveness.

Antoni Z. Kaminski received a Ph.D. in Sociology in 1974 from Warsaw University. He was an ACLS fellow in 1975–76 (affiliations: Columbia University and University of California, Berkeley). In 1980–81, he was a Visiting Professor at the University of British Columbia in Vancouver, and in 1988–89 he was Senior Research Fellow at the Workshop in Political Theory and Policy Analysis, Indiana University, Bloomington. From 1984 to 1990 he served as Head of the Institute of Sociology, Warsaw University, and in 1990–91 he was Deputy Director at the Department of Europe in the Polish Ministry of Foreign Affairs. From 1991 he has been Director of the Polish Institute of International Affairs. He is a national representative of the Society for the Advancement of Socio-Economic (SASE). His publications include three books and many articles on political and economic institutions. His most recent book is *Institutional Theory of Communist Regimes: Design, Function, and Breakdown of the Soviet System* (1991).

Akhmed I. Kitov is a Professor in Psychology at the Academy of Sciences in Russia and Chairman at the Russian Association of Economic Psychologists. He is the author of several books on psychology in Russia, for example, *Social Psychology and Management* (1984), *Economic Psychology* (1987), and *Personality and Restructuring—Individuals in Perestroika* (1990). He developed and headed the first ever Department of Management Psychology in the former Soviet Union in 1974 and the first Department of Economic Psychology in 1991.

Miroslav Klusák (b. 1957) earned a master's degree con *summa laude* in social sciences (psychology). His professional orientation has been influenced by participation in the Czechoslovak group of a UNESCO program on environmental perception. After summing up the main results of his work in "The Environmental Question and Psychological Research of Personality Development," he received his Ph.D. from the Czechoslovak Academy of Sciences in 1987. From 1987 to 1988 he worked for the Federal Government in the analysis of Czechoslovak participation in international nongovernmental organizations. From 1988 to 1991, he participated in the elaboration of a complex social and economic prognosis of the Czech Republic, specializing in research into changes in the culture of economic activities. He recently joined the Institute of Educational and Psychological Research at Charles University in Prague. He is an expert at the Confederation of Czechoslovak Employers' Unions and an established member of Prague's Employers' Unions and a founder of the Prague Group on School Ethnography.

Eva Mäsková (b. 1958) holds a master's degree in Economics and Information Technology. She has postgraduate studies in Economic Statistics and received her Ph.D. in 1991 from the Prague School of Economics. Between 1987 and 1990 she participated in the process of elaboration of complex social and economic long-term prognosis of the Czech Republic, specializing in participative ownership and financial and controlling structures of entrepreneurial subjects. She is an Associate Lecturer at the Prague School of Economics and an expert to the Slovak Cooperative Union. Since 1991 she has been a member of the Steering Committee of the European Association of Evolutionary Political Economy (EAEPE).

Maureen McKelvey (b. 1965) received her M.A. in Science and Technology Policy from the Research Policy Institute, Lund University, Sweden, in 1989 and her B.A. in Political Science and Economics from Rice University, Texas, in 1987. She is currently working on her Ph.D. at the Department of Technology and Social Change, Linköpings University, Sweden, and specializes in problems relating to technology in political economy. She is a member of the European Association for Evolutionary Political Economy (EAEPE). Her work includes *The European Economic Community: Research Policy, Political Ideology, and the Decision-Making Process* (1987), "How Do National Systems of Innovation Differ? A Critical Analysis" in a book edited by Geoff Hodgson (1991), and *High Tech Products and Productivity: A Study for the Swedish Productivity Delegation* (1991), written with Lars Edquist.

Pavel Mertlík (b. 1961) received his Ph.D. in Economics from the Prague School of Economics (Czechoslovakia) in 1991. He has been 1991 Senior Lecturer of Economics and History of Economic Thought in the Institute of Economic Sciences at the Faculty of Social Sciences, Charles University, Prague, since 1991. He is a Review Board member of the Czech Economic Society (ČSE) and a member of the European Association for Evolutionary Political Economy (EAEPE) and of the International Institute for Self-Management (IIS). He is an author or co-author of four papers published in the most prestigious

Czechoslovakian journals *Politická ekonomie* [Political Economy] and *Finance a úvěr* [Finance and Credit], which focus on problems of money, inflation, income distribution, and prospectives of workers' self-management, and he is a co-author of *Úvod do obecné ekonomie* [Introduction to General Economics] (1990), which is the first Czech textbook of modern economics, published twelve months after the November 1989 Czechoslovak "Velvet Revolution."

Klaus Nielsen (b. 1948) holds a M.A. in Economics from Copenhagen University. He is Associate Professor in Economics at Roskilde University Center. He is a member of the steering committee of the European Association of Evolutionary Political Economy (EAEPE). Among his recent publications are the following: *Nyere udviklingslinier i ökonomisk teori* [New Directions in Economic Theory] (1988), *Forhandlingsökonomi i Norden* [Negotiated Economies in Scandinavia] (1989), *From the Mixed Economy to the Negotiated Economy*, (1991), *The Politics of Flexibility. Restructuring State and Industry in Britain, Germany and Scandinavia* (1991), *Markets, Politics and the Negotiated Economy—Scandinavian and Post-Socialist Perspectives* (1991).

Douglass C. North was appointed Luce Professor of Law and Liberty in the Department of Economics at Washington University in the fall of 1983 and Director of the Center in Political Economy from December 1984 through June 1990. In April 1985, he was appointed editor of the Cambridge Series of books and monographs on "The Political Economy of Institutions and Decisions." Professor North's appointments at Washington University in St. Louis follow thirty-two years at the University of Washington at Seattle, where he was Director of the Institute for Economic Research for five years and Chairman for twelve years. He was the Peterkin Professor of Political Economics at Rice University in the fall of 1979, Pitt Professor at Cambridge University in England in 1981, and a Visiting Fellow of the Center for Advanced Studies in the Behavioral Sciences at Stanford University in 1987–88. He was editor of the *Journal of Economic History* for five years and President of the Economic History Association in 1972. He was a twenty-year member of the Board of Directors of the National Bureau of Economic Research, until 1986. In 1987, he was elected to the American Academy of Arts and Sciences. He has lectured at most major American and European universities and many Asian universities and is the author of more than fifty articles and eight books. His most current research has focused on the formation of political and economic institutions and the consequences of these institutions on the performance of economics through time. This research was published in *Institutions, Institutional Change and Economic Performances* (1990).

Marco Orrù is Associate Professor of Sociology at the University of South Florida. He received his Ph.D. in 1984 from the University of California at

Davis. His research on Japanese and other East Asian and Western European economies and business organizations has appeared in *Shoken Keizai* (1987), *Organization Studies* (1989), and in the book *The New Institutionalism in Organizational Analysis* edited by Walter Powell and Paul DiMaggio (1991). He is currently working with Gary Hamilton and Nicole Biggart on a monograph on *Patterns of East Asian Capitalism* and on another single-authored monograph titled *Institutional Typologies of Capitalist Economies*.

Tibor Palankai (b. 1938) graduated from the University of Economics, Budapest, in 1960 and received his Ph.D. in 1961. In the same year he was appointed to the Department of International Economic and Political Problems of the University of Economics as Assistant Professor. He has published widely on international economic integration, international energy problems, the British economy, problems of adjustment to world economic processes, economic warfare, and institutional transformations. Between 1977 and 1983 he was a Dean at the University of Economics, Budapest. Since 1982 he has been a full Professor and from 1983 Head of Department of World Economy in the same university. In 1986 he received his Ph.D. of the Economic Sciences from the Hungarian Academy. In 1966–67 he spent one year as a Ford Fellow in the United States; in 1971 he was a Visiting Professor at the University of Sussex in England; in 1987 he was Visiting Professor at the University of Pavia in Italy; and in 1989–90 he was a Senior Research Associate at the Institute of East–West Security Studies in New York. His most recently published book is *The European Community and Central European Integration: The Hungarian Case* (1991).

Ove K. Pedersen (b. 1948) is Associate Professor in Political Science at Roskilde University, Copenhagen, and Research Leader at the Center for Public Organization and Management, Copenhagen Business School. He was Chairman of this center, 1988–90, and is currently heading research projects that compare changes in public administration in the Scandinavian countries. He is a member of academic research associations, participates in think tanks, together with high-ranking politicians and managers from private firms and public organizations, and is a member of editorial boards for scientific journals. His internationally best-known writings are connected to the development of a theory for a negotiated economy: "From the Mixed to the Negotiated Economy—The Scandinavian Countries" (together with Klaus Nielsen) (in *Morality, Rationality, and Efficiency: Perspectives on Socio-Economics*, 1991), "At First They Were Two, Then Three and Now Four. Generalized Political Cooperation in Modern Danish Political History" (in *Tripartite Consultation and Cooperation in the Making of National Economic and Social Policy*, 1991), and "Nine Questions to Neo-Institutional Theory in Political Science" (in *Scandinavian Political Studies*, 1991) and *Politics of Flexibility* (1991, edited by Robert (Bob)

Jessop et al.). He has published three books in Denmark, one in Norway, and several articles in the United States, Sweden, Norway, Austria, Poland, Hungary, and Russia.

Charles B. Perrow received his Ph.D. in Sociology from the University of California, Berkeley, in 1960. He has been a Professor of Sociology at Yale University since 1981. He is a past Vice President of the Eastern Sociological Society, a Fellow of the Center for Advanced Study in the Behavioral Sciences, Fellow of the American Academy for the Advancement of Science, a former member of the Committee on Human Factors, National Academy of Sciences, and of the Sociology Panel of the National Academy of Sciences Foundation, and has been on the editorial boards of several journals. An organizational theorist, he is the author of six books, the most recent being *The AIDS Disaster: The Failure of Organizations in New York and the Nation* (1991). His internationally best-known writings include *Organizational Analysis: A Sociological View* (1970), *Complex Organizations: A Critical Essay* (1972; 3rd ed., 1986), and *Normal Accidents: Living with High Risk Technologies* (1984). His interests include the development of bureaucracy in the nineteenth century; the radical movements of the 1960s; Marxian theories of industrialization and of contemporary crises; accidents in such high-risk systems as nuclear plants, air transport, and chemical plants; and the prospects for democratic work organizations.

Sven-Erik Sjöstrand (b. 1945) received his Ph.D. from the Stockholm School of Economics (Sweden) in 1973. He has been Professor of Management and Organization Theory at this school since 1978 and Chairman of its Department for Management and Business Administration since 1989. He is a member of several boards, both in research associations and in large Swedish multinationals. Furthermore, he is the national representative and a board member of both the Society for the Advancement of Socio-Economics (SASE) and the European Association for Evolutionary and Political Economics (EAEPE). His internationally best-known writings include *A Taxonomic Approach to Some Problems of Company Organization* (1975), *Organizational Myths* (1978), *The Role Process: Towards an Integrating Device in Organization Theory* (1986), *The Dual Functions of Organizations* (1987), *Institutional Economics—An Overview* (1989), and *The Rationale Behind Irrational Institutions* (1992).

Piotr Strzalkowski is a Ph.D. student at the Institute of Sociology, Warsaw University. He has published several articles on entrepreneurship and changes in the private sector in Poland during the transition from a centrally planned to a market economy.

David Vail (b. 1943) received a Ph.D. in Economics from Yale University in 1971. He is Adams Catlin Professor of Economics at Bowdoin College in Maine, United States. In 1989–90 he was Visiting Professor and Senior Fulbright Scholar at the Swedish University of Agricultural Sciences. His book, *The*

Greening of Agricultural Policy: Swedish Innovations in a Comparative Perspective, with two Swedish co-authors, is currently in press. He is also a consultant to the Ecological Communities project at the Swedish University of Agricultural Sciences and a board member of the Swedish Program at Stockholm University. He has been an adviser on agriculture, economics, and environmental policy to United States Representative Thomas Andrews, the New England Governors and Atlantic Canada Premiers, and the Maine Commissioner of Agriculture. His previous books and monographs include *Sunrise Agriculture in the Northeast* (1982, editor), *The Family Farm in the Web of Community* (1986, with Richard Westcott), *Technology for Ujamaa Village Development in Tanzania* (1975), and *A History of Agricultural Innovation in Teso, Uganda* (1972).

Oliver Williamson (b. 1932) received his Ph.D. in Economics from Carnegie-Mellon University in 1963. He is Transamerica Professor of Business, Economics, and Law at the University of California, Berkeley. He is co-editor of the *Journal of Law, Economics, and Organization* and a Fellow of the Econometrics Society and of the American Academy of Arts and Sciences. He is a member of the Overseas Advisory Board, MITI (Research Institute), Japan and a Distinguished Senior U.S. Scientist, Alexander von Humboldt-Stiftung. His books include *The Economics of Discretionary Behavior* (1964), *Markets and Hierarchies* (1975), and *The Economic Institutions of Capitalism* (1985).

Andrzej Wojtyna (b. 1951) received his Ph.D. in Economics from Cracow Academy of Economics in 1982 and has been with this university since 1973. His main fields of research include the economic role of the state and contemporary economic thought. In the academic year of 1985–86 he was a visiting scholar at the Department of Applied Economics, University of Cambridge, and in the year 1990–91 he was Visiting Professor at the Economics Department, Stanford University.